THE POCKET

Beer Guide

STERLING EPICURE
New York

An Imprint of Sterling Publishing
387 Park Avenue South
New York, NY 10016

First Published in Great Britain in 2013 by Mitchell Beazley,
an imprint of Octopus Publishing Group Limited, Endeavor House,
189 Shaftesbury Avenue, London WC2H 8JY, an Hachette UK Company
www.octopusbooks.co.uk

© 2013 by Octopus Publishing Group Ltd

ISBN 978-1-4549-0647-6

Distributed in Canada by Sterling Publishing
c/o Canadian Manda Group, 165 Dufferin Street
Toronto, Ontario, Canada M6K 3H6

For information about custom editions, special sales, and premium and
corporate purchases, please contact Sterling Special Sales at 800-805-5489
or specialsales@sterlingpublishing.com.

Manufactured in China

2 4 6 8 10 9 7 5 3 1

www.sterlingpublishing.com

THE POCKET
Beer Guide

The Essential Handbook to the Very Best Beers in the World

Stephen Beaumont
and Tim Webb

STERLING EPICURE
New York

CONTENTS

HOW TO USE THIS BOOK

Sample entry:

① **RODENBACH (PALM)**
Roeselare, West Flanders ——— **②**

③ Unique 1899 brewery full of huge oak tuns, mostly ripening a single brown ale for up to two years. Blended into fresh beer this makes sour-edged, pleasant-enough **Rodenbach ★★** but in its raw form, filtered and slightly sweetened it becomes **Grand Cru ★★★☆**, an **④** ultra-tangy, red-brown ale of fine oak-aged character, often appealing to wine drinkers. Selected runs in larger bottles become **Vintage ★★★★**. **Vin de Céréale ★→★★★** is an occasional and experimental single tun bottling of a higher strength brew.

❶ Name: Breweries are identified by their most common name, with either their parent company or, in some cases, operating business name following in brackets. In languages where the local word for "Brewery" or "Brewing Company" ordinarily precedes the brewery name, that word has been deleted. However, where it usually follows, words such as "Brewing", "Brewery" or their linguistic equivalent have been retained in the title. So "Rodenbach" rather than "Brouwerij Rodenbach" and "Anchor Brewing" rather than "Anchor Brewing Company".

❷ Location: This gives the village/town/city and the province/state.

❸ Descriptions: Efforts have been made to summarize the brewery's personality and efforts in as concise a fashion as possible. Descriptive reviews and ratings are then provided for a maximum of five brands for each brewery.

❹ Ratings: Each beer has been rated on a scale of one to four stars, with most qualifying for this book with a minimum of two. An outlined star (☆) indicates a half.

★	Dependable quality but unexciting
★★	Above average character
★★★	Highly impressive, worth seeking out
★★★★	One of the world's great beers, a champion

Where a beer has year-to-year, format-to-format or batch-to-batch variation, an arrow (→) has been employed to denote the range of quality. So for example, bottles of Rodenbach's Vin de Céréale tasted thus far have varied between one to three stars in terms of quality and character.

Value: Although beer prices have been on the rise of late, we believe that, with but a small handful of special release exceptions, the overwhelming majority of ales and lagers produced today remain modestly priced. Thus, no consideration has been given to ratings in terms of value for the money, although we acknowledge that there may arise a need to introduce this in the future.

Cross references to other entries have been made where applicable and are marked in SMALL CAPITAL LETTERS.

Destinations: Throughout the book are listed specific Beer Destinations. In some instances, these are individual bars, restaurants or shops, while in others they suggest a specific city. In all cases, they represent what we view as the "best of the best" for local or regional beer enjoyment.

> **DESTINATION**
> **OOSTAKKER**
>
> Geerts Drankenhandel is the finest beer supermarket in Belgium (7 Ledergemstraat). Just off the Ghent ring road, it is well stocked, simply presented and full of rare Belgian and better imported beers. Good parking.

INTRODUCTION

There can be very little doubt that beer drinkers have never had it so good. In surveying the state of the brewing world for this book, we contacted experts and beer enthusiasts on six continents, from the classic European beer lands to the last places you might ever expect to discover a fine and flavourful ale or lager. And what we found is that worthy beer now resides almost everywhere.

Yes, there remain pockets where craft beer has not yet infiltrated, mostly for reasons religious, political or economic. But by and large, from New Delhi to New Orleans and Sussex to Singapore, entrepreneurial brewers and beer aficionados have brought craft beer to every corner of the globe.

Ironically, as this craft brewing juggernaut has multiplied exponentially, the large brewing corporations that control the bulk of the world's beer sales have grown fewer and fewer, thanks largely to their persistent acquisition of one another. As a case in point, at the time of writing the largest brewing company on the planet, Anheuser-Busch InBev, had just swallowed the 50% it didn't already own of the Mexican brewer Modelo, a move we anticipate will not only be ultimately successful, but also spark yet another round of "me too" purchases by others in the beer world's top 10, such as SABMiller, Heineken, Carlsberg and MillerCoors.

With expanding sales in their traditional bastions of North America and western Europe all but cut off, the world's leading convenience brewers have been forced to look for growth in emerging markets, notably China and eastern Europe, and the acquisition of their competitors. What often goes unmentioned in the financial pages, however, is that the driver behind this is the appreciation of better beers, which is slowly but methodically eating away at the market share of the global brewing corporations.

The personal journey involved in moving from drinking well-known brand beers to enjoying those of altogether greater character usually involves a walk down a one-way street accompanied by as many friends as will come, whether that be to discover cask-conditioned ales in the UK, perfectly formatted *landbier* in Franconia, the spontaneously fermented beers of Payottenland or Baltic porters from Poland. Or better still, all of the above.

In consequence, life in the craft beer segment is more or less rosy. In pretty much every nation where craft brewing has been established – and we claim there are now active craft beer cultures in over 45 – sales have been steadily increasing since the start of the new millennium, and we have no problem suggesting that such growth should be expected to continue through the next several years, and most likely significantly longer, despite the financial situation.

Which is not to say there are no hurdles to overcome. In youthful but developing markets such as Brazil and South Korea, where the big brewers are loathe to cede even a tiny fraction of their market share, any number of barriers conspire severely to limit craft brewery growth. Some of these are structural, such as the lack of a so-called "cold chain" of distribution in Brazil, whereby the beer is kept refrigerated from brewery to consumer, while others are legislative, like the regulation in South Korea that requires a distributing brewery to have a minimum fermentation and storage capacity of 1500 hectolitres. Most are surmountable.

In more mature markets, several of the global leviathans are fighting back, with varying degrees of success and, this far at least, minimal impact. Efforts have been made to stifle competition by tying up retail space, securing exclusive distribution deals or flooding the marketplace with diverse brands, buying established and successful craft breweries and even creating speciality beer portfolios that deliberately hide the identity of the parent company.

Yet through all of this, craft beer perseveres, indeed thrives, and perhaps more importantly, it evolves internationally. Which is why, although it was unquestionably true around the turn of the century, we do not believe it may still be said with veracity that the United States remains the most exciting country in the world for beer.

While the world's younger brewers and breweries accepted American craft beer guidance in the waning years of the 20th century and the early days of the 21st, embracing styles like American pale ale and IPA and being sure to attend events such as the ever-expanding, US-based Craft Brewers Conference, they were also poised to develop their own distinct and independent cultures. As the years have passed, these plans have come to fruition.

Thus, Italian brewers, at first influenced in equal parts by the Belgians and the Americans, are now developing a singularly Italian approach to brewing. Similarly, the fast-improving Brazilians are actively seeking their own way, using woods and fruits of the Amazon to influence and shape their brews, and Kiwi brewers are employing the singular nature of New Zealand hops to put a stamp on styles they can truly call their own.

The list goes on: Danes and their black beers; northern French *bière de garde*; Japanese brewers fermenting with sake yeasts; formerly underground Lithuanian brewers producing *kaimiškas alus*; and whatever the emerging breed of molecular-cuisine-influenced Spanish craft brewers have up their sleeves.

It is these pockets of local exploration, and many others like them, both existing and emerging, that we find most fascinating today, and expect to be the way forward for craft beer in the coming years. The most exciting place in the world for beer today is about to be in a bar or beer shop near you.

WHAT IS CRAFT BEER?

Although believed in some quarters to be a product of American small brewery marketers, the phrase "craft brewing" and its corollaries "craft brewed beer" and "craft beer" in fact date to at least the mid-1970s, during which time they were used to refer to small, artisanal and usually family-owned European breweries and their brands. Or more simply, whatever was not a large and usually multinational brewery or beer.

Today, the question of what makes a beer "craft" is a little thornier, but the answer remains in part the same. Brewing corporations that operate on a massive scale are, for the most part, devoted to the image of their beer rather than the flavour – although exceptions certainly do exist and where appropriate have been noted within these pages. Craft breweries are smaller by degrees – although with care it is possible to create assertively flavourful

beers in massive single brew runs, this is only provided no corners are cut in recipe or method, which omits most of the options for cost-cutting.

It is the flavour part of the equation that we consider most significant, and to that end there exist techniques generally used in convenience brewing that are normally shunned in the craft sector, beginning with high-gravity brewing.

Widely practised by multinational breweries, high-gravity brewing is the fermentation of beer to an alcohol content of 150% or higher than the intended packaging strength and the subsequent dilution of the beer at bottling, canning or kegging to that final potency. So, for example, a beer meant to appear in the bottle at 5% alcohol by volume might be fermented to 7.5% and watered back to 5% just prior to packaging, so rewarding a brewery with, say, 150,000 litres of bottled beer from a tank with a holding capacity of just 100,000 litres.

The use of brewing adjuncts is another area of differentiation between craft and convenience breweries. Where the latter often employ alternative sources of fermentable sugars, such as corn, rice or liquid sugar, to thin out and lighten the body of their already rather benign beers, craft breweries will tend to use smaller quantities of the same substances to achieve favourable flavour or balance, or both, moderating the weight of a strong ale, for example, or adding a grainy or caramelly accent to the taste of a weaker beer.

One rather romantic and superficially attractive definition of craft beer argues that it has "the brewer's thumbprint" on it, suggesting an ale or lager created by personality as well as technology and science. While we admire this notion, we would suggest that perhaps a less esoteric way to express it might be through a brewery's willingness to experiment, innovate and take risks.

Starting a business is always a risky undertaking, even more so when it must compete against established giants that not only dominate the market to near-exclusivity, but in many cases also control the means of distribution. Add in a determination to expand the market from the ubiquitous light lager to the rich tapestry of ales and lagers we enjoy today and it's clear that risk-taking and innovation are among the hallmarks of craft brewing.

On a related note, in a true craft brewing company, the ideas flow from the brewers to the marketing division, while in large-scale convenience brewing operations, the reverse is true. Looking at some of the delightfully illogical beers that craft breweries have created and made successful and comparing them with such big beer "innovations" as a can that changes colour when cold or a pink brew directed at the female market, it is an easy conclusion to draw.

Beyond size and risk and personality and intent, perhaps the single characteristic that most marks a craft brewery is a willingness and intent to lead. For all the most important steps forward the global brewing industry has taken over the last three or four decades have come as a result of craft beer instigation, marking the craft brewer as someone intent on changing the status quo, rather than being content to follow the herd.

BEER STYLES

The idea that a beer should be considered of a particular style was anathema to the 20th century industrialists who forged the notion of the universal beer. For them, the ideal was light gold, grainy sweet, almost bereft of bitterness and served as cold as possible, and the key was marketing.

The rise of modern craft breweries, on the other hand, has provoked a need for reliably recognizable terms to describe, distinguish and explain the myriad types of beer, old and new, that now adorn the shelves of bars, stores and home refrigerators around the world. The questions that remain are which terms to use and how to apply them?

We believe it was Michael Jackson, in his 1977 book, *The World Guide to Beer*, who first attempted to catalogue global beer styles, introducing readers to such beer types as "*münchener*," "*Trappiste*" and "(Burton) Pale Ale". His goal then was to provide readers with a context through which to discover – or rediscover – these beers. Our challenge, although addressed to a more beer-aware public, remains in essence the same.

While we would love to report that we have solved all the issues surrounding the current confusion and can provide readers with a simple map of the major beer styles of the world, this is not currently possible and, we admit, may never be. What we offer instead is a rough guide on how to pick your way through a linguistic and conceptual minefield in a fashion that adds to rather than detracts from understanding.

START WITH TRADITION
We believe the most reliable stylistic imperatives to be those based in centuries of brewing tradition and that most modern derivations are merely modifications of existing beer styles, however inventive or ingenious. Hence our first separation is according to method of fermentation.

Historically, the term **ale** has referred to a beer fermented at room temperature or higher, causing its yeast to rise to the top of the wort, or unfermented beer, hence references to top-fermentation or, sometimes, warm-fermentation. In contrast, a **lager** was fermented at a cooler temperature causing its yeast to sink, thus known as bottom-fermentation or, sometimes, cool-fermentation.

These main beer classes, comparable to red and white wine, still serve to define the overwhelming majority of beers, despite the temperature and yeast manipulation possible in a modern brewhouse. As a general rule, a beer

fermented at warmer temperatures with a yeast of the family *S. cerevisiae* and conditioned, or lagered, at relatively warm temperatures for short periods – an ale – should tend toward a fruitier character. Those fermented at cooler temperatures with a yeast of the family *S. pastorianus* and lagered for longer periods of time at cool temperatures – lagers – should not. Combine ale yeast with a lager-style conditioning and you have the hybrid styles of **kölsch** and **altbier**, respectively native to Cologne and Düsseldorf in Germany, as well as the American **cream ale**. Flip it to lager yeast and ale-type conditioning and you have **steam beer**, also known as **California common beer**.

Beers that have no yeast added to them, most famously the **lambic** beers of Belgium, are said to undergo spontaneous fermentation, effected by a combination of airborne and barrel-resident microflora, including *Brettanomyces* and *Pediococcus*, which yield complex flavours from mildly lemony to assertively tart. Those fermented with the same types of microbes introduced deliberately are becoming known as **wild beers** or **sour beers**.

ADD COLOUR AND STRENGTH

Colour is a powerful force in beer and often used to define beer by style, with some references to hue reserved exclusively for certain types of beer, such as "white" (*blanche*, *wit*, *weisse*) for **wheat beers**, even when such beers are relatively dark in colour. "Pale" or "light" (in colour, not alcohol or calories) are also popular adjectives, yielding the now-international **pale ale** and **India pale ale**, or **IPA**, the German *helles* and the Czech *světlý*.

"Amber" in North America was and to some extent remains synonymous with ordinary ales or lagers with a blush of colour, while "red" has varying degrees of Irish and Flemish (northern Belgian) authenticity, but is just as often used to describe a beer of uncertain style. "Dark" is also used in fairly random fashion in the English-speaking world, but retains validity in Bavaria where its translation, *dunkel*, should indicate a brownish lager of a style once strongly associated with Munich, and in the Czech Republic, where the term is *tmavý*.

"Brown" implies the use of more roasted malts and, while historically associated with a class of fairly winey **brown ales** from England or a tart, fruity *oud bruin* style native to northern Belgium (related to the Flemish red, above), may now apply to a wide variety of flavours, from sickly sweet to forcefully bitter, mild to alcoholic. "Black" is usually reserved for **porters** and **stouts**, although bottom-fermented German *schwarzbier* also deserves inclusion.

As for alcoholic strength, although commonly used around the world, few words are less useful to a beer description than "strong". The difficulty is in terms of context, since in parts of Scandinavia, strong beer (*starkøl*) is defined as being above 4.7% ABV, not far from where the British would place the definition, while most Belgians, North Americans and Italians would be hard-pressed to consider anything below 6% or 7% to be "strong".

The terms *dubbel*/**double** and *tripel*/**triple** are monastic in origin and have proved both durable and international. Historically used to indicate a beer fermented from a mash with greater malt sugar content – often the "first runnings" of grain then reused to make a second beer – the modern context of *dubbel*/double generally indicates a beer of 6–8%. Most commonly, it appears in reference to the malty and sweet Belgian abbey-style *dubbel*, the German *doppelbock* and related Italian *doppio malto* – although use of the latter term appears to be waning – and the modern American **double IPA**, usually an ale of significant strength and aggressive bitterness.

Tripel/triple likewise owes its origins to monastery breweries, although its advent is more recent, having been first employed in the 20th century. It usually describes a very specific type of blond, sweet-starting but usually dry-finishing strong ale, although is today sometimes used with **IPA** to suggest an even stronger and hoppier brew. *Quadrupel*/**quadruple**/**quad**, on the other hand, is a modern affectation, the first variant originally used by the Dutch Trappist brewery, La Trappe, to designate its new high-strength ale in 1998, hence the Dutch spelling – to imply heritage.

Historically, the term **barley wine** was used to indicate a beer of wine strength, though the modern interpretation sometimes brings it closer to **old ale** in its British guise, that is, a beer requiring some period of bottle-ageing, or high hoppiness in its American interpretation, and sometimes both.

Imperial has experienced a recent transformation from its original **Imperial Russian stout** designation, meaning a strong, intense, sometimes oily stout, to the suggestion that any style may be "Imperialized", which is to say made stronger and more intense. **Imperial pale ale** as a synonym for **double IPA** is the most common of these, although Imperial pilsner, Imperial *saison* and even the hopefully tongue-in-cheek Imperial mild have been sighted.

Brewers have for centuries used subtle nudge and wink systems to highlight alcohol content. The best-known remnant of this practice is the Scottish "shilling" system, whereby ales are measured from **60 shilling**, or **60/-**, for the lightest ale, to **90/-** for the strongest, the last sometimes also called "**wee heavy**". In the Czech Republic, the old Balling system of measuring wort gravity defines beers by degrees, from **8°** for the lightest to **12°** for a beer of premium strength and on up into fermented porridge territory.

FACTOR IN THE GRAINS

Besides the basic four ingredients of beer – water, barley malt, hops and yeast – numerous other grains are used with varying degrees of regularity, in all but a handful of specialized cases in combination with barley malt.

Wheat is the most common of these, creating whole categories of beer such as the German-style wheat beers variously known as *weizen*, *weisse*, *hefeweizen* or *hefeweissbier*, all normally indicating a beer with added yeast in the bottle, unless specified *kristall*, meaning clear. Also included in this family are the derivatives *dunkelweisse* and *weizenbock*, respectively meaning dark and strong wheat beers. Quite different is the more obscure *Berliner weisse*, kept light (usually +/-3.5%) and made tart through the use of lactic acid during fermentation.

Spontaneously fermented Belgian **lambic** is by law a wheat beer, though more common in Belgium and elsewhere is *witbier* (**white beer**, *bière blanche*), brewed with unmalted rather than malted wheat and spiced with orange peel and coriander, sometimes in conjunction with other spices.

Once ubiquitous but now more seldom seen are simple **wheat ales**, blond beers that have simply been made lighter of body through the use of malted wheat. Some craft brewers in the US and elsewhere have started to make strong wheat beers called **wheat wines**, referencing barley wine.

Other grains in general usage include oats, which brings sweetness and a silky mouthfeel to **oatmeal stouts** and other, more unconventional beers such as **oatmeal brown ales**; rye, which bestows a spiciness upon **rye pale ales** and **rye IPAs**, as well as the odd lager-fermented *roggenbier*, of German origin; buckwheat, blackened and used in the Brittany beer style, *bière de blé noir*; and an assortment of non-glutinous grains employed to create the growing class of **gluten-free beers**.

Malt and grain substitutes are mostly there for fermentable sugar to increase alcoholic strength, with or, more commonly, without adding flavour characteristics. The likes of maize (corn), rice, starches, syrups and candy sugar may bring balance to heavy beer by ensuring that it is suitably strong in alcohol, but are not seen as creating styles in their own right – though **Japanese rice beers** and a handful of related beers in the United States are having a go. The exception to this rule is where unfermentable sugars are added with the intention of adding sometimes considerable sweetness without alcoholic strength, fructose creating **sweet stout** and lactose contributing to **milk** or **cream stout**.

HOPS AND OTHER FLAVOURINGS

Hops have been the primary flavouring agent in beer since the Middle Ages, but only in the last century or two have beer styles begun to be defined by the variety of hop used.

Perhaps most famously, what the world knows as the **Czech-style pilsner** is seasoned with a single variety of hop, the floral Saaz, grown near where the style was invented. Equally, the typical hops used in a **British best bitter** have always been Fuggle and Golding, not necessarily because it was planned that way, but because they are what Kentish hop farms were and are still growing. (A wider variety are typically employed in the stronger, maltier **Extra Special Bitter**, or **ESB**, but Fuggle and/or Golding are often still used.)

When what we now recognize as the **American-style pale ale** was established in the 1970s, the hop used to give the beer its trademark citrus bite was Cascade, although now a variety of other so-called "C-hops" are considered acceptable, including Centennial and Chinook. By extension, these hops have also grown to be emblematic of the **American-style IPA** and its recently developed sibling, the **black IPA**, which might equally be described as a **hoppy porter**.

More recent hop-defined beer styles include two from New Zealand, the **New Zealand-style pilsner** and the **New Zealand-style pale ale**, both flavoured with grapey, tropical-fruity Kiwi hops, notably Nelson Sauvin and Motueka. As hop cultivation becomes increasingly scientific and more hybridized varieties are created, we may and most likely will see more beer styles identified by the variety of hops used.

While hops can be considered a core ingredient of any beer, other flavourings are distinctly optional, including herbs and spices. While we still see the odd beer identified as *gruut* (sometimes grut or gruit), which is to say seasoned with a selection of dried herbs and flavourings, but no hops, certainly the most famously spiced beer is the **Belgian-style wheat beer**.

Although all manner of herbs and spices were used prior to the widespread use of hops in brewing, before Pierre Celis pitched coriander, cumin and dried Curaçao orange peel into the *witbier* he revived in the Belgian town of Hoegaarden in 1966, the extent to which brewers, Belgian or otherwise, spiced beers is questionable. Today, however, beers can and frequently are flavoured with all manner of ingredients, to the extent that lumping them all into a single **spiced beer** category seems to us rather random. Unfortunately, failing the creation of all manner of sub-categories – black pepper beers, white pepper and allspice beers, grains of paradise beers, and so on – it remains the best available option.

We can blame popular modern Belgian brewers for the arrival of fruit syrups in beer. While cherries and raspberries have for centuries been steeped whole in Belgian **lambic** beers to create respectively *kriek* and *framboise*, the rash of beers made by adding juice, syrup, cordials or essence to ordinary lagers and ales is mostly a post-1980 phenomenon. While collectively known as **fruit beers**, this is often a misnomer as the additives are often a considerable distance from their time on the tree.

Stout in particular, but also **porter** and other types of **brown ale**, are increasingly having vanilla, cocoa and coffee added to them in formats that range from whole pods or beans to syrups and essences, with varying degrees of success.

One of the most curious additives is salt, once commonly and still variously used in **dry Irish-style stout** to fill out the palate, achieved with greatest aplomb in the 19th century by filtering the wort through a bed of shucked oyster shells, hence **oyster stout**. East German *gose* is essentially a salted wheat beer.

Italian brewers have sought to make a style out of adding chestnuts to their beer, whether in whole, crushed, honey or jam form. Whether it or any of the multitude of other additives and seasonings currently in use – from root vegetables to nuts to flowers and even tobacco leaf – stand the test of time once the initial excitement wears off, remains to be seen.

NATIONAL ADJECTIVES

Various nationalities and regionalities have grown in recent years into beer style descriptors. While some rankle – the term "Belgian" for a beer quite clearly brewed elsewhere than Belgium, for example – they do in most cases provide useful information.

Because some Belgian ales taste spicy, whether by dint of the yeast used or spices added, yeast propagation companies have developed yeast strains meant to mimic this effect, hence **Belgian-style** has come to mean a spicy or sometimes somewhat funky take on an understood beer style – i.e. Belgian pale ale, Belgian IPA, and so on.

Hop-related styles already discussed include **US** or **American-style** for pale ales and IPAs seasoned with Cascade and other such hops, and **New Zealand-style (Aotearoa-style)** pilsner and pale ale. **British-style**, usually used in conjunction with pale ale, IPA or barley wine, generally indicates not only the less aggressive hop character of a Golding, Fuggle or Northern Brewer hopping, but also a pronounced maltiness.

Scotch ale or **Scottish-style ale** suggests a beer of quite significant maltiness, with strength of up to 8% indicated by the former. Long-standing confusion about Scottish brewing methods means that beers so described sometimes also feature a potion of peated malt.

Other geographical qualifiers are more restricted. **Baltic porter** defines a beer that is not a porter at all, but rather a strong, dark and usually sweet bottom-fermented ale; **Irish red ale** is a popular descriptor of questionable authenticity; **Irish stout** has both legitimacy and utility in describing a low-strength, dry, roasty form of stout; **Bohemian-** or **Czech-style** generally modifies pilsner and suggests one more golden than blond, softly malty and floral; and **Bavarian** or **German** implies crisper, leaner and blonder when referencing pilsner, clovey and/or banana-ish when applied to a wheat beer.

AND THE REST

Several other old and new styles and derivatives also deserve mention here.

The need for beer during the non-brewing months of summer has historically led to the creation of several somewhat related styles, including *märzen* in Germany, *bière de garde* in France and *saison* in southern Belgium. Each is distinguished by a slightly elevated alcohol content and normally increased hopping rate, both employed for preservative effect.

Come harvest, German, Austrian, Dutch and Norwegian brewers would clear the stocks of malt from the previous year's barley by brewing a dark *bok* or *bock*, a custom mirrored in the spring in all but Norway with a pale *maibock* or *lentebok*. The latter fell in line with a tradition across much of northern Europe to produce stronger beers around the Lenten period.

The Germans also claim a host of local variants on usually blond lagers that are only partially filtered, sometimes known collectively as *landbier* and including types that are simply cloudy (*zwickelbier*), some which continue some fermentation in the pub cellar (*kellerbier*) and a few in which carbon dioxide is allowed to be released during lagering (*ungespundetes*).

Franconian brewers claim a slice of history by perpetuating the use of wood-smoked malt in their *rauchbiers* – at the same time inspiring a host of New World smoked beers – while Finnish and Estonian brewers do the same with their *sahti*, a beer filtered through juniper boughs and fermented with bread yeast, served by necessity very young and fresh.

Finally, the craft brewing renaissance has witnessed the emergence of a cacophony of new styles, both real and imagined, classifiable and almost ethereal. In the last group we place **barrel-aged** and **barrel-conditioned beers**, which begin in a multitude of styles and spend time in a variety of different sorts of barrels, from those which previously held wine, to bourbon barrels, to, in at least one extraordinary case, a barrel previously used to age maple syrup. Of particular interest in this area, we find, is what Brazilian brewers are currently doing with the exotic woods of the Amazon.

In a similar vein, fresh or unkilned hops are used in a new class of **wet hop beers**, mostly ales and primarily in the United States but otherwise of almost any hop-driven style the brewer wishes to brew. And beers named for occasions or seasons, including **Christmas** and **winter ales**, **summer beers** and **harvest ales**, suggest general character traits – heavier in winter, lighter for summer – but little else.

BEER AT THE TABLE

by Stephen Beaumont

Although through the millennia beer has been enjoyed in all manner of ways, from workplace restorative to meal accompaniment and evening refresher, over the past two centuries or so it has been largely confined to the role of social elixir, what you go out for "a couple of" with colleagues after work or enjoy with friends on a Friday or Saturday night.

With the emergence of craft breweries and their vast array of beer styles, however, beer has rediscovered its place at the table. And with the remarkable diversity of aromas and flavours currently being brewed, it's no wonder. Indeed, with its multiple ingredients and diverse fermentation possibilities, it can be argued that beer has even greater versatility in food pairing than does wine.

Included in that versatility are the myriad flavourings that may be used in brewing, from coffee and chocolate to a host of herbs, spices, fruits and so on. We have, for the most part, excluded these beers from our pairings — except for dessert — but they should be considered whenever the beer's flavouring is harmonious with the food's.

The following is our attempt to demystify the process of partnering food with beer, although we caution that while a well-orchestrated match can be a most delicious and enjoyable experience, the best pairing is always the beer you want with the food you desire.

BREAKFAST

Waiting "until the sun is over the yard-arm" before having a drink is a popular aphorism in parts of the world, but hardly a universal truth. Although it is becoming less common to find beer consumed early in the day, the practice is far from extinct and does come with certain gastronomic benefits.

Bagel and cream cheese: A not-too-hoppy pale ale.

Churros: A chocolaty stout or porter or, if you're feeling adventurous, a malty and not-too-strong barley wine.

Croissant: You'll likely be having this with an espresso or café au lait, but try a chocolaty porter for something different.

Eggs Benedict: Cut the richness of the hollandaise with a crisp *helles* lager.

French toast with fruit: Here a sweeter *kriek* or *framboise* is useful.

Fresh fruit with yogurt: A dryish fruit lambic or a *Berliner weisse* with or without syrup.

Full English breakfast: With so much on the plate, best keep the beer light. A golden bitter will do the trick.

Granola: If with milk, a nutty brown ale. With yogurt, a Flemish brown or red ale.

Oatmeal: Oatmeal stout, of course.

Pancakes with maple syrup: Oatmeal stout, preferably a sweeter and not so roasty example.

Raw or cured ham: A crisp pilsner, especially if mild cheese is also served.

Scrambled eggs: A Belgian-style wheat beer is a natural.

Smoked salmon: Dry stout or a softly smoky *rauchbier* or smoked porter.

Weisswurst: *Weissbier* is the traditional accompaniment, and for good reason.

LUNCH

While almost anything may be eaten for lunch, the key to pairing beer with the midday meal is to keep the alcohol content low and the refreshment element high, so the effect is restorative and invigorating rather than filling and dulling.

Chicken, fried: Anything light and hoppy, from US-style pale ale to pilsner or *kölsch*.

Chicken wings, spicy: For medium heat, pilsner; for hot, US-style pale ale or IPA.

Chicken sandwich with mayonnaise: *Bière de garde* or *märzen*.

Clam chowder: (New England-style) A hoppy blond ale or golden bitter; (Manhattan-style) Vienna lager or *altbier*.

Crab cakes: Dry porter or a *schwarzbier*.

Croque monsieur: A spicy, Belgian-inspired blond ale.

Hamburger: Dry, hoppy and aromatic US-style pale ale, or crisp pilsner.

Nachos: Spicy, cheesy and sloppy, this dish needs a beer to clean it all up: a crisp pilsner or restrained UK- or US-style IPA.

Oysters, raw or cooked: Dry stout, or *gueuze* lambic for a tasty variation.

Pizza: (Tomato) Vienna lager or *bock*; (White) *Weissbier* or, if cheesy, *weizenbock*; (With the works) A big US-style IPA.

Ploughman's lunch: Best bitter or UK-style pale ale.

Pulled pork: *Märzen* or *bock*.

Quiche Lorraine: *Altbier* or dark mild ale.

Salad, cobb: Pale ale or *saison*.

Salad, green with vinaigrette: *Helles* for a conventional approach; *gueuze* lambic for a refreshing alternative.

Salad, tuna: Brown ale if without pickles; porter or light stout if with pickles.

Soup, cream: Pilsner.

Soup, French onion: Pale ale or best bitter, or one of the hoppier and darker examples of *bière de garde*.

Veal schnitzel: Pilsner if greasy; *märzen* if not.

DINNER

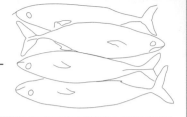

FISH

The key to pairing beer with fish is to start light and increase the weight of the beer according to the fattiness of the fish, the richness of the sauce, and so on. Also, fish generally don't take terribly well to hoppiness, often producing a metallic or minerally flavour in response, so well-hopped pilsners, pale ales, IPAs and the like should be employed judiciously.

Brandade: A simple, fruity blond ale.

Ceviche: The citrus makes this a fairly acidic dish, so match with the acidity of a fruit lambic or a tamer coriander-forward Belgian-style wheat beer or a *kolsch*.

Cioppino: This fennel and seafood stew from San Francisco pairs wonderfully with that city's beer claim to fame, steam beer, also known as California common beer.

Crab: Almost any way it's prepared, a sweetish porter will be crab's best friend. Make it hoppier if the crab is softshell and fried or heavily spiced.

Fish and chips: Best bitter or British-style pale ale, please.

Fish baked in a salt crust: This technique yields profoundly moist and flavourful flesh, suitable for pairing with a *märzen* or *schwarzbier*.

Haddock, halibut, cod and other firm and meaty fish, poached, sautéed or roasted: Meaty but light in flavour, these fish will accept almost any sort of non-hoppy ale or lager, from *bière de garde* to *bock* to light porters and dry stouts.

Lobster, cold with mayonnaise: *Bock* or malty *dubbel*.

Lobster, steamed with butter: A nutty and sweetish brown ale will accentuate the flavours of the lobster.

Mackerel, sardines, herring or other dark and oily fish, grilled: The fattiness of these fish beg for some hops to cut through the oil, so try a balanced, citrusy pale ale.

Monkfish, roasted: Oatmeal stout or Baltic porter.

Mussels: It's a myth that mussels should be enjoyed with the beer used to steam them, since a few cloves of garlic or a bunch of herbs can change the flavour playing field completely. Start with a Belgian-style wheat for lighter preparations such as lemon and parsley and increase the beer's weight as the flavours grow bolder. Avoid high bitterness in all cases, though.

Pad Thai: This dish mixes salty, sweet and sour, usually with a decent amount of spice, so reach for the workhorse of beer and food pairing, pale ale.

Paella: Garlic and a multitude of different flavours suits this to a Czech-style pilsner or British-style pale ale. Or if it's a very rich version, try one of the lighter Trappist ales.

Prawns (shrimp), barbecued New Orleans-style: This dish begs an IPA or double IPA. Alternatively, go for a severe, refreshing contrast with a crisp pilsner.

Prawns (shrimp), garlic: German- or Czech-style pilsner, light pale ales.

Red snapper, sea bass and other light and lean fish, poached, sautéed or roasted: Keep the beer light and fresh. Almost any wheat beer will work, or a *helles* if a little garlic or spice is involved.

Sablefish, black cod, sturgeon and other firm, oily whitefish, poached, sautéed or roasted: Although delicate of taste, the oils in these fish allow for a little hoppiness and their firm flesh invites a bit of weight. *Märzen*, or a not overly hoppy *altbier* or UK-style pale ale.

Salade Niçoise: Dressed with vinaigrette and prepared with the traditional canned tuna, this *salade composée* suits a *saison*.

Salmon, seared or grilled: Dry stout.

Scallops: On their own, sautéed or baked, their sweet and delicate taste begs for *kölsch* or Belgian-style wheat beer.

Seafood curry: Break out the pilsner and make it hoppier as the curry gets hotter. For a rich coconut milk curry, try an abbey-style *tripel*.

Sushi or sashimi: Varies according to the fish and other ingredients included, but if disinclined to drink sake, a *kölsch*, *altbier* or *schwarzbier* can be quite nice.

Trout, grilled or fried: New Zealand-style pilsner, if you can find it, or a light and fruity blond ale if you cannot.

Tuna, grilled or seared: Properly served raw in the middle, so any suggestion of hoppiness will bring out metallic tastes in the fish: stick to a *dubbel*, sweet *bock* or other medium weight and malty ale or lager.

MEAT

Red meat allows you to bring out the big guns of beer – abbey-style ales, double IPAs, barley wines and such. Poultry, on the other hand, allows for great leeway from lagers and lambics all the way to brown ales and porters. And everything German is good with pork.

Beef cheeks, braised: Imperial stout or strong abbey-style ale.

Beef, roast, medium to well done: The browner the meat, the browner the ale. Try a nutty brown ale for medium and head towards porter for more well-done beef.

Beef, roast, rare: Rich, meaty sweetness is best balanced by pale ale or best bitter.

Beef stew with potatoes, carrots, etc: Brown ale or porter.

Beef Stroganoff: Something big and beefy, like a malt-driven barley wine, strong abbey-style ale or even a whisky-barrel-aged stout.

Carbonade de boeuf: The Belgian equivalent to boeuf bourguignon, cooked with beer. A tart Flemish red or brown ale, or a moderately strong wild ale, is wonderful if the stew is finished with a little acidity, or a malty Trappist or abbey-style brown ale if not.

Cassoulet: Deliciously fatty, this dish calls for hoppiness without excess weight, meaning a *tripel* or traditional *saison*.

Chicken or turkey, roast: Traditional (*oude*) *gueuze* is a superlative match.

Chicken or prawn vindaloo: The ultimate accompaniment to spicy curries is, coincidentally, India pale ale.

Chilli con carne: A dish with many guises – meaty, bean-forward, spicy, turkey – calls for a beer with great flexibility of flavour, pale ale or, if very spicy, IPA.

Coq au vin: Properly deserving of red wine, but a brown ale can do in a pinch. (Or try coq à la bière.)

Duck or goose, roast: An ideal occasion for a proper *tripel* or a New World wine-barrel-aged strong golden ale.

Duck two ways (roast breast and confit leg): Hoppy *bocks* love this dish, or a new style "*hopfen*" *weissbier* otherwise.

Goulash: Balance refreshment with fat-cutting hoppiness and serve a restrained American-style pale ale.

Haggis: Whisky-barrel-finished porter or stout, peated malt ale or a single malt.

Ham, cooked: You can't go wrong with German beers whenever pig is on the menu. *Märzen*, *bock*, *rauchbier* and *weizenbock* can all be marvellous here.

Jambalaya: The hotter, the hoppier; start with a pale ale to partner with a mild spiciness and move to IPA when the hot sauce takes over.

Lamb, roast: Rare to medium-rare lamb is wonderful with a rich, malty and – dare we say it? – winey brew. Try an old ale, British-style barley wine or strong porter or brown ale. Medium-strength Trappist or abbey-style ales work, too.

Lamb rogan josh: A wonderful dish with lots of grease, calling for a malty double IPA or strong British-style IPA.

Pork, roast: An earthy *dunkel* or *bock*.

Rabbit: Full-bodied *dunkel*, sweetish brown ale or light porter.

Sausages: Best bitter for beef; *helles* or *bock* for pork; *weissbier* for veal. Choose hoppier styles like pilsner, pale ale and IPA for spicier sausages such as Italian, chorizo and merguez.

Shepherd's pie: Best bitter or brown ale; sweet porter if properly (but now rarely) made with lamb.

Spaghetti and meatballs in tomato sauce: *Bock* or *doppio malto*.

Steak and kidney pie or Steak in stout pie: Brown ale, porter or stout as a catch-all; Flemish brown ale for the kidneys and Imperial stout for the steak-in-stout as perfection.

Steak frites: Flavours that will crush any lager; choose instead an ESB or British style pale ale.

Steak tartare: A spiced or spicy strong abbey-style ale is a great match, or a malty pale ale if potency is a consideration.

Sweetbreads: The most elegant and balanced strong golden ale you can find, with extra points for a lean and spicy body.

Veal, roast: Brighten its character with a *bock*, or if served with gravy, a spicy *dubbel*. Berry-based and not overly sweet fruit beers are also an option.

Venison: Either a traditional (*oude*) fruit lambic with lots of fruitiness or a wild ale fermented with berry fruit.

Wild boar: Not to be treated as pork, boar deserves a strong *bock* or strong, rich, barrel-aged wild ale.

VEGETARIAN DISHES

Vegetarian food arrives in such a vast variety of flavours that it's difficult to make pairing generalizations. Below is a small sample offered for guidance.

Baked pasta dishes: Best is often a dark lager with a degree of hoppiness, an earthy *dunkel* or an *altbier*.

Cheese soufflé: A hoppy *kölsch* or wheat beer would work best.

Couscous with vegetables: Mild and light, a Vienna lager suits this to a T.

Grilled vegetables: With olive oil and herbs, a hoppy *helles* is a delight.

Lentils: *Altbier* is a great match for the earthy flavour, but a dry brown ale will do if none are available.

Macaroni cheese: Pair to the cheese, so a *bock* or brown ale if mild and best bitter or UK-style pale ale if sharper.

Mushrooms: Pair wonderfully with any beer that emphasizes dark, earthy malts, from *altbier* to stout.

Ratatouille: Richness plus garlic calls for a hoppy brown ale, equally hoppy *bock*, or perhaps a rye pale ale.

Spicy vegetarian dishes: Lager or ale suit, with pale ales/IPAs serving as well as hoppy *bocks* or 12°-or-stronger Czech or Czech-style lagers or Imperial pilsners.

Stuffed peppers: Green peppers call for a contrasting, cleansing flavour to balance, like a pilsner or *helles*. Switch to British-style pale ale if the peppers are sweet, and US-style IPA if the stuffing is spicy.

DESSERT

Beer shines when it comes to dessert, especially when chocolate is involved. It is wise in most cases to choose a beer that is at least as sweet as the dish, if not sweeter, to avoid the beer's flavour being trampled by the dessert's sugar.

Apple pie, strudel: An apple-flavoured, allspice- or cinnamon-spiced strong ale.

Cakes and cupcakes; sponge cake with icing: Pale, sweet *bock* or a sweet Belgian or Belgian-inspired golden ale.

Cheesecake: For a fruit-topped cake, pick a beer flavoured with the same or a complementary fruit. For liqueur-flavoured or caramel cheesecake, opt for a malty barley wine or more youthful old ale.

Chocolate: Pair flourless chocolate cake with Imperial stout; chocolate pudding with *doppelbock*; nutty chocolate truffle with brown ale; milk chocolate with sweet porter; chocolate cheesecake with milk stout.

Christmas pudding, mince pies: Barley wine or spiced winter ale.

Coffee desserts: Coffee-flavoured stout; regular stout and porter; or Imperial stout or Trappist ale for strongly flavoured dishes.

Crème brûlée: Strong and sweet blond ale, fruity or spicy or spiced.

Fruit: For a fruit salad, *hefeweizen*; for berries in cream, milk stout, Flemish red ale or chocolaty brown ale; for fruit tarts, match the custard with a sweet, fruity blond ale.

Lemon flavours: Wheat beers of varying types, selected according to intensity of the dish, or sometimes pilsners.

Nuts: Brown ale, some *bocks*, old ale.

Pecan pie: A bourbon barrel-conditioned stout or barley wine is a beautiful match.

Sticky toffee pudding: Sweet Scotch ale.

Tiramisú: Highlight the coffee with a sweet stout, or emphasize the creaminess with an abbey-style *dubbel* or stronger ale.

Trifle: Scotch ale.

CHEESE

Wine and cheese may get all the press, but beer and cheese is a more natural and harmonious pairing, as even many sommeliers now admit. The suggestions below are a mere starting point for a long and delicious journey.

Bloomy rind cheeses (Brie de Meaux or Camembert): Porter or oatmeal stout.

Firm, sharp and fruity-nutty cheeses (aged Cheddar, Gruyère, Manchego): Best bitter or UK-style pale ale (much the same thing) or dry porter or stout.

Goats' cheese, semi-soft and dry: Some hoppier versions of *kölsch*, *bière de garde* or *saison* fare well, but best is a traditional *oude* (old) *gueuze* lambic.

Goats' cheese, soft and moist: Belgian- or German-style wheat beer or *helles*.

Hard, grainy, crumbly and sharp cheese (Parmigiano Reggiano, aged Gouda): Nutty brown ale, malty porter or *rauchbier* is nice, but a bourbon-barrel-aged porter or strong brown ale is bliss.

Mild to moderately sharp and creamy blue cheeses (Cambozola, Cashel Blue, Stilton): Sweet stouts, strong, malty abbey-style *dubbels* and *doppelbocks* fare well with milder versions; for Stilton break out a malty, UK-style barley wine.

Semi-soft, mild-mannered cheese (Edam, Havarti, Morbier): *Bock*; Irish ale; Scottish ale; some light and sweeter versions of abbey-style *dubbel*.

Sharp, aggressive and mouth-drying blue cheeses (Roquefort, Cabrales, Gorgonzola): Break out the big guns, such as double IPA, US-style barley wines or strong Trappist or abbey-style dark ale.

Washed rind, strong and pungent cheeses (Epoisses, Münster, Chimay à la Bière): Strong spiced or spicy Belgian or Belgium-inspired ales, the strongest of almost any Trappist brewery's portfolio.

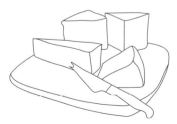

EUROPE

Norwegian Sea

NORWAY

OSLO

Shetland
Islands

North
Sea

DENMARK

COPENHAGEN

Hamburg

DUBLIN

IRELAND

UNITED
KINGDOM

ATLANTIC
OCEAN

LONDON

AMSTERDAM

NETHERLANDS

BERLIN

BRUSSELS

BELGIUM

GERMANY

LUXEMBOURG

Frankfurt

PARIS

PRAGU

CZEC

REPUE

Bay of
Biscay

FRANCE

Munich

VIEN

Bordeaux

Geneva

SWITZ.

ALPS

LIECH

AUSTRIA

LJUBLJAN

Toulouse

Pyrenees

MONACO

SLOVENIA

PORTUGAL

ANDORRA

SAN

MARINO

LISBON

MADRID

S

SPAIN

Barcelona

Corsica

ITALY

ROME

Balearic Islands

Sardinia

Mediterranean Sea

Sicily

MALTA

BELGIUM

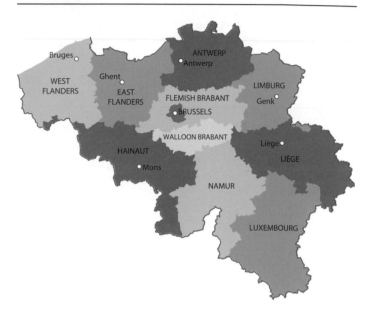

Belgian beers are revered for their uniquely broad styling, from the absurdly robust to the nearly impossibly delicate, from extreme sweetness to frank acidity; some are pungent with spicing while others reek of the stable, and they come in every colour and format. That said, the concept of a beer "style" remains alien to many Belgian brewers, who dislike conformity.

Modern Belgium's brewing heritage is built on diversity and mistrust, its lands having been invaded over 40 times by foreign powers in the past thousand years. They are outward-looking but inward-thinking, and they brew beers this way or that, because it seems right.

Brewing influences include the traditions of monastic brewing kept alive by six brewing abbeys of the Trappist Order; the lambic brewers of Payottenland, whose beers rely on wild fermentation and barrel-ageing; farmhouse traditions of seasonal brewing; and, since the country's last occupation ended in 1945, a plague of industrial lagers.

If Belgian brewing has themes they include a love of conditioning beers slowly to perfection at or near the brewery, while at the same time trying obsessively to bring balance to brews that are by any measure extreme and sometimes unique.

FLANDERS

The *gruut* barons of ancient Bruges may have been responsible for the modern Flemish weakness of putting spice in beer, or it might have been the influence of well-intentioned British beer writers of the late 20th century. It was certainly expat British brewers who earlier in the century had popularized sweet stout and lightweight pale ales called *speciaal*. However, firm brown ales, some aged to sourness, were a renowned feature of better Flemish taverns many centuries earlier, the oak-ageing tradition continuing to this day in West Flanders.

ACHEL
Hamont-Achel, Limburg

Newest Belgian Trappist brewery, near Hamont-Achel in Limburg since 1999. Delicate, hazy, hoppy, aromatic **5°
Blond ★★☆** appears only on draught and on-site; while the Trappist Achel bottle-conditioned beers are slightly spicy, straw-coloured lighter *tripel*, **Blond ★★☆**; more typically monastic, richer, fruitier *dubbel*, **Bruin ★★★**; and chestnut-coloured, sweetish, chocolaty barley wine, **Extra Bruin ★★★☆**.

ALVINNE
Moen, West Flanders

Restless craft brewery, now at Moen, south of Kortrijk. Mostly experimental,

sometimes wildly. Chinook and Amarillo hops dominate Belgo-US-style pale ale **Alvinne Extra Restyled ★★★**; the **Freaky** brands **★★** pack significant flavour into lightweight beers; and variants of the Three Wise Men Christmas beers **Gaspar**, **Balthazar** and **Melchior ★→★★★** repeat the same at the heavy end. Can try too hard.

ANKER, HET
Mechelen, Antwerp

Ages-old brewery at Mechelen, expanded after 1945 and kicked into shape by the current team since 1998. Its Gouden Carolus beers include clear, heavily caramelized, dark brown **Classic ★★★**; US-influenced strong, pale, hoppy-faced but modestly bitter

Hopsinjoor ★★☆; clean, precise, sweetish and light golden **Tripel** ★★☆; and premium-priced, annually recreated deep brown monster **Cuvée van de Keizer Blauw** ★★★→★★★★.

BAVIK
Bavikhove, West Flanders

Family-run brewery northeast of Kortrijk. Five low-alcohol *tafelbieren* ("table beers") like **Triple Bock** ★★ are of historic interest; summer and winter versions of **Wittekerke** wheat beer ★→★★ are popular; acidic, ultra-dry, oak-aged **Petrus Aged Pale** ★★☆ is an acquired taste; while ruby-tinted **Petrus Dubbel Bruin** ★★☆ coalesces polish with a nice malt mix and adequate hopping.

BOCKOR
Bellegem, West Flanders

The fifth Omer Vanderghinste to head up his family's 1892 brewery at Bellegem south of Kortrijk is changing things. A new strong golden ale was also christened **Omer** ★★☆; the blended, faintly sour brown ale has relaunched

as **VanderGhinste Oud Bruin** ★★; and the sour, zingy 18-month-old lambic-like beer has been released to the US market as **Cuvée des Jacobins Rouge** ★★★.

DESTINATION
KORTRIJK

Boulevard (15 Groeningelaan) is a beautiful, ancient, laid-back café bistro with a wide range of beers and simple delightful snacks to enjoy in Burgundian style inside or overflowing onto the grass.

BOELENS
St Niklaas, East Flanders

Brewery founded 1993 at a drinks merchant west of Antwerp. Former honey beer specialist evolving into a star brewer. **Waase Wolf** ★★☆ is a light copper-coloured, spiced ale best described as Flemish; brown **Dubbel Klok** ★★★ is confident, caramel-laced, fruity and robust; blond **Tripel Klok** ★★★☆ matches an intense herbal hop aroma to a substantial, mellow, grainy body; golden **Bieken** ★★☆ flys the flag for honey beer.

BOSTEELS
Buggenhout, East Flanders

Family brewery northwest of Brussels, famed for glassware. Candied amber **Pauwel Kwak ★★** is served in a stand-mounted coachman's flask; spicy blond **Tripel Karmeliet ★★☆**, sweetened by wheat and oats, has a painted goblet; and **DeuS ★★★** is presented in Champagne flutes; a production method like that of classic sparkling wine is used to create a highly carbonated, pungent and expensive pale blond sparkling barley wine.

CNUDDE
Eine, East Flanders

Not so much a brewery as a working antique, at Eine, near Oudenaarde. This occasional brewhouse puts out one brown ale, which it ages in metal tanks. **Cnudde Bruin ★★☆** is a dry, sourish, grainy brown ale with a strong lactic presence, in which cherries are sometimes steeped to create the rare, grab-it-if-you-see-it **Bizon Bier ★★☆**.

CONTRERAS
Gavere, East Flanders

Farm-based brewery south of Ghent. Gradual renovation of equipment and brands brought a reliable range of Valeir beers. Blond is better double-hopped as **Extra ★★**; **Donker ★★** is medium-brown and liquorice-laced; and **Divers ★★☆** is a soft light golden *tripel*. Light copper local pale ale **Tonneke ★★☆** baffles those drawn to big tastes and clear styles, as does its seasonal variant **Especial Mars ★★**.

DESTINATION
OOSTAKKER

Geerts Drankenhandel is the finest beer supermarket in Belgium, just off the Ghent ring road (7 Ledergemstraat), well stocked, simply presented, full of rare Belgian and better imported beers. Good parking.

DE KONINCK (DUVEL MOORTGAT)
Antwerp

Brewed in Antwerp and part of the city's soul. Saved from closure by a takeover in 2010. Its main beer, an amber quaffer made with 100% malt and Saaz hops, is **De Koninck**, which is best unpasteurized on draught, OK in bottle, rough when in cask **★→★★**. All other brands seem to fail, though neat and polished *dubbel*, **Winter ★★**, and clean, finely balanced, light amber **Triple d'Anvers ★★** may work.

DE RYCK
Herzele, East Flanders

Small century-old family brewery, between Ghent and Brussels. Pale ale

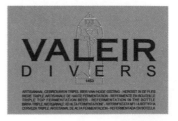

Special De Ryck ★★☆ is soft but rugged-edged; while the newish range of Arend beers includes the interesting, zesty and yeasty **Blond** ★★; a workmanlike, dryish, caramelled brown **Dubbel** ★★; and a nicely evolving orange-blond **Tripel** ★★★ in which floral, citrus and sweet elements complement each other.

DILEWYNS
Dendermonde, East Flanders

The Dilewyns family's 2011-built brewhouse at Dendermonde in East Flanders is their first in decades, arriving as precisely designed as their Vicaris beers. The **Tripel** ★★☆ is reliable, balanced, biscuity and full-flavoured; it is sometimes found blended with lambic as the clunky-sounding **Tripel-Gueuze 7%** ★★☆; while **Generaal** ★★★☆ is a star-quality, liquorice-laced, sumptuous brown ale, gifted by the brewer to her grandmother.

DOCHTER VAN DE KORENAAR
Baarle-Hertog, Antwerp

Brewery (founded 2007) at Baarle-Hertog, a Belgian enclave within the Netherlands. Its main beers have become themes on which variations are played. Blond Noblesse went from *kölsch* to *saison*, then excelled as **Extraordinaire** ★★→★★★; strong, spicy, rye-seeded **Finesse** ★★☆ is changed but not improved when barrel-aged; beefy brown **Embrasse** ★★☆ moves from strong porter to spiked when aged in whisky casks; and gently vanilla-imbued strong stout **Charbon** ★★☆ has yet to morph.

DESTINATION
ANTWERP

Kulminator (32 Vleminckveld) is a charming old drinks café just off the city centre, with perhaps the largest range of aged beers found anywhere, mostly Belgian but with some other extreme rarities.

DUVEL MOORTGAT
Breendonk, Antwerp

Belgium's most successful independent brewery, at Breendonk near Antwerp. Flagship strong golden ale **Duvel** ★★★ might have lost a step over the years, but is occasionally redeemed by its various **Triple Hop** incarnations ★★☆→★★★☆; the best light beer is **Bel Pils** ★★; while the best of the declining Maredsous brands, **8 Bruin** *dubbel* ★★ no longer cedes sweetness to complexity on ageing. Acquiring Liefmans of Oudenaarde led to an upgrade of its cherried ale to **Cuvée Brut** ★★★.

GAVERHOPKE, 'T
Harelbeke-Stasegem, West Flanders

Tiny brewery at Harelbeke near Kortrijk, sold on in 2007. Cursed by an earthy yeast strain, its beers are finally in transition, influenced by collaboration brewing. Variable strong blond **Zingende Blondine** ★★ can shine; and the unclassifiable old rascal **Den Twaalf** ★★☆ has recently become sharpish, multi-layered and more enjoyable.

GLAZEN TOREN
Erpe-Mere, East Flanders

Small brewery run by beer writer Jef Van Den Steen and friends at Erpe-Mere, near Aalst. Tries to use locally grown hops in sweetish beers like amber **Saison d'Erpe Mere** ★★☆ beyond any *saison* style we know; perfumed, citrus, murky oats and buckwheat "double *wit*" **Jan De Lichte** ★★☆; orange-blond and prominently hopped **Ondineke Oilsjtersen Tripel** ★★★; and the excellent dark, rich **Canaster Winterscotch** ★★★☆.

GRUUT
Ghent, East Flanders

Annick De Splenter's pub brewery in Ghent, established in 2009, makes her *gruut* beers without hops, a trick that is easiest in spicy, soft, citrus, clove and banana **Wit Bier** ★★☆; more difficult in the neutral, slightly citrus **Blond** ★★; not yet entirely credible in the slightly odd **Amber Ale** ★☆, but adequate in heavier, many-flavoured **Bruin** ★★☆.

HALVE MAAN
Bruges, West Flanders

The Vanneste family reacquired its brewery in Bruges in 2007. The Brugse Zot beers tend to be safe, though the grassy, pale **Blond** ★★ makes an excellent fallback beer and equally reliable **Dubbel** ★★ is growing pleasant edges. Straffe Hendrik brands are bolder: **Tripel** ★★☆ is a crisp, golden-amber strong ale; **Quadrupel** barley wine ★★★ is deep brown, rich and fruity. More is promised.

HOFBROUWERIJKE, 'T
Beerzel, Antwerp

One-man hobby brewery with a prodigious output, some impressive. Top of the tree is lightish, roasty, dry Irish-style stout **Hofblues** ★★★;

unmistakably Belgian pale ale **Hoftrol** ★★☆ is a reliable all-malt creation; and lighter, slightly tangy pale ale **Hofnar** ★★, with whisky malt, is worth sourcing.

HOF TEN DORMAAL
Tildonk, Flemish Brabant

A 2009 start-up on a smallholding at Tildonk, east of Brussels. The full plan involves growing its own barley and hops. Of the regulars, sweet, dark **Donker** ★★ and strongish, earthy **Blond** ★★ are the ones to go for. Experiments with ageing beer in spirits casks have produced **Barrel-Aged Project** beers ★→★★★, more often excellent than not. **Wit Goud** ★★, a strong blond beer with chicory, divides opinion.

KERKOM
Kerkom, Limburg

Brewing at the old farmstead in Kerkom, near Sint-Truiden in Limburg, has ceased for now, forcing the hire of facilities elsewhere to produce classically light, aromatic, super-hoppy **Bink Blond** ★★★; assertive, fulsome, golden **Kerckomse Tripel** ★★★☆ (US: Bink); ruby-brown, bittersweet and spiced seasonal **Winterkoninkske** ★★; and its blockbuster namesake, the huge and complex barley wine **Grand Cru** ★★★☆.

LEROY
Boezinge, West Flanders

In Boezinge, West Flanders since 1720 but averse to limelight. Owned by the same family as VAN EECKE. **Leroy Stout** ★★ is a dark, sweet, ruddy-brown, low-alcohol milk stout; **Sas Pils** ★★ is precise with true pilsner character; **Yperman** ★★☆ is a ginger-coloured and caramelized Flemish pale ale; and **Christmas Leroy** ★★☆ is deeper and richer, usually achieved at medium gravity.

MALHEUR
Buggenhout, East Flanders

Brewery (since 1997), added to a drinks merchant at Buggenhout in East Flanders. Regular Malheur beers include golden-blond **6** ★★, an English-style pale ale; and over-pepped blond *tripel* **10** ★★. Like near neighbour BOSTEELS it dabbles in classic-sparkling-wine-style, high-carbonation beers but without pungent spicing. Of these, straw-coloured **Bière Brut Reserve** ★★★ is strong and appealing; while **Brut Noir** ★★★ is an effervescent dark malt drink spewing coffee and chocolate in its after-burn.

NIEUWHUYS
Hoegaarden, Flemish Brabant

Tiny 2006 brewery at Hoegaarden in Flemish Brabant. Soft but tangy Flemish pale ale **Rosdel** ★★ is a rarity; as is faintly floral, lightly coriandered *witbier* **Huardis** ★★; though the limelight beckons for its accomplished heavyweight brown *tripel* **Alpaïde** ★★★.

PALM
Steenhuffel, Flemish Brabant

The second largest independent ale brewer in Belgium, at Steenhuffel, northwest of Brussels. Owns RODENBACH and half of **BOON**. Surprisingly good pilsner **Estaminet** ★★ is made with Saaz hops and tastes of a brewery; easy-drinking staple **Palm Speciale** ★★ is well made and clean; amber-blond **Royale** ★★ is smoother, sweeter and stronger; and **Steenbrugge Dubbel Bruin** ★★ is a polished interpretation with added *gruut*.

PROEF
Lochristi, East Flanders

Modern brewery at Lochristi, between Ghent and Antwerp, creating bespoke beers of high technical quality for hundreds of wannabe and established brewers. The in-house Reinaert range includes one of few examples of a 100% malt **Tripel** ★★☆; and heavy, chestnut-coloured barley wine, **Grand**

Cru ★★☆. Its efforts for others all too often go unacknowledged.

RODENBACH (PALM)
Roeselare, West Flanders

Unique 1899 brewery full of huge oak tuns, mostly ripening a single brown ale for up to two years. Blended into fresh beer this makes sour-edged, pleasant-enough **Rodenbach** ★★; but in its raw form, filtered and slightly sweetened it becomes **Grand Cru** ★★★☆, an ultra-tangy, red-brown ale of fine oak-aged character, often appealing to wine drinkers. Selected runs in larger bottles become **Vintage** ★★★★. **Vin de Céréale** ★→★★★ is an occasional and experimental single tun bottling of a higher strength brew.

ST BERNARDUS
Watou, West Flanders

Opened in 1946 to brew commercial scale beers for **WESTVLETEREN**. Went on to develop its own range, including highly spiced **Wit** ★★☆, a wheat beer of character; a blond, oddly bitter, lighter **Tripel** ★★★; dark, mellow, sweet, stronger *dubbel*, pear-dropped **Prior 8** ★★★☆; massive golden-brown, fruity, alcoholic barley wine **Abt 12** ★★★☆; and darker, spicy winter indulgence **Christmas Ale** ★★★.

SCHELDE
Meer, Antwerp

Began life in Dutch Zeeland, moving to Meer in northern Antwerp in 2008. Blond ales include sweet and spicy

Strandgaper ★★; standout is the newish, crisper edged and better hopped *tripel* **Hop Ruiter ★★★**; frustratingly noncommittal **Oesterstout ★★** is strong but not Imperial; and reworked pale barley wine **'n Toeback ★★** always seems too young.

SLAGHMUYLDER
Ninove, East Flanders

Family-owned 1860 brewery at Ninove, west of Brussels, becoming one of Belgium's first lager breweries in 1926. Its seasonal **Paas-** and **Kerstbier ★★☆** are variations on its regular pilsner. Better known for its Witkap range, including slightly peppery pale ale **Special ★★**; fruity, aromatic, light blond **Stimulo ★★☆**; and unusual, yeast-spiced, straw-coloured **Tripel ★★★**.

SMISJE
Mater, East Flanders

The hamlet of Mater's smaller brewery. The **Smiske Nature-Ale ★★** is an instantly likeable pale ale using Poperinge hops and 100% malted barley, appearing dry-hopped as **Extra ★★☆**. Newer are ruddy-brown work-in-progress **Bruin ★★** and the annually revamped heavyweight spiced barley wine **Winter ★★☆**.

STRUBBE
Ichtegem, West Flanders

Family brewery (1830) at Ichtegem in West Flanders. Well-hopped **Strubbe Pils ★★☆** is perhaps Belgium's best; though easy-drinking, sour-edged brown ale **Ichtegems Oud Bruin ★★**; and the slightly sweetened form of its oak-aged parent beer, **Grand Cru (6.5%) ★★★**, are better known. Brews many other beers every year incluing **Vlaskop ★★**, a wheat beer made with unmalted barley.

> ### DESTINATION
> ### OSTEND
>
> Bistronoom (22 Vindictivelaan) is a restaurant offering exceptionally fine dining with a unique range of around 150 Belgian beers in large bottles, for sharing over a carefully prepared and paired menu – book ahead.

STRUISE BROUWERS
Woesten, West Flanders

Rock-star craft beer makers, less well recognized at home, brewing mostly at Deca in Woesten, West Flanders. First attracted attention with aged variations on dark barley wine **Pannepot ★★★→★★★★**; twisting and turning with fruit-steeped, equally strong winter equivalent **Tsjeeses ★★★**; and creating an absurdly strong, surprisingly approachable Imperial stout **Black Albert ★★★☆**. To prove it can brew normal beers, try the disarmingly simple unfiltered, slightly hopped-up **Koeke Blond ★★☆**. Experimental and collaboration beers abound.

VAN DEN BOSSCHE
Sint-Lievens-Esse, East Flanders

Fourth-generation 1897 tower brewery at Sint-Lievens-Esse, south of Ghent.

Reputable for middle-strength dark ales like dryish, caramelled **Buffalo 1907** ★★☆, which spawned stronger **Belgian Stout** ★★☆ for the US market. Pater Lieven brands include moderately sweet and toasty **Bruin** ★★☆; and variable big brown spice-bomb **Kerst Pater Special Christmas** ★★→★★★, always with a smack of chocolate.

VAN EECKE
Watou, West Flanders

Small 1862 brewery at Watou, in the West Flanders hop belt. Its Kapittel range includes well-rounded, easy-drinking dry-hopped **Blond** ★★☆; and medium-dark *tripel* **Prior**, which becomes epic after a few years' cellaring ★★★ ·★★★★. Misty **Watou's Witbier** ★★☆ is light and lemony; while long-established, far-sighted, proto-IPA **Poperings Hommelbier** blossoms annually when brewed with new harvest hops ★★→★★★.

VAN STEENBERGE
Ertvelde, East Flanders

Started in 1768 and went commercial in the 1900s, at Ertvelde, north of Ghent. Once famed for sour brown ales, now concentrating on abbey beers and export. A huge and confused range includes well-judged stronger **Augustijn Blond** ★★☆; medium-strong brown ale **Leute Bokbier** ★★, part-German, part-Belgian, part-Dutch; and **Gulden Draak** ★★★, its opaque bottles obscuring a serious, intensely spicy barley wine finished with a vintner's yeast.

VERHAEGHE
Vichte, West Flanders

Fourth-generation family brewery at Vichte, near Kortrijk, making regular beers for its drinks warehouse and blends of aged brown ales for the world. Those who like their oak-aged browns sharper, lighter and woodier should prefer **Vichtenaar** ★★★☆; while for darker, sweet-sharp and buttery, choose **Duchesse de Bourgogne** ★★★☆; **Echt Kriekenbier** ★★☆ has whole cherries steeped in it. Best of the rest is **Noël Christmas Weihnacht** ★★☆, a yellow-ochre, lightly spiced seasonal ale.

VIVEN
Sijsele, West Flanders

Beer commissioner and wholesaler at Sijsele in West Flanders, helping create an excellent series of Viven beers with PROEF from simpler varieties like pale, hazy, rustic **Belgian Ale** ★★ and hazy golden, off-centre, spice-effect **Blond** ★★, to impressive US-influenced hoppy, roasty, aromatic **Porter** ★★★ and slightly over-hopped **Imperial IPA** ★★☆.

WESTMALLE
Westmalle, Antwerp

The largest of the Trappist brewers, located northeast of Antwerp. Responsible for popularizing the dark-*dubbel*, blond-*tripel* divide of stronger ales in the 1950s. Ruddy-brown Trappist **Westmalle Dubbel** appears in large and small bottles and on draught, simplicity rising and chocolaty-fruity edginess falling accordingly ★★→★★★; while stronger pale orange-golden benchmark **Tripel** ★★★ gains colour, allure and a honeyed glow with cellar ageing. Delicate, light golden **Extra** ★★★ is brewed occasionally for the abbey community and some of its friends.

enough grain; **Extra 8°** ★★★ is a liquorice-edged, strong *dubbel* that improves grudgingly in the cellar; and **Abt 12°** ★★★☆ is a dark, intense barley wine that used to grow with keeping but less so now. Special releases for a supermarket chain and US importer were unlikely to have been brewed here exclusively.

WESTVLETEREN
Westvleteren, West Flanders

A low-production Trappist brewery in West Flanders that has been afflicted by adulation, with the scarcity of its beers being mistaken for magnificence. The only one that uses whole hops is the skilful, light, rustic **Blond** ★★★☆, with its intense floral aroma and just

WILDEREN
Wilderen, Limburg

Up-and-coming, as yet tiny 2011 brewery near Sint Truiden in Limburg, whose early efforts with dryish, Limburg-style blond **Wilderen Goud** ★★ and heavier, light copper-coloured, polished, candied, if fussy **Tripel Kannunik** ★★ show promise.

BRUSSELS & WALLONIA

The beer of the south is *saison* and it probably does not exist – at least not as a single form. To one side, historically, is French *bière de garde*, ale stored in bottles and casks while its character matures like a fast-motion Alpine lager without the ice. To the other is agricultural practicality, farm brewing being easier in the winter for the availability of a workforce and the absence of insect life. In truth the Wallonian *saison* tradition is as authentically imprecise as that of German *landbier*.

ABBAYE DES ROCS
Montignies-sur-Roc, Hainaut

Second-generation family brewery southwest of Mons. The original **Brune** ★★★ is a huge, spiced, ruddy-brown ale; **La Montagnarde** ★★☆ is a

darkish amber *tripel* full of malt with spicy edges; while best of the lighter brews are **Blanche des Honnelles** ★★, a "double" wheat beer with malted oats and minimal spicing and complex, unspiced blond ale **Altitude 6** ★★☆.

ACHOUFFE (DUVEL MOORTGAT)
Achouffe, Luxembourg

Brewery (1982) in the Belgian Ardennes, absorbed in 2006. **La Chouffe ★★☆** is a strong, polished blond flavoured with coriander; darker **MacChouffe ★★** is a Scotch ale flavoured with liquorice; **Chouffe Houblon Dobbelen IPA Triple ★★☆** is a Belgian take on US-style double IPA; and Christmassy **N'Ice Chouffe ★★☆** is a heavy, sweet, black, spiced barley wine.

BLAUGIES
Blaugies, Hainaut

Brewery (1988) on the French border, southwest of Mons. Dry amber-blond, hazy, grainy **Darbyste ★★** has a dab of fig juice and is best drunk fresh; **Saison de l'Epeautre ★★★★** has clumpy turbidity, the aroma of a hay barn and a hop-yeast-buckwheat combo that delivers a rural idyll to the glass; and **La Moneuse ★★★** is a punchy, stronger *saison* tasting like a huge best bitter made with its characteristic yeast-hop double act.

BOCQ, DU
Purnode, Namur

Busy, successful, family-dominated brewery north of Dinant. **Blanche de Namur ★★** is a soft, unfiltered wheat beer; strong ale **Gauloise Brune ★★** has drifted from messy classic to cleaned-up also-ran; while **Corsendonk Pater ★★**, a medium-dark, sweetish *dubbel* is one of many contract brews, in this case for a pretend abbey that is really a drinks wholesaler.

CARACOLE
Falmignoul, Namur

Well-respected 1994 brewery in an ancient brewhouse at Falmignoul in the Meuse valley. **Troublette ★★☆** is an interesting, cloudy, lightly spiced wheat beer; flagship **Caracole ★★☆** is a strongish amber ale made with five malts and orange peel; **Saxo ★★** is a strong golden-blond ale; and **Nostradamus ★★☆** is the rich, warming, spiced barley wine.

CAZEAU
Templeuve, Hainaut

Farm brewery at Templeuve west of Tournai, in its third incarnation; the original started in 1753, this one in 2004. Tournay beers include solid, dependable, crafty-edged **Blond ★★★**; **Noire ★★★**, a roasted strong porter of promise; and **Noël ★★★**, a large, sweetish brown ale reminiscent of old-style Gauloise (*see* BOCQ, DU). **Saison Cazeau ★★☆** is a wispy summer ale that mixes floral hops with elderflower.

CHIMAY
Chimay, Hainaut

Second largest Trappist brewer, at the Abbaye Notre-Dame de Scourmont in southern Hainaut. Began small scale in 1862, expanding in the 1920s. Brewed and fermented at the abbey, bottled and matured in Bailleux. Adopts different names for 75cl bottles. **Rouge (Première) ★★** is a slim-bodied red-brown *dubbel* with light, crude bitterness; **Blanche (Cinq Cents) ★★☆** is an improving, well-balanced *tripel* that appears part-filtered on draught; and **Bleue (Grande Réserve)** ★★★ is a giant barley wine that avoids cloying.

DUBUISSON
Pipaix, Hainaut

Family-run brewery east of Tournai, that began brewing a super-strong English-style beer in 1931, its sole product until 1991. The original sweet, heavy, 12% ABV Bush (US: Scaldis) barley wine is now **Ambrée** ★★☆, which also comes oak-aged as Prestige ★★★☆; and again aged rather variably in old barriques of Nuits-St-Georges, hence **Bush deNuits** ★→★★★. Also makes lighter, hazy, spiced blond **Cuvée des Trolls** ★★.

DUPONT
Tourpes, Hainaut

Photogenic farm brewery with ultra-modern kit at Tourpes, east of Tournai. Its thumbprint yeast mix screams farmhouse. Brewing since 1844, in the family since 1920. Faintly musty, hopyard, barn-in-autumn, style-defining **Saison Dupont** ★★★★ even outshines its Wallonian *tripel*, **Moinette Blonde**

★★★☆. Other greats include curiously attractive, unfiltered **Rédor Pils** ★★★; and strong amber **Bière de Beloeil** ★★★. Makes many organic beers including florally hopped **Biolégère** ★★★, in an older, lighter *saison* style.

ELLEZELLOISE (LÉGENDES)
Ellezelles, Hainaut

This 1993 farmhouse brewery is the folksier half of Brasserie des Légendes (*see* GÉANTS), using flip-top bottles. **Blanche de Saisis** ★★ is a tasty dark blond unspiced wheat beer; **Quintine Blonde** ★★☆ is an unusually bitter, peel-edged stronger blond; but pride of place goes to Imperial-strength **Hercule Stout** ★★★☆, its chocolate and prune flavours offset by something Irish.

GÉANTS (LÉGENDES)
Ath, Hainaut

LÉGENDES' other half brews in a 21st-century brewery at a 12th-century castle east of Tournai. Sweetish, light amber **Saison Voisin** ★★ foils style junkies through low hopping but has genuine 1884 pedigree; **Gouyasse Triple** ★★☆ has a fulsome, grainy character with aged edges; while the most impressive regular is quirky, red-brown, off-peaty, yeast-spiced **Urchon** ★★★.

JANDRAIN-JANDRENOUILLE
Jandrain-Jandrenouille, Walloon Brabant

Brewery (2007) based in a converted barn at a double-barrelled village south of Brussels, using American kit and hops to make Belgian beers. **IV Saison**

★★★ is in the modern floral bitter style that influenced early US craft brewers; red-brown **V Cense** ★★★ would be a black *saison* if such existed; and **VI Wheat** ★★☆ is a mid-Atlantic wheat beer that begins with Simcoe hops, ends with Belgian spicing and does fresh bread throughout.

LEFÈBVRE
Quenast, Walloon Brabant

Efficient family-run 1876 brewery at Quenast, southwest of Brussels. Made its way in recent years with sweet and spicy beers for the abbey at Floreffe ★→★★; and honey ales like sweet, amber-blond, orangey **Barbãr** ★★. More impressive is its flip-top-bottled bitter, strong, golden ale, **Hopus** ★★☆.

MILLEVERTUS
Breuvanne, Luxembourg

Lovably adventurous 2004 Luxembourg province brewery that moved in 2011 to Breuvanne. An overly large portfolio includes plum-tinged, aromatic wheat beer **Blanchette de Lorraine** ★★; a Belgian take on US-style IPA called **La Bella Mère** ★★☆; and **La Douce Vertus** ★★, a lush, sweetish, full and dark French-style *bière brune*.

ORVAL
Villers-devant-Orval, Luxembourg

When the Trappist abbey of Orval, near Florenville in Luxembourg province, was reconstructed in 1926 the Order added a brewery to assist with costs. **Orval** ★★★☆ is a unique dry-hopped, bottled pale ale presented in a distinctive bottle, full of hops in the nose but not on the palate, flirting with genius by adding musty overtones to both by using brettanomyces in bottle-fermentation.

RANKE, DE
Dottignies, Hainaut

Small brewery at Dottignies, north of Tournai, run by a Flemish brewing team who led the return of hops to Belgian brewing and revived mixed fermentation beers. **Saison de Dottignies** ★★★ is the cleanest of the hoppier *saisons*; **XX Bitter** ★★★☆ is a pale golden ale of thirst-quenching bitterness; **Guldenberg** ★★★☆ is what happens when herbal hops are loaded into a well-made *tripel*; and dark, strong **Noir de Dottignies** ★★★ defies classification deliciously. **Cuvée de Ranke** ★★☆ is a sparkling musty concoction made by mixing blond ale with young lambic.

CUVÉE DE RANKE

70% BELGIAN SOUR ALE
WITH 30% LAMBIC ADDED

Unpasteurized - Unfiltered.

ROCHEFORT
Rochefort, Namur

Small Trappist brewery cursed by being considered among the best in the world. **Trappistes Rochefort 6 ★★☆** is a dark, dryish *dubbel* without complexity, praised by association; **8 ★★★☆** is the staple – an interesting, ruddy-brown, often hazy ale with firm chocolate backtastes; **10 ★★★★** is a supremely complex barley wine, best sipped or inhaled from a chalice, while seated next to an open fire.

DESTINATION
LIÈGE

Bars with a huge range of beers are rare in Wallonia, but the chain that began with suburban Vaudrée 1 (109 Rue du Val Benoit, Angleur) and central Vaudrée 2 (149 Rue St Gilles) has expanded to seven, each opening daily until the small hours, with 400+ beers and a huge menu.

RULLES
Rulles, Luxembourg

Small 1998 brewery in the southernmost part of the Belgian Ardennes. From a strong range we recommend in particular punchy, hop-packed, light pale ale **Estivale ★★★**; the original perfectly balanced, faintly spicy and characterful **Blonde ★★★**; the workmanlike **Brune ★★☆** with its dried- and tropical-fruit edges; and the superb **Triple ★★★☆**, a beer that manages distinctive character with meticulous delivery.

ST FEUILLIEN
Le Roeulx, Hainaut

Handsome 1873 brewery between Charleroi and Mons recently producing some confident new beers. **Saison ★★★** is up with the best; house staple **Blonde ★★☆** is well rounded and aromatic; newer **Grand Cru ★★★** is restrained and delicate for a heavyweight pale golden, *tripel*; and light-red-brown **Cuvée de Noël ★★☆** is an indulgent soup of spices. Occasionally sold in huge bottles.

DESTINATION
MONS

A dozen bars around the Grand Place have good selections of Wallonian beers, including two, Excelsior (no 25) and Cervoise (no 29), where the exceptional choice includes many that are hard to source.

SENNE
Brussels

Fully formed new arrival in Brussels, making beers that capture past and

future equally well. Hoppy light ale **Taras Boulba** ★★★ is best bottled or in Brussels; near-perfect prize-winning **Stouterik** ★★★☆ is a lighter stout that defies subtyping; precisely hopped pale ale **Zinnebir** ★★★ similarly avoids being American, British or a modern *saison*; while sweetish, yeast-spiced, orange-blond *tripel* **Jambe-de-Bois** ★★★☆ has snuck up to become one of Belgium's most enjoyable beers.

DESTINATION BRUSSELS

Poechenellekelder (5 rue du Chêne) is a delightfully eccentric drinks café opposite the Mannekin Pis, with a superbly chosen beer list, puppetry and an atmosphere that is hard to beat.

SILLY
Silly, Hainaut

This fifth-generation brewery at Silly, between Tournai and Brussels, has been commercial since 1950. Its light amber **Saison de Silly** ★★ is in the

less fashionable sweet style; the best newcomer is light blond, hazy and evolving **Abbaye de Forest** ★★☆; and the old trooper is chestnut-brown, rounded and warming sweet **Scotch Silly** ★★☆. To contract it makes slightly aged amber heavyweight **Cuvée des Hauts Voués de l'Avouerie d'Anthisnes** ★★☆.

VAPEUR, À
Pipaix, Hainaut

Saved from extinction in 1984 by idealists and still steaming away three decades later. The Vapeur brands are **Légère** ★★, a light ale sprinkled with vanilla and cinnamon; microbiologically odd, spiced, strong amber-blond **En Folie** ★★; and herbal, amber heavyweight **Cochonne** ★★☆. Frankly acidic and highly spiced **Saison de Pipaix** ★★ is as per the original, allegedly.

LAMBIC MAKERS OF BRUSSELS & PAYOTTENLAND

The lambic beers of Brussels and the rural area to its west, Payottenland, are the ultimate in folk brewing. In a tradition of dry to sourish wheat beers that had been present in western and central European brewing for centuries, they take variation to a new level by fermenting only with "wild" yeast, initially air-borne and found growing around the makers' storage areas and inside the oak casks in which lambics ferment. Few flavour characteristics are shared with ale or lager, most ending blended as *gueuze* or fruit-steeped as *kriek* or *framboise*.

BOON
Lembeek, Flemish Brabant

The southernmost and most influential lambic brewer. Kept aloft by a commercial cherry beer but better represented by surprisingly approachable, grapefruit-tinted **Oude Geuze ★★★** and sharp, slightly sour but high-fruited **Oude Kriek ★★★☆**. **Oude Geuze Mariage Parfait ★★★☆** is delightfully dry with a softness that comes from higher gravity. Also makes a lambic-free malt-driven dark brown ale with liquorice overlay called **Duivels Bier ★★☆**, for fun.

CAM, DE
Gooik, Flemish Brabant

Blender and steeper of other brewers' lambics at Gooik. Most frequently encountered are the tart, lemon-grapefruit and horse-blanket mélange called **De Cam Oude Geuze ★★★☆**; and the dark, vinous, sour-cherry, ultra-dry **Oude Kriek ★★★**; though the occasional, musty, lemony, late-bottled **Oude Lambiek ★★★** and sharp, spritzy, candy-coated, light amber bottled **Oude Faro ★★★** will amuse or amaze too.

CANTILLON
Brussels

Not far from Midi station, near central Brussels, part museum but mostly revered creator of astonishing drinks. 100% lambic and mostly organic ingredients. Half the output is accomplished, dry, slightly bitter, light citrus **Cantillon Gueuze 100% Lambic ★★★☆**. The rest is mostly fruit-steeped lambics such as the sharp, wild, lightly cherried regular **Kriek**, and its *grand cru* version **Lou Pepe ★★★→★★★★**; hybrid, black-graped **St Lamvinus ★★★☆**, aged in burgundy casks; and flowery, pink, extra dry and delicate *framboise* **Rosé de Gambrinus ★★★☆**. Darker, more assertive **Iris ★★★☆** cannot be a *gueuze* as it is all barley.

DESTINATION
BRUSSELS

Moeder Lambic Fontainas (8 Place Fontainas) is a modern café next to Anneessens metro, with the best range of rare draught Belgian beers in the country, a few special foreign beers and top-quality finger food.

DE TROCH
Wambeek, Flemish Brabant

Oldest of the surviving lambic makers, probably at Wambeek since 1780. Troubled for decades, fruit syrups being added to lambics drifting toward eccentricity. New dynamics are now in play and the latest stock of **Chapeau Cuvée Oude Gueuze** ★★☆ has raised heads. A dry and challenging **Oude Kriek** ★★ appears occasionally too.

DRIE FONTEINEN
Beersel, Flemish Brabant

Recently restyled 3F, a passionately committed lambic maker and now brewer. Its distinctive, dry and delicately bitter, pungent **Oude Gueuze** is also available as **Vintage** ★★★→★★★★; while its neatly balanced, big fruit and lambic **Oude Kriek** takes on historically traditional flavour as **Schaarbeekse** ★★★→★★★★★ when made with small, hard bitter Schaarbeek cherries. Ancient oddity **Doesjel** ★★★ is a bottled lambic beer from a cask that fails to ferment properly. For a modern twist try the near-black, mixed fermentation **Zwet.be** ★★☆, ale-fermented and brettanomyces-conditioned, its taste heads off towards oak-aged brown ale.

GIRARDIN
Sint-Ulriks-Kapelle, Flemish Brabant

Fourth-generation family brewers, on the farm at Sint-Ulriks-Kapelle since 1882. Most of the flat draught lambic found in Payottenland cafés will be its lightly carbonated, fungal, beery **Jonge**, or

sharper, flat, musty, vinous **Oude Lambic** ★★. **1882 Gueuze** still appears in white- and black-labelled versions, respectively dominated by filtered young lambic or else masterfully blended with older casks ★★→★★★★. The **1882 Kriek** is filtered and sweetish in the bottle but drier and hazy on draught ★★→★★★★.

HANSSENS
Dworp, Flemish Brabant

Longest established of the lambic caves, at Dworp. Tart and slightly bitter **Hanssens Artisanaal Oude Gueuze** ★★★ ages beautifully for five years and more to become slightly smoky; unusually, its well-cherried but sharp **Oude Kriek** ★★★☆ also gains maturity for a couple of years; while unique, must-try traditionally made **Oudbeitje** ★★★ gains little colour but much aroma from its strawberries. **Lambic Experimental** ★★★ beers in raspberry and blackcurrant are just that.

LINDEMANS
Vlezenbeek, Flemish Brabant

Seventh-generation lambic brewer at Vlezenbeek. The single lambic is lighter

in colour and strength than most and is put to best effect in sharp, light, lemony and faintly hoppy **Cuvée René Grand Cru Oude Gueuze ★★★** and steadily evolving **Kriek Cuvée René ★★★**. Among a clutch of sweeter beers, semi-authentic darkish **Faro Lambic ★★** is most enticing when iced on a hot day.

DESTINATION DWORP

Boelekwis is a great barn of a place on the road east from the E19 junction 20, south of Brussels (856 Alsembergsesteenweg), with reliable food and the widest selection of authentic lambics in Belgium.

MORT SUBITE (HEINEKEN)
Kobbegem, Flemish Brabant

Part of a global group possessing a handful of century-old, massive oak tuns in which its better lambics are aged. Most production is commercial fruit beer but two are made the old-fashioned way. Rarely encountered, faintly acetic and not so agricultural **Oude Gueuze ★★☆** is not as balanced as the sweeter-fruited, mouldy-in-a-good-way **Oude Kriek ★★★**.

OUD BEERSEL
Beersel, Flemish Brabant

Lambic cave in a preserved former brewery at Beersel, brewing own recipe lambics at **BOON**. These are blended to become an increasingly distinctive, bitter, citrus **Oude Geuze ★★★☆** that has begun to win prizes, and steeped to produce a pretty confident, sharpish, bottled **Oude Kriek ★★★**. The base beer, draught, flat, youngish **Oude Lambiek ★★★** can be found in a few dozen cafés locally and in Brussels.

TILQUIN
Bierghes, Walloon Brabant

New lambic cave and *gueuze* blender at Bierghes, just south of Payottenland, the first to include Cantillon lambics. Early releases of **Oude Gueuze Tilquin à l'Ancienne ★★☆** lacked any three-year-old lambic so were immature, though the potential was clear. The need to recoup investment has seen a *faro*, a plum lambic and more controversially a kegged mixed lambic, said to be typical of old Brussels.

TIMMERMANS
Itterbeek, Flemish Brabant

Brewery (1850) owned by a drinks and leisure group. Mostly commercial fruit beers but its **Oude Gueuze ★★☆** is perhaps the driest and tartest of all; as is experimental **Oude Kriek ★★☆**. Among the rest are lambic-*witbier* hybrid **Lambicus Blanche ★★**; and dark, fruity **Bourgogne des Flandres Bruin ★★**, made by mixing lambic into brown ale to imitate ageing.

GERMANY

As recently as 1980 half the breweries in the world and 80% of those in the EU were in Germany. Although the number of breweries in Germany has risen in recent years to nearly 1500, by the beginning of 2013 the equivalent proportions were roughly 15% and 30%.

German-style brewpubs, or *hausbrauereien*, began increasing in the mid-1980s, particularly in the north. More of the recent additions are tiny operations the size of mechanized home brew kits. Meanwhile, the old village and town breweries, typically small and family-owned for generations, are on the wane.

Most of the better-known beer brands are owned by the ever-conflating brewing groups that control much of the market. The global brewers are there, as in AB InBev's ownership of Beck's, Diebels, Löwenbräu, Franziskaner and others; Carlsberg's Holsten; Heineken's Paulaner and Hacker-Pschorr. Yet other groups, such as Bitburger, Radeburger, Oettinger, Ootker and Krombacher, remain in German hands.

German beer is delicate and pure. Its hallmarks are the dominance of the four "noble" (*edel* in German) hops: Hallertau, Spalt, Tettnang and Saaz – backed up by adherence to the now defunct *Reinheitsgebot* (*see* box overleaf). All that the big companies can bring to it are economies of scale, which often means cutting out the time-consuming parts that make all the difference to quality.

While German brewing is orderly, it is neither monochrome nor monotonous. To equate German beer with standardized blond lager is wrong. While 70% of the beer consumed in Germany would fit a broad definition of "pils", included within that are beers more correctly seen as *helles*, export, *märzen*, *spezial* or even the occasional longer-aged and deeper *lagerbier*.

More interesting are the types of beer that owe their origins to particular regions, the purpose behind our sub-division of the country into brewing regions.

BAVARIA

The Free State of Bavaria is home to 15% of the German population and over half its breweries. It only became part of Germany in 1919, though it had influenced brewing there for centuries. Made up of seven districts, of which two in particular warrant special attention from beer lovers – Oberfranken, or Upper Franconia, in the north around Bamberg and Bayreuth, and Oberbayern, or Upper Bavaria, in the south around Munich.

MUNICH & UPPER BAVARIA

While Munich's Oktoberfest, held annually in September, may steal the publicity, the city's famous beer halls are far more enjoyable and available all year round, while outside the great beer gardens of Oberbayern beckon visitors to sit under the linden trees from May to October, here to drink beer by the litre-sized *maß* in preference to the half-litre *seidla*.

THE REINHEITSGEBOT

The German beer-purity order, or *Reinheitsgebot*, was seen in turns as the world's first and longest-lasting piece of consumer protection law; a lucrative patronage scam; and ultimately, by the EU, a restraint of trade.

In 1516 at Ingolstadt, after price wars developed between brewers and bakers over the purchase of wheat, and concerns grew that brewers were polluting local beers with anything from pulses and root vegetables to mushrooms and animal products, the rulers of Bavaria instigated the *Surrogatvebot*, an order banning brewers from making beer from anything other than barley, hops and water, yeast escaping mention for being undiscovered.

Wheat was soon excluded from the ban, though brewers who used it had to be licensed directly by the royal household.

As the German states came together slowly over the centuries, then precipitately under Bismarck, the regulation spread northward, becoming woven into a notion of German-ness. By 1906 the *Reinheitsgebot* had become universal, Bavaria having made its adoption a precondition for becoming part of Germany, which it eventually did in 1919.

Critics of the *Reinheitsgebot* tend to decry the restraints it put on recipes and thereby the brewer's imagination, while its supporters cite exactly the same concerns, only from a different perspective.

ANDECHS, KLOSTERBRAUEREI
Andechs, Bavaria

Famous brewery below Andechs monastery, founded by Benedictine monks in 1455. Still owned by the order, but brewing is now carried out by secular staff. Andechser beers include **Export Dunkel ★★** with hints of bitter chocolate; the complex **Weissbier**

Dunkel ★★ with banana, chocolate and caramel flavours; clove- and banana-dominated **Weissbier Hell** ★★; and the frustrating **Doppelbock Dunkel** ★★☆ with insufficient weight to be a classic.

AUGUSTINER-BRÄU
Munich, Bavaria

One of only two large Munich breweries not attached to global brewers – Hofbräu is owned by the state of Bavaria – and so loved locally that it no longer needs to advertise. The name Augustinerbräu München is most associated with the sweet, pale **Edelstoff** ★★★; the bready **Lagerbier Hell** ★★★☆ sets the standard for *helles* lagers; the **Dunkel** ★★☆ does the same for darker beers; aromatic hop character abounds in the **Pils** ★★; while powerful **Maximator** ★★★ is all about molasses and dark fruits.

AYINGER
Aying, Bavaria

A family-run brewery located southeast of Munich and named after its village. Ayinger beers enjoy widespread distribution in the US. They are best known to enthusiasts for the rich and complex *doppelbock* **Celebrator** ★★★, of which there are echoes in the coffee- and caramel-accented **Altbairisch Dunkel** ★★☆. The stronger and more traditional of two citrus-spicy wheat beers is **Ur-Weisse** ★★★; while the pick is **Weizen-Bock** ★★★, which shows up just in time for Christmas.

BAUMBURG, KLOSTERBRAUEREI
Altenmarkt, Bavaria

Small brewery in a disused hilltop monastery outside Altenmarkt, brewing since 1612 and owned by the Dietl family since 1875. Ten solid enough beers are made, with lightly roasted, caramel-edged **Baumburger Dunkle Weiße** ★★ and creamy, citrus, seasonal **Weissbier Bock** ★★ hovering above the rest.

CAMBA BAVARIA
Truchtlaching, Bavaria

This 2008 pub brewery at Truchtlaching was opened to showcase the equipment of the brewery manufacturer Braukon but quickly gained a following for its wide range of ales and lagers, many of which are daringly experimental for Bavaria. The regular range of 20 or so Camba or Camba Bavaria beers includes the US-style citrus-hoppy **Pale Ale** ★★☆, and über-pepped **Eric's IPA** ★★☆, while the roasty **Eric's Porter** ★★☆ is head and shoulders above

most other German examples. Best of the indigenous beers is the dark and fruity **Truchtl'inger Wilderer Weisse** ★★☆, though the whole shebang is worth a detour.

CREW ALEWERKSTATT
Munich, Bavaria

Cuckoo brewers Mario Hanel and Timm Schnigula use the kit at Schlossbrauerei Hohenthann to make the two ales that, around Munich, seem to define those bars serving them as interested in the future of beer. Each is a work in progress US-style, the lighter **CREW Pale Ale** ★★ being hop-heavy, while *bock*-strength **CREW IPA** ★★ is rather subdued. They will get there.

ERDINGER WEISSBRÄU
Erding, Bavaria

The largest wheat beer producer in the world, still owned by the Brombacher family, at Erding just outside Munich. Erdinger beers enjoy global distribution and as often occurs with one so large, are predictably inoffensive. Its **Weißbier** ★☆ is for beginners, while **Urweisse** ★☆ manages to be thin and sweetish despite a claim to be brewed to an 1886 recipe. By far the best is the banana-spicy *weizenbock* **Pikantus** ★★.

ETTALER, KLOSTERBRAUEREI
Ettal, Bavaria

Another monastic brewery where secular staff produce the beer, in a high pass near Oberammergau. Of the Ettaler beers the best for regular drinking is the fruity-caramel **Kloster Dunkel** ★★☆; while the powerful and heavily roasted *doppelbock* **Curator** ★★★ should be approached with care.

FORSCHUNGSBRAUEREI
Munich-Perlach, Bavaria

Interesting small brewery in the Perlach district of greater Munich, founded in 1930, since when four generations of the Jakob family have made experimental beers, mainly for other brewers. Until recently, the only Forschungsbrauerei beers were the generously hopped yet malt-led **Pilsissimus** ★★★, described by the brewery as a *spezial* or export beer but by outsiders as a Bohemian-style pils; and **St Jakobus Blonder Bock** ★★★, which somehow starts out sweet but has a hoppy ending. Summer 2012 saw a new seasonal with the promise of more to come.

FREILASSING, WEISSBRÄU
Freilassing, Bavaria

As its name suggests, this tiny 1910 family brewery on the Austrian border near Salzburg makes only wheat beers. The two standard Weißbräu Freilassing beers are a pale, yeasty and citrus-tart **Hefe-Weizen** ★★☆ and equally impressive **Hefe-Weizen Dunkel** ★★. There are also two strong seasonal beers that we infer would reward finding.

GUTMANN
Titting, Bavaria

In the delightfully named Titting, close to the border with Franconia, this sizeable brewery makes mainly a full range of wheat beers, meaning pale, dark, strong, light and alcohol-free. The soft, banana-heavy, fruit-accented **Hefeweizen** ★★☆ is among the best in style; fruity-yeasty down-banana **Dunkles Hefeweizen** ★★ is not far behind; and the powerful yet quaffable pre-Christmas seasonal **Weizenbock** ★★★ also performs well.

HERRNGIERSDORF, SCHLOSSBRAUEREI
Herrngiersdorf, Bavaria

Founded in 1131 by Benedictine monks, this small brewery south of Regensburg has a strong claim to be the oldest brewery in the world in private ownership. Its main beer is the herbal-hoppy **Schlossbräu Trausnitz Pils** ★★☆;

though the equally interesting, aromatic, recent arrival **Hallertauer Hopfen-Cuvée** ★★☆ features Perle, Saphir and two types of Hallertau hops in its recipe.

HOFBRAUHAUS FREISING
Freising, Bavaria

First mentioned in 1160, this substantial brewery moved from the cathedral hill to the centre of Freising a century ago. Its range of six wheat beers sells as Huber Weisses and includes the classically banana-yeasty *weisse* **Original** ★★ and toffee-sweet, darker *weisse* **Dunkel** ★★. It also makes six regular beers under the brewery's name, of which the best is caramel-and-chocolate-dominated **Hofbrauhaus Freising Dunkel** ★★.

KARG
Murnau, Bavaria

This wheat beer brewery at Murnau makes some of the cloudiest beers known to man. Its Karg beers include chewy and yeasty **Helles Hefe-Weißbier** ★★☆; the often lump-infested but tasty **Dunkles Hefe-Weißbier** ★★; and star performer, the rich and fruity winter seasonal **Weizen-Bock** ★★★.

MAXLRAIN, SCHLOSSBRAUEREI
Maxlrain, Bavaria

Seventeenth-century castle brewery west of Rosenheim owned by Princess von Lobkowicz. Go for the chocolaty and bitter **Aiblinger Schwarzbier** ★★; bready and bittersweet **Schloss Trunk** ★★; and the rich and fruity Lenten *doppelbock* **Jubilator** ★★☆.

PAULANER (HEINEKEN)
Munich, Bavaria

Part of a group in which Heineken has virtual control, with around 50 beers made in the Munich brewery. Under the Paulaner brand it makes the solid **Hefe-Weißbier Naturtrüb** ★☆ and the legendary if diminished *doppelbock* **Salvator** ★★. Under the Hacker-Pschorr brand it makes the popular seasonal **Oktoberfest Märzen** ★★ and the group's most impressive beer, the stronger, toffee-raisin *doppelbock* **Animator** ★★☆. It makes the Thurn & Taxis brands too.

DESTINATION
MUNICH

To understand the whole Bavarian beer thing, find your way around Weisses Bräuhaus (7 Tal) for mid-morning white sausage and wheat beer; the Viktualienmarkt beer garden for a pre-lunch one from the cask; the Augustiner Bierhalle (27 Neuhauser Straße) for pomp and lunch; the Chinesischer Turm (3 Englischer Garten) for an afternoon in the park; Ayingers Speis & Trank (1a Platzl) for proper food and drink; finishing with the Hofbräuhaus (9 Platzl) for oompah, kitsch and the shadow of history.

REUTBERG, KLOSTERBRAUEREI
Sachsenkam, Bavaria

This small brewery was founded near Sachsenkam in 1677 and has been working as a cooperative since 1924. Its best Reutberger performers are the soft and aromatic **Export Hell** ★★; the nutty and drier than average **Export Dunkel** ★★; and the well-balanced, honey-tinged Lent seasonal **Josefi-Bock** ★★☆.

SCHÖNRAM, PRIVATE LANDBRAUEREI
Petting/Schönram, Bavaria

An eighteenth-century family-owned brewery located at Schönram, near the Austrian border not far from Salzburg. It is one of the first traditional brewers to introduce a range of bottled beers in foreign styles, called Bavaria's Best, at a price, among which the double IPA, **India Pale Ale** ★★☆, in particular, hints at more to come. Among the Schönramer beers available, the dry, crisp Pils is better when it is unfiltered and dry-hopped as **Grüner Pils** ★★; the dry **Altbayrisch Dunkel** ★★ is also nutty; and the **Saphir Bock** ★★☆ is so sweet and fulsome that it could easily be mistaken for a Belgian *tripel*.

STIERBERG
Stierberg, Bavaria

A small brewery in the village of Stierberg near Obertaufkirchen, from which few of owner-brewer Annemarie Kammhuber-Hartinger's four beers escape. If touring, try the aromatic and bittersweet **Stierberg Eispils Monte Torro** ★★ and copper-coloured, caramel-accented, fruity *Münchener* **Stierberg Hochzeitsbier** ★★☆ before the others.

UNERTL, WEISSBRÄU
Mühldorf am Inn, Bavaria

The second smallish brewery in the Unertl family (*see* UNERTL WEISSBIER) was founded at Mühldorf in 1929 and has been known to export its beers even to the UK. The best of these Unertl beers is the organic **Bio-Dinkel Weisse ★★☆** made with spelt; the yeasty and citrus **Oberland Export Weissbier ★★** is a new addition. The local **Steer Weiße ★★** and seasonal **Steer Weißbierbock ★★** are also currently made here by brewer Rudi Steer, whose own brewery is over capacity.

UNERTL WEISSBIER
Haag, Bavaria

One of two similarly named wheat beer breweries in the region (*see* UNERTL, WEISSBRÄU), owned by cousins. This one is in Haag and owned by the fifth generation of first-born males in the family to take the name Alois. The standard Unertl offering is a fruity and slightly acidic **Weissbier ★★☆**; the darker and sourer *dunkelweisse* **Ursud ★★** comes bottled only; and gently tart **Weissbier Bock ★★☆** hints at chocolate and dark fruit.

WEIHENSTEPHAN
Freising, Bavaria

Officially the world's oldest brewery, adjacent to a renowned brewing school of the same name. Owned by the state of Bavaria since the dissolution of the monasteries in 1803. Brewing began on this hill southwest of Freising in 1040 when Abbot Arnold obtained a licence from the town. The biggest-selling Weihenstephaner beer is the thinnish and banana-spicy **Hefeweissbier ★★★**; the **Hefeweissbier Dunkel ★★** has chocolate and banana but is light; the best is the powerful, citrus *weizenbock* **Vitus ★★☆**; and the odd one out is malty-sweet *doppelbock* **Korbinian ★★**.

DESTINATION
INTERNET: BIERKOMPASS.DE

Germany's leading internet beer shop, importing a fabulous selection of craft beers old and new from around the world, and shipping across the whole of Germany and beyond.

BAMBERG & UPPER FRANCONIA

Many Franconians will tell you, without rancour, that they do not wish to separate from Bavaria as they have never been a part of it. Those who live in Upper Franconia can harbour similar thoughts about their neighbours in Middle and Lower Franconia.

There are more breweries per head here than anywhere else in Europe, and possibly the world. Most have been established for several generations. Bamberg alone has 10, making it one of the great beer-exploring destinations.

As well as an abundance of local beers self-styled as *vollbier*, *landbier*, *zwickelbier*, *kellerbier* or *ungespundetes*, this is the spiritual home of rauchbier, a type of lager made with malted barley that has been smoked.

BAYRISCHES BRAUEREIMUSEUM KULMBACH
Kulmbach, Bavaria

In 2002 the world's first glass brewing vessels were installed here at the Bavarian Brewing Museum, formerly the Mönchshof brewery. The only regular beer is the unfiltered and grainy **Museumsbier** ★★, though there are half a dozen seasonals available periodically at the museum bar and adjacent pub.

BECHER-BRÄU
Bayreuth, Bavaria

The world's longest-standing brewery-borrower finally got its own brewery in 2011, having been using others since the small family firm was at Bayreuth in 1781. Until 1994 it used an old Kommunbrauerei, or community brewhouse, and thereafter commissioned another local brewer to make wort that

it would ferment. The best of its four regular beers is the herbal and slightly bitter **Becher-Bräu Kraußenpils ★★**.

DINKEL
Stublang, Bavaria

Tiny 1870 family brewery at Stublang, making one regular beer sold mostly at the tap on the edge of the village. **Stublanger Lagerbier ★★** has grainy malt character and finishes bitter. Also makes a November *bock*.

DREI KRONEN (MEMMELSDORF)
Memmelsdorf, Bavaria

Fifteenth-century pub brewery at Memmelsdorf a few doors up from HÖHN. Three beers are available year-round alongside one for each of the four seasons and a few experimental brews. Drei Kronen regulars include **Stöffla**

★★☆, a lightly smoked and sweeter than average *kellerbier*; and the draught-only, beautifully balanced, aromatic **Kellerpils ★★**.

Pils ★★ is stronger and maltier than most; the blond **Lagerbier ★★** is malty and herbal; and the city's strongest beer is the *doppelbock* **Bambergator ★★☆**.

DREI KRONEN (SCHESSLITZ)
Scheßlitz, Bavaria

A few kilometres up the road at Scheßlitz and unrelated to the Memmelsdorf **DREI KRONEN**. En route you will see the Drei Kronen at Straßgiech, a former brewery that is now the tap for **GÄNSTALLER-BRÄU**. The beers here are called Schäazer and include an aromatic **Original Premium Pils ★★☆** that finishes dry and bitter; and the maltier draught **Kronabier**, which loses something when bottled **★★☆→★★**.

EICHHORN
Hallstadt-Dörfleins, Bavaria

Small brewery at Dörfleins (Hallstadt) north of Bamberg, also known as Schwarzer Adler, unrelated to Eichhorn of Forchheim. Its five Eichhorn beers make it out of the village but not far. The crisp, well-rounded **Pils ★★☆** is better as a session beer than the more generously hopped **Export ★★**; but pick of the bunch is the pale, perfectly balanced **Kellerbier ★★★**.

FÄSSLA
Bamberg, Bavaria

Ambitious Bamberg brewery that has increased output tenfold in the past quarter century. All Fässla beers are well made. Nutty and bittersweet *dunkel* **Zwergla ★★** belies its strength; **Gold-**

GÄNSTALLER-BRÄU
Schnaid, Bavaria

The former Friedel brewery in Schnaid, now used by Andy Gänstaller to brew "extreme interpretations" of classic German styles. Beers are badged Drei Kronen when sold at the tap at Straßgiech but Gänstaller-Bräu elsewhere. The three regulars are the punchy, well-balanced **Kellerbier ★★☆**; the well-hopped **Zwickelpils ★★☆**; and stronger than typical **Zoigl ★★★**. Specials include the surprisingly subtle smoked *märzen* **FXA ★★☆**; and the astonishing smoked *doppelbock* **Affumicator ★★★☆**, brewed at the behest of Ma Che Siete Venuti a Fà in Rome but now sold elsewhere.

GOLDENEN ADLER
Rattelsdorf-Höfen, Bavaria

Diminutive 18th-century brewery in tiny Höfen, near Rattelsdorf, making a single amber, toffee-accented beer, **Goldenen Adler Ungespundetes Lager ★★☆**, brewed every couple of months and only available at the brewery.

GRASSER
Königsfeld-Huppendorf, Bavaria

Four regular Huppendorfer beers are made at this small brewery near Königsfeld, supplemented by a few seasonals. Optimistically described by the brewery as a *dunkel* is gently bitter amber standard **Vollbier ★★**; the **Hefeweizen ★★** has plenty of banana and clove; while in winter it offers herbal sweet and bitter **Heller Katherein-Bock ★★☆**.

GRIESS
Geisfeld, Bavaria

The village of Geisfeld, due east of Bamberg, manages to support two breweries (*see* **KRUG**). Output here barely reaches 1000hl a year and Griess beers are rarely seen elsewhere. The bestseller is dry and hoppy **Kellerbier ★★★**, which appears in a concentrated form in winter as **Bock ★★★**. Less well hopped but still excellent is the **Pilsner ★★☆**.

HEBENDANZ
Forchheim, Bavaria

Founded in 1579, one of four breweries in Forchheim. The standard Hebendanz session beer is the aromatic and well-rounded **Export Hell ★★**; equally good is the herbal-spicy **Edel Pils ★★**; chewy **Erstes Forchheimer Export-Hefe-Weissbier ★★** has banana in abundance; while its low-hopped, grassy, copper-coloured *märzen* **Jubiläums Festbier ★★** appears under different names through the year.

HÖHN
Memmelsdorf, Bavaria

Heavily rebuilt, substantial Memmelsdorf pub brewery and hotel a few seconds' walk from **DREI KRONEN**, housing a

wood-fired brewery that makes a single, unplaceable beer, a soft and herbal, unfiltered rustic pale lager called **Görchla ★★**.

HÖNIG
Tiefenellern, Bavaria

The Gasthof zur Post at Tiefenellern has brewed since 1478, the Hönig family taking over in 1812. Six Hönig beers are made, two of them seasonal. Best are the gently fruity and grassy **Lagerbier Ungespundet ★★** and **Posthörnla ★★☆**, a subtle *rauchbier* light on both smoke and colour.

HUMMEL-BRÄU
Merkendorf, Bavaria

The smaller of Merkendorf's brewers (*see* **WAGNER**) dates from the 16th century but is relatively adventurous, making more than a dozen Hummel-Bräu beers. Smoky but smooth **Räucherla ★★★** is possibly the best regular *rauchbier* made outside Bamberg; its golden, toffee-tinged **Kellerbier ★★★** has superb balance; the chewy Lent and Advent **Weizen-Bock ★★☆** drips with banana; and in winter the powerful **Räucherator Doppelbock ★★★☆** takes *rauchbier* brewing to a step beyond.

KEESMANN
Bamberg, Bavaria

The youngest of Bamberg's established brewers is not yet 150 years old. Exceptionally pale but impressively grainy **Keesmann Bamberger Herren**

Pils ★★☆ accounts for more than 90% of production and is the most widely available beer in the city. The best try-also is the nutty-caramel **Sternla Lager** ★★.

KNOBLACH
Schammelsdorf, Bavaria

Small, late-19th-century, family-run brewery at Schammelsdorf, east of Bamberg. The regular Schammelsdorfer beers are the fruity, dry and bitter **Ungspund's Lagerbier** ★★☆; spicy-fruity **Knoblach Weißbier** ★★; and **Räuschla** ★★, a malt-accented, dark, lightly smoked *märzen*.

KRAUS
Hirschaid, Bavaria

Family-run brewery and hotel in the centre of Hirschaid. Its nine Kraus beers have some local distribution. Best are the dryish and hoppy **Lager Hell** ★★☆; the lightly smoked **Hirschen-Trunk** ★★☆, an excellent *rauchbier* for the uninitiated; and good all-rounder, winter-only **Bock** ★★☆.

KRUG
Geisfeld, Bavaria

Geisfeld's other brewer (*see* GREISS) makes a single regular beer, rarely seen outside its traditional taphouse and summer terrace. Usually served in ceramic mugs, **Krug Lagerbier** ★★★ is actually a hazy, golden-amber *kellerbier* that is predominantly fruity and devilishly easy to drink. Three seasonal beers are rumoured to appear.

┌─────────────────────────────┐
DESTINATION
BAMBERG

Café Abseits (39 Pödeldorfer Straße), a couple of blocks out of town from the railway station, has accumulated a fine range of better Franconian beers and showcases some Weyermann experiments.
└─────────────────────────────┘

KULMBACHER
Kulmbach, Bavaria

Franconia's largest brewery traces its roots back to 1846, dropping Reichelbräu from its name in 1996 having acquired all of Kulmbachs's other sizeable brewers in the previous two decades. Around 30 beers are made, most under the EKU, Kapuziner, Kulmbacher or Mönchshof brands. **Mönchshof Schwarzbier** ★☆ is a smooth black beer that divides opinion beyond "playing it safe"; **Kapuziner Weißbier** ★★ has good flavour for one so mainstream. While its two strong *doppelbocks* are world famous but disappointing, try ruby-brown, sweet and powerful **EKU 28** ★☆; and not-so-strong, better balanced and more accomplished **Kulmbacher Eisbock** ★★.

KUNDMÜLLER
Viereth-Trunstadt, Bavaria

Family-owned brewery (since 1835) near Viereth-Trunstadt has expanded both its range and output in recent years. Among its Weiherer beers the bestseller is the flowery, golden, modestly proportioned **Lager** ★★; hoppy new addition

Urstöffla ★★☆ is billed as a *dunkel* but is more an amber *kellerbier*; hazy, herbal **Weiherer Keller-Pils** ★★☆ beats the ordinary one; and the amber **Rauch** ★★☆ is a lightly smoked, pale *rauchbier*.

LINDENBRÄU
Gräfenberg, Bavaria

This small brewery and distillery in Gräfenberg is at the end of the rambling railway line from Nürnberg Nordost. Of six Lindenbräu beers, two are seasonal. The bread-and-butter brand is the bitter but malt-led *dunkel* **Vollbier** ★★; the pale, citrus **Weizen** ★★ goes down best on a summer's day; while ruddy-brown and toasty **Festbier** ★★☆ is the Vollbier enhanced.

LÖWENBRÄU BUTTENHEIM
Buttenheim, Bavaria

The smaller of Buttenheim's two breweries, though its beers are fairly common in the region. Its Löwenbräu Buttenheim beers have changed a bit, the draught *kellerbier* known as **Ungespundetes Lagerbier** ★★ lacking the punch it once had, while the recently added **Pilsner** ★★ seems to have inherited some of its hops.

MAHR'S BRÄU
Bamberg, Bavaria

Family-owned Bamberg brewery almost opposite KEESMANN, well established in the US market, with a couple of export-only products. Best known of the Mahr's Bräu beers is the unfiltered,

light amber-coloured **Kellerbier Ungespundet** ★★★, best when served from the barrel; **Festtags Weisse** ★★ combines citrus and banana; the pale winter seasonal **Bock Bier** ★★☆ has bread and spice notes; while the other winter brew **Der Weisse Bock** ★★☆ is punchier.

MAISEL
Bayreuth, Bavaria

This, Bayreuth's last large brewery company, no longer has a second site in Bamberg but is otherwise expanding its horizons. Best known for its Maisel's Weisse wheat beers, the citrus-spicy flagship *weizen* **Original** ★★ and caramel-fruity **Dunkel** ★☆, new ventures include a range of Maisel & Friends craft-style beers and experimental up-hopped, organic and spiced beers.

> ### DESTINATION
> ### BAMBERG
>
> The world's best brewery crawl – 10 in all – must include Fässla and Spezial on Obere Königstraße, Mahr's and Keesmann on Wunderburg, Greifenklau on Laurenziplatz and the Schlenkerla tap on Dominikaner Straße.

MEINEL-BRÄU
Hof, Bavaria

Gisela Meinel-Hansen's family has run this brewery in Hof for 12 generations. Its Meinel-Bräu beers are fairly easy to find in the area but are rarely seen elsewhere. The hugely aromatic **Classic Pils** ★★☆ lives up to its name thanks to a generous dose of aromatic hops; while caramel features largest in the toasty **Märzen** ★★; and smooth, sweet, caramelized *doppelbock* **Absolvinator** ★★☆ travels from sweet to bitterish via fruity.

MEISTER
Pretzfeld-Unterzaunsbach, Bavaria

This is a small family-run brewery at Unterzaunsbach, near Pretzfeld. Brewer Georg Meister makes his copper-coloured, toasty and slightly bitter *dunkel*-ish **Meister Vollbier** ★★☆ year-round and sells it unfiltered in the spring and summer as **Zwickelbier** ★★☆. An amber-coloured *märzen*-ish winter offering called **Festbier** ★★☆ is stronger and a little sweeter.

MEUSEL-BRÄU
Dreuschendorf, Bavaria

Perhaps uniquely, three generations of the same family brew at the small Meusel-Bräu brewhouse in Dreuschendorf. Of the regular Meusel-Bräu beers, **Kellertrunk** ★★ is a little sweeter than most *kellerbiers*; while the deep red-brown **Bamberger Landrauchbier** ★★☆ might be termed a middle-smoke; and vanilla and clove are to the fore in soft **Ottmar Weisse** ★★. It will be interesting to see how the youngest generation's impressive charge into ever-changing seasonal beers (there have been 30-plus of these to date) settles down.

MÜHLENBRÄU
Mühlendorf, Bavaria

Small family brewery at Mühlendorf, a bus ride southwest of Bamberg. Typical Franconian village set-up, its Mühlenbräu beers rarely being seen elsewhere. Its **Dunkles Lagerbier** ★★☆ is full-flavoured with dabs of liquorice and caramel; while the **Pils** ★★ is light, malt-led and herbal.

MÜLLER
Debring, Bavaria

Recently rebuilt but still tiny brewery at Debring, between Bamberg and Würzburg. Another high-quality village brewery, making five Debringer beers, rarely seen beyond the parish. Go for the herbal, well-balanced **Pilsner** ★★☆, or **Micherla** ★★☆, its immediately likable unfiltered *kellerbier*.

OTT
Oberleinleiter, Bavaria

Seventeenth-century family-run brewery at Oberleinleiter, a village in the Franconian Jura. Its six beers are not as rare as some but rarely stray more than 20km (12 miles) from home. Herbal hops lift **Ott Edel-Pils** ★★ from its grainy base; and nutty malt is to the fore in the curiously named *dunkel*, **Ott Obaladara** ★★.

PENNING-ZEISSLER
Hetzelsdorf, Bavaria

Hillside brewery in tiny Hetzelsdorf, east of Forchheim. The eight Hetzelsdorfer beers are split equally between regular and seasonal and include the sweetish, malty **Pilsner ★★** and bready, bitter, *dunkel*-ish Fränkisches Vollbier, also available unfiltered and slightly diminished as **Lagerbier ★★**.

RECKENDORF, SCHLOSSBRAUEREI
Reckendorf, Bavaria

Decent-sized brewery dating from 1597, when it opened to serve the now-demolished Reckendorf castle. Recently rebranded Recken, its beers are readily found within a 30-km (19-mile) radius. Soft and aromatic **Edel-Pils ★★** just passes muster; while the citrus-spicy **Weissbier ★★** is perhaps its best everyday beer. A spicy, strong, seasonal **Weizenbock ★★☆** was introduced in 2010.

REH
Lohndorf, Bavaria

Early-20th-century family-run brewery at Lohndorf in the Eller valley. Its seven Reh-Bier brands do make it out of the valley and can be found up to 50km (31 miles) away. The local favourite is the fruity, hoppy **Pils ★★**; the **Zwick'l ★★** is fruity but dry; while winter-warmer **Der Dunkle Reh Bock ★★★** has sweet fruit initially, insinuates caramel and ends with a gentle bitter kiss.

RITTMAYER
Hallerndorf, Bavaria

Hallerndorf's larger brewery, Lieberth, has expanded its range of Rittmayer beers to more than 15 and also bottles in flip-tops for other brewers. One to watch for new directions, but for now head for the light brown, slightly sour *zoigl*-ish **Hausbrauerbier ★★**, a *kellerbier* created in remembrance of the citizen's right to brew; or the winter-only, banana-packed, slightly spicy, bit-too-sweet **Weizenbock ★★☆**.

ROTHENBACH
Aufseß, Bavaria

The largest of four small breweries in the municipality of Aufseß, a collection of 10 communities with a combined population of barely 1300. It's located in Aufseß village itself, hence Aufsesser beer. Its star performer is the dry and chocolaty **Dunkel ★★★**; with the herbal-hoppy **Pils ★★☆** and equally well-hopped winter **Bockbier ★★☆** not far behind.

ST GEORGEN BRÄU
Buttenheim, Bavaria

One of rural Franconia's larger brewers, next door to LÖWENBRÄU BUTTENHEIM. Best known of the St Georgen Bräu range is hoppy and darker-than-average **Keller Bier ★★★**; **Landbier Dunkel ★★☆** has caramel-chocolaty notes and is almost as good; the crisp, hoppy **Pilsener ★★★** is tastily balanced; while **Doppelbock Dunkel ★★☆** is more like the Landbier Dunkel on steroids.

SCHEUBEL
Schlüsselfeld, Bavaria

This small 1828 brewery with modern kit is run by the Scheubel family at Schlüsselfeld, where it makes two beers called Stern-Bräu for general consumption. The **Vollbier** ★★ is a well-hopped *helles*, while the superb **Festbier** ★★★ is a lightly smoked, fairly dry *rauchbier* that is among the best.

SCHLENKERLA (HELLER)
Bamberg, Bavaria

Legendary 16th-century Bamberg brewery better recognized by the name of its beers and brewery tap, Aecht Schlenkerla. Its most often encountered beer is the extraordinary and unrelentingly smoky **Rauchbier Märzen** ★★★☆; more subtle is the unsmoked wheat and smoked barley combination in **Rauchweizen** ★★☆; best is chewy autumn treat **Aecht Schlenkerla Rauchbier Urbock** ★★★★; the powerful winter special **Eiche** ★★★★ is sweeter and less assertively smoked; and **Fastenbier** ★★★☆ appears for Lent at the brewery tap only.

SCHROLL
Nankendorf, Bavaria

Mid-19th-century brewery at Nankendorf, out in the sticks between Bamberg and Bayreuth. The two regular Nankendorfer beers and one seasonal are seen occasionally elsewhere. Caramel and bitter hops are evident in the chewy **Landbier** ★★☆; while the toasty **Bockbier** ★★☆ starts sweet before aiming toward a stronger hop finish.

SCHWANENBRÄU BURGEBRACH
Burgebrach, Bavaria

A tiny brewery at Burgebrach that seems to have expanded from its pub brewery base. Its Schwanenbräu Burgebrach brands include a spicy, bittersweet, unfiltered amber *Münchener* called **Lagerbier** ★★☆; a stronger, grassier, golden **Kellerbier** ★★; and the elusive, powerful, slightly tart but interesting seasonal **Der Weisse Bock** ★★☆, which deserves wider attention.

SESSLACH, KOMMUNBRAUHAUS
Seßlach, Bavaria

This community brewery was built into the town wall of picturesque Seßlach. The only regular Seßlacher beer is the nutty, bittersweet **Hausbräu** ★★, which is joined occasionally by the similar but slightly stronger and hoppier **Festbier** ★★☆. Two pubs on the nearby square are supplied with wort that they lager themselves to make *zoigl* beers.

SPEZIAL
Bamberg, Bavaria

Smallish family-run Bamberg brewery, directly opposite **FÄSSLA**. Owner-brewer Christian Merz smokes his own barley malt as they do at fellow *rauchbier* specialists **HELLER**, only on a much

smaller scale. The "ordinary"
Spezial beer is the near-perfectly
balanced, understated **Rauchbier
Lager** ★★★★; the more robustly
smoked **Rauchbier Märzen** ★★★
is often preferred by those who are
seeking a SCHLENKERLA; the *kellerbier*
Ungespundet ★★★ is well-hopped
but completely unsmoked; and
Rauchbier Bock ★★★☆ again
involves subtle end smoking, this
time applied to quite a delicate but
interesting *bock*. Its Weissbier is
made by Schneider at Essing.

STAFFELBERG-BRÄU
Bad Staffelstein-Loffeld, Bavaria

The largest of five breweries along
the valley southeast from Bad
Staffelstein, named after the peak that
looms above its home town, Loffeld.
Best of the Staffelberg-Bräu range is
the **Hopfen-Gold Pils** ★★☆, which
manages to balance bitter hops with
quite intense malt; roasted malt and
caramel are to the fore in **Loffelder
Dunkel** ★★; while spicy banana
marks out the **Hefe Weißbier** ★★.

TRUNK
Lichtenfels, Bavaria

Located near Lichtenfels, just behind the
baroque basilica at Vierzehnheiligen.
This small family-run brewery, which
was founded in 1803, names its beers
Vierzehnheiligener Nothelfer, after the
14 holy helpers who are said to have
appeared on the site in 1446. **Trunk**
★★☆ is a nutty-caramel, dryish *dunkel*;
and **Bio-Weisse** ★★ a banana-fruity
organic wheat.

WAGNER
Merkendorf, Bavaria

Merkendorf's other brewery (*see* HUMMEL)
has an output of 17,000hl a year and its
Wagner beers are a relatively common
sight to the east of Bamberg. Its principal
product, a golden, moderately hopped,
grassy *kellerbier* called **Ungespundetes
Lagerbier**, sings on draught but mumbles
a few words in the bottle ★★→★★★;
Märzen ★★☆ is full-flavoured, biscuity
and hoppy; the fruity-hoppy **Festbier**
★★ appears so often it barely remains
seasonal; and bittersweet **Bock Hell**
★★☆ heralds Christmas.

WAGNER BRÄU
Kemmern, Bavaria

This small family-run brewery at Kemmern
near Bamberg is unconnected to WAGNER
or to a similarly named producer in nearby
Oberhaid. The best of its 10 Wagner-Bräu
Kemmern beers are grassy and bitter
Ungespundetes Lagerbier ★★☆; and
dry, hoppy **Pils** ★★☆.

WEISSENOHE, KLOSTERBRAUEREI
Weißenohe, Bavaria

They first brewed at this former
monastery near Gräfenberg around
1050. Urban Winkler's family took over
in 1827 and now brews around 20,000hl
each year. The signature Weißenoher
Klosterbrauerei beer is the nutty, copper-
amber, unclassifiable **Altfränkisch
Klosterbier** ★★; bread and caramel
come through in **Eucharius Märzen**
★★; and chocolate-raisin-caramel in Lent
seasonal **Bonator Doppelbock** ★★☆.

ZEHENDNER
Mönchsambach, Bavaria

Brewery established in the late-19th-century at Mönchsambach, a hamlet to the west of Burgebrach. Its five Mönchsambacher beers include well-rounded bestselling **Lagerbier ★★☆**; chewy banana milkshake **Hefeweizen ★★☆**; and fruity-alcoholic Christmas golden treat **Weihnachts-Bock ★★★**.

REST OF BAVARIA

Bavaria's five other districts are Lower and Middle Franconia, Schwaben (Swabia), Oberpfalz and Lower Bavaria. The lower number of breweries here is relative – Amberg alone has six – and there are more remnants of the *zoigl* tradition (*see* box, page 73). In the north one goes to the *bierkeller* and in the south to the *biergarten* – it amounts to the same thing. The west in particular is associated with the production of big, spicy, heavily clouded *hefeweizen* and other variants of wheat beer, while Lower Franconia is more of a wine region.

ADLER BRÄU
Stettfeld, Bavaria

Recently rebuilt and relocated close to the tap, this smallish brewery bottles for a number of even smaller brewers. Best of the Adler Bräu beers are light amber, toasty-caramel *kellerbier* **Alt Fränkisches Lagerbier ★★**; aromatic and hoppy pilsener **Stöpflder Classic ★★☆**; herbal-hoppy **Stettfelder Pils ★★**; and biscuity, beautifully hopped **Stettfelder Heller Bock ★★★**.

ALTSTADTHOF
Nuremberg, Bavaria

This Nuremberg pub brewery kick-started the German *hausbrauerei* renaissance in 1984. Better known for its smooth, roasted **Altstadthof Schwarzbier ★★**, it is its fruit-accented **Altstadthof Maibock ★★☆** that has the edge for being a dangerously sophisticated yet approachable beer.

ANDORFER, WEISSBRÄU
Passau-Ries, Bavaria

Tiny brewery on a hill above Passau, by the Austrian border, making only wheat beers. The Andorfer house staple is the grainy, rustic **Weizen ★★☆**; while orange and clove stand out in the slightly sour **Weizen-Bock ★★☆**.

AUTENRIED, SCHLOSSBRAUEREI
Autenried, Bavaria

Mid-17th-century brewery near Ichenhausen that grows and malts most of the grain it uses. Around 60,000hl of beer passes out of its gates annually, most of it toward northwestern Schwaben. Autenrieder brands include **Urtyp Hell** ★★, with a good presence of noble hops; a **Weizen** ★★ with clove and fruits to the fore; **Weizen-Bock** ★★☆, with so much spicy fruit presence you may want to chew before swallowing; and in contrast the understated, caramel-laced **Leonhardi Bock** ★★☆, which hides its strength well.

BAYER
Theinheim, Bavaria

This small family-run brewery at Theinheim is fast approaching its 300th anniversary. Its only regular beer is the excellent unfiltered, gravity-drawn **Bayer Theinheim Ungespundetes Landbier** ★★☆, a pale and grassy *kellerbier*. A pale *bock* appears for Lent.

BRUCKMÜLLER
Amberg, Bavaria

Sedate Amberg, on the river Vils, boasts six breweries, the largest of which began life in a Franciscan monastery in 1490. In 1803, following dissolution, the Bruckmüller family bought all bar the church. Still produces some beers under the Weizen Falk ("White Falcon") brand, leading to Germany's most confusing beer name, **Weizen Falk Dunkles Falk** ★★, for a nuts-and-toffee, bottom-fermented, bottle-conditioned brown beer without wheat. Of the Bruckmüller brands, the fruity-hoppy, golden-orange **Kellerbier** ★★ and lightish coloured, sweet-fruity-bitter *doppelbock* **Superator** ★★☆ are the best.

DESTINATION NUREMBERG

Few local places seem to stock a wide range of Franconian beers but Landbierparadies (60 Galgenhofstraße and other locations) is an exception, selling over 100 brands by the bottle and case.

EICHHOFEN, SCHLOSSBRAUEREI
Eichhofen, Bavaria

Late-17th-century village brewery near Regensburg. Six beers include the powerful treacle-toffee seasonal **Eichator Doppelbock** ★★☆; and the unfiltered, strongly chocolaty **Eichhofener Spezial Dunkel** ★★, sold as Premium Dunkel when bottled.

FALTER
Regen, Bavaria

The largest brewery in the Bavarian Forest was founded at Regen in 1649 and acquired for J B Falter and his descendants in 1928. Best of the Falter wheat beers is the soft and spicy **Weissbier Premium Gold** ★★, with typical banana and clove flavours; while best of the rest is **Regenator** ★★☆, an unusually dry, liquorice-fruity *doppelbock* for the carnival season.

FAUST
Miltenberg am Main, Bavaria

Miltenberg's only remaining brewery is the last left in what is principally a wine-producing area. The Faust beers from this small-to-medium-sized firm are widely available in the area and include the new heavily hopped US-style pale ale **Auswandererbier 1849** ★★☆; more traditional dry and yeasty **Kräusen** ★★☆; and an alcohol-infused **Doppelbock Dunkel** ★★☆ draped in molasses.

FISCHER
Höchstadt-Greuth, Bavaria

Norbert Fischer's family has been brewing at Greuth, near Höchstadt, since 1702. The pick of the three regular Fischer beers is the delicately smoked, none-too-assertive **Rauchbier** ★★☆, which makes a good starter for newcomers to the style; staple **Lagerbier** ★★ is bready; while the dark **Bockbier** ★★ is a sweet and malty winter warmer.

FRIEDEL
Zentbechhofen, Bavaria

Two kilometres from the previous entry, the village of Zentbechhofen is home to this 15th-century brewery, slightly larger than its near neighbour but every bit as local. Favourites of the Friedel range are the grassy **Vollbier** ★★; and darker, stronger and sweeter **Lagerbier** ★★.

FUCHSBECK
Sulzbach-Rosenberg, Bavaria

Small brewery immediately below the castle at Sulzbach-Rosenberg. Nine Fuchsbeck beers are made but they rarely travel further than Amberg. The bittersweet **Hell** ★★ makes

an excellent session beer, as does the stronger, more fragrant and sweet-bitter **Export** ★★; while **Primus** ★★ is a spring *weizenbock* that has been pleasantly toned down to make it more approachable.

FUCHSBERG, SCHLOSSBRAUEREI
Fuchsberg, Bavaria

A *schlossbrauerei* actually based in a castle rather than simply named after one. Its five Fuchsberger beers rarely get more than 30km (19 miles) from Fuchsberg, though **Urhell** ★★ is a remarkably easy-drinking, mild and grassy *helles*; and **Pilsener Premium** ★★ has great balance before a bittersweet finish.

GÖLLER
Zeil am Main, Bavaria

Dating from 1514 and in the Göller family for barely a century, this busy brewery at Zeil, between Bamberg and Schweinfurt, is in a wine town. It still brews on the original site but tanks beer to a newer bottling plant on the outskirts, which also bottles beers for other smaller breweries, some of which, particularly wheat beers, are made at Göller. The **Göller Rauchbier** ★★ is lighter than some; and its seasonal **Weizenbock** ★★ has a hint of tartness among the clove and banana.

GRAF ARCO
Adldorf, Bavaria

Sizeable brewery at Adldorf not to be confused with the south German giant Arcobräu of Moos. It makes 10 or so acceptable year-round Graf Arco beers but it is the seasonal brews that impress here. Autumn sees dependable golden **Grafentrunk Festbier ★★**, which starts sweet and finishes dry; while Lent sees the arrival of the raisin-scented, burnt-grain, darker *bock* **Arcolator ★★☆**.

HIRSCH
Dirlewang, Bavaria

Owned by Hans Lederle's family since opening in 1806, this small brewery in Dirlewang supplies few other places. Two Dirlewanger beers are made all year, the grainy and hoppy **Vollbier Hell ★★☆**; and softer, sweeter blond **Export ★★**; joined during winter by the fruity *märzen* **Festbier ★★**.

HÖSL
Mitterteich, Bavaria

Medium-sized, independent, family-dominated brewer at Mitterteich making around a dozen regular beers under its own name and numerous own-brand labels commissioned by others. They peak with **Hösl Whiskey-Weisse ★★☆**, an unusual, slightly smoky wheat beer brewed with Scottish whisky malt to celebrate 20 years of town twinning, now hopefully to remain.

IRSEER KLOSTERBRÄU
Irsee, Bavaria

The owners of this former monastic brewery have ducked the chance to claim that brewing started here in the 12th century – which it likely did – for an official founding date of 1803, the year

Bavarian monasteries were secularized. Of the Irseer beers, unfiltered **Kloster-Urtrunk ★★** is an unusual, malty-herbal, hazy, slightly musty golden beer, similar in ways to its darker, hazy sister **Kloster-Urdunkel ★★**, full of caramel and laced with chocolate.

JACOB
Bodenwöhr, Bavaria

Lakeside brewery at Bodenwöhr, a small town in the Upper Bavarian Forest nature park. Better known for its wheat beers, some brewed for other companies, the Jacob range of bottom-fermented beers includes an aromatic, bitter and oddly Bohemian **Edel Pils ★★☆**. The pale **Weissbier ★★☆** is assertively doused in banana and clove; the spicier **Dunkles Weissbier ★★** could be drier; but the dark **Weizen-Bock ★★★** manages a delicate balancing act best.

KNEITINGER
Regensburg, Bavaria

Brewery in the centre of Regensburg, dating from 1530 and used to producing two regular Kneitinger beers plus a winter *bock*. The **Edel-Pils ★★** has good herbal bitterness; nutty caramel and chocolate flavours are evident in **Dunkel ★★☆**; while the dark winter **Bock ★★★** is sweeter and stronger.

KREUZBERG, KLOSTERBRAUEREI
Bischofsheim an der Rhön, Bavaria

This small brewery is at a remote Franciscan monastery in the picturesque Rhön region. Although there are still monks here, they have no direct involvement in day-to-day brewing operations. Unusually for a brewery with 8500hl a year production, none of the beer is bottled. All four beers are unfiltered, among them the almost famous **Kreuzberger Klosterbier Dunkel ★★★**, a copper-coloured, bittersweet form of "liquid bread".

KUCHLBAUER
Abensberg, Bavaria

This substantial brewery at Abensberg claims it was founded in 1300. Best known for wheat beers, though there are also a couple of Kuchlbauer lagers. **Turmweisse ★★☆** is citrus and almost *bock*-strength; while well-intentioned **Aloysius ★★**, its dark and fruity *weizenbock*, has room for improvement.

MÄRKL
Freudenberg, Bavaria

A small family-run brewery dating from 1466, at Freudenberg, near Amberg. Its Freudenberger beers are delightfully straightforward, the **Pils ★★☆** being recognizably of the crisp, herbal Oberpfalz sub-style; while the **Dunkel ★★☆** has clear caramel and roasted malt flavours; and the powerful, no-nonsense *doppelbock* **Märkator ★★☆** is packed with molasses and dark fruit. Its wheat beer is brewed elsewhere.

NAABECK, SCHLOSSBRAUEREI
Naabeck, Bavaria

One of the larger breweries in Oberpfalz, close to Schwandorf. Brews about a dozen Naabecker beers for itself and a similar number under contract to other companies. Its golden **Edel-Märzen ★★** combines toasted malt and floral hops; while dark fruits dominate the slightly sweet **Bock Dunkel ★★**.

PYRASER
Thalmässing, Bavaria

This sizeable rural brewery south of Nuremberg has an extensive range of good-enough regular Pyraser beers such as the pale, sweet-and-sour **Angerwirts Weizen ★★**, but a smattering of better seasonal varieties such as unfiltered, hugely refreshing **Hopfenpflücker** ("Hop pickers") **Pils ★★★**; and the deceptively powerful, caramel-laden **Ultra ★★☆**. In 2012 it signalled an intention to experiment with making beers in foreign styles under a new Herzblut brand.

REINDLER
Jochsberg, Bavaria

Now in the eighth generation of ownership by the Reindler family, this small brewery at Jochsberg, west of Ansbach, makes seven beers, among them the fruity and relatively high-hopped **Hefe Weizen ★★☆**; dark toffee, roasted and dry **Dunkel ★★**; and a winter *doppelbock*, the sweetish, spicy-peach **Seckenator ★★**.

RHANERBRÄU
Schönthal-Rhan, Bavaria

Village brewery near Schönthal that claims to have originated in 1283. Its 14 Rhaner beers are fairly easily found in the region. The slight sweetness in the **Pils** ★★☆ fails to spoil great hopping; the **Panduren Weisse** ★★ has plenty of spice and clove; while **Lilly Bock** ★★☆ is a sweet, sour and spicy take on *weizenbock*.

RIEGELE
Augsburg, Bavaria

Sizeable brewery close to Augsburg's main railway station with a prodigious output of different beers for its own brands and numerous other companies. **Augsburger Herren Pils** ★★ is reliably crisp and bitter, aromatic and light; while at the other end of the spectrum its thick and malty *doppelbock* **Riegele Speziator** ★★☆ is full of toffee and caramel with burnt notes. Its alcohol-free wheat beers are remarkably tasty and 2011 saw a new range of premium beers, primarily ales, that we have yet to taste.

RITTER ST GEORGEN
Nennslingen, Bavaria

Knight-themed brewery at Nennslingen. Makes the best of packaging, with some distinctive labels and a couple of beers available in flip-top jeroboams. Hoppier-than-average **Ritter 1645 Ur-Märzen** ★★ celebrates the founding year of the brewery; while its winter offering is a spicy *weizenbock* called **Starker Ritter** ★★.

ROPPELT
Trossenfurt, Bavaria

Attractive little brewery at Trossenfurt. The two Roppelt-Bräu beers are the

Lagerbier ★★, a golden *kellerbier* with a grainy start and dry finish; and toasty, nutty, caramel-graced **Dunkel** ★★. We suspect its Steigerwald Gold Pils is brewed elsewhere.

SCHNEIDER
Kelheim, Bavaria

World-renowned Kelheim wheat beer producer originally from Munich, credited with the reinvention of high-quality wheat beers in Germany. Recent years have seen both extensive experimentation and rebranding of all beers as Schneider Weisse. The **Tap 7 Unser Original** ★★★★ is the rebadged spicy *weisse* against which all others are judged; while the remarkable **Tap 6 Unser Aventinus** ★★★☆ sets the same standard for *weizenbock*. Up-hopped **Tap 4 Mein Grünes** ★★★ is a better balanced, weaker version of **Tap 5 Meine Hopfenweisse** ★★☆, initially a collaboration with New York's Brooklyn Brewery. However, **Aventinus Weizen-Eisbock** ★★★★, a spit for Tap 6 with less water, is an intense, berry-loaded, Sauternes of the grains, best poured to release its CO_2 and become silky-smooth.

SEINSHEIMER KELLERBRÄU
Seinsheim, Bavaria

Seinsheim is a tiny town near Marktbreit with a suitably tiny brewery. Opened in 2002 by Frank Engelhardt and Winfried Zippel, next to the church, it opens for sales each Friday (brewing day). Its regular offering is the superbly balanced, ruddy-brown, bitter **Seinsheimer Kellerbier** ★★★.

SIMON
Lauf an der Pegnitz, Bavaria

One of two small breweries in Lauf and that rarest of beasts, a Franconian wheat beer specialist. There is one bottom-fermented Simon beer but its best works are the chewy, spicy **Weißbier ★★**; and the sweeter, darker **Schwarze Kuni ★★☆**, a seasonal *weizenbock*.

SPERBER BRÄU
Sulzbach-Rosenberg, Bavaria

Sulzbach-Rosenberg's other brewery (*see* **FUCHSBECK**) is another that keeps its ambitions local. Unusually it makes a couple of beers that mimic the *zoigl* style

of brewing, the more authentic being the generously hopped, citrus **Sperber Bräu Zoiglbier ★★☆**; while the refreshing and more mainstream **Rosenburg Pils ★★** is similarly well endowed.

ULRICH MARTIN
Schonungen-Hausen, Bavaria

Although founded as recently as 2008, this small firm in Hausen, near Schonungen, is run along strongly traditional lines. There was a brewery on the site from 1850 to 1965 and its modern day replacement is already well established in the locality. Citrus-hoppy **Ulrich Martin Pilsner ★★** is the best of the three regulars.

WELTENBURGER
Weltenburg, Bavaria

Dating from 1050 and perhaps the most attractively situated brewery in all of Germany. The Danube turns through 180° as it passes Weltenburg Abbey and, on occasion, has been known to pass through it. Most Weltenburger Kloster beers are brewed by Bischofshof in Regensburg but these are made on site. **Anno 1050 ★★** is a malt-driven amber lager; **Winter-Traum ★★** is a pale and seasonal *märzen*; **Barock-Dunkel ★★☆** is complex, bittersweet and dark, and appears super-charged as *doppelbock* **Asam-Bock ★★★**.

WIESEN, BÜRGERLICHES BRAUHAUS
Wiesen, Bavaria

A stone's throw from the border with Hesse, this small family-run brewery at Wiesen is at the northern end of the Spessart hills. It makes nine Wiesener beers of solid quality, among them the green-grassy **Pils** ★★; a copper-brown and hoppy **Keller Bier** ★★ that has echoes of the sᴛ ɢᴇᴏʀɢᴇɴ version; and **Räuber Weisse Dunkel** ★★, a spicy, characterful dark wheat.

THE ZOIGL BEER TRADITION

In Bavaria and Bohemia, the tradition of communal brewing goes back centuries, with town breweries gradually supplanting home brewing from the 11th century onward. In Oberpfalz five "*echter zoigl*" brewhouses remain, brewing wort that can be bought and taken away by customers to finish preparing on their own premises.

Though identical on leaving the brewhouse, the subtle effects of different ambient microflora in each of the *zoigl* houses, typically pubs, where this happens means that every version tastes different. At the last count there were about 25 such beers coming from brewhouses in Eslarn, Falkenberg, Mitterteich, Neuhaus and Windischeschenbach. Exploration may be assisted by *www.zoigl.de*.

WINKLER
Amberg, Bavaria

Seventeenth-century brewery tucked inside Amberg's city wall. Its annual output of 25,000hl includes beers brewed under contract to a couple of other brewery companies. The pick of its own Winkler range are the dry and grassy-hoppy **Amberger Pils** ★★☆; and sweet and nutty winter **Alt-Amberger Doppelbock** ★★☆.

WINKLER BRÄU
Lengenfeld, Bavaria

Winkler is a popular brewery name in this part of Germany. The beers from this 1628 brewery-hotel and bottler, between Regensburg and Nuremberg, are distinguished as Winkler Bräu Lengenfeld on its labels. The spicy and aromatic **Hefe-Pils** ★★★ remains bitter to the bottom of the glass; while a fruity lacing of dark caramel comes through the *dunkel*, **Kupfer Spezial** ★★☆.

WOLF
Rüdenhausen, Bavaria

One-man brewery at Rüdenhausen, founded in 1746. Output is around 500hl a year and the beers do not get far. We include it as typical of a dying breed of small brewhouse making worthy beers that deserve a wider audience, in this case dry and nutty **Wolf Urtyp Dunkel** ★★☆ and the **Wolf Pils** ★★, which tastes of the country.

BADEN-WÜRTTEMBERG

Germany's southwestern corner, bordered to its west by the Rhine, to the south by Switzerland and to the east by Bavaria, is famed for hazy beers. Baden-Württemberg shares a wheat beer culture with western Bavaria but is also the home of *kellerpils* and *zwickelbier*, lagered styles that are unfiltered on draught and find their way increasingly into bottles too.

ADLERBRÄU
Dellmensingen, Baden-Württemberg

There are six unrelated Adler ("Eagle") breweries in Baden-Württemberg. This one is at Dellmensingen, southwest of Ulm. Founded in 1349, its seven beers are rarely available elsewhere. Pick of the beers are **Haferbier ★★☆**, an unfiltered, top-fermented beer made with oats; and the aromatic, bittersweet **Keller Pils ★★**.

ANDREASBRÄU
Eggenstein-Leopoldshafen, Baden-Württemberg

One of many newish pub breweries around Karlsruhe, this above-average example can be found at Eggenstein-Leopoldshafen. Its only regular beer is the herbal, hoppy **Andreasbräu Pils ★★☆**, though there are also several worthy seasonal beers through the year.

BAISINGER BIERMANUFAKTUR
Rottenburg-Baisingen, Baden-Württemberg

Formerly badged Löwenbräu, this recently renamed family brewery, located near Rottenburg am Neckar, has been owned by the Teufels ("Devils"!) for nine generations. The full Baisinger range is typical of the region and features the citrus, grassy, unfiltered **Keller-Teufel ★★**; and peak performer, the yeasty **Teufels Weisse Helles Hefe ★★**.

BAUHÖFER
Renchen-Ulm, Baden-Württemberg

Mid-19th-century, family-owned brewery at Ulm village, near Renchen. Its Ulmer beers include the grassy **Keller No 5 ★★**, which is a little sweeter than might be expected; the slightly tart, fruity **Hefeweizen Dunkel ★★**; and a uniquely year-round, relatively dry and high-hopped **Maibock ★★**.

BRÄUNLINGER LÖWENBRÄU
Bräunlingen, Baden-Württemberg

Small family business in Bräunlingen, at the southern end of the Black Forest. Its four regular beers are all worthy of attention but the soft, spicy wheat beer **Bräunlinger Löwenbräu Weisser Leo ★★** and the hazy, hoppy **Bräunlinger Löwenbräu Keller-Pils ★★☆** stand out from the crowd.

GOLDOCHSENBRAUEREI
Spielbach, Baden-Württemberg

Much-loved farm brewery in Spielbach, a few kilometres from historic Rothenburg-ob-der-Tauber. Unchanged for many decades, its sole regular beer rarely travels beyond Rothenburg. **Spielbacher Spezial Hell ★★☆** is a soft, grassy, golden *helles* made with love.

HÄFFNER BRÄU
Bad Rappenau, Baden-Württemberg

Nineteenth-century Bad Rappenau brewery that has recently developed two distinct faces. The Häffner Bräu range of traditional beers includes the biscuity, unfiltered blond **Raban ★★** and spicy banana **Kurstadt Weizen ★★**. More edgy is the Hopfenstopfer range, among the first German beers to ape modern America. These include the grapefruity US-style pale ale **Citra Ale ★★**; and double IPA **Citra Strong Ale ★★☆**, a 10% ABV beer that suggests the brewery intends to get bolder.

HERBSTHÄUSER
Bad Mergentheim, Baden-Württemberg

Rural producer of over a dozen beers near Bad Mergentheim, in a part of the state that still sees itself as Franconian. The best Herbsthäuser beers tend to be the dry, herbal **Edel-Pils ★★**; fruity **Hefe-Weizen Hell ★★** with its slightly sour edge; equally fruity and moreish *dunkelweisse* **Alt-Fränkisch ★★**; and **1581 ★★☆**, the new yeasty *kellerbier* that recalls the year the brewery was founded.

HIRSCHEN-BRÄU
Waldkirch, Baden-Württemberg

Attractive, well-grounded, 19th-century regional brewery at Waldkirch, the home of German organ production. Its six-beer Hirschen-Bräu range is best represented by grassy, slightly spicy blond **Export ★★**; and banana-spice-laden **Hefe-Weizen ★★**, which is as pale as they come.

LAUPHEIM, KRONENBRAUEREI
Laupheim, Baden-Württemberg

Laupheim's last remaining brewery dates from 1753, supplying a handful of local pubs with beer made from their own barley malt. The staple Laupheimer beer, the biscuity **Kronen-Spezial ★★**, is slightly herbal, a characteristic it shares with the **Kronen-Pils ★★☆**. The recently arrived **Weisse ★☆**, the malted wheat for which is bought in, shows promise.

MÜLHAUPT
Lörrach-Brombach, Baden-Württemberg

Tiny front-room brewery at Andreas Mülhaupt's home in Lörrach, producing 350hl of beer a year, mostly for bottling. Each of his regular Hausbräu Mülhaupt beers is surprisingly good. The dry **Helles Lagerbier ★★☆** hints at raspberries; equally fruity, copper-coloured **Dunkles Exportbier ★★☆** finishes bitter.

PFLUGBRAUEREI
Hörvelsingen, Baden-Württemberg

Another of the small breweries around Ulm city that still harvests ice to keep its lagering cellars cool through the warmer months. This one is at Hörvelsingen and produces four year-round Pflug beers that include the soft, herbal **Pils** ★★; and the pale, citrus **Hefe-Weizen** ★★, which finishes drier than most.

ROTHAUS
Rothaus, Baden-Württemberg

Germany's highest brewery (959m/ 3145ft above sea level), in a hamlet of the same name, is owned by the state of Baden-Württemberg. It has been expanding rapidly in recent years, its three beers now being found far and wide. Assertively hoppy **Rothaus Pils** ★★ is the flagship; banana and citrus are to the fore in **Rothaus Hefeweizen** ★★☆; with the stronger **Rothaus Märzen Export** ★★ less impressive. In 33cl bottles, they are known respectively as Tannenzäpfle, Hefeweizen Zäpfle and Eis Zäpfle.

RUSS, KRONENBRAUEREI
Ulm, Baden-Württemberg

This is another "Crown" brewery, but unrelated to KRONE at Tettnang. It is located at Söflingen, a suburb of Ulm city, where its Söflinger beers are mostly found. It is one of the few remaining breweries (*see* PFLUGBRAUEREI) to harvest ice for lagering. Its **Kronen Bier Keller Pils** ★★ is a little sweeter than most. The bittersweet and aromatic **Kronen Bier Spezial Hell** ★★ is the standard light session beer, contrasting with the year-round, spicy and warming **Kronen Bier Natureis-Bock Hell** ★★☆.

SCHÖRE
Dietmannsweiler, Baden-Württemberg

Traditionally presented but modern-kitted pub brewery, distillery and farm, deep in the Tettnang hop region at tiny Dietmannsweiler. It grows and uses its own hops in dry, bitter **Schörepils** ★★☆; the more subtly constructed, unfiltered **Schörebräu Hell** ★★☆; and the superb full-bodied, fruity **Schöre Weisse** ★★★.

SONNE
Herrenzimmern, Baden-Württemberg

Brewing again for barely a decade, this revived pub brewery sits at the centre of Herrenzimmern, a village high above the Neckar north of Rottweil. There are two regular beers, the toasty and bittersweet **Sonne Spezial** ★★ and **Sonne Weizen** ★★, dominated by banana but with a spicy side; **Sonne Keller-Pils** ★★ is the easy-drinking summer special.

TETTNANGER (KRONE)
Tettnang, Baden-Württemberg

As you might expect from a brewery found in Tettnang, hops are generously used by this small family business, which is located in the town centre. The Tettnanger range of beers includes three pilsners, of which the organic **Keller-Pils** ★★☆ is the hoppiest and best; while their **Kronen-Bier** ★★ is a bittersweet, herbal *helles*, and their sweet, fruity **Coronator Dunkel** ★★☆ is one of two winter *doppelbocks* that are on offer.

VOGELBRÄU
Karlsruhe, Baden-Württemberg

Representative of a new trend in German brewing, Rudi Vogel opened his first pub brewery at Karlsruhe in 1985 and has added two others at nearby Durlach and Ettlingen. These make and serve a regular range of 22 seasonal brews covering most of the compass of German brewing, plus one year-round regular, the unfiltered and lavishly hopped **Vogelbräu Pils** ★★☆.

WALDHAUS
Waldhaus, Baden-Württemberg

This smallish but not insignificant brewery dominates its hamlet. The wide range of beers is headed up by the beautifully balanced, generously hopped **Diplom Pils** ★★★; a second, unfiltered, extra-hoppy pilsner, **Ohne Filter Extra Herb** ★★☆, deliberately contains hops from all round the country; the low-alcohol **Classic 2.9** ★★ has far more character than most light beers; while **Schwarzwald Weisse** ★★☆ shows how to up-hop a wheat beer.

COLOGNE, DÜSSELDORF & NORTH RHINE-WESTPHALIA

Germany's most populous state is home to two genuine regional beer styles and one foreign misunderstanding. Düsseldorfer *altbier*, or *alt* for short, is a darkish pale ale, while *kölsch*, from arch-rival Cologne (Köln) is light blond. Each is brewed and fermented as an ale before being lagered for about six weeks, and is found at its best served straight from an uncarbonated upturned cask on the bar. They share qualities recognizably with other northern European beers such as British bitter, Belgian *speciaal* and lighter forms of French *bière de garde*.

The imaginary style is Dortmunder, a term misapplied to beers that Germans would term export or *märzen*, which is to say a slightly sweeter, usually stronger, blond lager. Other than as a brand name, you will not find it here.

BRAUSTELLE
Cologne, North Rhine-Westphalia

Street-corner pub brewery in the Ehrenfeld suburb of Cologne that was for a time single-handedly changing the face of

German beer. Around 100 different beers have been made here to date including several dozen for beer commissioners Freigeist Bierkultur in Stolberg and Fritzale of Bonn. With the range ever-changing, our best advice is to try any of the beers that bear one of these three brands. The most reliably encountered tend to be the bestseller, **Braustelle Helios ★★**, a hoppy, unfiltered *kölsch*; **Freigeist AbraxXxas ★★☆**, a stronger modern interpretation of a traditional and defunct style of salty, smoked and sour wheat beer called a *Lichtenhainer*; and any of the various incarnations of **Fritzale India Pale Ale ★★→★★★**, which go as hoppy as any German beer gets.

DESTINATION
COLOGNE

Cologne's two genuine taphouses are Päffgen (64 Friesenstraße) and beautiful Malzmühle (6 Heumarkt). Nevertheless, renegade Pfaffen (62 Heumarkt) and big boy Früh (12–18 Am Hof) have a presence too.

FRÜH
Cologne, North Rhine-Westphalia

Probably the best known of the *kölsch* producers for its export presence and its legendary tap near Cologne's towering Gothic cathedral. The brewery is now in an industrial area outside the city and makes just the one alcoholic product, the soft, light and predictably understated **Früh Kölsch ★★** that like all of its ilk is far superior when served fresh from the upturned, uncarbonated barrel.

FÜCHSCHEN
Düsseldorf, North Rhine-Westphalia

The Little Fox, one of the four remaining established *altbier* producers located in Düsseldorf's old town. Three Füchschen beers are made, the soft and dry hoppy classic **Alt ★★★**; yeasty-citrus *weizen* **Silber Füchschen ★★**; and a slightly stronger and hoppier version of the ordinary *alt* called **Weihnachtsbier ★★★**, available bottled for six weeks before Christmas and sold on draught at the tap only on Christmas Eve.

GAFFEL
Cologne, North Rhine-Westphalia

Brewery operated by the Becker family for over a century, with a flagship pub near the famous cathedral. **Gaffel Kölsch ★★☆** is oft-derided as too commercial a brand, with production of over 400,000hl in bottles, cans and kegs, but its hop-forward, aromatic and only marginally fruity character makes it worth a visit.

GEMÜNDER
Gemünd, North Rhine-Westphalia

Smallish village brewery at Gemünd in the northern Eifel. It produces more than a dozen beers under various names including the unfiltered, herbal-hoppy blond **Eifeler-Landbier ★★**; and the nutty, fruity, deep ruby-brown winter-only *bock*, **Eifeler-Böckchen ★★☆**.

GLEUMES
Krefeld, North Rhine-Westphalia

Handsome traditional pub brewery in Krefeld, dating from 1807 and the last of its kind in the city. Three Gleumes beers are made. The slightly roasty, bitter, light amber **Lager ★★☆** is an *altbier* in disguise; the banana-yeasty **Weizen** ★★ is an incomer; and the newish, unexceptional but well-constructed **Pils** ★★, introduced to replace a perfectly respectable *helles*.

HÜCHELNER URSTOFF
Hücheln, North Rhine-Westphalia

Small brewery just west of Cologne, named after its principal product. Four beers are made here, all top-fermented and then lagered. The best are **Bartmann's Kölsch** ★★, typically soft, light, fruity and bittersweet; and fruity-yeasty and refreshing **Hüchelner Urstoff** ★★, another rare example of the type of unfiltered *kölsch* traditionally called *wiesse*.

IM DOM
Neuss, North Rhine-Westphalia

Revived *hausbrauerei* in the old town at Neuss. It was brewing here from 1601 until 1971 and again between 2008 and

2010. New owner intends to make the arrangement permanent, thus far making only the dark, unfiltered, fruity and toasty-bitter **Dom's Alt** ★★.

KÜRZER
Düsseldorf, North Rhine-Westphalia

Three-year-old brewery in the city's Altstadt, producing a fairly full-bodied and sweetish **Altbier** ★★ with some dried-fruit notes and a comparatively ale-like character, attributable no doubt to its two-week brew and fermentation cycle. Worth a visit if only to see the unique "glass cask" used for dispense.

MALZMÜHLE
Cologne, North Rhine-Westphalia

Small brewery at the southern end of Cologne's old town. Until recently it made just one beer, the classically made, light but somehow grainier than average **Mühlen Kölsch** ★★★★. However, summer 2012 saw a pale summer *bock* called Von Mühlen, made with Champagne yeast at a price to match.

PÄFFGEN
Cologne, North Rhine-Westphalia

The most traditional of the Cologne breweries, Päffgen makes a single *kölsch* available only from the (usually wooden) barrel. The perfectly balanced, hoppy **Päffgen Kölsch** ★★★☆ is available only in four pubs, all in the city. The only nod to the modern world is that it can now be bought in siphons, filled to order, to take away.

PFAFFEN
Lohmar, North Rhine-Westphalia

Following a difference of opinion with brother Rudolf, owner of the aforementioned family brewery, Max Päffgen founded his own small brewery on a farm near Lohmar. As his Pfaffen (roughly "faffing about") beers are brewed outside the area of metropolitan Cologne designated for the production of official *kölsch* beers, it is better to term his pale blond, light-bodied, fruity, malt-driven, top-fermented and lagered **Original ★★☆** of indefinable style. A second beer, the bready and sweet-bitter pale **Bock ★★☆** appears in the spring and at Christmas. Both are sold mostly at the tap, Zum Pfaffen in Cologne.

PINKUS MÜLLER
Münster, North Rhine-Westphalia

Pinkus Müller, a Münster institution, boasts one of the most traditional taprooms of any north German brewery and was the first brewer anywhere to be certified organic. The beer range is gradually increasing to include the unfiltered, yellow-golden, dry and grassy **Müller's Lagerbier ★★**; the deep golden, crisp and malty **Original Pinkus Obergärig** (US: Münster Alt) **★★☆**, available with fresh fruit syrup at the tap, sadly; and dark, fruity, well-malted *dunkel* **Pinkus Jubilate ★★**.

RATINGER BRAUHAUS
Ratingen, North Rhine-Westphalia

Pub brewery (since 2005) at Ratingen, between Düsseldorf and Essen, making only **Ratinger Alt ★★☆**, a fine, traditionally designed, produced and tasting *altbier* that comes close to the classics, an impression boosted by the fact that as in Düsseldorf, it is served by *kobes*, the essential wise-cracking and blue-aproned waiters.

SCHLÜSSEL
Düsseldorf, North Rhine-Westphalia

Brewery in the heart of Düsseldorf's old town (Altstadt) that makes the lightest of the classic *alts*. Deep amber in colour, with dabs of fruit and nut, **Schlüssel Alt ★★☆** has a lasting bitterness. A stronger *alt* called **Schlüssel Stike ★★★** is available on two days each year, in March and October.

DESTINATION DÜSSELDORF

Düsseldorf's Altstadt hosts four taphouses – Füchschen (28 Ratinger Straße), Schlüssel (41 Bolkerstraße), Kürzer (18 Kurze Straße) and must-see Uerige (1 Berger Straße), all serving *alt* from the cask. A fifth, Schumacher (123 Oststraße), sits halfway to the railway station.

SCHMITZ MÖNK
Anrath, North Rhine-Westphalia

A pub brewery at Anrath, due north of Mönchengladbach, founded around the turn of the 20th century. The flagship Mönk beer is the toasty-nutty **Alt ★★☆**, slightly paler than those of Düsseldorf but almost on a par; the **Kellerbier** ★★☆ is a relatively recent introduction and has a whiff of smoke; appearing several times a year is the **Bock** ★★☆, essentially a stronger *alt* in the manner of *sticke* beer but lightly smoked.

SCHUMACHER
Düsseldorf, North Rhine-Westphalia

The oldest of Düsseldorf's traditional *altbier* producers is said to be where the term "*alt*" was first coined. In 1871 the brewery moved to its current location on the eastern edge of the old town. **Schumacher Alt** ★★★ has a roasty twang and dry, bitter finish. Its stronger malty *alt* **Latzenbier** ★★★☆ is available on the third Thursday of March, September and November.

SÜNNER
Cologne, North Rhine-Westphalia

Of the 10 breweries remaining in Cologne, this is the oldest, dating from 1830. It makes more than just *kölsch*

here, producing a number of beers under contract for dormant breweries elsewhere and a Sünner brand lager and *weizen* for itself. Its **Kölsch** ★★ is very well balanced, tangier and lighter than most; and it also makes an organic, citrus-fruity *wiesse* called **BioColonia** ★★.

UERIGE
Düsseldorf, North Rhine-Westphalia

Perhaps the best known of the brewers still making *altbiers* in Düsseldorf, Uerige is unusual for actively courting an export market to the US, originally making the extraordinary DoppelSticke exclusively for there. It produces four variations on Uerige *alt*. The regular dry and bitter **Alt** ★★★★ is occasionally available unfiltered as **Alt Nicht Filtiert** ★★★☆. The stronger *alt*, **Sticke** ★★★☆, appears on draught at its wonderful rambling old tap, one block off the Rhine, on the third Tuesday of January and October, but is more widely available bottled; as is the aforementioned **Uerige DoppelSticke** ★★★☆.

REST OF GERMANY

In other parts of Germany, the obsession with beer is modified. The northward spread of the *Reinheitsgebot* (see box, page 51) destroyed numerous local beer styles, as did physical, political and economic war damage after 1945.

Reunification after the Berlin Wall came down in 1989 coincided with the re-emergence of black beers (*schwarzbier*) from the east. Production of *gose* beers around Leipzig recommenced, while light, bone-dry *Berliner weisse* has struggled to survive.

Elsewhere localism in beer making is highly dependent on a great rash of brewpubs, typically sporting a predictable triptych of one white, one blond and one dark, though experimentation is increasingly likely.

ANKERBRÄU
Steinach, Thuringia

Thuringian brewer at Steinach, occupying premises formerly inhabited by GESSNER. The two regular beers are the soft and grainy bittersweet **Anker Pils ★★☆**; and the deep amber, toasty, slightly sweeter **Ankerla Dunkel ★★☆**, in the Franconian style.

BAYERISCHER BAHNHOF
Leipzig, Saxony

Millennium pub brewery at Leipzig's former railway terminus for trains to the south, remarkable for focusing on beer styles with a stronger East German heritage. Speciality of the house is **Original Leipziger Gose ★★☆**, a less acidic version of this revived style when compared to some; the exceptionally tart **Brettanomyces Lambicus ★★★** is brewed with lambic yeast but in the manner of a *Berliner weisse*; while the smooth, roasted-chocolate **Heizer**

Schwarzbier ★★☆ is the best of the more conventional beers.

BERGSCHLÖSSCHEN
Lieske, Saxony

Small brewery in the Missionshof Lieske, a project for disabled people near Oßling in Saxony. Four Bergschlößchen beers are made, all available from the nearby tap or from a few other outlets across the state. Go for the caramelled, bittersweet **Dunkel ★★** and citrus-grassy **Zwickel ★★☆**.

BRAUBERGER ZU LÜBECK
Lübeck, Schleswig-Holstein

Atmospheric pub brewery on the edge of Lübeck's historic old town, which is a UNESCO World Heritage Site. Its sole beer is the hazy, dark blond, unplaceable, bready and caramel-edged **Brauberger Zwickelbier ★★**, only available at the tap, where it is dispensed without carbonation direct from wooden barrels – the only pub we know that does this so far north.

BREWBAKER
Berlin

Ambitious, experimental craft brewery that opened in 2005 under a railway arch in Berlin's Tiergarten, expanding in 2011 into its current location at the

Arminus Martkhalle. Fifteen other bars are supplied, most in Berlin. Owner-brewer Michael Schwab has made over 60 different beers so far in a wide variety of German and other styles. Regulars include hoppy, aromatic and bitter **Bellevue Pils** ★★☆; and refreshing and impressive citrus pale ale **Berlin IPA** ★★★.

DESTINATION BERLIN

Mommsen-Eck (45 Mommsenstraße), in the Charlottenburg district, is one of Germany's few emporium beer bars, showcasing around 100 German beers, the best range in the capital.

BRUCH
Saarbrücken, Saarland

One of only two traditional Saarland breweries to have escaped the clutches of regional giant Karlsberg. Based at Saarbrücken. Citrus-fruity **Bruch Zwickel** ★★ has some herbal notes; while **Weizen** ★★ has a clove-citrus-banana mix of flavours. It is unclear whether a pub brewery next to the main brewery's tap is still in operation.

FALLERSLEBEN, ALTES BRAUHAUS ZU
Fallersleben, Lower Saxony

Pheonix-like Lower Saxony pub brewery that rose from the ashes of a 2007 fire. Located in the grounds of Fallersleben castle, its beers are only available there. Signature brew **Fallersleber**

Schlossbräu ★★ is an unfiltered but clean, hoppy golden lager; while the well-hopped **Fallersleber Weizen** ★★ has spicy banana notes.

GESSNER
Sonneberg, Thuringia

Close to the Franconian border in Thuringia, this modern brewery at Sonneberg relocated from nearby Steinach in 1997. Among the many Gessner beers, bittersweet, roasted, dark caramel lager **Alt-Sumbarcher Dunkel** ★★☆ and the similar-tasting but stronger **Dunkler Bock** ★★☆ stand out.

GOSLAR, BRAUHAUS
Goslar, Lower Saxony

Pub brewery in the UNESCO World Heritage Site at Goslar, on the northern edge of the Harz Mountains in Lower Saxony. This is the town where *gose*, a sour, salted wheat beer flavoured with coriander, originated. Two Brauhaus Goslar varieties of this have been revived here, the more citrus and wheat-led **Helle Gose** ★★, and the sweeter, faintly sour **Dunkle Gose** ★☆, though each can be seen as safe compared to the Leipzig area recreations.

GROHE
Darmstadt, Hesse

Small Hessen brewery in the centre of modern Darmstadt. Its five Grohe beers remain remarkably local to the city and its environs. Malt and grassy hops pervade the **Pils** ★★; the **Weizen** ★★

has spicy-citrus notes; and the winter seasonal dark **Bock** ★★ has a nutty, caramel flavour.

HARTMANNSDORFER BRAUHAUS
Hartmannsdorf, Saxony

Medium-sized Saxony brewery not far from Chemnitz. Makes several brands of beer in addition to its own. Since the closure of Leipzig's Bauer brewery it has made the incomparable **Original Ritterguts Gose** ★★★☆, a citrus-sour beer with a salty finish, a beer that was popular in the area before it was *Reinheitsgebot*-ed out in 1919.

HOMBURGER BRAUHAUS
Homburg, Saarland

The first phase of the German beer revival began in the 1980s with a rash of pub breweries spreading across the north and middle of the country. This one is at Homburg in Saarland and is found on the first floor of a shopping centre. Here it makes two Wirtsbräu beers all year, supplemented by several others as seasons dictate. The dry and hoppy year-round **Hell** ★★ could pass for an unfiltered pils; while best of the seasonals is the bitter-chocolate **Bock** ★★☆ that appears in winter.

HOPS & BARLEY
Friedrichshain, Berlin

Formerly a butcher's shop, this bohemian pub brewery in the Friedrichshain district of Berlin opened during 2008 and has already expanded, likely for the popularity of its 20+ seasonal or occasional Friedrichshainer beers and the fact that its three regulars are well above average for a modern pub brewery. These are the fruity-hoppy-bitter **Pilsner** ★★☆; chocolate-roasted-coffee **Dunkles** ★★☆; and soft-banana-spicy **Weizen** ★★.

> ### DESTINATION
> ### BERLIN
>
> Ambrosetti (103 Schillerstraße) is a beer store in the Charlottenburg district stocking in the order of 300 different German beers and maybe 100 imports. By far the biggest selection in the capital.

KLOSTER MACHERN
Wehlen, Rhineland-Palatinate

Pub brewery (since 2004) in a former monastery near Bernkastel-Keus, in the Mosel valley wine country, again distinguished for the above-average quality of its standard triptych. The Kloster Machern beers are all unfiltered and include a yeasty, aromatic **Hell** ★★; banana and sharp-citrus **Weizen** ★★☆; and roasted, fruity-hoppy **Dunkel** ★★.

MEIEREI
Potsdam, Brandenburg

Visitors to Berlin increasingly spend time in Potsdam. The setting of this pub brewery in a former pumping house is superb, appreciated best when approached by boat from the city centre. Its single regular beer is the slightly sweet and gently bitter **Meierei Hell**

★★; with among a dozen seasonals the smooth, almost black, roasty and fruity autumn **Bock Sollator** ★★☆ also impressing.

METZLER
Dingsleben, Thuringia

Small brewery in the village of Dingsleben, southern Thuringia, not far from the Franconian border. Best of the Dingslebener bunch are the flowery **Edel-Pils** ★★, and **Lava** ★★, a strong and rich, chocolaty *schwarzbier*.

NEUSTÄDTER HAUSBRAUEREI
Dresden-Neustadt, Saxony

Small brewery in the Neustadt district of Dresden, producing half a dozen beers found in local bars and shops across the city. **Hecht Alt** ★★ is a fruity, unfiltered *alt* that has less bitterness than the Rhineland classics; citrus and grassy **Neustadt Hell** ★★ is drier than might be expected; while oddball **Lenins Hanf** ★★ is a fruity, herbal beer made with hemp.

RATSHERRN
Hamburg

Revivalist brewery (since 2012) that has obtained the right to brew Ratsherrn beers, once the brand of Hamburg's Elbschloss brewery, which closed in 1997. Located in an old slaughterhouse in the city centre. The three regular beers are the crisp and dry **Pilsener** ★★; dry and bitter caramel-fruity **Rotbier** ★★; and the as yet somewhat subdued, US-inspired **Pale Ale** ★☆.

DESTINATION
HAMBURG

Bierland (10 Seumestraße) is a small but impressive beer shop near the Wandsbeker Chaussee U- and S-bahn stations, famed for sourcing rare and obscure German beers.

REICHENBRAND
Chemnitz, Saxony

Twenty years after the Berlin Wall came down East German brewers are slowly starting to find their voice. This small-to-medium suburban brewery at Chemnitz, also known as Bergt-Bräu, is widely seen around the city though not much yet in wider Saxony. Its Reichenbrander beers include an aromatic, dry and golden **Kellerbier** ★★; and strong, spicy, Czech-style **Premium Pils** ★★.

ST MICHAELIS (BRAUHAUS EUTIN)
Eutin, Schleswig-Holstein

Pub brewery (since 1989) on Eutin's market square, midway between Lübeck and Kiel, on the eastern side of Schleswig-Holstein. The three regular St Michaelis beers plus half a dozen or so seasonals include its bestseller, dry and bitter **Pils** ★★☆; and **Tafelbier** ★★, a grainy and slightly sweet unfiltered *helles*.

SCHMITT
Ilmtal-Singen, Thuringia

This small brewery at Singen in Thuringia was one of only a handful to remain in private hands throughout the DDR period. Formally protected since 1976, there has been little significant investment here in more than a century and it is a now a working museum. This really is brewing as performed in days gone by, complete with a steam engine powering all manner of belt-driven equipment. Its sole offering, **Singer Bier** ★★, is golden, grassy, herbal and surprisingly nice.

SPECHT
Ehrenfriedersdorf, Saxony

Small brewery in the Erzgebirge ("Iron Mountains"), midway between Chemnitz and the Czech border, serving about 30 pubs in the area with six beers. The pick are the grainy and lightly bitter **Greifensteinquell Landbier** ★★; aromatic and grassy **Specht Pilsener** ★★; and **Schwarzer Specht** ★★☆, a *bock*-strength, dark-fruity *dunkel*.

STÖRTEBEKER BRAUMANUFAKTUR
Stralsund, Mecklenburg-Vorpommern

Known as the Stralsunder Brauerei until 2011, this convert to craft brewing in the far northeast of mainland Mecklenburg-Vorpommern changed its name to reflect the increasing importance of its premium Störtebeker range, named after a 14th-century privateer. The fruity-sweet **Roggen-Weizen** ★★ is made with rye, wheat and barley; **Atlantik-Ale** ★★☆ is a new golden, grapefruit-flavoured ale; and **Stark-Bier** ★★☆ is an almost black beer that might justify the description *schwarzbierbock*.

WATZKE
Dresden, Saxony

Lavish riverside pub brewery in Dresden, converted from a ballroom. Owned by Rudi Vogel of Karlsruhe pub brewery fame, this far-flung outpost of his empire has two regular beers: the aromatic and bitter **Das Pils** ★★☆; and fruity, bittersweet, light golden-brown **Altpieschener Spezial** ★★. There are also a dozen or more seasonal beers through the year.

WEESENSTEIN, SCHLOSSBRAUEREI
Müglitztal, Saxony

Small pub brewery within the bowels of Weesenstein Castle, in the Müglitz valley south of Dresden. Due to the narrow lane through the castle, malt and spent grain are transported by donkey. Owner-brewer Ulrich Betsch is a keen player of the bagpipes but this does not appear to upset his beer, **Weesensteiner Schlossbräu Original** ★★☆, which is a soft and malty *vollbier* with grassy hops.

WIPPRA
Wippra, Saxony-Anhalt

Small 15th-century brewery and museum of traditional brewing at Wippra on the southeastern edge of the Harz Mountains in Saxony-Anhalt. Its Wippraer beers are often seen in litre bottles in the region's shops, as far away as Braunschweig. The unusually dark **Pilsener** ★★ has a malty, herbal flavour; while roasted coffee and caramel dominate the **Schwarzbier** ★★☆.

AUSTRIA

Austrian beer is underrated. The German purity law (see *Reinheitsgebot*, page 51) was never adopted here, though the quality of brewing in the Innviertel region, bang up against the Bavarian border, gives the neighbours a run for their money. Ruddy-brown Vienna lagers, while as distinctive as Munich's light and dark, and Pilsen's blond golden, do not share the limelight.

However, for exploration and surprise, Austria has much to offer. Its classic lagers, in all the major styles, include one of the world's best pilsners, while some newer, smaller breweries interpret foreign craft beer styles with aplomb. It even has its own Trappist abbey brewery.

1516 BREWING
Vienna

Austria's foremost American-style brewpub, in the centre of Vienna since 1998. Specializes in top-fermented beers

but always carries **Helles** and/or **Lager** ★★ on tap. Guest brewers collaborate to make favourite beers, some becoming regulars, such as the heavily hopped US-style IPA **Hop Devil** ★★★, with characteristic grapefruit aroma and some alcoholic warmth inspired by its namesake from VICTORY BREWING in the US; **Eejit Oatmeal Stout** ★★☆ is a full-bodied, roasty interpretation of the style showing hints of smoke; while the **Amerikansky Pale Ale** ★★ is a light-bodied, yet quite bitter pale ale.

AUGUSTINER KLOSTER MÜLLN
Salzburg

Former Augustine abbey brewery founded in 1621 just outside the city centre. Famed for the beer halls and garden at its memorable brewery tap, where beer is still dispensed fresh from large wooden barrels. Most of the output is its **Märzen** ★★☆, a darker golden, lighter-bodied Austrian interpretation of the style.

BIERWERKSTATT WEITRA
Weitra, Lower Austria

Small brewery in the town of Weitra,
near the Czech border. Claims to
have the oldest brewing privilege in
Austria, dating back to 1321. Taken
over by the much larger Zwettler, from
the neighbouring town, in 2002 and
has since specialized in producing an
organic, amber-coloured Vienna-style
lager called **Hadmar ★★☆**.

DIE WEISSE
Salzburg

Austria's oldest pub brewery, founded in
1901 in the part of Salzburg on the north
bank of the Salzach. Focuses almost
entirely on brewing wheat beers, in a
wide number of styles. The regular Die
Weisse beers include the original **Hell
★★**, a classic dark-blond *hefeweizen*
with strong banana and a little clove
aroma, low-to-medium body and a dry
finish; and fuller-bodied **Dunkel ★★☆**
with hints of caramel and butterscotch.
It also has a *weizenbock* and has played
with making a wheat-based *märzen* and
even a *doppelbock*.

EGG
Egg, Vorarlberg

Small brewery in the village of Egg in
Vorarlberg, not to be confused with the
much larger Egger brewery in Lower
Austria. Beer is only generally available
in the region, notably the straw-coloured,
moderately hopped, yet very dry **Edel
Pils ★★**; and the **Wälder Senn ★★☆**,
a surprisingly flavoursome light lager,
under 3% ABV, brewed with whey from
a nearby dairy.

ENGELSZELL, TRAPPISTENBRAUEREI
Engelhartszell, Upper Austria

The surprise package of 2012 was the
reopening of a small brewery at the
Trappist cloister in Engelhartszell, on the
Danube. The first beer was **Gregorius
★★☆**, a hazy, mahogany-brown, slightly
sweetish ale with a plum-like aroma,
much like a strong *dubbel*. It remains a
work in progress but shows potential.
A lighter, spritzy blond ale with hints of
lemon zest and a robust bitterness has
also appeared but is to be reformulated.

FORSTNER BIERE
Kalsdorf bei Graz, Styria

Tiny brewery operating a 2.5hl
brewhouse. Started out as a brewpub
in 2002, though the tap is now closed.
Gerhard Forstner's wide range of
bottled brews includes **Styrian Ale
★★☆**, a bottle-conditioned pale ale
with sulphury and roasty notes; an
intensely fruity Belgian-style *tripel* called
Fünf vor 12 ★★☆; and barley wine
Bonifatius Barrique ★★★☆, matured

in wine casks, sporting aromas rich in raspberries, kiwi fruit and fresh yogurt.

DESTINATION
VIENNA

Känguruh (20 Bürgerspitalgasse) is an evenings-only bar near the Westbahnhof with the capital's largest beer selection by far, mostly from Germany, Belgium and increasingly Austria, including several house exclusives.

GÖSS (HEINEKEN)
Göss, Styria

Large brewery in a former cloister in the hop-growing province of Styria, now part of the (Heineken-owned) BrauUnion group. Gösser beers include one of Austria's most popular beers, a golden, medium bodied **Märzen ★★** characterized by a nutty flavour; fuller-bodied and slightly stronger **Spezial ★★☆** has a robust hop bitterness; while annual **Reininghaus Jahrgangs Pils ★★★** varies despite an identical recipe, highlighting the differences between each year's harvest of the piney Styrian Celeja hops with which it is made.

GUSSWERK, BRAUHAUS
Salzburg

All-organic small craft brewery founded on the outskirts of Salzburg in 2007. **Regular Edelguss ★★** is a golden ale with medium body and bitterness; **Nicobar IPA ★★☆** has a nutty brown colour with a lot of haze, a tobacco-like aroma and a complex bitterness; **Cerevinum ★★** is a dry ale with little hop character that undergoes secondary fermentation with a priming of red grape juice; while barley wine **Dies Irae ★★★** has a complex aroma of dried pears and plums.

HOFSTETTEN
Sankt Martin, Upper Austria

Arguably one of the oldest breweries in the country, first mentioned in 1229. Its unfiltered **Hofstettner Kübelbier ★★** is a balanced lager with a grainy aroma; while brown **Granitbock ★★★☆** is a *steinbier*, boiled by the immersion of glowing hot granite stones into the wort, imbuing burnt and smoky tastes.

HUBER, FAMILIENBRAUEREI
Sankt Johann in Tirol, Tyrol

Regional brewery established 1727 in Tyrol with the brewery tap on top of the malt silo with impressive views of the

AUSTRIA

Alpine landscape. **Meisterpils** ★★☆ has an impressive head, a herbal, almost peppery hop aroma and a dry aftertaste. **Augustinus** ★★ is a dryish dark brown *dunkel* with hints of toasted bread; and the seasonal amber **Bock** ★★★ is sweet on the palate but dry in the aftertaste.

KADLEZ BRAUHAUS FLORIDSDORF
Vienna

Pub brewery (2006) at Floridsdorf, a northern suburb of Vienna, which also produces some bottled beers, notably **Florido Pale Ale** ★★, moderately hopped with some nutty aroma and hints of sulphur; and the straw-coloured **Helles** ★★ in a light and slightly grainy version of the style.

LONCIUM, PRIVATBRAUEREI
Kötschach-Mauthen, Carinthia

Small 2007 brewery close to the Italian border making mostly bottom-fermented beers. **Austrian Amber Lager** ★★☆ is currently a seasonal beer in the Vienna style, slightly hazy and moderately hopped with a touch of roasted malt; while **Schwarze Gams** ★★★ is a very dark *bock* with caramel and coffee notes.

MOHRENBRAUEREI AUGUST HUBER
Dornbirn, Vorarlberg

Austria's westernmost brewery, at Dornbirn, established in 1834. Its Mohren beers include a stronger than average standard lager, **Spezial** ★★☆, with robust malty body and a bold bitterness; and the stronger and sweeter **Bockbier** ★★, rich in esters and honey-like aromas, followed by a surprisingly dry bitterness in its aftertaste.

OTTAKRINGER
Vienna

Vienna's only industrial-size brewery (1837), still operates in historic 19th-century buildings. A tribute to the founding period is **Rotes Zwickl** ★★☆, an unfiltered Vienna-style lager with a reddish appearance and distinctive sweet malty backtastes, found only on draught; golden **Goldfassl Spezial** ★★ has slightly more alcohol and shows caramel notes before finishing rather bitter.

RIED
Ried im Innkreis, Upper Austria

Regional brewery owned by the tenants of taverns in the Innviertel beer region. While Rieder has a full portfolio of lagers and wheat beers it takes pride in brewing a *weizenbock* called **Rieder XXX Weisse** ★★☆, with an intense banana and not so prominent clove aroma, full, slightly sweetish body and tart finish.

SCHLOSS EGGENBERG
Vorchdorf, Upper Austria

Regional brewery in an old palace, famous for its strong beers. Golden *doppelbock* **Urbock 23** ★★☆ has a sweet malty character, with good ageing potential at 9.9% ABV. Production of the originally Swiss super-strong lager Samichlaus moved here in 1999 and now comes in several versions, all 14% ABV. The brownish **Classic** ★★★ has some chocolaty aromas; while the regular **Hell** ★★★ is more on the sweet side, with some vintages going on to be matured in wine casks as **Holzfass** ★★★☆, showing distinct astringency.

SCHWECHATER (HEINEKEN)
Schwechat, Lower Austria

The brewery where the Vienna style of lager was invented in 1841 has sadly not brewed one for decades. However, the pale **Schwechater Zwickl** ★★★ is arguably the smoothest of all unfiltered Austrian lagers, helped by malted wheat appearing on the grain bill to balance an aggressive hop profile.

STIEGLBRAUEREI ZU SALZBURG
Salzburg

Established in 1492 and now the largest independently owned brewery in Austria. Malty, somewhat nutty **Stiegl Goldbräu** ★★ is the bestselling beer in the country and style-defining for Austrian *märzen*.

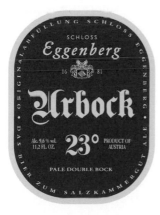

The brewery also makes regular seasonal beers in small runs, including a fruity **Double IPA** ★★★, some going on to become regular products such as the unfiltered, rather flat organic *zwickelbier* **Paracelsus** ★★; and medium-bodied, unfiltered *weizen* **Stiegl Weisse Naturtrüb** ★★.

> **DESTINATION SALZBURG**
>
> The Friesacher Einkehr (6 Brunngasse, Anif) is a large, smart, *heurige*-style restaurant in a village 5km (3 miles) south of the city, featuring a remarkable selection of perhaps 50 beers including draughts mostly from the region, a bottled selection from further afield and a collection of strong, cellar-aged stronger beers including dozens of vintage *bocks*.

TROJAN
Schrems, Lower Austria

Regional brewery, northwest of Vienna. Its **Schremser Roggen** ★★☆ is a hazy, amber-coloured ale brewed with organically grown rye, featuring fruity aromas, a medium-to-full body and a mild bitterness in the finish.

TRUMER PRIVATBRAUEREI JOSEF SIGL
Obertrum, Salzburg

Independent brewery, founded in 1601 and in the Sigl family since 1775. Josef Sigl pioneered the German style of pilsner in Austria, perfecting a straw-coloured classic of the genre, the Austrian icon, **Trumer Pils** ★★★☆, also brewed in Berkeley, California. Fermented in open vessels, it ends crisp with a hay-like aroma, and stands head and shoulders above most rivals. Its other beers have been peripheral, though a new range of interesting seasonal beers is starting to appear.

VILLACHER
Villach, Carinthia

The largest brewery in Kärnten province, not far from the borders with Italy and Slovenia. Since becoming Vereinigte Kärntner Brauereien in 2009 its Villacher brands have been reviewed and now include the straw-coloured and medium-hopped **Pils** ★★; Vienna-tweaked, copper-coloured *bock* **Selection Red** ★★☆, with hoppy aromas and a malty

body; and lightweight, Sapphire-hopped **Pur** ★★, aimed at a younger audience wanting more flavour and less alcohol.

VITZTHUM, PRIVATBRAUEREI
Uttendorf, Salzburg

Traditional family-owned regional brewery in the Innviertel region dating back to 1600. Its straw-coloured **Uttendorfer Pils** ★★☆ has great head retention and a soft mouthfeel, despite intense bitterness; while **Falstaff** ★★ is a malty, Oktoberfest-style *märzen* with a sweet start and hoppy finish.

ZILLERTAL BIER
Zell am Ziller, Tyrol

Small 1500 brewery attached to a hotel in a remote Tyrolean valley. Brews light golden, herbal, dry and deceptively light-bodied **Gauder-Bock** ★★☆ for the Tyrol's largest folk festival each May, hiding its 7.8% ABV well. Recent addition **Weißbier Bock** ★★☆, of the same strength, is rich in banana and hazelnut aromas and dangerously easy to drink. Best consumed locally.

ZIPFER (HEINEKEN)
Zipf, Upper Austria

Sizeable brewery making the speciality beers for the (Heineken-owned) BrauUnion group. **Zipfer Urtyp** ★★ is a straw-coloured, crisp lager with a hoppy finish; **Zipfer Pils** ★★☆ shows the character of whole-leaf Tettnanger hopping; amber-coloured *weizen* **Edelweiss Hofbräu** ★★★ has a fruity, banana aroma and a full, but not overly sweet body.

UNITED KINGDOM

British beer is in transit. The end of the 20th century saw an unlikely revival of cask beer, or "real ale", a phrase originally intended to mean any that is cask- or bottle-conditioned and served without additional carbon dioxide. The bulk of this revival involved paler beers of 3.5 to 4.5% ABV.

The challenge for brewers is that the rest of the world is taken with older and grander types of British ale that their predecessors stopped making. In the UK, too, these are starting to attract attention from people not naturally drawn to lighter beers consumed in traditional pint (568ml) measures.

Lower alcohol beers that leave the brewery as soon as they are made are an inevitable by-product of the rules that have governed UK beer excise duty since 1914. However, this has also meant that the country that first brought the world porter, stout, bitter beer, pale ale, IPA and many others is now underperforming badly in international craft beer markets, with few products designed to meet today's more old-fashioned preferences.

Some newer exponents, and older hands sensing change in the air, show a growing desire to create more challenging beers. While this has caused some truly awful pastiches to appear, the idea that the key to Britain's brewing future lies in its past is beginning to take root.

UK brewing has a way to go before it becomes as bold and meticulous as the modern beer consumer demands but if it keeps reworking old beer designs, using fresh ingredients and the no-cut-corners approach adopted by many US craft brewers, all it will need is time and practice.

ENGLAND

It was England, as opposed to other parts of the UK, where the revival of interest in cask-conditioned beers first flourished in the late 1970s, helping to fuel the revival in beer's fortunes globally. However, while locally made beers have made impressive inroads into pubs, persuading hotels, restaurants and others to stock better-quality beers has proved a more difficult challenge.

ACORN BREWERY
Barnsley, South Yorkshire

Celebrated locally for slightly brackish, resinous revival of its home town's **Barnsley Bitter** ★★ using the same yeast strain as the original. Better known nationally for its series of 40-plus single-hop cask **IPAs** ★★→★★★; oily, slightly astringent **Old Moor Porter** ★★; and hoppy Imperial stout **Gorlovka** ★★☆, full-flavoured despite modest strength.

ADNAMS
Southwold, Suffolk

Long-established, family-dominated independent brewery on the Suffolk

coast. Revered for benchmark cask ales like **Southwold Bitter** ★★☆, with complex marmalade and peppery Fuggle flavours; and richer, nuttier **Broadside** ★★. Cultivating a contemporary edge with a plethora of new creations including pear-tinged "Champagne beer" **Sole Bay Celebration** ★★★. The revived, rich barley wine **Tally-Ho** ★★★ improves with ageing.

ARBOR ALES
Bristol

Inventive Bristol brewery winning admirers since 2007. Beers include chaffy and honeyed best bitter **Brigstow** ★★☆; distinctive chocolaty, leafy **Mild West** ★★☆; and smooth and smoky **Oyster Stout** ★★☆ with real oysters added to the mash. Numerous experimental ales appear under the name **Freestyle Fridays** ★★→★★★.

BLACK SHEEP BREWERY
Masham, North Yorkshire

Set up in 1992 by a far-sighted wayward son of the local Theakston brewing family, brewing no-nonsense ales in the traditionally dry regional style using Yorkshire Square fermenters. The **Best**

Bitter ★★☆ is balanced, honeyed and slightly tannic; the **Ale ★★★** is an understated heavier, almost austere stronger bitter; and darker stronger **Riggwelter ★★☆** – local dialect for a sheep stranded on its back – is firm and chocolaty with burnt-fruit notes.

BLUE ANCHOR INN BREWERY
Helston, Cornwall

Former monks' hostel that is one of the world's longest-surviving pub breweries, able to prove three centuries of continuous brewing. Fruity, sweetish **Spingo Middle ★★☆** follows a 1910s recipe; spicy, berry-edged **Spingo Special** sometimes upgrades to **Extra Special** form **★★→★★★**. **Bragget ★★** nods to a medieval heritage with added apple and honey.

BRAKSPEAR BREWING (MARSTON'S)
Witney, Oxfordshire

The historic Brakspear brewery at Henley-on-Thames closed in 2002, its brands heading upstream to Witney,

on an Oxfordshire tributary, via a tortuous route. **Brakspear Bitter ★★☆** has retained its rooted, fruity, slightly sulphurous character; and powerful bottle-conditioned **Triple ★★☆** has notes of almonds and whisky.

BRISTOL BEER FACTORY
Bedminster, Bristol

Avowedly contemporary brewer in a corner of a defunct brewery at Ashton Gate in Bristol. Regular beers include creditable, cloved British *weizen* **Bristol Hefe ★★**; Citra-hopped, chewy US-style pale ale **Independence ★★**; a smooth, poised and slightly smoky **Milk Stout ★★★**; and massively floral, grapefruited and bitter UK-style **Southville Hop IPA ★★★**. Innovation continues with projects like "The Twelve Stouts of Christmas".

BRODIE'S BREWERY
Leyton, Greater London

Pub brewery in Leyton, East London that enjoys wider distribution for a prolific series of creative, sometimes eccentric, occasionally superb specialities. It makes the cheerful but complex single-hop golden ale **Citra ★★☆**; the well-judged **Dalston Black IPA ★★☆**; pine-and-grapefruit-peel **Hackney Red IPA ★★☆**; and cherry-dabbed, roasty old ale **Olde Ardour ★★☆**.

BUTCOMBE BREWERY
Wrington, North Somerset

One of the longest standing revivalist cask brewers, from 1978. For two decades it produced a single beer, a dry, generously grainy cask **Bitter ★★☆** that remains a best-practice example of its style. Its appropriately well-engineered, crisp English-hopped **IPA ★★☆** shows promise too.

BUXTON BREWERY
Buxton, Derbyshire

New and keenly contemporary brewery in the eponymous spa town, within the Peak District National Park. Offers a sweetish, herbal, hoppy **Bitter ★★** but is better known for more adventurous bottle-conditioned beers like its curiously fruity Imperial stout **Tsar ★★★**; piney and sweetish US-style IPA **Wild Boar ★★★**; and the Amarillo- and Nelson Sauvin-infused double IPA **Axe Edge ★★★**.

CAMDEN TOWN BREWERY
Kentish Town, Greater London

This hi-tech modern plant in London's Kentish Town produces technically flawless kegged and bottled beers in mainly European styles. Clean and malty **Hells ★★→★★★** appears also in unfiltered form and occasionally a

US-hopped version that challenges some German originals. **Ink ★★** is a creditable craft-brewed dry nitro stout.

DESTINATION
LONDON

Craft Beer Co has pubs at 55 White Lion St, Islington, 82 Leather Lane, Clerkenwell, and 11 Brixton Station Road, with extensive ranges of cutting-edge cask ales, and better UK and imported bottled beers. The Cask & Kitchen at 6 Charlwood Street, Pimlico is similar, or for craft beer celeb-spotting in bijou surroundings, try the Rake at 14a Winchester Walk, Borough Market.

CHILTERN BREWERY
Aylesbury, Buckinghamshire

Buckinghamshire farmhouse brewery founded in 1980. Particularly adept at making stronger ales such as the outstanding long-matured **Bodgers Barley Wine ★★★**, rich with marzipan and fresh orange notes. Less hefty is the chewy chestnut- and raspberry-edged **300s Old Ale ★★☆**.

CONISTON BREWING
Coniston, Cumbria

Housed in a modest plant behind the Black Bull pub, a stone's throw from Coniston Water in the Lake District National Park. Renowned for refreshing lime- and ginger-tinged golden bitter **Bluebird**, which appears in cask, US export and bottle-conditioned versions

★★→★★★. Other options include the smoky and herbal dark mild **Old Man ★★☆**; and **No 9 Barley Wine ★★★☆**, which has smooth vanilla, sherry and orange toffee tones.

CROUCH VALE BREWERY
South Woodham Ferrers, Essex

One of Britain's oldest (1981) new generation brewers at South Woodham Ferrers in Essex. Best known of its "fine Essex ales" is multi-award-winning golden ale **Brewers Gold ★★☆**, with grape and tropical-fruit flavours. Also hop-forward and golden is stronger, apricot-tinged **Amarillo ★★☆**; while sacky, figgy **Essex Boys Bitter ★★** is flavoursome for its strength.

DANIEL BATHAM & SON
Brierley Hill, West Midlands

Tiny, traditional, family-owned independent brewery at Brierley Hill near Dudley, producing sweet, grainy ales. The **Mild Ale ★★★** is classically sappy and robust with chocolate-biscuit notes; while the paler **Best Bitter ★★☆**, added in the 1950s, is full and sweetish with increased English hopping.

DESTINATION BIRMINGHAM

The Post Office Vaults (84 New Street) is a relatively new beer bar next to the main station, with a wide range of contemporary British beers in cask and a wide selection of craft beers in bottles and kegs.

DANIEL THWAITES
Blackburn, Lancashire

Family-owned regional independent now in its third century at Blackburn. Among its regulars is a smooth, chocolaty mild **Nutty Black ★★**, available also as the stronger bottled **Very Nutty Black ★★**; while full-bodied golden ale **Wainwright ★★☆** celebrates a renowned local outdoor writer. **Old Dan ★★☆** is a sweetish, buttery old ale. A Signature range of more adventurous ales is developing.

DARK STAR BREWING
Partridge Green, West Sussex

Former pub brewery that span off from PITFIELD in 1995 and landed near Horsham in West Sussex. Produces reliably outstanding beers with contemporary appeal. **Original ★★☆** is a distinctive roasty old ale; bestselling session beer **Hophead ★★☆** is fruity, citric and well balanced; **American Pale Ale ★★★** bursts with grapefruit and pineapple flavours without excessive bitterness; while its black-

brown, estery **Imperial Stout** ★★☆ is the biggest of numerous specials.

DONNINGTON BREWERY
Stow-on-the-Wold, Gloucestershire

A small, picturesque brewery with its own trout lake, near Stow-on-the-Wold in Gloucestershire. The rarity of its beers beyond a limited estate of Cotswold pubs fuels cult status of a sort, though quality can vary. The standard bitter **BB** ★★ is smooth and sweetish; darker, premium bitter **SBA** ★★☆ is drier and hazier; and neglected, toffee-nosed, fruity-bodied **Double Donn** ★★ is as hard to place as it is hard to find.

DURHAM BREWERY
Bowburn, Durham

A reliable source of big, often bottle-conditioned beers inspired by its home city's ecclesiastical heritage, such as the peach-liqueur-tinged *tripel* **Bede's Chalice** ★★★; the spicily hoppy barley wine **Benedictus** ★★☆; and the cakey, bitter Imperial stout **Temptation** ★★★ and its sour mutation **Diabolu** ★★★. Bold session casks include the mineral and plum-noted golden ale **Cloister** ★★☆.

EVERARDS BREWERY
Narborough, Leicestershire

Family-owned independent at Narborough, near Leicester, known for its much-improved dry end cask ales. Its stronger bitter **Original** ★★ is tawny, fruity and nutty; while the best bitter **Tiger** ★★☆ is subtly fruity with a burst of English hops. There are numerous seasonal beers too.

EXMOOR ALES
Wiveliscombe, Somerset

Founded in 1980 at Wiveliscombe in the Somerset part of Exmoor National Park, this first-wave microbrewer prospered partly from inventing the golden ale style with still tasty, slightly peppery **Gold** ★★. More distinctive is the fruity and coffee-ish porter called **Beast** ★★☆.

FREDERIC ROBINSON'S
Stockport, Cheshire

Big regional independent, family-dominated brewery at Stockport southeast of Manchester, a former stronghold of the hat industry. The best of its cask beers is the smooth and slightly whisky-ish light mild **1892** ★★, formerly Hatters. Star of range is the deep brown barley wine **Old Tom** ★★★ with rich, coffee-ish, slightly tart flavours.

FREEDOM BREWERY
Abbots Bromley, Staffordshire

An early pioneer of newer, smaller-scale, higher spec lager brewing in the UK, this brewery started in London in 1995 and has now transferred to new owners in rural Staffordshire. Uses *Reinheitsgebot*-compliant, vegan-friendly methods, real Burton brewing water and a minimum of four weeks' lagering. The *helles* **Organic English**

Lager ★★ is full and crisp with good leafy hops; the **Organic Dark Lager** ★☆ is a light, toffee-ish and likeable *dunkel*; and the annoyingly reasonable **Pils** ★☆ makes you want them to try out 12-week lagering.

FULLER, SMITH & TURNER
Chiswick, Greater London

Long-standing, independent, family-influenced brewery producing a strong portfolio of Fullers beers in numerous styles from a wisteria-clad riverside site at Chiswick, west London. Well known for cask beers like delicately hoppy and refreshing **Chiswick Bitter** ★★☆ and marmalade-tinged, style-defining **ESB** ★★★, it is gaining new respect for historical revivals such as its slightly smoky amber ale **1845** ★★★☆ and its annually released barley wine **Vintage Ale**, which usually becomes more complex and port-like with age ★★★→★★★★. The brewery occasionally releases a steel-aged sourish version of the classic oak-aged barley wine **Gale's Prize Old Ale** ★★☆, which it acquired by takeover

GEORGE BATEMAN & SON
Wainfleet All Saints, Lincolnshire

Picturesque, family-owned brewery, under a windmill in Lincolnshire. Its characterful Good Honest Ales include chewy, russet best bitter **XB** ★★; grainy and complex **Combined Harvest** ★★☆; dryly fruity and beautifully balanced dark mild **DM** ★★; and rich, fruity and stronger **Victory Ale** ★★☆.

GREENE KING
Bury St Edmunds, Suffolk

This national brewer, founded in 1799 at Bury St Edmunds, is caught between the revered status of being the UK's largest independent brewing company, and, at the same time, being an industrial predator. Ubiquitous light bitter **Greene King IPA** ★☆ is out of step with current expectations of its name. In contrast it is the only UK brewer to continue maturing a strong stock ale in oak vats: the vinous, slightly sour **Old 5X** ★★★☆, which makes rare solo appearances but is mostly blended with fresh ale to create bottled classic **Strong Suffolk** ★★☆. Its old-fashioned cask dark mild **XX** ★★ is only slightly less rare.

DESTINATION
CAMBRIDGE

The Cambridge Blue (85 Gwydir Street) is currently the best of various beer bars off Mill Road, having expanded its cask beer interest to include 100 mainly UK, US and Belgian bottled brews.

GREEN JACK BREWING
Lowestoft, Suffolk

Britain's most easterly brewer, from Lowestoft, Suffolk, launched an improving range of 75cl flip-top bottled speciality beers in the late 2000s, including the roasted, blackcurranty export stout **Baltic Trader ★★☆**; the fruity, gracefully ageing barley wine **Ripper ★★★**; and the more sessionable, soft, chocolaty **Lurcher Stout ★★★**.

HAMBLETON ALES
Melmerby, North Yorkshire

Much-expanded 1991 brewery at Melmerby, north of Ripon, that produces beautifully judged, consistent, tasty beers. The beer names and logo nod to a white horse figure carved into a nearby hillside. Best known for its dreamy, slightly pursing stout **Nightmare ★★★**, which has physalis and raisin notes; the sweetish roasted porter **Black Lightning ★★☆** and dry golden bitter **Stud ★★** are good too.

HARDKNOTT BREWERY
Millom, Cumbria

Creative newer brewery producing boldly flavoured beers. The range includes floral and lemony contemporary bitter **Continuum ★★☆**; treacly but hoppy dry stout **Dark Energy ★★☆**; and extreme beers like sherry- and mature-cheese-scented barley wine **Granite ★★★** and riotous strong stout **Vitesse Noir ★★☆**, infused with coffee, vanilla and cocoa.

HARVEY & SON
Lewes, East Sussex

Revered, family-dominated regional brewer at Lewes, East Sussex, with a classic Victorian-design tower brewery. Best known for dryish, beautifully balanced and slightly toffee-ed **Sussex Best Bitter ★★★**; and internationally for benchmark grainy, leathery, slightly sour and long-ageing historic recreation **Imperial Extra Double Stout ★★★★**. Numerous cask and bottled specialities, often in endangered styles, include a generously malty dark **Mild ★★☆**; hoppy, woody barley wine **Elizabethan Ale ★★★**; and indulgently sweet and complex **Christmas Ale ★★★**.

HAWKSHEAD BREWERY
Staveley, Cumbria

Begun in a barn at Staveley in the Lake District National Park and expanding rapidly on the strength of solid cask beers with a contemporary edge, like its appealingly creamy and astringent flagship **Bitter ★★★**; a blackberry-shaded porter called **Brodie's Prime ★★★**; fruity **Lakeland Gold ★★★**; and dark golden, grapefruity and peachy occasional cask bitter **Cumbrian Five Hop ★★★☆**, which shows a new hop-forward direction.

HEPWORTH & CO BREWERS
Horsham, West Sussex

Technically accomplished newer brewer at Horsham in West Sussex, producing numerous bottle-conditioned ales, mostly under contract to others. Its own brands include smooth and orchard-influenced traditional bitter **Pullman ★★**; and sacky, liquoriced and comforting winter seasonal **Classic Old Ale ★★☆**.

HOBSONS BREWERY
Cleobury Mortimer, Shropshire

In a former granary at Cleobury Mortimer in south Shropshire. Best known for its low-gravity but surprisingly flavoursome malty **Mild ★★☆** but also good for sooty double brown **Postman's Knock ★★☆** with added vanilla, and perfumed flowery bitter **Town Crier ★★☆**.

HOGGLEYS BREWERY
Litchborough, Northamptonshire

Underrated former home brewery that outgrew the garden shed in Litchborough to become Northamptonshire brewing's best-known "best kept secret". Notable for bottle-conditioned beers in traditional styles. **Northamptonshire Bitter ★★☆** is golden with a citric floral tang; **Mill Lane Mild ★★☆** blackcurranty and dry; while **Solstice Stout ★★★** is a skilful blend of roast and hop flavours.

HOGS BACK BREWERY
Tongham, Surrey

Perched on a pretty chalk ridge in Surrey, this smallish farmhouse brewery majors on tasty mainstream session ales like distinctly hoppy but mellow bitter **Traditional English Ale**, or **TEA ★★☆**; stronger double brown **OTT ★★☆** has hints of black treacle and banana; while rum-edged **Advent Ale ★★☆** is a seasonal treat.

HOOK NORTON BREWERY
Hook Norton, Oxfordshire

Established independent brewer in the eponymous Oxfordshire village, its Victorian tower brewery still partly steam-powered. Best known for its rooted, earthy ESB **Old Hooky ★★**. More interesting are **Double Stout ★★☆** with its long, roasted finish; full-bodied and chocolaty, low-gravity **Hooky Mild ★★**; and new seasonals that include the plummy and unashamedly English bottle-conditioned IPA **Flagship ★★★**.

HOP BACK BREWERY
Downton, Wiltshire

Outgrown 1980s brewpub that changed drinking habits in the 1990s with **Summer Lightning ★★☆**, a gooseberry-tinged cracker of a golden cask ale also sold bottle-conditioned, designed to compete with premium lagers. **Entire Stout ★★☆**, its roasted coffee notes softened by malted milk ones, is at least as good.

HOPSHACKLE BREWERY
Market Deeping, Lincolnshire

One-man operation in south Lincolnshire, producing meticulously crafted historical recreations and flavoursome originals in bottle-conditioned form, such as the sternly roasted, cherry- and geranium-tinged **Historic Porter ★★★**, also found in aniseed and vanilla versions. **IPA Resination ★★★** is sherbert-like and peppery; while the **Extra Special Bitter ★★★** is complex and chewy; and vintage barley wine **Restoration ★★★** is fruity and medicinal.

HYDES BREWERY
Salford, Greater Manchester

Long considered one of the most conservative brewers in the UK, with some recipes unchanged for 50 years, this Manchester independent has rebranded its straightforward though notably dry and herbal dark mild as **1863** ★★, and its equally old-school bitter as **Original** ★★. Spicy, whisky-tinged, reddish-amber, stronger winter ale **XXXX** ★★★ is one of several seasonals.

ILKLEY BREWERY
Ilkley, West Yorkshire

Recent set-up in the town of Ilkley by the eponymous moor near the Yorkshire Dales National Park, this brewery is rapidly winning admirers for its contemporary session beers like the earthy but cheerily refreshing golden ale **Mary Jane** ★★★; and the caramelled mild **Black** ★★. There is US influence in brews like the eucalyptus-tinged **Lotus IPA** ★★☆; and oddball specials like the lively, tart "rhubarb *saison*" **Siberia** ★★☆.

JENNINGS BREWERY (MARSTON'S)
Cockermouth, Cumbria

A classic Victorian small-town brewery at Cockermouth on the Cumbrian coast. Still uses well water for traditional ales like its dryly malted, earthily hopped **Bitter** ★★; and distinctive darker speciality **Sneck Lifter** ★★☆, rich with treacle toffee, burnt toast and tangy orange-peel flavours.

J W LEES
Middleton, Greater Manchester

Manchester-based regional independent that supplements cask ales like the classic creamy, fruity mild **Brewer's Dark** ★★★ with strong bottled specialities like the caramel-smooth and persistently bitter barley wine **Moonraker** ★★★ and the widely exported oak-aged barley wine **Harvest Ale** ★★★☆, this last made annually with new season's ingredients, with a nutty, sherried and slightly salty, olive-imbued complexity.

KELHAM ISLAND BREWERY
Sheffield, South Yorkshire

Seminal small brewery that brought beer making back to Sheffield in 1990, under the stewardship of the late Dave Wickett, a visionary among smaller brewers. Popular light but robust golden ale **Pale Rider** ★★★ has a tropical-fruit aroma and helped steer Britain toward higher-hopped paler beers. Also noted for jet-black, fruit and chocolate stout **Bête Noire** ★★☆, and numerous specials and collaborations.

DESTINATION
SHEFFIELD

The Sheffield Tap is the restored refreshment room on Platform 1B of Sheffield's main station, with a range of interesting casks and a clever selection of kegged and bottled British and foreign craft beers.

KERNEL BREWERY
Bermondsey, Greater London

Determinedly artisanal young Bermondsey brewery widely lauded and awarded for authentic historic recreations of pale ales, porters and stouts. These include spiky **Export Stout London 1890 ★★★☆** with tobacco and liquorice notes; an elegant prune-tinged **Imperial Brown Stout London 1856 ★★★★**; and big, hop-forward but always well-judged contemporary pale ales, IPAs and black IPAs, recipes for which change from brew to brew (usually **★★★**). Mainly bottle-conditioned, a few in keg.

LEEDS BREWERY
Leeds, West Yorkshire

Highly professional and ambitious 2007 set-up in the city where Tetley was king until Carlsberg closed it down. Its calling card is the treacly, vermouth-tinged mild **Midnight Bell ★★★**; the bestseller is the grainy, easy-going **Pale ★★☆**; with the lusciously flavoursome, woody stout **Gathering Storm ★★☆** and sweetish, lemony cask lager **Leodis ★★** also of interest. A small, high-quality pub estate.

DESTINATION LEEDS

North Bar (24 New Briggate) is a pioneering, contemporary, minimalist, right friendly beer bar with cask and now craft bottled UK beers and a good range of sometimes unusual imports.

LIVERPOOL ORGANIC BREWERY
Bootle, Merseyside

Ambitious and inventive new Merseyside brewer offering a diverse range including flavoured beers. Strong brews like its oily and blackcurrant-edged **Imperial Russian Stout ★★** are light for the style. Grassy and grapefruity **Shipwreck IPA ★★☆** appeals to contemporary craft beer fans; while orangey and mellow **24 Carat Gold ★★☆** and the floral and biscuity revival of **Higsons Best Bitter ★★** are more sessionable.

LOVIBONDS BREWERY
Henley-on-Thames, Oxfordshire

Keg and bottle specialist helmed by a US expat in the regatta town of Henley-on-

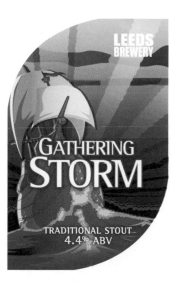

Thames, Oxfordshire. Products include aromatic piney, US-style **69 IPA** ★★☆; fruity and chocolaty porter **Henley Dark** ★★; and tart, herbal, complex fruit beer **Sour Grapes** ★★☆, a World Beer Cup gold medallist.

MAGIC ROCK BREWING
Huddersfield, West Yorkshire

This Huddersfield craft brewer has been commanding youthful attention since 2011 with a bold, heavily US-influenced hop-forward range, including piney but rounded **Cannonball IPA** ★★☆; its intense chilli-dipped double brother **Human Cannonball** ★★☆; fruity and spicy red ale **Rapture** ★★; and a charred ooze of an Imperial stout called **Bearded Lady** ★★☆, which is also the basis for some impressive barrel-aged specials.

MARBLE BEERS
Ancoats, Greater Manchester

Originally located in the Marble Arch heritage pub on the northern

edge of Manchester city centre, this brewer expanded off site back in 2009 following its deserved success for consistently excellent and innovative output. Fine session ales like the creamy, golden, perfumed **Manchester Bitter** ★★☆, evoking the once-legendary Boddingtons at its peak, and the luscious, stronger, dark mild **Chocolate Marble** ★★★☆ are supplemented by big bottle-conditioned specialities such as the complex and fruity Imperial stout **Decadence** ★★★★ and the delightful tea- and bergamot-infused **Earl Grey IPA** ★★☆.

DESTINATION
MANCHESTER

Port Street Beer House (39 Port Street) is a stylish specialist beer bar in the city centre's Northern Quarter with an ever-changing range of exciting brews from hand-pulled local ales to rare and exotic imports.

MARSTON, THOMPSON & EVERSHED (MARSTON'S)
Burton upon Trent, Staffordshire

One of only two historic breweries left in the old brewing town of Burton upon Trent. Retains a Burton Union fermentation system of interlinked banks of wooden casks, to make the creamily dry flagship pale ale **Pedigree**, said to retain the struck match or "Burton snatch" aroma. Designed to be a cask beer edified by good keeping, it rarely is, while other formats diminish it ★→★★★. Others brews include salty, liquoriced **Oyster Stout** ★★; the apple-edged mid-Atlantic IPA, **Old Empire** ★★☆; and, for now, London's much misunderstood, low-alcohol, sweet heritage ale, **Manns Brown** ★★.

MAXIM BREWERY
Houghton-le-Spring, Tyne and Wear

Risen from the ashes of Sunderland regional brewer Vaux to perpetuate celebrated oily, dry brown ale **Double Maxim** ★★☆; higher-strength sweet and slightly sherry like **Maximus** ★★; and biscuity **Ward's Best Bitter** ★★, restoring a lost Sheffield brew.

MEANTIME BREWING
Greenwich, Greater London

Smallish brewery near the Thames at Greenwich, exploring life beyond real ale since 1999. Good at lagers such as notably nutty Vienna-style **Union** ★★☆, alongside clean and pineapple-edged **London Pale Ale** ★★☆ and outstanding historical revivals in 75cl bottles like **India Pale Ale** ★★★ and **London Porter** ★★★☆.

MIGHTY OAK BREWING
Maldon, Essex

Well-respected small Essex brewery at Maldon, on the Blackwater Estuary. Best known for award-winning mild **Oscar Wilde** ★★☆ – rich, roasty and bracing for the style. Other beers include pleasantly floral and easy-drinking **Maldon Gold** ★★.

MOOR BEER
Pitney, Somerset

This small, rural Somerset brewery was rejigged in 2007 by a Californian expat, retaining and improving the signature old, strong brown ale, the tart, malt-bread- and fruit-tinged **Old Freddy Walker** ★★★; and the complex and roasty Amoor, aka **Peat Porter** ★★★. Contemporary flavours were added with the nettly, chocolate black IPA **Illusion** ★★★; and the huge cracked-pepper and peach tones of US-style **JJJ IPA** ★★★☆. Moor also makes numerous cask and unfined keg beers.

MORDUE BREWERY
North Shields, Tyne and Wear

Reviving the name of a defunct 18th-century company, this award-winning small brewery by the Tyne Tunnel at North Shields flaunts Geordie character in its zesty, grapey blond bitter **Five Bridges** ★★☆; grainy, hoppy **Geordie Pride** ★★☆; and deep, peppery and deliciously autumnal flagship dark bitter **Workie Ticket** ★★☆, meaning "troublemaker" in local dialect.

NETHERGATE BREWERY
Pentlow, Suffolk

Suffolk-Essex-borders brewer that played a key role in the revival of porter when it produced full-flavoured, cakey and tangy **Old Growler ★★★**, still one of the best. Also reintroduced spiced beers to the UK with coriander-laced, flowery, copper **Umbel Ale ★★** and the deliciously complex, spiced porter **Umbel Magna ★★☆**. The recipe for **Augustinian ★★☆** has varied but is currently a big toasty ESB.

OAKHAM ALES
Peterborough

An early adopter of light-coloured, higher hopped ales, its success prompted a move from Rutland to Peterborough in 1998. Bestseller is elegant, lychee-tinged, pale golden bitter **JHB ★★☆**. Straw-coloured **Bishop's Farewell ★★☆** has lime and passion-fruit notes; while **Green Devil IPA ★★★** is one of the better US-influenced British IPAs. Seasonal **Asylum ★★☆** adds big hops to a British bitter.

O'HANLON'S BREWING
Whimple, Devon

Reliable escapee from London that honours its Irish ancestry through its softly malty **Dry Stout ★★☆**. Complex, cedary **Original Port Stout ★★★** is dosed with ruby port; while **Gold Blade ★★** is a creditable English spiced *weizen*. Sadly, its custodianship of legendary barley wine **Thomas Hardy's Ale ★★★☆** has ceased,

though bottles of the last brew in 2009 will keep improving for years.

OKELL & SON
Douglas, Isle of Man

Long-established independent brewer on a semi-autonomous island in the Irish Sea that still has a local beer purity law. Its cask-conditioned session **Okells Bitter ★★** is slightly nutty. More recent specialities play on Celtic and historical themes, like tarry, leathery, smoked porter **Aile ★★☆**; light and lemony **Doctor Okell's IPA ★★**; and big, burry, citrus wheat beer **Mac Lir ★★☆**.

PITFIELD BREWERY
Moreton, Essex

Founded in London in 1982 as the first successful new London brewery for decades, and relocated to rural Essex in 2008. Grows its own organic barley. Pioneered single-varietal bitters with a decently rounded session beer, **East Kent Goldings ★★**. More substantial are strong historical recreations like **1792 Imperial Stout ★★★**, **1850 London Porter ★★★** and annually released **Vintage Stock Ale ★★☆**.

REDEMPTION BREWING
Tottenham, Greater London

Another of the better new-wave London brewers launched since Young's departed in 2006, producing individual but approachable beers at its Tottenham base. Standout is golden ale **Trinity ★★★**, only 3% ABV but packed with floral and tropical fruits; also sappy, roasted brown mild **Urban Dusk** ★★☆ and easy-drinking, blackcurranty **Fellowship Porter** ★★☆.

REDWILLOW BREWERY
Macclesfield, Cheshire

This Macclesfield-based former home brewer, turned pro in 2010, is already making waves with an eclectic range of flavoursome ales including one of Britain's best modern double IPAs, sesame- and lavender-scented **Ageless** ★★★☆; fruity smoked porter Smokeless ★★☆; aromatic US-style pale **Wreckless IPA** ★★★; and the always interesting series of **Faithless** experimental beers ★★→★★★.

RINGWOOD BREWERY (MARSTON'S)
Ringwood, Hampshire

Founded in 1977 at Ringwood, on the edge of Hampshire's New Forest, by Peter Austin, a one-man wellspring of craft brewing, who made and sold kit that revived smaller scale commercial brewing across Britain and around the world. Best known for nutty ESB **Old Thumper**

★★☆, also brewed by Shipyard in Portland, Maine; golden bitter **Fortyniner** ★★☆; and warming, marmalade-tinged **XXXX Porter Winter Warmer** ★★★.

ROOSTER'S BREWING
Knaresborough, North Yorkshire

This early UK champion of US hops, brewing at Knaresborough near Harrogate, has been under new owners since 2011. The award-winning cheerful golden ale **Yankee** ★★☆ has lime and mandarin notes; while the **Wild Mule** ★★ foregrounds Nelson Sauvin; and the citric, fruity **YPA** ★★ is more English in style. The Outlaw brand has started to mark out numerous inventive specials.

RUDGATE BREWERY
Tockwith, North Yorkshire

Reputable small brewery on a disused airfield near York. Noted for lemony, quinine-bitter, light golden ale **Jorvik** ★★☆, and malty but bracing **Ruby Mild** ★★★. It has absorbed Marston Moor brewery but has retained the brand for pruney, woody **Matchlock Mild** ★★ and others.

ST AUSTELL BREWERY
St Austell, Cornwall

The last surviving independent regional brewer in Cornwall deploys a canny sensibility by securing national success for its lemon-pepper premium bitter **Tribute** ★★☆, made with a purpose-specific own-design malt, alongside citrus-and-strawberry, hop-led IPA

Proper Job, made to different specs for cask and bottle ★★→★★★; the newer, crisply bitter and caramelled IPA **Proper Black** ★★★; and experimental brews from an in-house nano-brewery, such as the occasional, massive **Smugglers Ale Grand Cru** ★★★☆.

ST PETER'S BREWERY
St Michael South Elmham, Suffolk

Small high-tech brewery in an Elizabethan manor near Bungay in north Suffolk, producing widely exported specialities in designer bottles. Its fruit and spiced beers do not always work but stylish **Hoppy Grapefruit** ★★ wheat beer stands out. Better are the light but tasty **Cream Stout** ★★☆; cola- and candy-tinged **Ruby Red Ale** ★★; and toffee-ish double brown **Winter Ale** ★★☆.

SALTAIRE BREWERY
Shipley, West Yorkshire

Award-winning small brewery in a disused power station by the Saltaire UNESCO site in Shipley. Makes citric, slightly bitter **Cascade Pale Ale** ★★ and flavoured specialities such as delicate, floral **Elderflower Blonde** ★★; nutty but restrained **Hazelnut Coffee Porter** ★★☆; and cakey but tart stout **Triple Chocoholic** ★★.

SAMUEL SMITH OLD BREWERY
Tadcaster, North Yorkshire

The oldest brewery in Yorkshire, founded 1758 at Tadcaster. Eccentric, taciturn, determinedly independent and successful, its single cask ale **Old Brewery Bitter** ★★ and own-brewed lagers contrast with bottled specialities aimed at the US and other export markets, where they impacted decades before the rest. Get the point with the silky-smooth, sweetish, mellow **Oatmeal Stout** ★★★; rich and vinous **Nut Brown Ale** ★★☆; creamy but dryly bitter **Taddy Porter** ★★★; and oak-aged, red-fruit and spiced-toffee barley wine **Yorkshire Stingo** ★★★☆.

SARAH HUGHES BREWERY
Sedgeley, West Midlands

Brewing was restored at the Beacon Hotel in Sedgeley near Wolverhampton in 1987 after a 30-year break, reviving recipes used by ancestral proprietor Sarah Hughes. **Dark Ruby** ★★★☆ is a benchmark strong dark mild, moreishly drying with blackcurrant and ripe plum tones; while subtly citric **Sedgeley Surprise** ★★☆ is a more contemporary premium bitter.

SHARP'S BREWERY (MOLSON COORS)
Rock, Cornwall

Brewing under a spotlight since taken over by MoCo, at Rock on the north Cornwall coast, its ubiquitous sweetish bitter **Doom Bar** ★☆ appears simplified, leaving its session bitter, flowery golden **Cornish Coaster** ★★ superior. Less often found are its bottle-conditioned specialities such as wild-fennel-infused wheat beer **Chalky's Bite** ★★☆ and the big and bitingly spicy **Honey Spice Tripel** ★★☆, among other experimental brews of promise.

SHEPHERD NEAME
Faversham, Kent

Family-infused independent with a claim to be Britain's longest established licensed brewery, founded in 1698 at Faversham, in the hop country of Kent. Flagship premium bitter **Spitfire ★★** has lost something while ascending to national brand status, but recent speciality launches like meaty, plummy barley wine **Generation Ale ★★☆** and rich, honeyed English-style **India Pale Ale ★★★** have restored respect. **Sappy Late Red ★★** is the tastiest of the regular casks.

SUMMER WINE BREWERY
Honley, West Yorkshire

Though its name nods to a much-loved British TV sitcom about misbehaving pensioners, filmed around nearby Holmfirth, this determinedly modern operation foregrounds bold flavoured beers like "double black Belgian rye pale ale" **Cohort ★★** – black American, not pale Flemish; floral, grapefruity IPA **Diablo ★★☆**; berried and tropical amber ale **Rouge Hop ★★☆**; and roasted, smoky, coffee-grounds, 10-malt, Imperially stout **Teleporter ★★☆**.

T & R THEAKSTON
Masham, North Yorkshire

This respected 19th-century brewery has been back in family hands since 2003. The once self-governing market town of Masham had a 12th-century ecclesiastical court called a Peculier, after which **Old Peculier ★★★** is named, an old ale that turns remarkably dry after a complex, sweetish start. Slightly chalky, straightforward, tasty best bitter **XB ★★** is worth a try. The notably malty and stronger **Masham Ale ★★** lies somewhere between complex and uneven.

THORNBRIDGE BREWERY
Bakewell, Derbyshire

Hailed by many as Britain's leading 21st-century brewery. An offshoot of KELHAM ISLAND and originally based at a Derbyshire stately home, it now brews at Bakewell. Its flagship is the resinous but approachable **Jaipur IPA ★★★★**, perhaps the archetype for a new UK hop-forward version of a style originally made at the other end of the county. An imaginative and consistently excellent range also includes lighter and more citric **Wild Swan ★★★**; toasty Vienna lager **Kill Your Darlings ★★★**; superb Imperial stout **St Petersburg ★★★** (**★★★→** in whisky-cask-aged versions); and the unique dark, sweet and spicy honey beer **Bracia ★★★**.

SHARP'S BREWERY
— CONNOISSEURS —
CHOICE
HONEY SPICE
TRIPEL
FINEST BOTTLE CONDITIONED BEER

STUART HOWE HEAD BREWER

Nº3 | BREWED IN CORNWALL | VINTAGE 2011

THREE TUNS BREWERY
Bishops Castle, Shropshire

A small but classically designed tower brewery near the Welsh border at Bishops Castle in Shropshire, active from 1642 and holding the oldest known brewing licence in Britain, with possible interruptions. The main products are figgy, mellow bitter **Cleric's Cure** ★★☆; fruity, sticky barley wine **Old Scrooge** ★★☆; and grainy, grassy golden bitter **XXX** ★★★.

TIMOTHY TAYLOR
Keighley, West Yorkshire

Recently expanded family-owned brewery at Keighley in the south Pennines, making characteristically dry, chalky beers. The peppery, slightly gingery best bitter **Landlord** ★★★, as endorsed by Madonna as the "champagne of ales" on *The Jonathan Ross Show*, looms large, overshadowing lower-powered but smart cask ales like the delicate and flowery light mild **Golden Best** ★★★; the nutty, substantial **Dark Mild** ★★☆; and the distinctive plum- and raisin-edged old ale **Ram Tam** ★★☆.

INNOVATION · PASSION · KNOWLEDGE

Thornbridge

WILD SWAN

WHITE GOLD PALE ALE
3.5% ABV

500ml℮

TITANIC BREWERY
Burslem, Stoke-on-Trent

This consistently high-achieving 1985 brewery is located at Stoke-on-Trent, home city of the captain of the SS *Titanic*. The intense, roasted and mocha-tinged **Stout** ★★★ is occasionally available in limited-edition fruited versions. There also is a soft, slightly appley **Mild** ★★☆; a stronger, more citric winter mild **Black Ice** ★★; and flowery US-hopped wheat beer **Iceberg** ★★.

WELLS & YOUNG'S
Bedford, Bedfordshire

Young's abandoned centuries of brewing in London by merging its brewing into Bedford-based Wells in 2006. Young's **Bitter** ★★ remains distinctive and faintly winey. **Double Chocolate Stout** ★★☆ fulfils the promise of its name; while the complex, liquorice-laced seasonal **Winter Warmer** ★★★ is said to be based on a 19th-century Burton pale ale. The 2011 relaunch of the legendary **Courage Imperial Russian Stout** ★★☆ will benefit from a little more ageing, and courage.

WILLIAM WORTHINGTON'S BREWERY (MOLSON COORS)
Burton upon Trent, Staffordshire

Brewing giant Molson Coors (MoCo) acquired the site of the old Bass brewery at Burton upon Trent and in 2011 created an impressive small brewery within the National Brewing Centre, which is located there. That most adept of survivors, the classically English pale ale **White Shield**, is far better bottle- than cask-conditioned ★→★★★, and is once more nationally distributed, alongside the more floral, golden **Red Shield** ★★. Other recreations that appear occasionally, include the estery, vinous Imperial stout **P2** ★★★; and a distinctly tea-like version of upmarket bitter **Worthington's E** ★★☆, from before the age of kegging.

WINDSOR & ETON BREWERY
Windsor, Berkshire

This accomplished new brewery, which can be found in the shadow of Windsor Castle, is steering skilfully between "real ale" and innovation. Seductive golden ale **Windsor Knot** ★★☆ showcases fruity New Zealand hops; while black IPA **Conqueror** and its stronger **1075** version ★★→★★★ expertly marries chocolate and resinous hops. Pollen-dabbed, bitterish **Republika** ★★ is a pale lager that uses Czech yeast.

WOODFORDE'S NORFOLK ALES
Woodbastwick, Norfolk

Award-winning 1980 regional brewery in the Norfolk Broads best known for its cheerful, blackcurranty and slightly astringent golden bitter **Wherry** ★★☆. Also good are the earthy, dark **Nelson's Revenge** ★★☆ and the resinous stronger ale **Headcracker** ★★☆. The bottle-conditioned heritage barley wine **Norfolk Nip** ★★★ is sadly rarely seen.

DESTINATION
KINGS LYNN

Beers of Europe, at Setchey, south of Kings Lynn, is a beer warehouse in the middle of nowhere that stocks over 2000 beers from all over the world for walk-in supermarket-style purchase or delivery across the UK.

WYCHWOOD BREWERY (MARSTON'S)
Witney, Oxfordshire

A different plant on the same site as **BRAKSPEAR** produces cakey, dark bitter **Wychwood Hobgoblin** ★★.

WYE VALLEY
Stoke Lacy, Herefordshire

Reliable, well-settled 1985 brewery at Stoke Lacy, near Hereford, often using local hops. Crisp and grapefruity golden cask bitter **HPA** ★★☆ and softer, stronger bitter **Butty Bach** ★★☆ are supplemented by impressive bottle-conditioned ales fronted by fictional forces' sweetheart Dorothy Goodbody, including her generously malty and sharply roasted **Wholesome Stout** ★★★☆; and nutty, darkish pale **Country Ale** ★★☆.

SCOTLAND

In the late 19th century, sugar refining became a major industry in Scotland, fuelling a shift in the Scottish diet – the influence of which remains to this day. Around that time strong, sweet beers nicknamed and sometimes branded "wee heavy" emerged, later gifted to the world via Belgium and elsewhere as "Scotch ale". In the 20th century, the independent brewery sector fell to mergers and takeovers more swiftly in Scotland than in England, though its revival has seen determined small breweries emerge in some remarkably remote places.

BELHAVEN BREWING (GREENE KING)
Dunbar, East Lothian

This medium-sized brewery in the ancient coastal town of Dunbar, east of Edinburgh, boasts a longer history of continuous brewing than any other brewery in Scotland, beginning as far back as 1719 and possibly earlier. Part of Greene King since 2005, Belhaven produces its own brands, notably the thick, malty and gooseberry-fruity cask **80/-** ★★☆; more berry-fruited, dry-hopped **St Andrews Ale** ★★; dry and slick but disappointingly nitro-kegged stout, **Black** ★☆; and the more interesting low-gravity "light" **60/-** ★★☆.

BREWDOG
Ellon, Aberdeenshire

The UK's most provocative and, for its size, successful brewer exports to the world from Fraserburgh, on the east coast of northern Aberdeenshire. Brewdog's style, vocabulary and edgy marketing are US-influenced, while its UK-wide chain of evangelical beer bars (*see* box, below) comes from a mixture of business sense and passion. Its unpasteurized, often coarse-filtered, kegged and bottled beers include the flagship grapefruit-hoppy **Punk IPA** ★★☆; the chewy modern amber ale **5am Saint** ★★☆; and the crude but reliable hop bomb **Hardcore IPA** ★★★☆. Its range of specials is unsteady in more ways than one and includes massive weird stuff like the 18.2% ABV, viscous cranberry stout **Tokyo** ★★★★; and a complex series of **Paradox** whisky-barrel-aged Imperials ★★★→★★★★.

DESTINATION
ENGLAND AND SCOTLAND

The growing BrewDog chain of beer bars has set up in a dozen UK cities, including Bristol (58 Baldwin Street), Nottingham (20 Broad Street) and Edinburgh (143 Cowgate) with its own beers on draft and international craft nobility in bottle.

CALEDONIAN BREWING (HEINEKEN)
Slateford, Edinburgh

The only brewery in Edinburgh in continuous production since the 19th century still uses direct fired coppers. New corporate owners have smoothed out the charmingly flowery, bestselling golden ale **Deuchars IPA ★★☆** and creamily malty, fruity, traditional **80/- ★★☆**, unfortunately. Numerous specials include nutty and more complex **Merman ★★★**.

FYNE ALES
Achadunan, Argyll & Bute

Farm brewery overlooking Loch Fyne in Argyll & Bute, with a rapidly improving range that includes the outstanding zesty, lychee- and kiwi-fruit-tinged, hoppy golden cask ale, **Jarl ★★★☆**; slightly stronger, sweeter and more floral **Avalanche ★★☆**; and deeper, richer **Highlander ★★☆**, which airs aromatic specialist malt notes.

HARVIESTOUN BREWERY
Alva, Clackmannanshire

Now one of Scotland's oldest breweries, founded in 1985 and since moved to Alva in Clackmannanshire. Pioneered lighter, hoppier styles with grassy, citric **Bitter & Twisted ★★★**; and flowery, resinous, blond lager **Schiehallion ★★**, which is better in the keg or bottle. Notable thick, chocolaty, oated porter **Old Engine Oil ★★★** is matured in various whisky casks to produce varieties of enormously enjoyable, complex, Scotch-pepped **Ola Dubh ★★★→★★★★**.

HIGHLAND BREWING
Swannay, Orkney

Accomplished small brewery in an old cheese factory at Swannay, on Orkney. Producing nectary, citric, strong pale ale **Orkney Blast ★★**; bitterish, tasty and spicy, if underpowered **Orkney IPA ★★**; and a fruity, liquoriced, easy-drinking **Porter ★★☆**.

ORKNEY BREWERY
Quoyloo, Orkney

The longer-established of the Orkney brewers, located near the neolithic village at Skara Brae, Orkney Brewery is known for its malt-led, sweetish, and lightly tart dark brown ale **Dark Island ★★** and its peaty, fruity, whisky-barrel-aged and massive big brother **Dark Island Reserve ★★★☆**. The slightly lighter **Skull Splitter ★★☆** is a walnut- and apple-tinged barley wine that is named after a former Norse ruler of the islands. The brewery also brews the Atlas brands, such as grassy and floral cask-conditioned "pilsner" **Latitude ★★**.

STEWART BREWING
Loanhead, Midlothian

Newish, highly regarded brewer near Edinburgh making traditionally styled malty Scottish ales with contemporary flair, including comfortingly biscuity **80/- ★★★** with tobacco and dark fruit notes; olive- and toasted-coconut-tinged bitter **Embra ★★☆**; determinedly malty and cindery **St Giles ★★☆**; and chaffy, plummy **Edinburgh No 3 Scotch Ale ★★**. Often even better bottle-conditioned.

TEMPEST BREWING
Kelso, Borders

Contemporary craft brewer at Kelso, Borders, establishing a reputation for big flavours since launching in 2010. IPA **Brave New World ★★☆** spews out mango, apricot and menthol; four-grain, strong stout **Double Cresta ★★** is creamily fruity; fruit-charged golden ale **Long White Cloud ★★☆** is oily, tropical and rich; while the porter **Red Eye Flight ★★★** has coffee and ash.

TRAQUAIR HOUSE BREWERY
Innerleithen, Borders

Oldest inhabited stately home in Scotland where the late laird revived the 16th-century brewhouse in the grounds in 1965 to create benchmark revivalist strong beers. **Traquair House Ale ★★★☆** is a dark delight of rich malt with tart fruit and vermouth tones; while sweetish, complex, liquoriced, coriander-spiced **Jacobite Ale ★★★** reflects in its name the family's historic loyalties.

TRYST BREWERY
Larbert, Falkirk

Former home brewery named after Falkirk's historic cattle market. Distinctive and reliable cask- and bottle-conditioned ales include refreshing, summery, elderflower-dosed golden **Blàthan ★★**; rare chocolaty Scottish-style mild **Brockville Dark ★★☆**; smooth but cuttingly roasted **Carron Oatmalt Stout ★★☆**; and sage-and-cinder, toffee-tinged **Drovers 80/- ★★☆**.

VALHALLA
Haroldswick, Shetland

Small brewer on the island of Unst in Shetland, the UK's northernmost community, once part of Norway and closer to Bergen than Edinburgh. Fittingly for a remote producer, its sweet, golden brew **Island Bere ★★☆** is unique, made from an ancient form of barley called bere, offset by Cascade hops; delicate, fruity pale ale **White Wife ★★** is bulkier in the bottle; while easy-drinking **Sjolmet Stout ★★** is a good all-rounder.

WEST BREWERY
Bridgeton, Glasgow

Pub brewery owned and run by a German brewster, in one of Glasgow's quirkier landmarks, a former carpet factory modelled on Venice's Doge's Palace. Flagship citric-hoppy but honeyed *helles* **St Mungo** ★★☆ is one of the UK's best-tasting craft lagers. There is also a decent chewy and chocolaty **Dunkel** ★★☆; and a drinkable, slightly fruity **Munich Red** ★★.

WILLIAMS BROTHERS BREWING
Alloa, Clackmannanshire

The only brewery in the once great brewing town of Alloa, Clackmannanshire. The enterprising inventors of distinctively infused **Fraoch Heather Ale** ★★☆, which changed perceptions of Scottish brewing history when launched in 1992, have gone on to create refreshingly tart gooseberry **Grozet** ★★; floral but firm golden ale **Seven Giraffes** ★★ with elderflower and lemon zest; and fruity, substantial and elegant **Profanity Stout** ★★☆.

> #### DESTINATION GLASGOW
>
> The Blackfriars (36 Bell Street) is a large pub and eating house in the fashionable Merchant City area, with Scottish cask ales and craft beers and a more eclectic range of bottles, especially from the US.

WALES

Indigenous beer styles that would distinguish Welsh brewing from that of heavy industrial or deserted rural areas in neighbouring England are yet to be recognized, though localism thrives in the principality, so something will emerge in time, no doubt.

BRYNCELYN BREWERY
Ystradgynlais, Powys

Tiny pub brewery expanded to become a small stand-alone brewhouse on the river Tawe, upstream of Swansea. Its subtle, cheerful beers owe their names to Buddy Holly, for some reason. The soft, slightly smoky dark mild is **Buddy Marvellous** ★★☆; the flowery golden ale, **Holly Hop** ★★; and the more toffee-ish pale ale, **Oh Boy** ★★.

MŴS PIWS (PURPLE MOOSE BREWERY)
Porthmadog, Gwynedd

This small brewery, established in 2005, is located at Porthmadog on the coastal strip of Wales' Snowdonia National Park, in Gwynedd. It wins accolades in particular for its **Ochr Tywyll y Mŵs (Dark Side of the Moose)** ★★☆, an unusual hoppy dark ale with citrus and pineapple notes. The resinous fruit-salad-tinged bitter **Cwrw Madog (Madog's Ale)** ★★ is good too.

OTLEY BREWING
Cilfynydd, Rhondda

Otley Brewing Company was originally created at Cilfynydd in Pontypridd to supply a small family-owned pub chain found in the South Wales valleys.

Brewing flair and hip presentation have since driven national recognition and expansion of the company. Their beers include the award-winning, tangy, lemony pale ale **01** ★★☆; the audaciously named orangey *witbier* **O-Garden** ★★; the fruity, toasted, seed-toned strong IPA **mOtley Brew** ★★★; and the autumnal ruddy bitter **03 BOss** ★★☆. Badly designed beers are rare here.

PEN-LON COTTAGE BREWERY
Llanarth, Ceredigion

A fine range of sporadically distributed bottle-conditioned beers from a small farmhouse in Llanarth, rural Ceredigion. These include the smooth, pastille-like **Chocolate Stout** ★★★; a strong ale with notes of coal tar and orchard fruit, called **Ramnesia** ★★☆; the robust and characterful pale ale **Tipsy Tup** ★★☆; and occasional specials made with local fruits, like the chewy, tannic plum stout **Torwen** ★★.

S A BRAIN
Cardiff

One of only two long-established Welsh independent brewers, Cardiff-based S A Brain & Co is still under family influence. Its cask ales include the sharpish, slightly perfumed mild **Dark** ★★☆; winey, gooseberry-tinged bitter **SA** ★★★; and **SA Gold** ★★☆, with notes of apple pie and ice cream. More interest should come from a work-in-progress range of experimental and collaboration beers made in smaller kit and marketed under the Brains Craft Brewery brand.

TINY REBEL BREWERY
Newport

Youthful contemporary brewery grabbing
attention soon after opening in 2012 with
bold-flavoured beers like raspberry-ish red
ale **Cwtch** ★★; luscious but assertively
charred 10-malt stout **Dirty Stop Out**
★★☆; grapey New Zealand-hopped pale
ale **Full Nelson** ★★☆; and flowery,
thistley, lightish **Urban IPA** ★★.

NORTHERN IRELAND

The politics differ in north and south but the island of Ireland shares a
common beer culture, built on the historic preference for porter and stout.
Where the north differs is in having some pioneering "real ale" brewers who
managed to introduce limited choice into the market 15 years ahead of their
southern colleagues.

CLANCONNEL BREWING
Craigavon, County Armagh

Small brewery set up near Craigavon in
Co Armagh and making mainly bottled
beers, among which **McGrath's Irish
Black Stout** ★★★ is a corker of a
traditional dry stout, with an earthy hop
that defines its Irishness.

HILDEN BREWING
Lisburn, County Antrim

Northern Ireland's first new brewery in
decades appeared in 1981 near Lisburn,
County Antrim, and is still flourishing
under family ownership. **Scullion's
Irish Ale** ★★ is a distinctively gritty
and fruity session beer; and golden,
zingily citric and bitterish **Twisted
Hop** ★★☆ is a recent arrival. Also
brews College Green beers for Belfast,
notably the light cola-tinged **Molly's
Chocolate Stout** ★★.

WHITEWATER BREWING
Kilkeel, County Down

This successful new small brewery in the
fishing port of Kilkeel, is now Northern
Ireland's largest brewery. Minerally
reddish-amber **Belfast Ale** ★★☆ is
substantial and distinctive; **Belfast Lager**
★☆ is grainy, floral and unusually heavy;
and **Clotworthy Dobbin** ★★☆ is a very
dry, tart, full-flavoured porter.

REPUBLIC OF IRELAND

Porter and stout were invented in London but by 1800 Ireland had made them her own, qualifying their strength and style by use of terms like "plain", "extra" and "export" and creating drier, less malted varieties by the addition of salt to the mash, sometimes by filtering the wort through shucked oyster shells.

The question still stands whether, historically, there was also a local "red" style of pale ale.

Opening a new brewery was nigh-impossible for decades, due to the absence of genuinely independent shops and pubs. As these have returned, so has a wave of entrepreneurial smaller brewers bringing international beer styles, cask ales and a full range of stouts and porters to a new, younger audience, something at which Guinness and Murphy's, which hold most of the market, have signally failed.

CARLOW BREWING
Bagenalstown, County Carlow

The O'Hara family's successful 1996 brewery expanded in 2009 to Bagenalstown in County Carlow, its beers bearing the family name.

Comes into its own as a brewer of stouts like medium-bodied, drier end, near-black **Irish Stout** ★★☆, with more coffee than chocolate; and heavier **Leann Folláin** ★★★, with a whiff of molasses and toasted malt, liquorice and dark fruit.

CHORCA DHUIBHNE (WEST KERRY BREWERY)
Ballyferriter, County Kerry

Tiny 2008 brewery on the Gaelic-speaking Dingle peninsula. Increasingly fêted for its cask- and bottle-conditioned, six-weeks-aged strong porter, **Cúl Dorcha** ★★★, which has smoke, spice, bitter chocolate and the rest bursting forth; and its little sister, fruity pale golden ale **Beal Bán** ★★, which has a bitter follow-through.

DUNGARVAN BREWING
Dungarvan, County Waterford

This neat little 2010 brewery is located at Dungarvan in County Waterford. The year-round brews they produce are an interesting, floral, grassy, citrus but honeyed blond **Helvick Gold ★★☆**; a surprisingly good "Irish red" called **Copper Coast ★★☆**, fruity and caramelled before a hoppy finish; and a medium-bodied, roasted malt and coffee bean stout **Black Rock ★★☆**. Seasonals appear too.

EIGHT DEGREES BREWING
Mitchelstown, County Cork

A start-up (2010) at Mitchelstown in County Cork, run by an Australasian duo. Crisp, citrus-edged US-style pale **Howling Gale Ale ★★** is edgy for Ireland; **Sunburnt Irish Red ★★** breathes life into its subject with NZ and Australia hops; while top dog **Knockmealdown Porter ★★☆** is a malt-driven, nutty, dryish beer with firm bitterness

FRANCISCAN WELL (MOLSON COORS)
Cork City

Early in 2013 Molson Coors took over Franciscan Well, a senior citizen of Irish craft brewing that has been located in Cork City since 1998, with the intention of increasing production massively. **Rebel Red ★★** is fruity with a faint bitterness, its pale cheeks suitably rouged; roasted **Shandon Stout ★★** is creamier and more approachable than most; while the unexpected star is a hazy orange, banana-laced *hefeweizen* with a touch of new-mown hay, **Friar Weisse ★★☆**.

DESTINATION CORK

The Abbot's Ale House (17 Devonshire St), bang in the centre, has likely the best selection of beer in all Ireland. The bottle shop on the ground floor stocks well over 500, while the first-floor bar rotates craft Irish taps and limitless bottled beers from round the world.

GALWAY BAY BREWERY
Salthill, Galway City

The Galway Bay pub brewery, which was established in 2009 at Salthill in Galway City, serves its own chain and other bars nationally. Its early beers include the typical fruit-and-nut, copper-coloured **Galway Bay Ale ★★**; and the dryish, malt-driven toasted porter **Stormy Port ★★☆**.

DESTINATION GALWAY

The Salt House (4 Ravens Terrace) pub-restaurant is leading a trend in the west toward craft beer, majoring on 25+ Irish brews with a larger number of quality international ones, some of considerable note.

GALWAY HOOKER
Roscommon, County Roscommon

This careful small brewery is making its way unusually with a floral, citrus, honeyed light blond ale **Irish Pale Ale** ★★☆, made with local malt and US hops. No other regular beers yet but the occasional **Bonaparte's Stout** ★★☆, brewed for a pub in Galway, turned heads.

METALMAN BREWING
Waterford City

Brewing since 2010, with its own place at Tycor in Waterford since 2012. First beer **Pale Ale** ★★ is an enjoyable, mostly keg, occasionally cask US-style pale ale with a touch of mandarin in the citrus. New beers likely to spring from seasonal experiments. Made of sound stuff.

PORTERHOUSE BREWING
Dublin

Dublin-based firm that restarted it all. Tried and tested range includes three cleverly measured black beers. **Plain Porter** ★★★ is straightforward and unenhanced, doing simple so well that some may not get it; fuller **Oyster Stout** ★★☆, with whole oysters, seems fruitier rather than drier; while heavily roasted **Wrassler's XXXX** ★★★☆ has a dab of rusty nail and dark fruit. UK-hopped citrus pale ale **Hop Head** ★★☆, revived from brewpub days, recalls its prescience.

DESTINATION
DUBLIN

Always a great place for pubs but not beer, the Irish capital is now starting to even things up. Try gorgeous, foody W J Kavanagh's (4 Lower Dorset St), Porterhouse Central (45–47 Nassau St) and original (16 Parliament St) branches, the Buckley steakhouse chain's Bull & Castle (5 Lord Edward St) and L Mulligan Grocer (18 Stoneybatter), all bars that stock 100+ beers, a healthy share of which are new Irish.

TROUBLE BREWING
Allenwood, County Kildare

Tiny 2009 brewery at Allenwood in Kildare that pitched up with accomplished **Dark Arts Porter** ★★☆, a lighter-bodied, near black, malt-led beer with a touch of caramel, and has struggled to find it a soul mate, though fruity, golden **Ór** ★★ is starting to get there.

FRANCE

Surprisingly perhaps, the term "craft beer" was most likely first coined in France, where the description *bière artisanale* was in use by the early 1970s at the latest.

Parts of France, particularly around Lille in the north, and Alsace-Lorraine in the east, have always enjoyed a strong brewing culture, though the 400 and more new breweries that have opened in recent years are spread pretty evenly across the country. As with Italy, a country inextricably associated with wine production is rapidly developing one of the most exciting beer scenes in Europe.

The concept most closely associated with traditional French brewing is that of *bière de garde*, or "stored beer", referring to the practice of cool-conditioning ales at or near the brewery for some months, before bottling either unfiltered or reseeded. The tricolour brewing habit of producing one blond, one brown and one amber beer is also deep-rooted, as is the use of 75cl bottles for sharing.

The newer brewers are a mixed bag influenced by the brewing practices of Belgium, the US, the UK, Germany, the French north, modern Italy and nowhere in particular. Many will likely flounder but in their midst will be many of Europe's great brewers and beers of the future.

ALIÉNOR
Saint-Caprais-de-Bordeaux, Gironde

Start-up (2012) of great promise, in an old wine store at Saint-Caprais-de-Bordeaux, southeast of the city, run by a young Belgian vintner turned brewer. Blond, brown and white are for starters, with seasonals in development; first brew **Alienor Blanche** ★★ being a creamy *witbier* with slight sourness and, unusually, well-balanced bitterness.

AN ALARC'H
Huelgoat, Finistère

Small 1998 brewery at Huelgoat on Brittany's Finistère peninsula, collaborating with TRI MARTOLOD to make a wide range of beers including UK-style ales and stouts. Standouts are Breton-style stout, **Hini Du** ★★★, a black ale with liquorice tastes and well-balanced bitterness; and a lighter-end Imperial stout with burnt malt, dark chocolate, expresso, smoked and cocoa flavours, called **Kerzu ★★★**, which improves with a few years cellaring.

ATELIER DE LA BIÈRE
Villedieu-sur-Indre, Indre

Industrious, hands-on 2004 brewery and beer shop at Villedieu-sur-Indre, near Châteauroux in central France. Regular beers include light blond ale **La Yote ★★**, with herbal aromas; **Tournemine Real Ale ★★**, a floral, copper-coloured bitter with peppery notes; dark ruby-brown **Une Inquiète ★★☆**, a slightly tart, mocha-edged stout; and **Touraille ★★★**, an amazing, full-flavoured smoked porter.

BARON, AU
Gussignies, Nord

Charming, tiny family-run bistro brewery at Gussignies, on the Belgian border south of Mons. Seasonal blond *bière de garde* **Cuvée des Jonquilles ★★☆** has become year-round for its exceptional floral and citrus aroma and

Hini Du

Bier du Menez Arc
Bière noire des Monts d'Arree
4,7%vol.   75cl

freshness, with less well-known **Saison St Médard ★★** worth trying too.

BELLEFOIS
Neuville-de-Poitou, Vienne

Handsome, small 2003 brewery north of Poitiers, with its own auberge and restaurant. Friendly enough with ORVAL in Belgium to be allowed use of its yeast to ferment golden-amber **732 Charles Martel ★★☆** and others.

BERCLOISE
Bercloux, Charente-Maritime

Tiny brewery at Bercloux, inland from La Rochelle on the Atlantic coast, brewing in a Charentais still designed for making Cognac. **Bercloise au Cognac ★★** is a light brown ale infused with brandy; while newer, smoked and fruity **Stout ★★** has an Irish coffee aroma.

BRETAGNE
Kerouel, Finistère

Operates breweries at Trégunc on Brittany's south coast and Tréguier on its north, and produces over a dozen ales under the Ar-Mon, Britt, Celtika, Dremmwel and Gwiniz Du brands, as well as all-grains blond special **St Erwann ★★☆**, made with barley, wheat, buckwheat, oats, rye, spelt and millet.

CAUSSENARDE
Saint-Beaulize, Aveyron

Small farmhouse brewery at Saint-Beaulize, northwest of Montpellier in the south of France. Malt made from its own barley is used in accomplished Caussenarde beers like the biscuity sweet **Blonde** ★★☆, with an intense floral hop and long, bitter finish; a toffee and nutty **Ambrée** ★★; and a velvet-bodied **Blanche** ★★★ that is an amazing fruity-spicy interpretation of a *hefeweizen*.

CHOULETTE, LA
Hordain, Nord

A small farmhouse brewery located at Hordain, near Cambrai, south of Lille, making a wide range of beers. Traditional *bière de garde* **Choulette Ambrée** ★★☆, with caramel, malt and hop flavours, is perhaps the best; with safer, blond **Sans Culottes** ★★ more of a starter beer.

DESTINATION
LILLE

La Capsule (25 rue des Trois Mollettes) is a slightly downmarket but candle-lit bar near the cathedral, with a world-class selection of local and international ales on tap and in bottle, welcoming all.

DAUPHINÉ
Saint Martin d'Hères, Isère

Small brewery at Grenoble in the French Alps, making beers called La Mandrin. The summer **Blanche** ★★☆, made with seven herbs, is light, dry and herbal; **Aux Noix** ★★ has subtle flavours from walnuts; **Noire au Réglisse** ★★

is a black ale with roasted malt and liquorice root; and **Au Sapin** ★★☆ is a strong fruity, sweet winter beer gaining freshness from fir tree sap.

DER, DU
Montier-en-Der, Haute-Marne

Village brewery (2006) with modern kit and local ways, at Montier-en-Der, northeast of Troyes. La Dervoise beers include **Mellite** ★★, a dryish golden ale with chestnut-honey aroma and slight honey aftertaste and a hoppy note at the finish; while **Nuisement** ★★☆ is an intensively roasted stout with hints of coffee and a spicy end.

DUYCK
Jenlain, Nord

Successful family-run, fourth-generation (1922) brewery southeast of Lille, better known by the name of its brand and village of origin, Jenlain. Best in 75cl bottles, its **Jenlain Ambrée** ★★☆ remains a classic of its kind, though newer products seem simpler in comparison. Into canning too, an odd concept for *bière de garde*.

ENTRE 2 MONDES
Mouthier-Haute-Pierre, Doubs

Small 2008 brewery at Mouthier-Haute-Pierre, between Besançon and the Swiss border, started by an experienced craft brewer from Quebec – hence the name. Bold blond ale **Eau de Pierre** ★★☆ has a strong malt aroma and flowery notes; and reddish **Indian** ★★★ is a delightful reinterpretation of IPA, with fresh hops and piney flavour, strong bitterness and an oaky, dry finish. There are others, untried.

ENTRE DEUX BIÈRES
Mauriac, Gironde

Tiny but interesting 2009 brewery at Mauriac, in the Entre-Deux-Mers wine region east of Bordeaux, experimenting with local twists. **L'Entre 2** ★★☆ is an organic blond beer, bottom-fermented with some white grape juice before being lagered in wine barriques; and **La Tchanquée Brune** ★★ is a roasty light stout with oyster brine added to the brew, ending slightly acidic, with a coffee taste.

FLEURAC
Ydes, Cantal

Small 2008 brewery run by a Belgian near Ydes, deep in the Auvergne. Shows great promise with newer beers like US-style IPA **Cowboy & Indien Pale Ale** ★★; stronger, self-explanatory **Triple Brune IPA** ★★★; and **Grains de Folie No 2** ★★★☆ Imperial stout, as rich in hop flavours as coffee and spices. Best sampled locally.

FONTAINES, DES
Les Verchers-sur-Layon, Maine-et-Loire

Small brewery at Les Verchers-sur-Layon, south of Angers, in the vineyards of the Loire valley. **La Fosse Blonde** ★★ is rich, with a malty, spicy character; malted amber ale **Diabolik** ★★☆ has a warming character; while full-bodied stout, **Sarcophagus** ★★, has a smoky finish.

FRANCHE, LA
La Ferté, Jura

Tiny brewery southeast of Dijon in Franche-Comté. **Profonde Blonde** ★★☆ has aromatic hops and a distinctive, fresh, long finish; while regular **Ipane Brune** ★★ becomes an intense, sweet barley wine with a unique caramelized character, in its winter version **Hivernale** ★★★.

GAILLON
Courpalay, Seine-et-Marne

The second generation of the Rabourdin family to brew on their farm at Courpalay, southeast of Paris, badge their ales Bière de Brie. The **Blanche** ★★ is a French interpretation of *witbier*, spicy with a lemon aroma; the tasty **Blonde** ★★ is biscuity and goes well with Brie cheese; while the **Ambrée** ★★☆ is a more malt-driven *bière de garde*.

GARLAND
Algans, Tarn

Farm brewery east of Toulouse, longest established of the region's small breweries. Concentrating on organic Karland beers, such as **Ambrée** ★★, which has a smoked malt, rich body and dry finish.

GARRIGUES
Sommières, Gard

Creative small brewery west of the southern city of Nîmes. Bottle-conditioned beers inspired by British and northern French brewers include delicate **Saison des Amours** ★★☆, with candied-fruits aroma and *faux* bitterness; NZ-hopped strongly aromatic IPA, dry-hopped **Frappadingue** ★★★ is best at room temperature; and **Nuit de Goguette**, its stout brand, now comes with oats, with rye, barrel-aged or smoked ★★→★★★.

JOLI ROUGE
Canals, Tarn-et-Garonne

Promising brewery with a beer shop, at Canals, north of Toulouse. Its **Pils** ★★ has a herbal aroma and bittersweet profile; impressive UK-influenced **Bitter** ★★☆ is hopped with Aramis, an Alsace variety derived from Strisselspalt; **India Pale Ale** ★★ is hopped UK style, while **Amber Ale** ★★☆ is made with rosehips, giving it slight acidity.

LANCELOT
Le Roc-Saint-André, Morbihan

Pioneering and successful 1990 Breton brewery, now expanded into a former gold mine. Best known for **Cervoise Lancelot** ★★, a pale ruddy-amber ale, flavoured with herbs said to have been used by the Gauls; and **Telenn Du** ★★☆, a *blé noire* beer, brewed with the blackened buckwheat used in local crêpes.

LEPERS
La Chapelle-d'Armentières, Nord

Small, century-old firm making mainly paler beers, both in its own name and as L'Angelus. **Lepers 6** ★★ is light golden and balanced; **Lepers 8** ★★ is stronger and dry for the style; **L'Angelus Blonde** ★★☆ is a *bière de garde* take on wheat beer, conjuring the aroma of fresh-cut hay, a smooth bitterness and slight acidity.

LUTINE, LA
Limeuil, Dordogne

Pocket-sized brewery at Limeuil, in the Dordogne. The **Blonde** ★★ has a generous body, grassy with spicy notes; while occasional brew **Aux Noix** ★★ has a roasted caramel flavour, sour notes, a subtle taste of nuts and a spicy finish.

MAISON DE BRASSEUR
Pont-d'Ain, Ain

Interesting if tiny brewery at Pont d'Ain, northeast of Lyon, making two beers of note: pale ale **Rivière d'Ain** ★★, with

wild hops; and **Bresse** ★★, a caramel-sweet amber ale with a long finish.

MATTEN
Matzenheim, Bas-Rhin

Inventive, prize-winning boutique brewery with attitude, south of Strasbourg. Its well-rounded **Red Fox IPA** ★★☆ uses mostly local Alsace hops with cooked apple aromas; while **La Schwortz** ★★★ is a black stout, with a strong coffee aroma, creamy, toasty, chocolate malt flavours and a fruity finish. Expect more.

MAUGES
Beaupréau, Maine-et-Loire

Well-organized, small 2010 brewery whose Rombière beers include smooth and refreshing **Blanche** ★★, a *witbier* with oats; and **Noire** ★★☆, a smooth, roasted stout with subtle coffee flavours.

MÉLUSINE
Chambretaud, Vendée

Small brewery southeast of Nantes. **Love & Flowers** ★★ is a wheat beer aromatized and flavoured with rose petals and hop flowers; **Mélusine Bio** ★★☆ is a pretty, sweet amber ale with peach notes; and **Barbe Bleue** ★★★ is a stewed brown ale with roasted malts and a hint of liquorice.

MONT SALÈVE
Neydens, Haute-Savoie

Rising star near Neydens, south of Geneva, creating a skilful, additive-free range of Salève beers. **Sorachi Ace Bitter** ★★★ is an amazing low-strength beer with fruity, herbal aroma and exceptional body; the **Blanche** ★★★ is a daring, citrus, hoppy take on *witbier*; Nelson Sauvin-hopped IPA **Amiral Benson** ★★★ follows intense fruit-pine aromas with a full flavour and long finish; **Mademoiselle Aramis IPA** ★★★☆ showcases Aramis hops from Alsace; and winter's **Tourbée** ★★★☆ tastes of its smoked malts with toasted peach notes.

ORGEMONT
Sommepy-Tahure, Marne

Distinctive 2001 farm brewery at Sommepy-Tahure in the western Ardennes, surrounded by the vineyards of Champagne. Orgemont beers include a strong yellow-blond **Triple** ★★☆ full of grain, with citrus notes and cracked peppercorn; while the contract brewed Valmy brands include **Blanche** ★★, a *witbier* with spicy aroma and grainy body.

> ### DESTINATION BOUGUENAIS
>
> Bières et Chopes (2 chemin de la Vaserie) is an amazing beer store near Nantes, with northern French specialities among 500+ bottles, high-quality advice and a small cellar café-restaurant.

PARADIS, LE
Blainville-sur-l'Eau, Meurthe-et-Moselle

Punchy little 2009 brewer at Blainville-sur-l'Eau, southeast of Nancy in Lorraine.

Flagship UK-leaning IPA **La Sylvie'cious** ★★★ begins and ends with herbal hops, fresh fruits and flowers; **Corinne-Louise** ★★☆ is a rare French dark mild, with subtle hops and an astonishing spicy finish; and red-amber ale **Hop'ss Marie-Magdeleine** ★★ is a good French take on an ESB. One to watch.

PLEINE LUNE
Chabeuil, Drôme

Inventive and eye-catching new brewery at Chabeuil, south of Lyon. Its red-amber, grainy but grapefruity IPA **Aubeloun** ★★★ has turned experienced heads with its measured bitterness; while altogether more traditional amber ale **Lunik** ★★☆ has toffee aromas and hints of caramel and red fruits.

RATZ
Fontanes, Lot

Small, efficient 2001 brewery near Cahors, north of Toulouse, little-known elsewhere but achieving much in this wine-growing area. **Ratz Ambree** ★★ is sweet and nutty, in a range that now includes organic beers and occasional specials.

ROUGET DE LISLE, LA
Bletterans, Jura

Small 1994 brewery at Bletterans in the Jura, between Dijon and Geneva, making beers that absorb regional produce. Soft wheat beer **Griottines** ★★☆ has the juice of Franche-Comté cherries added during brewing, ending in a slightly acidic blend of malt and fruit, with a surprisingly clean finish; the grainy, nutty

blond version of **La Ventre Jaune** ★★ is made with grilled cornflour; while **Perles Noires** ★★★☆, a four-grain black barley wine aged in wine barriques for three years before bottling, has raised it to a new level.

SAINT ALPHONSE
Vogelgrun, Haut-Rhin

New brewery created by a Belgian on the Rhine between Strasbourg and Basle in southern Alsace. His Saint Alphonse beers show promise with a classic 8.5% ABV **Brune** ★★, with roasted and spicy flavours. The 6.5% Blonde and 7.5% Ambrée are yet to be tried.

SAINTE COLOMBE
Sainte-Colombe, Ille-et-Vilaine

Gradually evolving 1996 Breton brewery near Sainte-Colombe, south of Rennes. Apart from a sound normal range there are also **Pie Noire** ★★★, with moderate bitterness overrun by strong flavours from rye and smoked malts; and a unique barley wine **Grand Cru** ★★★, with an amazing buttery caramel aroma, full and sweet, with caramel and hints of oak and cherry.

ST GERMAIN
Aix-Noulette, Pas-de-Calais

Small, active brewery at Aix Noulette, southwest of Lille, making the Page 24 beers. **Reserve Hildegarde Ambrée** ★★ is brewed with local hops, giving strong bitterness alongside toasty notes; and **Reserve Hildegarde Brune** ★★ is dark with intense aromas of roasted and chocolate malts and light liquorice.

SAINT LÉON
Créon, Gironde

This pub brewery and music venue, which is surrounded by vineyards, located at Créon, east of Bordeaux, is likely to expand. Its tasty and grainy **Saint Léon Blonde ★★** is an aromatic, well-rounded, soft pale ale that is brewed from home-made malt.

SAINT RIEUL
Trumilly, Oise

Farmhouse brewery, established in 1998, located at Trumilly in Picardy, named after an early Christian evangelizer, spearheading the return of craft beer to this once brewery-rich area. The Saint Rieul range includes above-average 7% ABV blond, amber and brown ales and also **Blanche ★★**, a fresh-tasting *witbier* with coriander and orange peel; and triple-fermented **Grand Cru ★★☆**, a well-rounded stronger ale with rich biscuit and vanilla flavours.

ST SYLVESTRE
Saint-Sylvestre-Cappel, Nord

This successful 150-year-old family brewery, located at Saint-Sylvestre-Cappel, between Dunkirk and Lille, is best known for its instantly likeable strong blond ale **3 Monts ★★☆** and its amber equivalent **La Gavroche ★★☆**. Seasonal offerings include big, strong brown but uninspired **Bière de Noël ★★**; and the aged-over-winter Easter release, golden **Bière Nouvelle ★★☆**.

THEILLIER
Bavay, Nord

One-man operation near the Belgian border south of Mons. Among France's oldest breweries (1835), with some period kit, likely to close when its owner retires. Produces two near-perfect lagered ales called La Bavaisienne, in the *bière de garde* tradition. The rustic **Blonde ★★★** is malt-led with fruity edges; while the **Ambrée ★★★☆** has toasted, caramel malt aroma and beautifully judged bitterness. Neither travels too well.

THIRIEZ
Esquelbecq, Nord

Pioneering small brewery (1996) south of Dunkirk. **Blonde d'Esquelbecq ★★☆**, is a crisp, golden, modern interpretation of a traditional farmhouse ale; **Etoile du Nord ★★★** uses richer, flavourful hops to bring grapefruit notes; incredible double IPA, **Dalva ★★★☆**, has intense hop, fruit and floral flavours but manages to be well rounded and refreshing too; while **Fièvre de Cacao ★★☆** has cocoa beans added at the end of the fermentation, bringing a silky mouthfeel and hints of cacao on a bed of dark malt.

DESTINATION CASSEL

Hill town south of Dunkirk blessed by the supremely authentic Kerelshof (31 Grand Place) and Kasteelhof (8 rue St Nicolas) beer cafés, the Traditions du Nord beer shop and much *bière de garde*.

TRI MARTOLOD
Concarneau, Finistère

A small 1999 brewery and craft produce store collaborating with **AN ALARC'H** since 2006 to make Tri Martolod beers like not-too-spicy, *hefeweizen*-style **Blanche** ★★; and well-balanced smoked *dunkelweisse* **Fumée** ★★, with toasted malt.

TROIS FONTAINES
Fenay, Côte-d'Or

Early new-wave brewer in Burgundy, south of Dijon. Uses regional malts and French hops in its La Mandubienne beers, such as dark and rich **Brune** ★★☆, with roasted malt character and strong coffee bitterness. Also makes Téméraire brands with additives, such as **Ambrée au Cassis** ★★ with blackcurrant seeds; and **Blanche au Pain d'Épices** ★★, a *witbier* with gingerbread notes.

VALLÉE DE CHEVREUSE
Bonnelles, Yvelines

Small 2008 brewery in parkland southwest of Paris, recently moved to organic. Best so far of its Volcelest brands is cloudy, fruity **Ambrée** ★★, with a malty aroma and similar fruit and malt flavours.

DESTINATION
PARIS

La Fine Mousse (6 avenue Jean Aicard) is the capital's best café for French craft beers, topping 100 varieties with a dozen on draught.

VEXIN, DU
Théméricourt, Val-d'Oise

Low-key 1992 farm brewery northwest of Paris. **Blonde du Vexin** ★★☆ is a pale ale that looks, tastes and smells like crushed grain juice, with more bitterness than many; **Veliocasse Ambrée** ★★ is a smooth, honey-flavoured amber ale.

DESTINATION
PARIS

La Cave à Bulles (45 rue Quincampoix) is France's premier beer boutique, between the Pompidou Centre and Les Halles, fronting French craft beer among the galleries and fashion houses.

VIGNES
Graulhet, Tarn

Challenging small brewer experimenting with spontaneous fermentation and barrel-aged beers for French palates, from a wine country perspective. **Clandestine Blonde** ★★ has a vinous finish; **Bulle de Vignes** ★★☆ and **Vent d'Ange** ★★☆, brewed in alternate years, each with a sour, lactic character and fruity flavours and fermented in oak wine barriques, divide opinion.

NETHERLANDS

By the early 1980s Dutch beer production consisted of two large combines, Heineken and Skol; a few mostly southern smaller breweries making safe lagers; and a single ale brewer, the Trappist abbey of Koningshoeven, near Tilburg.

A small chain of independent cafés, ABT, fostered interest in Belgian craft beers, persuading a few Dutch home brewers to chance going into small-scale commercial production. Quality was notoriously unpredictable but interest thrived. In the past decade, inspired pivotally by the efforts of De Molen brewery at Bodegraven, professionalism has spread, leading to a wave of smaller brewers using flair to design their beers and technical expertise to ensure they remain in good order.

Brewers have tended to ape beers styles from elsewhere, though dark autumnal "*bok*", off the same tree as German *bockbier*, has migrated far enough to be considered a Dutch speciality.

The list of recommended brewers that follows errs away from safety.

ALFA
Schinnen, Limburg

Brewery (1870) steadfastly failing to move with the times. Superior strong blond lager **Super Dortmunder** ★★☆ has a flowery nose and balanced bitterness but is steered away from greatness by its sweet side; while autumn's **Bok Bier** ★★, ironically perhaps, sidesteps the very sweetness that blights many similar beers.

BERGHOEVE
Den Ham, Overijssel

Tiny but impressive brewery brewing larger runs at MOLEN, DE, pending expansion. **Donkerbruin Vermoeden** ★★★ is a black IPA with strong burnt coffee and subtle fruity bitterness; quaffable, hoppy blond **Khoppig** ★★☆ is a light US-style pale ale; golden ale **Vuurdoop** ★★☆ has citrus hopping and added coriander; warming **1842 Hammer Brand** ★★☆ is a chilli-stained porter drinking well above its lowly weight.

BRAND (HEINEKEN)
Wijlre, Limburg

Solid if unspectacular smaller brewery claiming to be the oldest in the Netherlands, with a heritage back to 1340. Best known for its impressively full-bodied, malty **UP** ★★☆, short for Urtyp ("Original") Pilsner, the best blond lager in the Heineken stable; while its seasonal **Dubbelbock** ★★ has nice caramel tinges but insufficient bitterness.

BREUGEMS
Zaandam, North Holland

Small brewery making solid-to-excellent beers that could be more adventurous. Richly tempting **Stoutert** ★★☆ balances chocolate notes with bitter coffee; well-rounded dryish **Dubbel** ★★ has a smoky edge and bitter finish; hazy golden-blond **Tripel** ★★ is full-bodied and bitter.

BUDELS
Budel, North Brabant

Fourth-generation family-run 1870 brewery producing standard and organic ranges with dependable results. Blond barley wine **Zware Dobbel** ★★☆ is richly warming without overbearing sweetness; above-average **Goudblond** ★★ is balanced by a light, dry bitterness; and

aromatic, off-mainstream, **Capucijn** *dubbel* ★★☆ has a slightly sour edge.

7 DEUGDEN, DE
Amsterdam

Small brewery that experiments with adding stuff to established styles with interesting results. **Spring+Tijm** ★★☆ is a thyme-infused *meibok* with herbal freshness and bitter finish; intensely dark, mid-strength **Stout+Moedig** ★★☆ uses three types of malt and some coffee; the spices in **Dubbel+Dik** ★★☆ give a rounded warmth; and **Wijs+Neuzig** ★★☆ is a *dunkelweisse* with faint clove hints.

DESTINATION **AMSTERDAM**

The Bierkoning (125 Paleisstraat) is a warren of a beer shop, off Dam Square in the bustling heart of the city, somehow packing in 1100 beers including a strong range of Dutch, Belgian and American.

EEM, DE
Amersfoort, Utrecht

Gypsy brewer often using PRAEL, DE and PRAGHT among others, with plans to settle down in Amersfoort. Golden-blond **Eem Bitter** ★★ does what it says, both on the palate and in its follow-through; likeable **Tasty Lady** ★★ is a spiced blond ale with subtle bitterness; while the dark, rich Christmas ale **Eem Kerst** ★★☆ tastes of toffee but with a bitter kick.

EMELISSE
Kamperland, Zeeland

Interesting and ever-improving brewery, now up there with the best. Accomplished **DIPA** ★★★ is a double IPA that packs a mighty bitter punch into an increasingly delicious ale; deep and rich **Rauchbier** ★★☆ is an ale made with smoked malt from Bamberg; rich, black, coffee-tinged **Espresso Stout** ★★★ is becoming a classic of its kind; while the one-off series of barley wine or Imperial stout aged in whisky casks, called **White Label** ★★☆→★★★★☆, can be sensational.

FRIESE BIERBROUWERIJ
Bolsward, Friesland

Us Heit beers are Friesland's contribution to modern Dutch beer culture, defying the sober reputation of locals since 1985. First brew, light amber **Buorren Bier** ("Local Beer") ★★ would be a *vollbier*, were it only German; richly rounded golden-blond **Dubbel Tarwe** ★★☆ is a bigger-than-average *witbier* with fulsome sweetness and citrus edges; while stronger amber **Elfstedenbier** ★★☆ has a fine bittersweet balance.

GOEYE GOET, 'T
Arnhem, Gelderland

Tiny brewery set incongruously amid heritage buildings at the national open-air museum near Arnhem. In distinctive stone bottles it sells an impressively refreshing and malty **Pilsener** ★★☆, exceptional for one so small; an abbey-style **Dubbel** ★★ with a slight sourness we hope is deliberate; and a dark autumn **Herfstbock** ★★ with unintrusive sweetness.

GULPENER
Gulpen, Limburg

1825 brewery at Gulpen in Limburg, producing a huge range of beers, from agreeable to mediocre. Crisp, malty **Chateau Neubourg** ★★ is a dry-ish and bitter pilsner; Gerardus **Wittems Kloosterbier Dubbel** ★★ opts for dryness above cloying caramel and polish over haze; while rock-solid, dryish *witbier* **Korenwolf** ★★☆ is a cut above many Belgian peers.

HEMEL
Nijmegen, Gelderland

Best of the Dutch pub breweries, found in Nijmegen and sometimes beyond. Makes simple beers like citrus *witbier* **Serafijn** ★★; but more in its element with lightly smoked, deep and fruity winter ale **Moenen** ★★☆; rich, well-balanced, dark golden-blond *tripel* **Helse Engel** ★★☆; and lovable giant amber barley wine **Nieuw Ligt** ★★★, warming and soft when young and magnificent as spicy, cellar-aged **Grand Cru** ★★★☆.

3 HORNE, DE
Kaatsheuvel, North Brabant

Hobby brewery (1991) that grew with improving quality. Often rented to wannabe brewers and not averse to smaller-scale contract brewing. Dark, pleasing **Horn's Bock** ★★ has marshmallow hints but avoids cloying sweetness; finely balanced bittersweet **Trippelaer** ★★ is intended to be easy-drinking; and balanced pale **Meibock** ★★ has caramel with bitterness.

IJ, 'T
Amsterdam

Amsterdam's oldest brewery, dating from 1983, always phasic but currently on a roll. Latest star attractions are double-strength **'t IJ Wit** ★★☆, which leans neither to Bavaria nor Belgium; and hazy golden-blond **IPA** ★★☆, still finding its way in the bitterness stakes. Old troopers include strong *tripel*-ish, orange-amber **Columbus** ★★, a collage of clashing flavours; and seasonals like dry, rounded superior amber winter brew **IJndejaars** ★★☆.

DESTINATION
AMSTERDAM

Proeflokaal Arendsnest (90 Herengracht) is one of the driving forces behind the Dutch brewing revival, serving exclusively beers from the Netherlands since opening in 2000 and often the first café outlet for many brewers in the capital.

JOPEN BIER
Haarlem, North Holland

Finally blessed with its own brewery, in a former church at Haarlem, North Holland, a well-practised range is now supplemented by one-offs, some of which stick. The dry and hoppy blond ale **Hoppen** ★★☆ is starting to push its bitterness envelope; the intensely hopped **Jacobus RPA** ★★☆, an IPA with rye, is ahead of its time in Europe; the triple-grain **Trinitas Tripel** ★★★ is gaining confidence with time; and the four-grained **Bokbier** ★★★ has so much bitter cocoa taste that it is almost a porter.

KLEIN DUIMPJE
Hillegom, South Holland

Tiny brewery in the bulb-growing part of South Holland. Too many beers but some decent. Dryish **American Pale Ale** ★★ has a pleasing fruity hop; well-practised **Hazelnoot Porter** ★★☆ is less nutty than its name suggests; **Blackbird Schwarz** ★★☆ has roasted barley and bitterness to the fore with some chocolate notes; and rounded **Imperial Russian Stout** ★★☆ tastes coffee'd.

LA TRAPPE
Berkel-Enschot, North Brabant

The Netherlands' only Trappist brewery, known as Koningshoeven in some places. Operated by commercial brewers Bavaria of Lieshout, but brewing within the walls of Koningshoeven abbey near Tilburg and answerable to the Order. Simpler beers like pale ale **Isid'or** are better bottled than on tap ★→★★; golden-amber **Tripel** ★★ has hints of bitter orange; while its slowly evolving, year-dated barley wine Quadrupel, full of nuance, loses gooey-ness and can gain gravitas when **Oak Aged** ★★☆→★★★★.

DESTINATION
OIRSCHOT

Buitenlust (5 Spoordonkseweg) is a charming, simple, but welcoming, small-town local café northwest of Eindhoven boasting likely the longest and among the best beer lists of any in the country, totalling over 800 much of the time.

LECKERE, DE
De Meern, Utrecht

Utrecht brewer (1887), the first to go organic and found in health food stores nationally. Quality varies, most reliable being balanced barley wine **Blauwe Bijl** ★★, an elegant high-malt beer with a gentle, bitter finish; *dubbel* **Crom Hout** ★★☆, with dabs of cocoa painted onto a slightly sour background; and dark autumn *bok*, **Rode Toren** ★★.

LEIDSCH BIER
Leiden, South Holland

Accomplished brewer making some beers on a tiny scale in Leiden and commissioning larger runs from elsewhere. Own-brew standouts thus far are assertive, highly attenuated, English-hopped **Morsporter** ★★★, with chocolate and cocoa to the fore; and pine-scented, fragrant, highly spiced Christmas ale, **Kerstbomenbier** ★★☆. Its flagship US-style IPA **Leidsch Aaipiejee** ★★☆ is brewed at PROEF in Belgium.

LINDEBOOM
Neer, Limburg

Another 1870 brewery from Limburg, this time at Neer. Slowly breaking out of its mould but held back by safety. Developing a range of Gouverneur beers, abbey-style with polish, of which bittersweet *dubbel* **Brune** ★★ was the first; German-facing Venloosch brands include an **Alt** ★☆ yet to be marketed, in vertical wooden casks; while **Herfst Bock** ★★☆ remains trad Dutch.

MAALLUST
Veenhuizen, Drenthe

Small brewery of promise in a converted grain mill at Veenhuizen in Drenthe, a former colony town for vagrants and beggars, now home to a prison. Malty, bitter **Vagebond Vienna ★★☆** is one of very few Dutch takes on a Vienna amber lager; citrus **Kolonist Weizen ★★** is well rounded and tangy; bittersweet **Weldoener Blond ★★** is satisfyingly malty; and **Zware Jongen Tripel ★★☆** has enough grass to conjure summer meadows.

MAXIMUS
De Meern, Utrecht

New-wave Utrecht brewer, outstanding from day one. Superbly rich, fruity hoppy **Brutus ★★★☆** amber lager is a real star, rich in US influence; US-style IPA **Pandora ★★★** has a lovely floral aroma and major bitter finish; while its variant, immensely likeable golden IPA **Highhops ★★★** is different again; and **Stout 8 ★★★**, the stronger, almost Imperial stout is dry and bitter.

MOLEN, DE
Bodegraven, South Holland

For some years the guiding light of modern Dutch brewing, at Bodegraven in South Holland, now a world leader in craft brewing. Experimentation bordering on insane alchemy at times, has produced a range of 15 regular beers and upward of 200 one-off variants and collaborations. Stunningly aromatic six-hop but only modestly bitter, **Vuur**

& Vlam ★★★★ is one of the world's great IPAs; equally wonderfully hopped, intensely floral double IPA **Amarillo ★★★☆** plays the hop-monster role; varieties of **Tsarina Esra ★★★★** Imperial stout or super-strong porter have treacly whisky tinges when oak-aged as Reserva; while bitter, coffee-tinged **Hel & Verdoemenis ★★★☆** is another Imperial stout with an almost smoky finish. It even has the audacity to brew US-hopped British-style bitter **Op & Top ★★★☆** better than most UK brewers could.

MOMMERIETE
Gramsbergen, Overijssel

Small riverside brewery in Overijssel whose outstanding beers belie its small stature. Its regular **Blond ★★★** is an excellent example of simple done well, a pale ale that smells like a hay barn; the fragrant, malty and complex **Meibock ★★★** is among the best in class; perfectly balanced **Rookbock ★★☆** juggles smoky notes with a fruity, bitter finish; while the two Van Gramsbergen barley wines come in her warming, bittersweet, alcoholic toffee **Vrouwe ★★★**; and his addictive rich, smoky and dry **Heer ★★★**.

MUIFELBROUWERIJ
Berghem, North Brabant

North Brabant brewer with some tiny kit, mostly brewing at PROEF in Belgium and Sint Servattumus in North Brabant. Showing potential are blond ale **Graaf Dicbier ★★**; decidedly off-centre **D'n Osse Bock ★★**; barley wine **Zuster Agatha ★★☆**; and sometimes **1851 Bik & Arnold Dubbel ★★**.

NATTE GIJT, DE
Weert, Limburg

Talented Limburg brewer renting time at Anders in Belgium or **DE 3 HORNE**. **Hop met de Gijt** is a US-style IPA with flowery nose, fruity, hoppy taste and a bitter finish, even better in some of its single-hop special editions ★★☆→★★★.

PRAEL, DE
Amsterdam

Remarkable state-funded rehabilitation project, morphed into a successful small brewery that is starting to experiment. Nelis Bock now has a dry-edged smoked version **Met Pijp** ★★; blond **Johnny** ★★ is just bitter enough to work; bittersweet **Mary** ★★ is an amber *tripel* with a fruity finish; malty, warming **Willy** ★★☆ is a spiced barley wine for winter.

PRAGHT
Dronten, Flevoland

Small brewery in the Flevoland beer void, creating above-average beers. Lovely multi-textured Imperial **Extra Stout** ★★☆ is chocolaty throughout, with raspberry on the nose and a dry bitter finish; darkly complex **Blackbox** ★★★ *doppelbock* has a hint of liquorice and plenty of coffee; while rock-solid **Tripel** ★★ is dry-edged and bitter.

RAMSES BIER
Wagenberg, North Brabant

Moving from **DE 3 HORNE** to its own brewhouse as we write, with a top-table place beckoning. Superb dark amber IPA **Den Dorstige Tijger** ★★★☆ blends fruity notes with rampant bitterness; full-bodied, rounded **Mamba Porter** ★★★ has a fruity, bitter centre and coffee-cocoa edges; impressive golden **Antenne Tripel** ★★★ balances bitter and honey; while lovely rounded Imperial **Shire Stout** gains further in its barrel-aged version ★★★.

RODENBURG
Rha, Gelderland

Small-scale rural brewery in Gelderland making beers called Bronckhorster, rarely less than excellent. Pleasingly bitter Christmas ale **Scrooge** ★★★ is full-mouthed and rounded; treacly **Night Porter** ★★☆ has the full rainbow of coffee, cocoa and dry bitterness; while fruity **Angus Tripel** ★★☆ has a restrained sweet finish.

> ### DESTINATION
> ### ERMELO
>
> Burg Bieren (45 Putterweg) is the country's largest beer retailer and within its 1000+ range has probably the best Dutch range anywhere, some way off the beaten track in the Veluwe region of western Gelderland.

ROOIE DOP
Utrecht

Utrecht brewer launched in 2012, developing mini test brews in a canalside cellar bar and brewing larger volumes at DE MOLEN. The strongly dry-hopped and aggressively bitter **Chica Americana IPA** ★★★ has 10% oats in the mash to round it out; while the **Double Oatmeal Stout** ★★☆ gives off cocoa and rich chocolate.

DESTINATION
UTRECHT

De Drie Dorstige Herten (47 Lange Nieuwstraat) is a small street-corner beer café with a carefully chosen list made up almost entirely of beers from small, hard-to-source local producers.

ROOS, MUSEUMBROUWERIJ DE
Hilvarenbeek, North Brabant

North Brabant brewing museum doubling as a working brewery, with a huge range veering from noteworthy to so-so. Golden-blond **Arnoldus** ★★☆ honeyed *tripel* has enough bitterness to balance both sweetness and strength; decently balanced dry, fruity **St Jansrogge** ★★☆ is a blond ale made with rye.

SCHANS, DE
Uithoorn, North Holland

Brewery-distillery eschewing commercial success to make Schans beers when it feels like it. Spiced **Saison** ★★☆ balances bitter and sweet with clove and ginger; inky-black 7% ABV **Stout** ★★☆ is nowadays seen more commonly than its acquired historic brand, **Van Vollenhoven's Extra** ★★; the **Imperial** ★★★ is similar with 25% less water.

SINT CHRISTOFFEL BIER
Roermond, Limburg

Trading was suspended at this 1986 brewery as we went to press but its renown should attract a buyer. Famed for its up-hopped unpasteurized pilsner **Christoffel Bier** ★★★; well-made Vienna lager **Christoffel Robertus** ★★; and fruity, delicious, dry-hopped **Christoffel Nobel** ★★☆. Even better is **Bramling Cross** ★★★, a strong, bottom-fermented, unfiltered beer lagered for 10 weeks.

TEXELSE BIERBROUWERIJ
Oudeschild, North Holland

Small 1999 brewery on the island of Texel, off the North Holland peninsula. A solid range in established styles, with no show-stoppers but beginning to accrue prizes, especially for seasonal *bocks*. **Skuumkoppe** ★★ was the first Dutch *dunkelweisse*; old trooper **Tripel** ★★☆ is growing in complexity; but for prowess try the increasingly popular **Bock Bier** ★★★, and less subtle strong *doppelbock* **StormBock** ★★☆.

VOLENDAM
Volendam, North Holland

Tiny brewery also known by its brand, 't Vølen Bier. Often favours larger bottles. Its scale promotes laterality but reduces reliability. Dark seasonal **Vølenbock** ★★ has a sharpish finish countering sweetness; strong golden *tripel* **Ootje** ★★☆ has a touch of the barley wines; hazy amber, sweetish strong ale **Øster** ★★☆ might be great if more reliable.

SCANDINAVIA

The two big influences on Scandinavian beer culture in the 20th century were innovative microbiological research by the Carlsberg brewery and punitive beer taxes imposed by temperance-affecting politicians who preferred wine. Folk traditions live on, as in Finnish *sahti*, but this century's brewers are led the by the adage that if it must be expensive, it should taste superb. Expect big, assertive stouts, porters and pale ales.

DENMARK

The speed with which the Danish beer scene has shifted from dependable but dull to verging on psychedelic took even its most ardent supporters by surprise.

About a decade ago, confronted with the prospect of other global brewers coming to Scandinavia and taking slices out of Carlsberg's home market, the Danish giant decided to inject a little unpredictability into the game by enabling the growth of new smaller players.

Whether those who decided on this tactic foresaw the arrival of 13% ABV stouts infused with the world's most expensive coffee beans, or delicate blond ales ruined by the addition of asparagus is unclear. Either way, the explosion of interest in beers of all dimensions in this normally conservative nation knocks even the enthusiasm of the Italians into second place.

Older campaigners fear progress may have been so rapid that inspired brewers will shoot off into the distance leaving the drinking public behind. The absence of infrastructure and a financial commitment to stay in business also worries them, as many of the most creative exponents do not bother with the inconvenience of having to own or maintain a brewery, or employ people.

No one visiting the countless Copenhagen bars where the world's great beers are now matched in quality by little-known local products, or touring the Danish countryside to discover the shops and taphouses run by many of the country's 130 or so new breweries can be left in doubt that something impossibly wonderful is occurring here.

AMAGER
Copenhagen, Capital

Energetic Copenhagen craft brewer with a large but reliable range, strong local following and growing export trade. Interesting beers include **Sloth** ★★☆, a super-dry single malt, Simcoe-only pale ale designed with US colleagues; new regular **Rugporter** ★★★ with rye to add a spicy sweetness; monstrous juicy double IPA **Gluttony** ★★☆, loaded with C-hops; and **Hr. Frederiksen** ★★★☆, a heavily dry-hopped, massively roasted and powerful Imperial stout.

BEER HERE
Copenhagen, Capital

Revolutionary beer commissioner actively involved in designing the brews it has produced at PROEF in Belgium. Delightful sounding **Dead Cat** ★★☆ is a pine and melon amber ale with Simcoe hops; **Kama Citra** ★★★ is an alternative take on brown ale hopped only with Citra; super-hopped, coppery **Hopfix** ★★★☆ an IPA high in alpha acids; while at the opposite end milk stout **Ammestout** ★★★ brims with smooth, sweet flavours from a solid roast base.

BØGEDAL
Jerlev, Southern Denmark

Farmhouse brewery in the rolling hills outside Vejle in Southern Jutland using ancient techniques to make lost Danish beer styles. No two brews are identical but individually numbered gyles are themed. So **Lys #1** ★★☆ is a rustic type of IPA with citrus aroma; biggest seller **Hvede** ★★ is an ultra-sweet type of *witbier*; and **Mork #8** ★★★ is a full-bodied Christmas brown ale made with muscovado and orange peel.

CROOCKED MOON
Copenhagen, Capital

One-man enterprise based at a Copenhagen pub, hiring other Danish breweries when they need to produce. Fat and moist **All Blacks** ★★★ is a pale ale showcasing New Zealand hops; **Bad Karma** ★★☆ is a rich, pruney coffee stout with vanilla and overripe fruit; while IPA **Stonewall** ★★★ is a no-frills, powerful hop punch-in-mouth.

COPENHAGEN

Ørsted Ølbar (13 Nørre Farimagsgade) is a cosy cellar and sports bar catering to a relaxed mix of beery students, football fans and businessmen. A dozen mostly Danish craft taps and a huge list of bottles, in a district awash with eating options.

DET LILLE BRYGGERI
Viby, Zealand

Innovative hobby brewery at Viby, southwest of Copenhagen, making an impressive range with many experimental beers and one-offs. Fairly regularly come **Lakrids Porter** ★★☆, the subtle roastiness of which allows the added raw liquorice to shine; **Columbus Ale** ★★★, an IPA with eponymous hops from the US and both malt and yeast from the UK; and the ever-changing incarnations of **Barley Wine ★★★☆**, each perfectly balanced and warming.

DJÆVLEBRYG
Copenhagen, Capital

Copenhagen-based beer commissioner currently contracting INDSLEV to brew its invariably dark, gothic-imaged beers. **Dark Beast ★★★** is a black IPA in which hops overpower the high-roasted malts; **Mareridt ★★☆** a challenging beer that combines smoked malt with brettanomyces; and **Gudeløs ★★★☆** is a pitch-black Imperial stout that balances its roasts with some light sweetness.

EBELTOFT GÅRDBRYGGERI
Ebeltoft, Central Denmark

Small farmhouse brewery in countryside overlooking the sea, east of Aarhus. At the lighter end **Gårdbryg ★★☆** is a crisp Bohemian pilsner with lots of grassy hops; **Porter Special ★★★** is dark brown and strong, with sweet liquorice and dried fruit playing amid the roasted malts; while in powerful *doppelbock* **Bock No. 4 ★★☆** they are complemented by pumpernickel and burnt caramel.

EVIL TWIN BREWING
Copenhagen, Capital

Danish company fronted by New York-based Jeppe Bjergsø, twin brother to Mikkel, of MIKKELLER. Commissions the beers it designs from breweries in many countries to sell on to even more. **Bikini Beer ★★☆** is a citrus, hop-forward, low-alcohol pale ale; **Soft Dookie**

★★★☆ a filling Imperial stout with a gentle edge of milk chocolate; while **Imperial Biscotti Break ★★★★** is a super-potent porter loaded with coffee and bitter dark chocolate.

FANØ
Nordby, Southern Denmark

Small brewery at Nordby, on the island of Fanø, off Esbjerg, brewing for beer commissioners but also with its own lateral-thinking clutch. Low-strength IPA, 2.7% ABV **Havgus ★★☆** packs lots of hop punch into not much; stronger **Vestkyst ★★★** is a classic American pale ale with crisp and piney hop aromas; **Forår ★★☆** is a dead straight seasonal spring pale *bock*; while massive **Imperial X-mas Porter ★★★★** will knock out any Christmas dinner with its overload of roasted malts, spices and alcohol.

FLYING COUCH
Copenhagen, Capital

The brewer from the brewpub run by NØRREBRO, who also freelances at HERSLEV, has a third job selling promising beers he commissions from his employers. **Paint It Black ★★☆** is called a black IPA but is more like a strong, roasted stout with light aromatic hops; while sweet, mellow **Phister de Noël ★★★** is a winter Imperial stout made with vanilla.

FREDERIKSODDE HAANDBRYGGERLAUG
Fredericia, Southern Denmark

Two home brewers recently turned pro, currently commissioning a solid range of beers from the Kvajj brewery in Vejle. **6 Juli Ale** ★★ is a light, quaffable American-style pale ale loaded with Cascade; **Etlars IPA**★★ is another beer called a black IPA but needing its stout-like hop profile tuned up; and **Lundings Porter** ★★☆ is rustic and strong with notes of tar and smoke.

GRAUBALLE
Grauballe, Central Denmark

Farmhouse brewery and 2002 pioneer of the Danish beer revolution, making solid, no-nonsense beers. **Enebær Stout** ★★☆ is a mid-strength British stout with juniper spicing; subtle Scotch ale **Mørk Mosebryg** ★★☆ combines smoked malts with First Gold hops; Christmas's strong **Peters Jul** ★★ offers no spice but has a rich, warming caramel base.

HERSLEV
Herslev, Zealand

One of Denmark's older small breweries, at Herslev, west of Copenhagen. Going green, using malted home-grown barley. **Økologisk India Dark Ale** ★★☆

is basically a strong brown ale made zippy by NZ hops; **Four Grain Stout** ★★★ comes rich and smooth with an amazing aroma; and **Mjølner** ★★☆ is a powerful seasonal barley wine with occasional consistency problems.

HORNBEER
Kirke Hyllinge, Zealand

Small brewery that enjoys immense popularity with regular Danish beer lovers, despite brewing some challenging beers. **Dryhop** ★★☆ is a lager with the hopping of an IPA; **Hophorn** ★★☆ is a full-throttle strong black IPA heavy on both roasted malts and aromatic hops; darker and stronger comes **Caribbean Rumstout** ★★★, a sweet Imperial stout spiced with rum; while multiple-award-winner **The Fundamental Blackhorn** ★★★★ is an Imperial stout that has undergone dry-hopping, barrel-ageing and the addition of walnuts.

INDSLEV
Nørre Aaby, Southern Denmark

Small brewery off the motorway northwest of Odense, brewing Indslev wheat beers, a separate range of Ugly Duck ales and much contract brewing for various beer commissioners. **Indslev Sort Hvede** ★★☆ is a wheat beer that looks and tastes like a stout, Breton-style; while **Spelt Bock** ★★☆ is a creamy *weizenbock* with dark chocolate from the roasted spelt. **Ugly Duck Hopfest** ★★☆ is an IPA celebrating US aromatic hops; and strong **Imperial Vanilla Coffee Porter** ★★★ keeps the hops and blends them with mocha and a layer of vanilla.

JACOBSEN (CARLSBERG)
Copenhagen, Capital

Carlsberg's smallish speciality brewhouse within the grounds of its old brewery in Copenhagen. The best of a careful range are **Extra** ★★, a clean, crisp pilsner infused with juices of sea-buckthorn; strong hybrid **Pale Ale** ★★ spiced with German hops; and **Abbey Ale** ★★★, a warming, vinous and surprisingly authentic take on a Belgian *dubbel*.

KRAGELUND
Kragelund, Central Denmark

Small village brewery near Silkeborg, west of Aarhus, that is impressing some tough judges. **Steam Beer** ★★☆ is pale beer with a dry-grape character, hopped by Nelson Sauvin; **Katarinas Mild** ★★★ is an original "small beer", designed as a UK dark mild but made from the first run-off from the monstrous Imperial **Katarinas Stout** ★★★; while **Pramdrager Porter** ★★★ elegantly runs smooth vanilla into a roasted beer with a tar-like edge.

KRENKERUP
Sakskøbing, Zealand

Small brewery in an ancient barn on the Krenkerup estate, near Sakskøbing in the south of Zealand, making mostly German-style beers. **Lolland og Falster Guld** ★★☆ emphasizes rich, clean and sweet malts balanced with flowery hops; **Rauch** ★★ has just enough smoked malts to count as a subtle *rauchbier*; while the gem is **Doppel**

Bock ★★★☆, rich in caramel with pumpernickel accents, an excellent example of the style.

MIDTFYNS
Brobyværk, Southern Denmark

Brewery (2004) at Brobyværk, south of Odense, owned by an American expat, a fact reflected in its range. The aptly named **Chili Tripel** ★★ is highly praised, though perhaps more on reputation than merit; **Rough Snuff** ★★☆ is another strong Belgian, this time dark and rich with a tobacco and molasses character; while strong black IPA **Gleipner** ★★★ offers fresh citrus hops on a base of roasted malts.

DESTINATION
ODENSE

Christian Firtal (31 Vintapperstræde) is a traditional pub with a strong emphasis on Danish craft beers, set in the historic city centre, appealing to locals, beer geeks and tourists alike. Twenty taps and as many bottles with enough food to survive.

MIKKELLER
Copenhagen, Capital

The world's most prolific brewer of idolized new beers owns no brewhouse. Mikkel Bjergsø's reputation is such that with a call he can brew all over the world, or get others to do it for him. Occasionally makes a dog but more fairly profiled by **Jackie Brown** ★★★, which set new standards for hopping brown ale when first released; wittily concocted, fabulously delivered, complex coffee stout **Beer Geek Breakfast ★★★☆**, ratcheted up to the beautifully absurd Imperial stout **Beer Geek Brunch Weasel ★★★★**, flavoured with coffee beans that have passed through an Asian civet cat; and voyage of discovery **Nelson Sauvignon ★★★☆**, a refined, Belgian-pointing, Bretty strong ale aged in Austrian white wine barriques.

NØRREBRO
Copenhagen, Capital

Pioneering US-style brewpub in Copenhagen that spawned a busy production brewery. **Ravnsborg Rød ★★** is a deceptively slick, smart and easy-going red-amber ale; **La Granja Stout ★★☆** is a rich and sweet coffee stout; while **Little Korkny Ale ★★★☆** is a warming, English barley wine served from a snifter and not far off the perfect after-dinner drink. Numerous rotating and one-off beers too, rarely dull.

OKKARA
Velbastaður, Faroe Islands

The newer of two sound independent breweries on the semi-autonomous Faroe Islands, in the north Atlantic. When the island's council legalized stronger beers recently, **Portari ★★★** evolved into a rich and filling strong porter with liquorice and coffee notes; **Olavur ★★** is a sweet golden ale with balancing flowery hops, brewed for the islands' national day in July; and flagship stone beer **Rinkusteinur ★★☆** is brewed by the immersion of glowing lava rocks.

SKAGEN
Skagen, North Denmark

Pub brewery near the northernmost point on the Danish mainland, offering a solid range. **Skawskum ★★** is a clean *dunkel* rich in Munich malts, with a dry and hoppy finish; **Bundgarn ★★☆** a rugged, lightly smoked porter with English liquorice in the boil; while **Væltepeter ★★☆** is a filling, warming *doppelbock* with a slightly salty edge.

SØGAARDS
Aalborg, North Denmark

Pub brewery at Aalborg, south of the last entry, with an extensive range of bottled beers. **Stout Noire ★★☆** is a complex brew blending lightly smoked malts with salty liquorice; potent **Bispens Trippel ★★☆** offers the expected yeastiness but with a note of refined almonds; and **Fort Dansborg IPA ★★** is a well-crafted if modest example of the style.

SØKILDEGAARD
Vipperød, Zealand

Tiny farmhouse brewery at Vipperød, west of Copenhagen, selling its beers only on its premises. A roast coffee aroma from **Farfars Favorit** stout ★★★ preludes a smooth and sweet oatmeal follow-through; **Humleguf** ★★☆ is a far from traditional pale ale with interwoven coriander, orange peel and American hops; while New Year beer **Nytårsøl** ★★★ is a sophisticated blend of the farm's own grapes with American hops in a strong Belgian ale base.

STRONZO BREWING
Copenhagen, Capital

The new naughty boy of Danish beer making may have fun with exports to Italy, even when he gets his own brewery in the near future. **Hop Lunch** ★★☆ is a quaffable, low-alcohol IPA, dry-hopped with Cascade; simple golden ale **Proud Stronzo** ★★☆ is made enticing by loads of crispy aroma hops; quadruple-mashed, the almost vulgar **1000 EBC** ★★★ may be the world's blackest Imperial stout; while **Honey Badger** ★★★☆ is an extreme Imperial stout that manages to make honey and booze strike a balanced stand-off.

SVANEKE
Svaneke, Capital

Denmark's easternmost brewery, on the island of Bornholm, has a second smaller brewpub plant for experimental beers. Straight, well-made **In Your Pale Face IPA** ★★★ offers an overload of resinous piney hops; **Liquorice Stout** ★★☆ comes with locally produced sweet liquorice added; super-clean and fresh **Session Pilsner** ★★☆ is rich in citrus hops; while the oddly named **Den Udødelige Hest** ("The Immortal Horse") ★★★☆ is a rugged take on Baltic porter.

TO ØL
Copenhagen, Capital

Experimental brand created by two Copenhagen-based MIKKELLER pupils who now commission for themselves. **Raid Beer** ★★☆ is a lager hopped as an IPA; **Ov-ral Wild Yeast IPA** ★★☆ is what happens if you add brettanomyces into the fermentation of a double IPA; adding lactose and coffee to a strong brown ale makes **Mochaccino Messiah** ★★★; and making a super-strong milk stout then putting it in a whisky barrel creates **Sort Mælk** ★★★.

> ### DESTINATION
> ### COPENHAGEN
>
> The Mikkeller Bar (8 Viktoriagade) is a trendy hang-out for in-crowd beer geeks, with minimalist décor, 20 taps split 50–50 between Mikkeller own beers and guests, and extensive bottles. Beer snacks too and an annoyingly excellent, unrivalled choice of beers.

WINTERCOAT
Sabro, Central Denmark

Tiny brewery at Sabro near Aarhus, brewing beers in styles imported from

Britain that could usefully be exported back. **Double Hop ★★☆** is what a British double IPA might taste like; creamy and nutty **Oatmeal Stout ★★☆** is loaded with malts and oats; and Christmas's **Yule Ale ★★** is a fresh and dark British strong ale with bitter orange for a citric zest.

DESTINATION
AARHUS

The Fairbar (66 Nørre Allé) is a small, eco-friendly, collectively run café just off the centre, with 10 taps of frequently rotating, top-quality Danish brew from smaller producers, and rather more bottles in the same ilk. Adequate food is set to become broader.

XBEERIMENT
Copenhagen, Capital

Another Copenhagen beer commissioner using HERSLEV to give life to its plans. **Crisp Madraz IPA ★★★** blends US with NZ hops; thicker, juicier hops bring some semblance of balance to huge **Hoppenheimer Imperial IPA ★★☆**; while another massive beer, Imperial stout **Black Force One ★★☆**, narrowly avoids getting sticky-sweet by being lightly peaty.

NORWAY

The astonishing rate of tax levied on Norwegian beer was until a decade ago met with an unimaginative response by the handful of medium-to-large breweries that survived its intentions. From being the place where the Gulating code compelled every farmer to brew beer, independent Norway became a nation for ordinary lagers and *lettøl*, sweet light beer of 2% ABV.

Then a lateral-thinking brewery called Nøgne Ø decided to try a different approach. If beer drinkers were forced to pay a shocking amount for a sawn-off glass of decent but dull light lager, why not suggest they part with an outrageous sum for an overfull glass of heavy but superb ale made to uncompromising standards.

So was born the small miracle that brought full-on craft brewing to the fjords and fjells of the country with the world's crinkliest coastline.

AASS
Drammen, Buskerud

One of only two remaining older independent breweries, in the family since 1867, southwest of Oslo. The best example of how things used to be. Uninspiring Vienna lager **Classic** ★☆ and its *dunkel* equivalent **Bayer** ★☆ are of historic interest; its two dark Christmas beers, modest **Juleøl 4.5** ★★ and robust **Juleøl 6.5** ★★☆ summarize the tradition but; while the autumnal dark **Bok** ★★★ is the best of a breed similar to Dutch *bokbier*.

ÆGIR
Flåm, Sogn og Fjordane

Tiny brewery next to a famous end-of-fjord railhead at Flåm, northeast of Bergen. **Bøyla Blonde Ale** ★★☆ is the easy-drinking golden session brew; **India Pale Ale** ★★★☆ is a superb, floral, heavily hopped bitter but fruity IPA; the near-black Imperial stout **Natt Porter** ★★★☆ gains nuance and depth as **Lynchburg Natt** ★★★★, steeped in bourbon casks; while barley wine **Tors Hammer** ★★★ perhaps takes intensity too far at 13.5% ABV.

DESTINATION
BERGEN

Henrik (10 Engen) is a town-centre, first-floor bar with smart but minimalist décor and a huge range of tap beers topping 50, yet still dwarfed by its bottled list. Popular with the university crowd but not so much with students.

BERENTSENS
Egersund, Rogaland

Interesting small brewery at Egersund, south of Stavanger, an offshoot from a long-established cider maker. **RAV Amber Ale** ★★ is fruity and bittersweet; **Sorte Får Stout** ★★☆ is dry and bitter with a taste of unsweetened prunes; and heavy-duty but mid-strength **Jules Avec** ★★★☆ is one of the finest Christmas beers in Scandinavia.

DESTINATION
STAVANGER

Just off the harbour, sporting pub décor from London *circa* 1980, the Cardinal (21 Skagen) is a nicely positioned, remarkably well-stocked bar with 400+ beers including many from the region and some real rarities.

HAANDBRYGGERIET
Drammen, Buskerud

Questing small brewer in the same town as **AASS**, making hand-crafted beers that do not always work but can be spectacular. **Røyk Uten Ild** ★★★ is a dark beer loaded with smoked malt but not oppressive; the mid-strength **Porter** ★★★☆ is robust but smooth and fruity; **Bestefar** ★★★ is a hefty black beer made for winter; **Dark Force** ★★★ is an Imperial stout with a high wheat content; and unique **Norwegian Wood** ★★★☆ is an interpretation of Gulating beer with smoked piney flavours.

KINN
Florø, Sogn og Fjordane

Small brewery, set to expand, at Florø, between Bergen and Ålesund, making mainly UK- and Belgian-inspired beers. **Pilegrim** ★★ is a bottled English bitter; **Svart Hav** ★★☆ is a toasted, bitterish dry lighter stout sometimes found in cask; **Bøvelen** ★★☆ is a Norwegian take on a Belgian *tripel*; while **Vestkyst** ★★★ is more successfully like a US-style IPA.

LERVIG
Stavanger, Rogaland

Small, commercially driven 2005 brewery making standard lagers plus three off-centre Brand beers, including hoppy US pale alc **Lucky Jack** ★★☆. Its Brewers Reserve range of craft oddities are most interesting: **Rye IPA** ★★★, a double IPA to which rye adds fruity sweetness; and **Konrad's Stout** ★★☆, Imperial made approachable, thanks to oatmeal.

NØGNE Ø
Grimstad, Aust-Agder

One of the world's greatest craft breweries, pronounced "nurg-na ur", based at a former hydroelectric plant in Grimstad, northeast of Kristiansand. Can brew anything well but excels with its ordinary strength **Brown Ale** ★★★☆; virtually perfect, middleweight **Porter** ★★★☆; an **India Pale Ale** ★★★★ that is rarely if ever bettered; and an **Imperial Stout** ★★★☆ that is quite restrained for a blockbuster; with **# 100** ★★★☆, a super-strong IPA created by pure self-indulgence.

DESTINATION
KRISTIANSAND

Patricks (10 Markensgate) is a pub-restaurant that has brought top-quality Norwegian and imported beers to the country's most southerly city and ferry port, the range building impressively with the clientele.

SCHOUSKJELLEREN
Oslo

Oslo pub brewery (2010) that is making waves. Creates dozens of new beers each year for its own pub and a few others. Most frequent performers are golden summer ale **Blondilox** ★★; light-bodied but tasty, grown-up **Thunderbear Stout** ★★★; work-in-progress US-style IPA **Empress of India** ★★; and more fully formed lighter pale ale **Female of the Species** ★★☆.

DESTINATION
OSLO

Beautiful, historic and stark in turns but never less than stiflingly expensive, the Norwegian capital has spawned many fine beer venues recently, among the best being two ornate restaurant pubs, Håndverkerstuene (7 Rozenkrantz'gate) and Olympen (15 Grønlandsleiret), though we keep going back to the original, Lorry (12 Parkveien), near the Royal Palace.

SWEDEN

Sweden's notoriously high taxes on alcohol have not deterred 40 or more new breweries setting up since the mid-1990s, with several others intent on joining the fray. The main influences are old UK styles that have become more American with time, though Swedish precision seems to demand high design and delivery standards.

As in the rest of Scandinavia, variations on porter and strong stout are becoming the national and regional speciality.

DUGGES
Landvetter, Västra Götland

Small, prolific 2005 brewery at Landvetter, east of Gothenburg, started by a home brewer. **Avenyn Ale ★★☆** is a US-style pale ale with a fresh, grapefruit flavour from Chinook, Centennial and Simcoe; **Holy Cow ★★★** is a much-malted IPA, its alcohol cleverly hidden by slight sweetness and a large, lingering, five-hop bitter finish; while anything called **Idjit ★★☆→★★★☆** will be dark, generous, strong and portery.

JÄMTLANDS
Pilgrimstad, Jämtland

Small 1996 brewery near Östersund, midway up the country in the unpopulated part, winning countless national awards for beers like well-made, pleasantly balanced amber lager **Bärnsten ★★☆**; **Postiljon ★★☆**, an ESB with a fruity malt character and lingering bitterness; and deep reddish winter ale **Julöl ★★☆**, with a strong earthy hop aroma, some malt sweetness and straight bitterness.

MALMÖ BRYGGHUS
Malmö, Skåne

Pub brewery in an old chocolate factory in Malmö, an expensive bridge-hop from Copenhagen. **Veteöl ★★** is a refreshing *witbier* with coriander and citrus peel; **Beerssons IPA ★★☆** is medium-bodied with a grapefruit hop aroma and lingering bitterness; **Cacao Porter Criollo ★★☆** is robust, real cacao punctuating a sweet, malty flavour; and occasionally released **Grand Crew ★★☆** is a much-praised oddball sour "lambic", aged for 14 months in Cognac barrels before bottling.

MOHAWK
Täby, Stockholm

Beer commissioner (2010) based at Täby, north of Stockholm. Its hazy **Unfiltered Lager** ★★☆ has a Vienna-style foundation but US and NZ hopping; **Black Rocket Porter** ★★★ is strong and Baltic-style but brewed with American hops, giving it some spice; **Mohawk Extra IPA** ★★★ is American-influenced, made by heavily dry-hopping an already high-hopped double IPA.

NÄRKE KULTURBRYGGERI
Örebro

Närke Kulturbryggeri at Örebro, west of Stockholm, is small in size but big on flavour and adulation. **Örebro Bitter** ★★★ is in the delicate English style, with more Goldings and Cascade than most; **Närke Slättöl** ★★☆ is a simple, refreshing, lighter pale ale; **Black Golding Starkorter** ★★★☆ is a heavy-middleweight dark porter; while

Stormaktsporter ★★★★ is maybe the best Baltic porter anywhere, full-figured with a long, lingering finish and ageing beautifully.

NILS OSCAR
Nyköping, Södermanland

Small brewery (1996) that moved from Stockholm to Nyköping in 2006, with its own distillery and maltings. First brew **God Lager** ★★ is a Vienna lager with Spalt Select and Tettnanger imparting aroma and bitterness; **India Ale** ★★ is an IPA with Amarillo supplying impressive bitterness; **Rökporter** ★★☆ has a caramel, dried-fruit aroma and fairly slight smoky character despite 80% of its malt being beechwood-smoked; while the star is a great full-bodied **Barley Wine** with slight sweetness, which ages to perfection ★★★→★★★★.

NYNÄSHAMNS ÅNGBRYGGERI
Nynäshamn, Stockholm

This early brewery (1997), located at Nynäshamn, south of Stockholm, enjoys a loyal following. Its amber coloured **Bedarö Bitter** ★★☆ is full-flavoured with English malt but US C-hops; its blond **Landsort Lager** ★★☆ is the Swedish style, slightly sweet with medium bitterness from Perle, Tettnanger and Saaz; the rounded **Brännskär Brown Ale** ★★☆ is US-style, brewed with four malts, honey and cane sugar; and its **Mysingen Midvinterbrygd** ★★★ is a spicy winter ale whose flavour is enhanced by nutmeg, cumin, cloves, vanilla and fresh orange peel.

OCEANBRYGGERIET
Gothenburg, Västra Götland

Started in 2007 in the grounds of the old Lyckholms brewery. **Ocean India Pale Ale** ★★☆ is American, malty and rounded with a distinct hoppy finish; **Göteborgs Porter** ★★☆ is full-bodied in the London style, with blackcurrant on the nose, liquorice on the palate and chocolate throughout; and **Julöl** ★★☆ is a fussy winter ale with a grassy, blackcurrant aroma from a six-malt mash and five-hopped boil.

OPPIGÅRDS
Hedemora, Dalarna

This small farmhouse brewery (2004) northwest of Uppsala is brewing some of the best beers in Sweden. Its nicely balanced **Golden Ale** ★★☆ mixes Goldings, Pacific Gem and Cascade; **Amarillo** ★★★ is a single-hopped American pale ale dry-hopped for aroma but perfectly balanced to give a full-bodied ale with lingering bitterness; and its **Indian Tribute** ★★★ is an American IPA with citrus aroma, all the flavours

expected from the style, a malty body and a long, fresh, bitter finish.

ST ERIKS
Gothenburg, Västra Götland

Beer commissioner contracting beers from SIGTUNA. Its US-style session **Pale Ale** ★★☆ is complex for one so small, with a nice citrus finish; the **Porter** ★★☆ is robust, with hints of coffee, chocolate and dark rye bread; **#1 Enbär** ★★☆, created in collaboration with chef Mathias Dahlgren, is a refreshing lager brewed with juniper and spruce tips; and **BIPA** ★★★ is a good example of a Cascadian-laced black IPA.

SIGTUNA
Arlandastad, Stockholm

A 2006 operation brewing for itself and others. Its **East Coast IPA** ★★☆ is American with an intense hop aroma but balanced bitter finish; **Prince of Darkness Black IPA** ★★★ has a roasted malt character with hints of chocolate and coffee and big Cascade hopping; **Red Ale** ★★☆ is an up-hopped, almost mahogany ale with Centennial and Amarillo.

FINLAND

Commercial beer making in Finland has been rendered bizarre by well-meaning but ineffectual laws aimed at reducing alcohol misuse in the country. This has led, tortuously, to the government-controlled national chain of liquor stores discriminating against smaller Finnish brewers, and the long-established culture of trans-generational drinking in well-regulated pubs being priced out in favour of solitary consumption at home.

Meanwhile, massive volumes of cheap beer continue to be brought over on the ferry from Estonia and the country's great heritage beer style, *sahti*, struggles to survive. It takes determination to make one's way as an entrepreneurial small brewer here, but some exceptional people have done so.

FINLANDIA SAHTI
Sastamala, Pirkanmaa

Legendary maker of traditional *sahti*, west of Tampere, saved from extinction in 2011 but still tiny. Two versions are made, both flat as pancakes, sweet and full of banana, allspice, juniper and bread pudding, the light brown **8% Sahti ★★★** less so than the murkier, heavier and darker **10% Strong Sahti ★★★☆**.

LAITILAN
Laitila, Finland Proper

Beer and beverage maker, established in 1995, that has enjoyed some strong commercial success and is now making numerous supermarket labels. It splits its brands into the simpler Kukko and the more interesting Kievari beers, the latter showing willing but still too restrained. Best are its **Portteri ★★☆**, an upscale porter with some raisin and coffee; and its seasonal *weizen*, **Vehnänen ★★☆**.

LAMMIN SAHTI
Hämeenlinna, Tavastia Proper

Small specialist brewery, set up in 1985 to make traditional *sahti* at Lammi hamlet, southeast of Tampere. Now the largest producer but still tiny. **Original Lammin Sahti ★★★☆** is a murky brown symphony of spiced rotting fruit with super-smooth undertones, which are lost to some extent in the filtered version, **Juhlaolut ★★☆**, which appears in the national chain of liquor stores at Christmas.

MALMGÅRDIN
Malmgård, Uusimaa

Small brewery in a beautiful old country house at Malmgård, northeast of Helsinki, that is brewing beers under both the Malmgård and Huvila brands. Among the former, the standout is **Ceci n'est pas une Belge ★★★**, a strong, copper-brown beer with yeast-led spiciness and cleverly understated hopping; while the best Huvila beers are a Goldings-hopped **ESB ★★☆** that beats what most British brewers would dare make; mid-range **X-Porter ★★☆**, which veers toward creamy and nutty; and chestnut-coloured, juniper-laced **Arctic Circle Ale ★★★**, which has a nice bitter finish.

NOKIAN
Nokia, Pirkanmaa

Commercially successful small brewery with an odd mix of dull and interesting beers, usually sold under the name Keisari and often appearing in different formats. Black lager **Året Runt 4.5% ★★** is better at **5.7% ★★☆**; likewise, the slightly stronger bottled version of **EloWehnä** *weizen* **★★☆** is far better than its canned lighter version; and dark winter brew **Talvi ★★☆** is better when stronger.

PLEVNA
Tampere, Pirkanmaa

A pub brewery, sometimes called Koskipanimo, that can be found in

Finland's second city Tampere, and is regarded as the country's best craft beer producer. Its dozen or so regular Panimoravintola Pevna Tampere brands include a high-wheat *hefeweizen* called **Vehnäolut ★★★**; the better and stronger of two soft, sweetish Czech-style dark lagers, **Tumma ★★☆**; the sharply hopped US-style **Severin Extra IPA ★★★☆**; the sweet and soft German-style amber-coloured **Bock ★★★**; and the surprisingly approachable, tar-coloured, fruity, roasted **Siperia Imperial Stout ★★★★**.

DESTINATION TAMPERE

The country's second city has its next-best pub crawl, and peaks with two self-styled gastropubs, Tuulensuu (16 Puutarhakatu) for more breadth and imports, and Nordic (3 Otavalankatu) for a more regional focus in terms of both beer and food.

STADIN
Helsinki, Uusimaa

This tiny brewery, located in Helsinki, is obsessed with experimentation and has produced over 400 beers in 15 years, some of them more than once. The most frequently produced are semi-predictable **American Pale Ale ★★☆**; almost reliable **American Dark Ale ★★★**; steady but uninspiring **Weizen ★★**; and a Finnish interpretation of *doppelbock*, **Ultimator ★★☆**.

The capital's best-known beer pubs are One Pint (Sinikaislankuja) and St Uhro's (10 Museokatu); the best for the beers of smaller Finnish breweries is Villi Wäinö (4 Kalevankatu); and the easiest to find, by the main railway station, is Kaisla (4 Vilhonkatu). The smoothest, best run and stocked and most informative is Pikkulintu (11 Klaavuntie), hidden in a dreary shopping precinct out near Puotila metro station – best of luck!

STALLHAGEN
Godby, Åland Islands

Small brewery at Godby on the Åland Islands, midway between the Finnish mainland and Sweden. Some dull beers, more that are interesting and a few excellent, occasionally brewed differently for the Swedish market. Highlights include a gentle *dunkel* called **Delikat Dark Lager ★★**; much-praised American-style amber **US Red Ale ★★★**; a steady **Baltic Porter ★★☆**; and variable but never dull Easter seasonal **Påsköl ★★☆→★★★**.

SUOMENLINNAN
Helsinki, Uusimaa

Pub brewery on Suomenlinna, one of the islands that shelters Helsinki harbour from the Baltic. Recently invested in a bottling line so that its fame may spread. Reliable beers include copper-coloured

UK-style pale **Coyet Ale ★★**; equally English in spirit, **Spithead Bitter ★★**; Bohemian-style Saaz-accented **Höpken Pils ★★**; and an homage to London porters called **Helsinki Portteri ★★**.

TEERENPELI
Lahti, Päijänne Tavastia

Small brewery in Lahti with franchised brewpubs at Tampere, Turku and Kamppi (Helsinki), making mostly solid beers. **Hippaheikki TESB ★★** is a reasonable bash at a stronger British bitter; *hefeweizen* **Vauhtiveikko ★★☆** is one of Finland's best; and **Pakkaspaavo ★★** is a sort of Scotch ale produced in winter.

VAKKA-SUOMEN
Uusikaupunki, Finland Proper

Small 2008 brewery in the port of Uusikaupunki on the west coast, making an increasingly interesting range of beers under the Prykmestar brand. The ordinary **Pils ★★** is more German than most, with Perle hops; Finland's first regular *weizenbock*, **Wehnäbock ★★☆**, arrived to warm applause in 2012; evolving and increasingly impressive **Double IPA ★★★** is set to go far; and the stronger of two *rauchbiers*, juniper-smoked heavyweight **Savu Kataja ★★★**, removes any doubt that it means business.

ICELAND

Some visitors to this brilliantly lit land of fire and ice conclude that it is not much interested in beer, ignoring the fact that until its decriminalization in 1989, beer brewing had in effect been absent for over 70 years. The fact that Icelandic brewery numbers will soon reach double figures, several making beers fit for substantial export, and that the first speciality beer bar has taken root suggests healthy growth rather than lack of interest.

GÆÐINGUR ÖL
Sauðárkrókur, Skagafjarðarsýsla

Best and most authentic of the recent clutch of newcomers, brewing with British equipment on the northwest coast. Beers thus far have included quite a zippy **Pale Ale** ★★☆; a less impressive blond **Lager** ★★; and a generous light-to-medium **Stout** ★★★ that gives liquorice and chocolate. Seasonals have started too.

ÖLVISHOLT BRUGGHÚS
Selfoss, Árnessýsla

A 2007 start-up on a 1000-year-old farm at Selfoss in the southwest, rapidly making accomplished beers. **Fósturlandsins Freyja** ★★ is Iceland's first and lightly spiced wheat beer; blond lager **Skjálfti** ★★☆, named after the quake that nearly levelled the farm in 2000, has more bite than judder; **Móri** ★★☆ would be a Vienna lager were it not an ale; and **Lava** ★★★☆ is a heavy, smoked Imperial stout named after the active volcano seen from the brewery door.

VIKING ÖLGERÐ
Akureyri, Eyjafjarðarsýsla

Part of the Vífilfell beverage group. Brewing began to expand at its remote brewhouse in Akureyri, a fishing port at the end of a sheltered inlet on the north coast in 2008, with firm, dryish **Íslenskur Úrvals Stout** ★★☆; extending to include similar but sweeter **Black Death** ★★☆ in 2011. It now brews four Einstök Icelandic brand beers for a US-orientated beer commissioner, including **Toasted Porter** ★★☆ and a lightish **Doppelbock** ★★★.

> ### DESTINATION
> ### REYKJAVIK
>
> The Micro Bar (6 Austurstræti) is a simple place between the cathedral and the trawler harbour, that manages to stock 100 beers. Strong Icelandic presence, with Scandinavian in second place and better world beers next.

IBERIA

There is little brewing tradition on the Iberian peninsula beyond international-style lagers and a spat with Watneys Red and its ilk in the 1970s. Yet just as El Bulli taught Spanish chefs to cook outside the box, so the region's brewers are exploring the art of the possible, tantalizing with their potential, from plain to seismic.

SPAIN

First it was Italy that surprised the drinks world by daring to park a host of imaginative new beer makers on the wine world's front lawn. Then the beer bug swarmed across the vineyards of France. Next to fall will be Spain.

Thankfully Iberian beer has moved on since British expats ensured the survival of Watneys Red Barrel on the Costa del Sol long after it had died off elsewhere. Rather, it is young Spaniards touring the world and bringing back their experiences of far better beers and entrepreneurs, especially in Barcelona and around Catalonia, who are making the running.

The clear intention is that excited young brewers are about to do for Spanish brewing what El Bulli did for the country's culinary profile.

ALES AGULLONS
Sant Joan de Mediona, Barcelona

One of the pioneers, at Sant Joan de Mediona, west of Barcelona, creating ales with an English soul. Beautifully simple **Pura Ale ★★☆** might even appeal to some of those homesick Brits when it appears cask-conditioned; **Bruno ★★☆** is light brown from Crystal malts and aromatic from a mix of Cascade and Fuggles; while well-off-beat **Setembre ★★★** is produced each year to a different recipe but typically

is a blend of Pura Ale and one-year-old lambic from Belgium's DRIE FONTEINEN.

ART CERVESERS
Canovelles, Barcelona

One of the pioneers of the Barcelona craft beer boom, its brewery and tap outside Canovelles reflecting the architectural splendour of the city itself. Of its Art beers, **Orus ★★** is a solid *märzen*; **Flama ★★☆** is an IPA more British than American in character, best sampled near to home; while **Coure** ★★☆ is an unhopped winter ale, spiced with nutmeg, cinnamon and sweet gale.

DESTINATION BARCELONA

With the craft beer scene exploding, the rate of change in bars is rapid but Ale & Hop (10 Basses de Sant Pere) near the Olympic stadium is currently leading the field, with cosy La Cerveteca (25 Guinàs) and tiny Bar SF (48 Carrer de les Carretes), near the port, the other must-dos. For take-home find Rosses i Torrades (192 Consell de Cent), a beer cellar near Hostafrancs metro.

DOMUS
Toledo

Highly professional and growing brewery at Toledo, which has gained a good reputation in the highly competitive Barcelona scene. Its **Aurea** ★★☆ is a highly aromatic and refreshing IPA that prefers balance over loud bitterness, in contrast to its pale ale **Europa** ★★, brewed with six kinds of European hop, and the winter beer, disconcertingly called **Summa** ★★☆, which is a Scotch ale.

DOUGALL'S
Liérganes, Cantabria

The creature of British beer enthusiasts who moved to Liérganes in Cantabria, not far from Santander. Its **942** ★★★ is a light-bodied pale ale with notes of earth, fruit and citrus that make it interesting;

Leyenda ★★☆ is an ESB with fruit, apple, citrus and an intriguing spice note; and **Tres Mares** ★★ is a roasty brown ale with a surprising hoppy finish.

GUINEU
Valls de Torroella, Barcelona

Not a dedicated brewing company but rather the beer brand of a brewery supplies company at Valls de Torella, north of Barcelona. **Riner** ★★☆ is a well-above-average low-alcohol pale ale with a rabid hop bite giving it spirit; **Antius** ★★ is an ordinary bitter that could cope in an English pub despite American hops; and **Montserrat** ★★★ is an inspired, multi-layered stout with a surprise with almost every sip.

MONTSENY
Sant Miquel de Balenyà, Barcelona

The biggest and most ambitious of the Spanish newbies, north of Barcelona in northern Catalonia, aiming for a wider audience. **Lupulus** ★★ is a fresh, balanced and refreshing mainstream IPA; whereas **Malta** ★☆ is pedestrian in its

raw form but interesting after a year in wine barrels as **Malta Cuveé** ★★☆, the love child of pale ale and oak-aged Chardonnay. Winter ale **HivernAle** changes recipe slightly every year but is always spice-loaded with a pinch of muscovado sugar ★★→★★☆.

ZZ+ ★★☆ is a refreshing, complex amber beer of contrasts, with syrup and caramel on one side, pine and herbs on the other and rock 'n' roll at its heart.

NAPARBIER
Noáin, Navarre

A cooperative at Noáin near Pamplona that has quickly earned respect beyond Spain and seems to improve with every batch. **Janis Porter** ★★ is roasted, with coffee and citrus bringing some lightness;

ZARAGOZANA, LA
Zaragoza

Spanish industrial brewers do not enjoy the best reputation but Ambar beers from La Zaragozana are often excluded from the generalization. The **1900** ★★ is a summery English pale ale with a firm body; **Negra** ★★ is a sweet *dunkel*; and **Export** ★★ is more of a pale *bock* than a standard stronger lager.

PORTUGAL

While beer is popular in Portugal the scene is dominated by a small number of industrial brewers, mostly foreign-owned, with Unicer, maker of the unadventurous Super Bock brands the only significant independent. Visitors confused by the repeated presence of *cervejarias* – literally "breweries" – need know that these places, though often wonderfully atmospheric and almost always fine locales in which to spend an evening, are typically beer halls or restaurants without brewing facilities, in the fashion of many French brasseries.

We know of two tiny new craft brewing set-ups around Oporto. Os Três Cervejeiros is making its Sovina beers in the city, and the Fermentum brewery makes its Minho beers at Braga, just to the north. Both look promising. A few beer commissioners are dipping a toe in the water too, and there is a brewpub called Praxis at Coimbra, between Lisbon and Oporto.

THE BALTIC STATES

The post-Soviet Baltic pecking order sees Latvia and Lithuania normally competing for second place behind Estonia. In brewing the rule is reversed, as a countryside tradition of folk brewing from the Lithuanian highlands vies with rising Latvian interest, leaving Estonia in the starting blocks.

ESTONIA

Well over 95% of Estonian beer is brewed by three foreign-owned companies. The largest, Saku, is part of Carlsberg; the historically important A Le Coq is now owned by Olvi of Finland; and the smallest, Viru, by Harboe of Denmark. Like the other Baltic States recent years have seen efforts to bring new beers to the market, with most wildly off the mark, or else poorly promoted. Hence the inclusion of only two small producers here.

SILLIMÄE ÕLLETEHAS
Sillamäe, Ida-Virumaa

The fourth-largest Estonian brewer, a minnow founded in 1993 at the Baltic port of Sillamäe, near the Russian border. Makes four München brand beers that include variable blond lager **Hele** ★★; dark brown **Tume** ★★; and stronger, copper-coloured Vienna lager, **Vaskne** ★★, with syrupy backtastes.

TAAKO
Pihtla, Saaremaa

This may be the only remaining commercial producer of what some term Estonian blond *sahti*. Its **Pihtla Õlu** ★★☆ is a hazy, sharpish, herbal and clove-laden ale with a taste profile not far off the Finnish speciality. Like-minded producers on the island congregate occasionally to show their beers, though whether or not these are licensed brewers we do not know.

DESTINATION
TALLINN

Two bars in the capital's old town are trying hard to raise awareness of quality beers, relying more on imports than local producers. Drink Baar (8 Vaike Karja) is a nice UK-style pub run by an expat, attracting increasingly unusual brews; Hell Hunt (39 Pikk) is a groovy youthful hang-out that tolerates older beer travellers and has a slightly wider range of Estonian brews.

LATVIA

Watching the Latvian beer scene is like being in a school biology class waiting for a seed to germinate. Its three largest breweries, Aldaris, Cēsu and Līvu-Lāčplēša, are all part of large Scandinavian groups, the better-organized independents remain conservative and the growing band of enthusiastic and competent home brewers has yet to dare to plunge. Someone will sprout soon.

For now the words to master are *gaišais* ("pale beer"), *tumšais* ("dark beer") and *nefiltrētais* ("unfiltered").

ABULA
Brenguļi, Vidzeme

This former farm brewery was established on the Abula River near Valmiera in the north of Latvia in 1969. It hired a German brewer once it grew, following independence and privatization. Its two Brenguļu beers are as typical of Latvian beer as it gets, **Gaišais ★★** being a hazy, sweetish stronger pale lager; and **Tumšais ★★☆** being a murky-brown country *dunkel* with sweet caramel, raisins and subtle roasting.

ALDARIS (CARLSBERG)
Riga

Latvia's largest brewery, located in Riga (*see* box, right), makes roughly half the nation's beer. Its generic, safe pale lager **Luksus ★☆** has won prizes, inexplicably; while its unusually impressive **Porteris ★★☆**, a medium-to-full-bodied, dark ruby-brown Baltic porter with a bitter chocolate aroma and roasted malt, liquorice and molasses, deserves prizes.

> DESTINATION
> **RIGA**
>
> ALEhouse (12 Lāčplēša) is a newish craft beer bar and shop in the embassy district serving a brilliant range of 200 beers to a local audience keen to learn. Food all day, every day.

MADONAS ALUS
Bodnieki, Vidzeme

Tiny 2009 brewery associated with an old country house near Madona, 100km (62 miles) east of Riga, producing a well-offbeat, honeyed, cloudy pale draught beer, **Madonas Bodnieku Gaišais** ★★, unfiltered, musty and medicinal. There is a strong beer too.

PIEBALGAS ALUS
Jaunpiebalga, Vidzeme

Operating since 1989 in the picturesque Jaunpiebalga region, Piebalgas Alus has thus far produced a range of safe, dull but clean, unpasteurized lagers, of which the best are pale **Jubilejas** ★☆ and copper-brown **Tumšais Lux** ★★, a sort of simple lightish *dunkel*. Fingered as a possible "first mover" to create more interesting beers.

TĒRVETES (AGROFIRMA)
Kroņauce, Zemgale

Collective farm brewery (1971) with its own maltings, at Kroņauce, near Tērvete, southwest of Riga. Generally regarded as the best of the established smaller brewers, making five different pale Tērvetes lagers. Top beer is **Oriģinālais** ★★☆, a full-bodied, deep golden, wholesome-tasting lager with a bitter finish; with the *zwickelbier*, **Nefiltrētais** ★★, also worthy.

UŽAVA
Užava, Kurzeme

Small brewery (1994) at Užava, south of Latvia's largest port, Ventspils. Essentially brews two Užavas brand beers that are better in their unfiltered form, a lighter, balanced and sweetish **Gaišais** ★★→★★☆; and slightly stronger **Tumšais** ★★→★★☆, a chewy, toffee-laced comfort beer with mild roasty flavours and caramel.

VALMIERMUIŽA
Valmiera, Vidzeme

Small brewery (2009) in the same town as ABULA, and with the same range of types as UŽAVA, though its presentation is slicker and the beers less immediate, being drier from greater attenuation. The unfiltered versions are only available on draught and notably better, whether **Gaišais** ★☆→★★ or **Tumšais** ★☆→★★.

LITHUANIA

Lithuania has a special place in the world of beer.

Most of the country enjoys a culture typical of many Eastern European nations 20 years on from the fall of the Berlin Wall – a few larger breweries owned by foreign companies, some smaller ones seeking to grow and a handful of brewpubs from which entrepreneurial craft brewers will likely emerge at some point, from the 70 that existed in Spring 2013.

However, in the northeastern Aukštaitija region, literally the Highlands, there remain two dozen breweries making *kaimiškas alus*, or "country beers", unique relics of brewing practices long-gone elsewhere.

These are run mainly by local people looking to make a living by supplying their wares to a few villages. Until recently, few were ever seen outside the region, but then a couple of beer bars in the capital, Vilnius, began to obtain supplies, and since then interest in the countryside beer culture has started to grow.

Locally honed brewing traditions include that, instead of being added to sweet wort in a separate boil, hops are boiled separately and added directly to the mash in the form of a tea. Fermentation then takes place in open vessels, sometimes kept underground, using yeast strains that have mutated without being refreshed over the lifetimes of several generations of brewer.

The extent to which the Soviet authorities knew about these local brewing activities is a moot point, though they had been going on for decades before the end of Russian rule in 1990. Ironically perhaps, since independence and European Union membership, the number of these ethnic brewhouses, some quite primitive, has dwindled as licensing regulators insist that equipment be modernized.

These are not entrepreneurial enterprises hungry for publicity and few can be visited on a whim. Rather they are run by people of modest means, survivors of a craft tradition, baffled by and wary of the renaissance of interest that is enabling them to sell their idiosyncratic products into an entirely alien market in the capital, their plastic bottles speaking of ill-preparedness.

Kaimiškas alus are not robust and should be discovered as fresh and close to source as possible. They are unlikely ever to be suitable for export, varying hugely in flavour and character, and with few reference points to compare their often raw character to more conventional types of beer. Star-rating them is thus made difficult, but we have tried.

BUTAUTŲ DVARO BRAVORAS
Biržai, Panevėžys

This establishment is located in an old manor at Biržai, near the Latvian border, that was once used by Soviet officials to "relax". Their **Šviesus** ★★☆ is a quenching, mineral vehicle with toasted cereals and herbal hops; while **Tamsus** ★★☆ has earthy nuances and strays from heavy caramel to evolve bready and spicy flavours.

CIŽO ALUS
Dusetos, Utena

This tiny brewery, located in a house outside Dusetos village, Utena, oozes with local colour. It is quite possibly the last remaining brewer of authentic Lithuanian *keptinis*, a beer in which malted barley is baked into a bread before being steeped in water and mashed with hops. The resulting unnamed beer ★★☆ is a near-flat, earthy, woody, slightly smoky, rough-and-ready time-travel brew.

DAVRA
Pakruojis, Šiauliai

Small, purpose-built brewery at Pakruojis, in the heart of Lithuania's brewing region. Its stalwart offering, **Varniuku** ★★★ is a rich, raisiny dark brew, or *tamsus*; whereas its **Daujotų** ★★★ is a supremely toasty blond affair; and **Linksmieji Vyrukai** ★★☆ is an equally toasty but slicker amber-hued companion. A remarkably luxurious tasting room is available for use if you call ahead.

JOVARU ALUS
Jovarai, Utena

An unmarked house in the hamlet of Jovarai that is the domain of the queen of Lithuanian traditional brewing, whose main beer bears her name. **Aldona Udriene** ★★★ is a toasty, fruity and quenching brew that is the house beer at Šnekutis (*see* box, below). Mashed with its hops and fermented at nearly 30°C (86°F), it ends up tasting like an ancient rustic ESB. The honey-infused bottled version, **Su Medumi** ★★☆ is sweeter and smoother.

> ### DESTINATION
> ### VILNIUS
>
> The capital's best outlet for draught countryside beers is Šnekutis (7a Polocko Gatvé), which we expect to move shortly; while for bottled ones the highly civilized, stone-walled Bambalyne (7 Stiklių Gatvé) cellar bar and shop is better. Alaus Namai (8 Alberto Goštauto Gatvé) is a grungier basement bar near the river, with a mix of home-grown and international beers.

KUPIŠKIO ALUS
Kupiškis, Panevėžys

Inside a former food bunker in the town of Kupiškis, with a tiny shop on site. **Magaryčių Alus** ★★☆ is brewed with roasted hazelnuts to make a balanced marvel of local *je-ne-sais-quoi*; **Keptinis** ★★☆ is a polished modern take on a forgotten smoky style; **Patulo Alus**

★★☆ aligns citrus fruitiness with lightly toasted malts; while **Salaus Alus** ★★ is an elegant *šviesus* with honey and citrus accents.

KURKLIŲ BRAVORAS
Kurkliai, Utena

Tiny brewery in Kurkliai, part of the Aukštaitijos brewing group that tries to protect and grow the area's unique beer culture. Its only beer is the extraordinary **I O Boiko** ★★★, which adjoins rye to spicy hops, haystack and banana esters creating huge character. Some batches are brewed and bottled at BUTAUTŲ.

MORKŪNO ALUS
Pasvalys, Panevėžys

A modest, one-man operation in an unmarked house in the country town of Pasvalys. **Morkūno** ★★☆ has typical *kaimiškas alus* earthiness with herbal elements in a faintly carbonated, highly drinkable liquid.

PINIAVOS ALUTIS
Piniava, Panevėžys

Small brewery in an apartment building outside Panevėžys, unofficial capital of the Highlands. **Seklyčios** ★★★ is a thirst-quencher in which fresh toasted malts and elegant honeyed sweetness converge; **Laukinių Aviečių** ★★☆ is the same beer filtered through raspberry bush branches; while using a bed of red clover to filter **Raudonųjų Dobilų** ★★ lends it floral character.

SU PUTA
Paliūniškis, Panevėžys

In a small warehouse at Paliūniškis, with a bottle-filling shop for walk-in patrons. **Senovinis-Senolių** ★★☆ is a powerful yeasty wheat beer with a potent hop character; **Sidabrinė Puta Šviesus** ★★ is toasted and floral; **Paliūniškis Medutis** ★★ has mild honey flavours balanced out by leafy hops; and **Stiprus Tamsus** ★★☆ is a winter showcase of bready caramel and warming alcohol.

TARUŠKŲ ALAUS BRAVORAS
Irakiškio, Panevėžys

This excellent small brewery near Panevėžys is also part of the Aukštaitijos group. **Šviesus** ★★★ delights with modest barnyard character and spicy hop bitterness; **Kanapinis Tamsus** ★★ is a textbook brown ale; and **Su Kanapemis** ★★ is a quaffer, brewed with hemp seeds.

ITALY

Italy is a wine land, no doubt, but it is also very much a gastronomically inclined nation and it is this fact that has allowed the Italian craft brewing industry to develop, grow and indeed prosper in a relatively short period of time.

From almost the moment craft beer appeared on the Italian scene, its creators have made the dining table their focus, creating beers that harmonize well with the local cuisine, packaging in ornate, restaurant-friendly bottles and marketing their wares at the kind of prices that almost demand respect. It has been a successful strategy, establishing in short order Italian craft beer as a comparable alternative to wine, rather than a cheaper substitute better suited to quenching thirst than complementing dinner.

It helps, of course, that Italian craft breweries have shown steady improvement since they came on the scene in force around the year 2000. The past several years in particular have seen remarkable progress in both the quality and quantity of Italian craft beers, to the point that some breweries might now be said to rival the best in northern Europe in terms of brewing creativity and flavour complexity.

While brewing remains still most concentrated in the north, Rome is emerging as the centre of Italian craft beer, with the populace growing increasingly enamoured of ales and lagers of quality and character.

---

32 VIA DEI BIRRAI
Pederobba, Treviso

Brilliant brewery in the Veneto region named for the Belgium telephone country code and known for its clever marketing ideas. Flagship **Oppale** ★★★ is a hoppy ale with a bitter finish reminiscent of chives; cloudy, spiced **Curmi** ★★☆ is brewed with spelt and barley malt; **Audace** ★★ is a fruity, spicy strong golden ale; local chestnut honey flavours the full-bodied **Nectar** ★★.

ALMOND '22 BEER
Spoltore, Pescara

Brewery located in a disused almond-processing plant – hence the name – near Pescara in coastal Abruzzo. Organic spelt and honey lend a sweet nuttiness to

Farrotta ★★; smoky, plummy, cinnamony **Torbata** ★★★ is brewed with peated malt; and **Pink IPA** ★★★ is named after the pink peppercorns that give the beer an appealingly zippy spiciness.

AMIATA
Arcidosso, Grosseto

Small sibling-operated Tuscan brewery that has had its problems in the past, but appears more reliable now. Tropical-fruit and pine flavours dominate **Contessa** ★★, billed an "Italian pale ale"; while saffron-spiced **Crocus** ★★ combines fruitiness with a spicy floral character. Best is the chestnut beer, **Vecchia Bastarda** ★★★, aged in wine barrels for a sweet, vanilla-accented nutty fruitiness.

BALADIN, LE
Piozzo, Cuneo

Italy's most famous craft brewery, founded in mid-1990s by creative

innovator Teo Musso in Piedmont. **Isaac** ★★☆ is a pioneering Belgian-style wheat beer, rich in exotic fruit flavours; **Wayan** ★★☆ is a zesty, fruity *saison*; ancient Egypt-inspired **Nora** ★★★ is spiced with ginger and myrrh; former flagship brand, the warming, nutty **Super** ★★★, was designed to pair with food; targeted oxidization give sherry flavours to the still, intense and already classic **Xyauyù** ★★★★.

BARLEY
Maracalagonis, Cagliari

Brewery in the south of Sardinia that began the Italian trend of using wine must in brewing. **Friska** ★★☆ is a characterful, quenching wheat ale; local orange-blossom honey makes **Zagara** ★★☆ a pleasant, refreshing session beer; the amber, malty **Sella del Diavolo** ★★☆ is an Italian take on the French *bière de garde*; **Toccadibò** ★★★ is a warming golden ale with dryly bitter and amaretto-ish finish; strong and vinous **BB10** ★★★☆ is an astonishing barley wine made with local Cannonau grapes.

BEBA
Villar Perosa, Turin

Pioneering brewery in Piedmont near the French border, one of the first eight craft breweries in Italy. Pioneering roots show in beers like **Uno** ★★, a pale lager seemingly aimed at the Moretti drinker who wants a change for the better, and **Toro** ★★, a *doppio malto* – roughly equivalent to a *doppelbock* – with toffee-ish maltiness and a lightly warming finish.

BI-DU
Olgiate Comasco, Como

Located near Lake Como, this brewery is best known for its bravely hoppy beers. **Rodersch ★★☆** is a flowery, herbal, hoppy take on a *kölsch*; **ArtigianAle ★★★** is well balanced and strong; generously hoppy **Confine ★★☆** is a coffee-ish and smoky porter; **H10op5 ★★☆** is highly hopped with 10 varieties added in five stages; quenching, dry, flowery **Saaz of Anarchy ★★** is a tribute to Saaz hops and anarchist ideology.

BIRRA DEL BORGO
Borgorose, Rieti

Successful brewery located northeast of Rome, specializing in interesting seasonals and experimental brews. Citrus-fruity and piney flagship **Re Ale ★★★** pioneered the US-style pale ale in Italy; refreshingly sweet and mellow **Duchessa ★★☆** uses local spelt; strong and hoppy pilsner **My Antonia ★★★** is a collaboration with DOGFISH HEAD BREWING in the US; smoky, roasted **KeTo RePorter ★★☆** is well balanced despite being infused with tobacco leaves from Kentucky.

> ### DESTINATION
> ### ROME
>
> Bir&Fud (23 Via Benedetta) is aptly named, with a gastronomic delight of a menu, including excellent pizzas, complemented by 18 taps of usually all-Italian craft beers and a select domestic and international bottled-beer list.

BIRRANOVA
Triggianello, Bari

Puglia brewery with an adjoining taproom. **Abboccata ★★** is a strong amber ale, sweet and malty with medium hop bitterness; **Arsa ★★** is a rare example of smoked porter mixing ancient local wheat and smoked barley malt; cooked must of Primitivo grapes and dried figs are the main seasoning of the warming barley wine, **Primatia ★★☆**.

BIRRA OLMO
Arsego di San Giorgio delle Pertiche, Padua

Young craft brewery in Padua area, aspiring to become the Italian version of Scottish iconoclasts, BREWDOG. Hops from US, New Zealand and Japan make **Mundaka ★★**, a light, refreshing summer ale; **White Rabbit ★★** is a spiced, peppery wheat ale brewed with unmalted spelt; golden ale **Butterfly ★☆** reveals citrus and exotic fruit flavours; **Guerrilla IPA ★★** is an aggressively hoppy pale ale.

BIRRA PASTURANA
Pasturana, Alessandria

Lower Piedmont craft brewery, museum and brewing school. **Filo d'Arianna ★★** is a fresh, fruity, sessionable pale ale; **Filo di Fumo ★★** is an elegant, gently smoked ale; **Fil Rouge ★★☆** is a slightly sour ale brewed with lees from Brachetto wine; the vinous flavours and warming mouthfeel of **Filo Forte Oro ★★☆** come from the addition of Muscat grape must.

BREWFIST
Codogno, Lodi

Young brewery taking southern Italy by storm from its base in Lombardy. **24K Golden Ale** ★★☆ shows citrus and peach notes when bottled but is more best bitter-like on cask; a perfumey start to **Spaceman India Pale Ale** ★★ is obliterated by mid-palate hoppiness; **Burocracy India Pale Ale** ★★☆ fares better with caramel maltiness and herbal, citrus hops; **Fear Milk Chocolate Stout** ★★☆ delivers on its name with a creamy, roasty character.

BRÙTON
San Cassiano di Moriano, Lucca

Export-minded brewery and restaurant offshoot of a successful Tuscan winery, located near Pisa. **Flagship Brùton** ★★ is light and fragrantly spicy; **Stoner** ★★☆ is loaded with tropical-fruit notes balanced by hop and rye spiciness; pale ale **Lilith** ★★ has a restrained hoppiness and lots of yeasty character; the spelt, wheat and barley brew **Bianca** ★★☆ is floral and quenching.

CARROBIOLO, BIRRA DEL CONVENTO
Monza, Milan

Milan-area brewery that unusually names all its beers after their original gravity (OG). **O G 1045** ★★★ is a *kölsch*-style ale with pineapple and gooseberry notes from New Zealand hops; **O G 1043** ★★ is a fragrant and floral wheat beer that finishes citrus and off-dry; **O G 1056** ★★ is a dryly spicy pils; and ultra-strong **O G 1111** ★★★ is a barely carbonated, peaty warmer loaded with flavours of raisin and date.

CIVALE
Spinetta Marengo, Alessandria

Rapidly improving craft brewery near Alessandria. Quaffable **Alica** ★☆ is a blond ale with bready and malty flavours; flagship **Lùmina** ★★★ is an irresistible pale ale with a clean, dry finish; amber ale **Ulula** ★★ is the brewery's most bitter beer, with aggressive citrus and exotic-fruit flavours.

CROCE DI MALTO
Trecate, Novara

Brewery touting itself as "the evolution of tradition," situated in Trecate, between Milan and Turin. Orange-hued **Temporis** ★★ is a spiced ale with lovely bitter and peppery notes; **Magnus** ★★ is a dark and strong ale, spicy and roasty with dried-fruit flavours; flagship **Triplexxx** ★★★ is a sweet and fruity, internationally awarded strong golden ale.

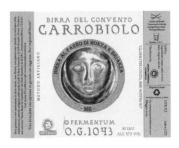

DADA
Correggio, Reggio Emilia

Young, enterprising craft brewery in
Emilia-Romagna, named after the avant-
garde art movement. **Tzara** ★★ is a fresh
wheat ale with exotic-fruit flavours; **Lop
Lop**★★ is a peppery, gently hoppy IPA;
Gattomao ★★☆ is a fruity, hoppy amber
ale take on the French *bière de garde*;
Rrose Sélavy ★★★, named for one
of artist Marcel Duchamp's pseudonyms,
is a peppery, zesty and yeasty *saison*.

DEL DUCATO
Roncole Verdi di Busseto, Parma

From the Parma village where Verdi
was born comes this much-awarded
brewery. **Verdi Imperial Stout** ★★★
is a lovely mix of peppery spice and
espresso, better still in barrel-aged
Black Jack ★★★ version; **Chimera**
★★★☆ is warming, faintly cinnamony
and spicy, evoking thoughts of a fine
Barolo wine; flagship **VIÆMILIA** ★★★
is a crisp and ideally balanced lager;
and seasonal **Winterlude** ★★★ is
tropical-fruity and herbal, with a more
bitter and warming finish.

DOPPIO MALTO BREWING
Erba, Como

Lombardy brewery attached to an
American-style restaurant. **Bitterland**
★★☆ is a dry, crisp golden ale made
with five different American hops;
Mahogany Ipa ★★ is as dark, citrus
and hoppy as its name suggests;
liquorice and coffee notes are obvious
in the chocolate stout, **Old Jack** ★★.

EXTRAOMNES
Marnate, Varese

Belgian-inspired Lombardy brewery
with a taste for experimental brewing.
Blond ★★☆ is a light golden ale with
impressive complexity; special offering
Zest ★★ is similar, but more peppery and
lemony thanks to the use of Citra hops;
Tripel ★★★ is sweetish with preserved
lemon notes and a warming finish;
Donker ★★☆ has a sweet espresso
flavour accented by chocolate-raisin notes.

FOGLIE D'ERBA
Forni di Sopra, Udine

Much-awarded brewpub in the
Dolomites, focused on brewing with
local and Fairtrade spices. **Babél** ★★☆

is a pale ale with a bitter, long finish; **Hopfelia** ★★★ is a strong IPA spiced with local mugo pine to a fresh and resiny bitterness; black IPA **Ulysses** ★★☆ is a successful mix of roasted wheat and barley malts and with ample hoppiness; **Song from the Wood** ★★☆ is a strong, coffee-ish Imperial stout.

FORST
Lagundo, Alto Adige

Family-owned brewery, over a century and a half old, near the Austrian border. Beers are crafted steadfastly in the Germanic tradition, as in the slightly grainy, export lager-ish **Kronen Speciale** ★☆ and the more mainstream **1857** ★☆. Best is *doppelbock* **Sixtus** ★★☆, light for the style but with a pleasing mix of caramelly, toasty maltiness.

FORTE, DEL
Pietrasanta, Lucca

Young and dynamic craft brewery in touristy Versilia coast area. Thirst-quenching, zesty, dry **Gassa d'Amante** ★★☆ is the house session beer; **2 Cilindri** ★★★ is a coffee-ish and roasty porter with a slightly smoky finish; ripe fruit notes are detectable in the golden strong ale **La Mancina** ★★★, which becomes **La Mancina XL** ★★☆ in its stronger and spiced version.

GRADO PLATO
Chieri, Turin

Pub and brewery located near Turin in Piedmont, with brands instantly recognizable thanks to its elegant swing-top bottle. **Strada S. Felice** ★★★ is a nutty, toffee and orange brandy-ish chestnut ale; unusual **Weizentea** ★★☆ combines wheat with green tea and American hops, and successfully so; **Sveva** ★★☆ is a quaffable homage to Bavarian *helles*.

ITALIANO
Lurago Marinone, Como

Technically focused brewery midway between Milan and the Swiss border. **Tipopils** ★★★ drinks like an homage to the best of Czech brewing, with marvellous balance and structure; **Extra Hop** ★★☆ is similarly German pils inspired; **Bi-Weizen** ★★ is a malty, slightly heavy *hefeweizen*, **Bibock** ★★☆ offers toffee-ish malt with a drying finish; **Vùdù** ★★★ is a delicious clove and cocoa take on a slightly potent *dunkelweisse*.

DESTINATION
NEMBRO

Birroteca The Dome (15 Via Caso Sparse Europa) is a large pub deserving of more success than yet realized, with an extensive rotating selection of taps and bottles emphasizing emerging craft breweries, especially local ones.

KAMUN
Predosa, Alessandria

Young, lower Piedmont craft brewery, located in Predosa, making promising ales. **Prima Lux** ★★★ is a crisp, dry-hopped session beer; much-awarded oatmeal stout **Nocturna** ★★★ is soft, velvety and silky on the palate; **Occasum** ★★ is a surprisingly balanced amber ale generously spiced with hibiscus flowers, orange peel, ginger and cinnamon.

KARMA
Alvignano, Caserta

Located near Naples, this brewery emphasizes local ingredients and spices. **Cubulteria** ★★ is a full-bodied, malty and strong wheat ale; reddish **Carminia** ★★ is a sessionable English-style IPA with a herbal and bitter finish; **Lemon Ale** ★★☆ is a refreshing, zesty wheat and rye ale with coriander and local lemon peel; **Centesimale** ★★☆ is a warming and vinous strong ale made with grape must and local apple jam.

L'ORSO VERDE
Busto Arsizio, Varese

A Lombardy brewery that produces uncompromising ales. Golden ale **Wabi** ★★★ is irresistibly flowery, fruity and extremely dry; **Back Door Bitter** ★★☆ is rich in caramel, citrus-fruit flavours with a long and dryly bitter finish; robust porter **Nubia** ★★☆ features roasty, liquorice and coffee flavours; **Rebelde** ★★ is a strong amber ale made sweet with Belgian malts and bitter with American hops.

LAMBRATE
Lambrate, Milan

Pioneering Milan brewpub founded in 1996 and still highly popular. **Domm** ★★☆ is a hoppy, not-too-fruity *hefeweizen*; **Montestella** ★★☆ is a hoppy lager with a salty flavour; black and roasty **Ghisa** ★★★ taught Italians to appreciate smoked ales; **Ligèra** ★★☆ is an American-style pale ale with refreshing tangerine and bitter-orange flavours; golden and British-inspired **Ortiga** ★★☆ boasts a long and dryly bitter finish.

LARIANO
Dolzago, Lecco

Creative and versatile brewery in Lombardy. English-style bitter, **Miloud** ★★, is well balanced between malt and hops; **Aura** ★☆ is a sweet blond ale spiced with coriander and orange peel; strong golden ale **Tripè** ★★ is malty, fruity and warming; the addition of salt and coriander make **Salada** ★★ a citric wheat ale take on a Leipziger *gose*.

LOVERBEER
Marentino, Turin

Punning on his own name, homebrewer Valter Loverier went pro with this exceptional enterprise. The best brands are barrel-aged, like the tart, sour cherry-ish, appetizing **Dama Brun-a ★★★**; spontaneously fermented **BeerBera ★★★**, fermented with Barbera grapes; and plummy, sweet-and-sour **BeerBrugna ★★★**. Fresher, grapey and cinnamon-ish **D'uuvaBeer ★★** is lovely, as well.

> DESTINATION
> **TURIN (AND OTHER LOCATIONS, INCLUDING TOKYO AND NEW YORK CITY)**
>
> Eataly (230/14 Via Nizza) is a chain of large grocery stores-cum-dining destinations which, despite their overtly corporate appearance, feature an impressive selection of craft beers including some exclusive to the chain and others brewed on site.

MAIELLA
Casoli, Chieti

Central Italian brewery using local ingredients also prized by area's renowned pasta makers. Durum wheat and lavender flowers are used in refreshing, herbal, bitter **Noviluna ★★☆**; **Cluviae ★★** is a fruity, flowery, green-apple-flavoured golden ale; acacia honey makes amber ale **Matthias ★★★** sweet, soft and fruity; **Bucefalo ★★☆** is an elegant foreign extra stout with roasty, balsamic flavours.

MALTOVIVO
Capriglia Irpina, Avellino

Experienced craft brewery in the Campania region. Fresh, flowery, dry **Tschö! ★★** is an interpretation of the *kölsch* style; coppery **Noscia ★★☆** is a well-balanced US-style IPA with resinous herbal notes; robust **Black Lizard ★★** is a coffee-ish, roasty and slightly smoked porter; and vinous, warming **Memoriae ★★★** is a dark strong ale successfully aged in oak barrels that previously held local Taurasi wine.

MALTUS FABER
Genoa

Environmentally aware Genoa brewery focused on interpretations of Belgian styles. **Bianca ★★** is a refreshing, unspiced Belgian-style wheat beer; **Blonde ★★☆** is herbal and hoppy; well-balanced **Ambrata ★★☆** has biscuity and nutty flavours; **Triple ★★☆** is a dangerous, quaffable, strong and fruity ale; Belgian-inspired **Extra Brune ★★★** is soft, dark and warming.

MANEBA
Striano, Naples

Promising operation near Naples brewing interpretations of classic styles. Blond ale **L'Oro Di Napoli ★★** is malty and zesty with a dry finish; **Clelia ★☆** is a peppery and lemony take on a Belgian-style wheat beer; **Vesuvia ★★** is a fruity, warming amber ale spiced with coriander; fruity flavours and a bitter finish place **Masaniello ★★☆** somewhere between an IPA and a dark strong ale.

MANERBA BREWERY
Manerba del Garda, Brescia

The Manerba is Garda's lakefront brewery and restaurant. **La Bionda** ★★ is a classic *helles*, malty with gentle hop flavours; a hoppier, unfiltered lager simply called **Pils** ★★★ is dry and crisp; **Route 66** ★★ is a clean, dry-hopped US-style pale ale with grapefruit flavours; **Rebuffone** ★☆ is a roasty, fruity brown ale close to a Belgian dubbel.

MENARESTA
Carate Brianza, Monza and Brianza

Gastronomically inclined brewery located near Milan. Bread yeast-fermented **Birra Madre** ★★☆ has a gently tangy, pear-ish fruitiness; quaffable **Bevara** ★★ is dry with peppery peach-pie notes; elderflower-flavoured **Flora Sambuco** ★★☆ recalls elderflower cordial with a peppery finish; **22 La Verguenza** ★★☆ is a strong IPA with piney, almost garlicky hoppiness, which drinks better in its lighter **La Verguenza Summer IPA** ★★★ edition.

DESTINATION
NICORVO

Sherwood Music Pub (7 Via Giarone) is a temple for beer enthusiasts near Milan, featuring tasty pizzas, Italian craft beers and many rare selections from Belgium and Germany collected by the passionate owner-traveller.

MISTER DRINK
Cervia, Ravenna

The town of Cervia in Ravenna is known for its salt, which makes an appearance in everything from chocolate and beauty products to a beer called **Salinae** ★★★. Light in alcohol content and colour, it has a minerally aroma, a gentle body with lemony, salty notes and a sustained minerality that gives the impression of a health drink as much as a beer.

MONTEGIOCO
Montegioco, Alessandria

Named for the Alessandrian town in which it is based, this impressive brewery makes excellent use of wine barrels, as per its star, **La Mummia** ★★★★, a spicy-tart, vanilla-accented golden ale aged in Barbera barrels. It also brews the mildly fruity **Runa** ★★★, a golden ale used as a base beer for other brands; **Tentatripel** ★★★, a spicy, candied-pear nightcap; and **Tibir** ★★☆, a peachy, passion-fruity ale.

OLMAIA, L'
Sant'Albino di Montepulciano, Siena

Tuscan wine country brewery. Hoppy, quaffable **La 5** ★★☆ is a basic blond ale; local grains are the secret of the dry and thirst-quenching **PVK** ★★★; **La 9** ★★ is a strong, complex amber ale with caramel and dried-fruit flavours; **BK** ★★ is a gentle dry stout with liquorice and coffee flavours and a dry finish.

OPPERBACCO
Notaresco, Teramo

Enterprising craft brewery in Abruzzo region, using pure water from Gran Sasso mountain. Fresh and tangy wheat ale **Bianca Piperita ★★** is unusually spiced with peppermint; roasty, coffee-ish **10 e Lode ★★★** is a strong dark ale that turns smoky when infused with tobacco to become **Extra Vecchio ★★☆**, and vinous when barrel-aged for **Barricata 050 ★★☆** and **Sour 050 ★★☆**.

PANIL (BIRRIFICIO TORRECHIARA)
Torrechiara, Parma

Craft brewery near Parma, pioneering in spontaneous fermentation. Former flagship **Panil Ambrè ★★** is a fruity, roasty amber ale; flat lambic-like **Divina ★★★** is spontaneously fermented by local bacteria and wild yeasts; brown ale **Panil Barriquée ★★★** is fermented 15 days in stainless steel, then 90 days in oak and 30 days in the bottle; sour version **Panil Barriquée Sour ★★★☆** has lactic, vinegary flavours.

PAUSA CAFÈ
Turin

A "social cooperative" café in Turin dedicated to assisting producers in the developing world, and crafting some decent beers as well, the brewing of which takes place off-site. Most successful include **Tosta ★★★**, made with Costa Rican chocolate and evocative of a fruity chocolate liqueur; **Chicca ★★**, brewed with Huehuetenango coffee and full-bodied but subtle and balanced

in its coffee flavour; and a very floral, herbal, hoppy pils called **PILS ★★☆**.

PETROGNOLA, LA
Piazza al Serchio, Lucca

Tuscan craft brewery using locally grown spelt in of its all beers. Unique **Farro ★★★**, brewed from 100% malted spelt, is fruity and spicy; flagship **La Petrognola ★★☆** is a flowery, roasty amber ale that also has a lighter version called **Mezza Petrognola ★★**; **Petrognola Nera ★★☆** is a coffee-ish, black ale; and **Sandy ★★** is a reddish, nutty ale named after brewer's daughter.

RETORTO BIRRIFICIO ARTIGIANALE
Podenzano, Piacenza

Open since only the spring of 2012, this brewery midway between Parma and Milan made an almost immediate impact on the Rome beer scene. The four regular brands include **Morning Glory ★★**, a fragrant but light-bodied pale ale; a highly aromatic IPA with soft citrus notes and a dryish finish, called **Krakatoa ★★☆**; and a plummy, lightly peaty Scotch ale, **Daughter of Autumn ★★★**.

DESTINATION
ROME

Ma Che Siete Venuti a Fà (25 Via di Benedetta), informally known as the "football pub", sits across the street from Bir&Fud (*see* page 166) and offers a casual, friendly atmosphere for enjoying one of the city's most carefully assembled beer selections.

RURALE
Vigevano, Pavia

Lombard farmhouse brewery founded by a group of homebrewers in 2009. Basic brands include a most refreshing and orange blossom-accented Belgian-style wheat beer, **Seta** ★★☆; the beautifully reserved, perfumey **Terzo Miglio** ★★☆, fashioned as a US-style pale ale; and **Blackout** ★★★, a dryly roasty stout that tastes more Irish than many Irish stouts.

SAN PAOLO
Turin

Brewery in San Paolo district of Turin specializing in bottle-conditioned beers. **Fraké** ★★☆ is a caramelly, citrus amber lager; **Pecan** ★★ is *kölsch*-inspired and authentically balanced; flagship IPA **Ipè** ★★★ is American-inspired with caramel malt contrasting citrus and piney hops; golden ale **Robinia** ★★ is sweetened with organic dandelion honey and bittered by aromatic American hops.

THERESIANER, ANTICA BIRRERIA
Nervesa della Battaglia, Treviso

Rooted in the era of Austrian rule over Trieste, this family-led brewery fares best when focused on lager rather than ale. **Premium Pils** ★★ is light and crisp, with hoppiness growing to a dry, pleasingly bitter finish; **Vienna** ★★★ is off-dry and softly roasty, with nutty hoppiness; ale success is found in the winter seasonal, **Birra d'Inverno** ★★☆, strong, chocolaty and mildly spicy.

TOCCALMATTO
Fidenza, Parma

Parma-area brewery with a passion for bottle-fermentation and hops. Pale ale **Re Hop** ★★☆ offers soft citrus hoppiness on appley malt; **Skizoid** ★★☆ is a subdued and amber-hued, nutty IPA; **Zona Cesarini** ★★☆ uses Pacific hops to create big, fruity-spicy, food-friendly flavours; **Dudes Barley Wine** ★★★ shows brandy-ish, almondy complexity, and turns phenolic and smoky when aged in whisky barrels to become **Salty Dog** ★★☆.

TROLL
Vernante, Cuneo

Nestled in the mountains of Piedmont, this brewpub gained so much popularity that it now bottles. **Dau'** ★★☆ is a low-alcohol summer seasonal with peppery spice; **Shangrila** ★★☆ is brewed with a kitchen full of spices, emerging complex and warming; **Dorina** ★★ is lavender-spiced and suitably floral; **Febbre Alta** ★★★ is a herbed *gruut* with hops that manages vaguely to resemble an amaro.

DESTINATION
QUINTO VICENTINO

Drunken Duck (77 Via degli Eroi) is a genuine country pub not far from Venice, featuring a clever rotation of craft lagers, ales and lambics in addition to exclusive house beers commissioned from various brewers.

LUXEMBOURG

One of the few countries in Europe to have a stagnant beer culture, despite being, or perhaps because it is, surrounded by countries that do it far better.

BOFFERDING
Bascharage, Capellen

Officially the Brasserie Nationale, the largest independent brewery in Luxembourg, at Bascharage, which took over and closed the second largest, Battin, in 2005. Technically perfect but rather dull lagers include **Bofferding Pils ★★**, which is crisp but lacks depth; and maltier **Gambrinus Pilsener ★★**, satisfactory but without hitting a home run.

SIMON
Wiltz

Family-run brewery at Wiltz, in the north. Its new Okult range was resurrected from the former Redange brewery and includes **No 1 Blanche ★★**, a *witbier* with obvious orange peel; while simple but satisfying **Quaffit Stout ★★☆** needs more oomph. Simon brands include fresh-tasting golden-blond spelt beer **Dinkel ★★**, with a light, bitter finish; and **Noël ★★☆**, the slightly too sweet Christmas ale.

SWITZERLAND

In the latter half of the 20th century Switzerland mimicked the pan-European style of variants on blond lagers and was a late starter in regard to craft brewing. However, progress is now strong, with up to 100 new breweries either up and running or in the works, prompting some of the longer-established independents to brush up their act. The best of the new breed are starting to impress.

BOXER
Yverdon-les-Bains, Vaud

The last sizeable regional brewery in the French-speaking part of the country at Yverdon in Vaud canton makes **Premium** ★★, a decent crisp, flowery take on pilsner for such a large producer.

BRASSERIE DES FRANCHES-MONTAGNES
Saignelégier, Jura

BFM is the brewery that put Switzerland on the craft beer map of the world, at Saignelégier in Jura. Its flagship brew, the vinous, fruity, sour dark red **Abbaye de St Bon-Chien** ★★★☆ is a blend of oak-aged beers, while its one-off **Grand Cru** varieties ★★★→★★★★ usually come from a single cask. Offbeat spicy, warming Imperial stout **Cuvée Alex le Rouge** ★★☆ is worth a try, as is sage-infused, funky blond **La Meule** ★★★.

FELSENAU
Bern

Small independent brewery in the northern suburbs of the capital, Bern, and ubiquitous in and around the city. Smooth, roasty, toffee-ish **Bärni** ★★ is a good example of a Swiss *dunkel*, while fragrant, crisp **Junkerbier** ★★☆ is an excellent pilsner, especially when on draught.

DESTINATION
BERN

The country's top beer outlet is found in the southwestern suburbs of the capital, between Köniz and Liebefeld railway stations. Erzbierschof (276 Könizstrasse, Liebefeld) began life as the shop of a specialist beer importer, expanding to include a cellar bar. Between them they stock 300+ hand-picked Swiss and imported beers, with a dozen on tap.

LOCHER
Appenzell, Appenzell Innerhoden

Medium-sized, independent, family-dominated brewery at Appenzell, southeast of Zurich. Its Appenzeller brands include soft, unfiltered pale lager **Naturperle** ★☆, the first organic Swiss beer; vanilla-edged, woody, oak-aged amber lager **Holzfassbier** ★★; and **Schwarzer Kristall** ★★★, a rounded, roasted, smoky, chocolaty and rich *schwarzbier*, far above the usual standard for beers of this type. Lots of contract brewing for others too.

RAPPI, BIER FACTORY
Rapperswil, St Gallen

Promising newish small brewery at Rapperswil on the southernmost tip of Lake Zurich. Its smooth **Blackbier** ★★ is a good, dry session-strength stout, while peppery, earthy UK-style IPA **XXA Xtra Bitter Strong Ale** ★★☆ is a seasonal beer that is roughly as its name suggests.

SAN MARTINO
Stabio, Ticino

Small brewery in Stabio, at the southern-most tip of Tessin, also known as the

Ticino Brewing Co, producing the UK-US-Italian-influenced range of Bad Attitude beers, far removed from the Germanic beer traditions of the area. These include dry, fragrant and fruity golden session bitter **Kurt** ★★☆; earthy-citrus, fruity rye **IPA Hobo** ★★; and rounded, rich, warming, treacly, roasted **Two Penny** ★★☆ strong porter.

SCHÜTZENGARTEN
St Gallen

Famous for its medieval abbey, St Gallen is also home to the oldest (1779) and largest remaining independent Swiss brewery. Soft, fragrant, flowery **Klosterbräu** ★★ is one of the country's best unfiltered bottled lagers; while light brown, fruity, dry, spicy, juniper-infused **Gallus 612 Old-Style Ale** ★★ is a bold recent departure for a normally reserved company.

STILLMAN'S, THE
Gurmels, Fribourg

At Gurmels, north of Fribourg, this small spirits importer matures a brown ale brewed by Haldemann at Sugiez, in hogsheads used to import single malt whiskies. The **Darach Mòr** series necessarily varies depending on both cask and beer, but is an intriguing if sometimes slightly over-the-top contribution to Swiss beer diversity ★★→★★★.

SUDWERK
Pfäffikon, Zurich

Newer craft brewery at Pfäffikon, east of Zurich, making US-influenced beers toned down for local palates, such as the crisp, peppery, golden bitter **Gold Miner ★★**; occasional roasty, rounded mid-strength **Liborator Stout ★★**; and easy-drinking, smooth, chocolaty, treacly **Pacific Pioneer Porter ★★**.

TROIS DAMES
Ste-Croix, Vaud

Small brewery at Ste-Croix in the Jura mountains, at the northern end of Vaud, the first to introduce true-to-style Anglo-US-Belgo ales to Swiss palates. Its bready, smooth, nutty Irish red ale **Rivale ★★** is complex but light; citrus, peppery, earthy **India Pale Ale ★★★** has become a Swiss classic; fruity, spicy **Fraîcheur du Soir ★★** is a lush, double-strength *witbier*; and unique, heretical **Grande Dame Oud Bruin ★★★☆** is made from a blend of strong stout with fermented apricots but ends stunningly close to a Belgian sour brown ale.

EASTERN EUROPE & THE BALKANS

In Soviet times, Czechoslovakian beers were delicious while those of the occupiers were not. It took Czech brewers two decades to muster the confidence and influence to invest in new brewing talent, followed recently by Poland. Progress elsewhere is patchy but several countries now have hero innovators and one or two – Hungary and perhaps Slovenia – show promise.

CZECH REPUBLIC

Beer in Bohemia is entitled to obey different rules. This is the place where hops were first cultivated in the seventh century, that first began using them routinely in brewing, had by the 11th century established a network of town breweries to supplement home brewing and then, in 1842, first trumpeted a blond lager – in the then German-speaking town of Pilsen.

Ironically, the preservation of small regional breweries making beers to careful standards long into the 20th century owes more to neglect than anything. Failure to invest after 1945 by the occupying Soviets forced brewers into a make-do-and-mend mentality, although as many foreign investors learned to their cost after the Russian occupation ended in 1989, the beer-obsessed Czechs had come to appreciate the slow and careful methods this preserved.

Until recently, few if any Czech brewers sought to set the world on fire by making swaggering, assertive and shocking beers. Rather they concentrated mainly on making lighter beers, perfectly.

Pale (*světlý*) and dark (*tmavý*) Bohemian lagers typically use hops from around Žatec (Saaz in German) and malt from the Hanà valley in Moravia, to make decoction-mashed, bottom-fermented, 8–12-week lagered beers, classified by degrees Plato, 8° signifying light, 10° standard and 12° premium.

After 1989 the network of sometimes decrepit or dilapidated local breweries was put up for sale to the highest bidders. Many closed, and glitzy modern ways were introduced into others, to the disdain of local drinkers. A couple of decades on, numerous smaller companies using older ways have returned, along with some new brewers with a broader vision.

ANTOŠ
Slaný, Central Bohemia

Small pub brewery at Slaný, in the heart of the hop-growing region around Žatec, making excellent traditional lagers and newer creations for its tap, bottles and kegs landing as far away as Prague. **Antošův Ležák** ★★★ is a Bohemian pale lager with a pronounced hop bite; *hefeweizen* **Slánská Pšenka** ★★☆ presents a classic Bavarian clove and banana slate; while **Tlustý Netopýr Rye IPA** ★★☆ melds US hops with peppery rye.

BERNARD
Humpolec, Vysočina

Neglected old brewery at Humpolec, midway between Prague and Brno, declared bankrupt in 1991 and bought by the Bernard family, who made it a national exemplar, with hands-off Belgian co-owners DUVEL MOORTGAT investing in 2001. Biscuity, malt-focused pale **Sváteční Ležák** ★★☆ is now the brewery flagship; food-friendly **Černý Ležák** ★★☆ is one of the best wider-distribution dark lagers, with chocolate and cola notes; and amber lager **Polotmavý Ležák 11°** ★★ can impress too.

BŘEVNOV
Prague

On the site of a long-past 10th-century brewery at Prague's Břevnov Monastery, where a new facility opened in 2012, creating an instant classic in **Benedict Světlý Ležák** ★★★☆, the unusually minty, vegetal hop flavours that derive from an old-growth Saaz yard; while imported traditional styles have thus far included a spiced *dubbel*, **Abbey Ale** ★★, and a deceptively easy-drinking 8% ABV pale lager, **Imperial Pilsner** ★★☆.

BŘEZŇÁK (HEINEKEN)
Velké Březno, Ústí nad Labem

In northern Bohemia, now owned by Heineken but still a remarkable beast

for its continued use of traditional open fermenters. **Březňák Světlý Ležák ★★**, the flagship pale lager, remains unusually fragrant and peppery when fresh.

BROUMOV
Broumov, Hradec Králové

Regional brewer at Broumov in northern Bohemia, exporting significantly across the nearby Polish border. The beers bear the brand name Olivětinský OPAT, with favourites being the up-hopped **Bitter ★★☆**, with pronounced Saaz cedar notes; and the holiday seasonal **Sváteční Speciál 17° ★★★**, a stronger amber lager with rich stewed-plum and gingerbread flavours.

BUDWEISER BUDVAR
České Budějovice, South Bohemia

The Budějovický Budvar brewery at České Budějovice in Bohemia is becoming best known for its long-running trademark battle with Anheuser-Busch that leads to its flagship beer **Budvar** being called **Czechvar** in the US. Formally **Budějovický Světlý Ležák ★★★**, it is well-attenuated pale lager with crisp, crackery malt and well-rounded bitterness that maintains excellence by cutting no corners; less well known **Budvar Dark**, or **Tmavý Ležák ★★★** is a classic dark lager with deep toffee and coffee notes.

CHOTĚBOŘ
Chotěboř, Vysočina

Small independent brewery at Chotěboř, midway between Prague and Brno,

unusual for being new (2009) and purpose-built. Produces exemplary lagers in which hops take a backseat to crackery malt. **Premium ★★☆** is the standard-bearing pale lager; **Černé Premium ★★** employs dark malts for interest; and rich butterscotch heightens the caramel-inflected stronger **Speciál ★★☆**.

DESTINATION BRNO

U Modrého (19 Česká) is a neat, modern beer shop near the centre of Brno with over 200 Czech and foreign beers, mostly chosen for interest.

CHÝNĚ
Chýně, Central Bohemia

Pub brewery in Chýně village, just outside of Prague, producing beers that are long-standing favourites in many of the capital's speciality bars. In particular, its **Světlý Ležák ★★★** is a textbook Bohemian pilsner, blending punchy Saaz notes with more citrus fruit than Carmen Miranda's hat.

DALEŠICE
Dalešice, Vysočina

Once-shuttered brewery at Dalešice in Moravia, where the pre-revolutionary cult film comedy *Postřižiny* (*Cutting it Short*) was shot. Reopened in 2002 with a few star beers like **Dalešická 11° ★★☆**, a pale lager with a berries-and-cream flavour; amber **Dalešické Májové 13° ★★☆**, which starts malty but finishes with prickly hops; and dark lager **Fledermaus 13°** ★★, which typically emphasizes bitterness over sweetness.

DOBRUŠKA
Dobruška, Hradec Králové

Based in eastern Bohemia, this now-you-see-me-now-you-don't regional brewery has returned to produce beers under the name Rampušák, such as impressive **12° Kvasnicový Ležák** ★★★, with a lot of body and long, hoppy finish; plus lighter but equally traditional beers named Dobruška, such as **Kvasnicový Světlý Ležák 11°** ★★☆, with buttery malt and a pronounced bready feel from its yeast.

FALKON
Žatec, Ústí nad Labem

Beer commissioner at Žatec run by one of the brewers at **ANTOŠ**, creating beers for his own label. Beyond common-or-garden craft fare like US-inspired bittersweet **Stalker IPA** ★★☆ are experiments in alien and overlooked styles like the sweet and roasty **Milk Stout** ★★☆.

FERDINAND
Benešov, Central Bohemia

Regional producer at Benešov, south of Prague, still operating its own maltings. Grain trumps hops in its **Sedm Kulí 13°** ★★☆, a gingery dark beer made with seven malts and four kinds of spice; the strong pale lager **d´Este 15°** ★★ blends crackery barley with a bitter counterpunch; and model pale lager **Premium 12°** ★★ finishes crisp and dry.

HEROLD
Březnice, Central Bohemia

Solid regional brewery in the grounds of a castle, south of Prague. Still has its own floor maltings, balancing tradition and innovation. Classically **Czech Premium Lager** ★★☆ emphasizes malt over hops, as also in roasty and bitter **Bohemian Black Lager** ★★★ and sweetly malty **Bohemian Wheat Lager** ★★☆.

JIHOMĚSTSKÝ
Prague

Stylish František Richter brewpub (*see* **U BULOVKY**) set among the *paneláky* estates of south Prague. The specials bring in the curious, though local fans stick to standards like house lager **Jihoměšťan** ★★, with a very spicy Saaz nose; clove-scented *hefeweizen* **Weissbier** ★★☆; and **Tmavý Speciál** ★★★, a beer that takes dark lager toward stout territory.

DESTINATION
PRAGUE

Zlý Časy (5 Čestmírova) has an airy street-level bar and atmospheric cellar offering 30+ draught beers from rural producers, plus international and rare local beers in bottle, also in its shop.

KOCOUR
Varnsdorf, Ústí nad Labem

New-school brewery located at Varnsdorf near the German border, making largely top-fermented beers, including many collaboration brews. High points include **Samuraj** ★★☆, an aggressive, US-style IPA brewed with Toshi Ishii from Guam; **Gypsy Porter** ★★☆, a citrus-inflected Baltic porter produced with UK Brewer, Steel City; and low-octane pale ale **Sumeček** ★★☆, with plenty of (mostly US) hops.

KOUT NA ŠUMAVĚ
Kout na Šumavě, Plzeň

Cult favourite from a renovated small town brewery in western Bohemia, making four lagers – two pale, two dark. **Punchy Kout 10°** ★★★ has more Saaz character than many 12° premiums; sharply bittersweet **Kout 12°** ★★★★ balances spicy hops with a rich, caramel body; the two darks, **Kout 14°** ★★★ and **Kout 18°** ★★★☆ share the same grain bill, each offering similar gingery spice and cola notes.

KRAKONOŠ
Trutnov, Hradec Králové

This solid regional brewer near the Polish border, is named after the legendary giant of the Krkonoše, or Giant Mountains. The premium pale lager, **Světlý Ležák 12°** ★★☆, is an easy-drinking favourite for its full malt body and delicate finishing hop aroma.

KRUŠOVICE (HEINEKEN)
Krušovice, Central Bohemia

Before 1989, the hop-popping pale lager from Krušovice was a high spot of any Prague beer hunt. The brewery once owned by King Rudolf II and now by Heineken, uses its region's renowned soft water to make frustratingly solid but unexciting beers, the best of which is likely **Krušovice Černé** ★★☆, a dark lager balancing sugary malt with a gently spicy hop note. Needs de-renovating.

LOBKOWICZ
Protivín, South Bohemia

A small but important new brewing group has gained the rights to the name Lobkowicz, given to beers made at Platan in southern Bohemia. Its flagship pale lager, **Premium** ★★☆, offers round, almost buttery malt sweetness finishing with a whiff of noble hop aroma

---

MATUŠKA
Broumy, Central Bohemia

A small family brewery based at Broumy, west of Prague, run by father-and-son master brewers, and producing classic beers from across the continent and beyond, including one of the country's best *hefeweizens*, citrus and well-balanced **Pšeničné Pivo 13°** ★★★; plummy, fruity **Weizenbock** ★★★; and modern craft styles including a crisp, US-style pale ale, Sierra Nevada homage to **California** ★★☆ and a pugnacious, bittersweet IPA, **Raptor** ★★☆.

NA RYCHTĚ
Ústí nad Labem

A new pub brewery located at Ústí nad Labem in industrial northern Bohemia, founded by former employees of the nearby Heineken-owned Zlatopramen brewery, and making beers that hark back to the heyday of classic lager brewing. Its pilsner-style **Mazel** ★★★☆ pushes Saaz bite into C-hop territory; while its pale, caramel and Munich malts make up the rich backbone for sugary dark lager **Vojtěch** ★★☆.

NOMÁD
Prague

Prague-based beer commissioner run by Honza Kočka, formerly prime mover at KOCOUR, creating innovative beers like all-Czech IPA, **Karel** ★★☆, which showcases the lemony, raspberry-scented, Saaz-related Kazbek hops; **Black Hawk** ★★☆, which pairs various American C-hops with Moravian dark malts; and **Pelikán** ★★★, a peppery double IPA that cuts Kazbek and Czech Agnus hops with US Chinooks and Cascades.

PERNŠTEJN
Pardubice

Regional brewer east of Prague with a stable of solid but standard brews and one eye-catching special, a Baltic porter washed up miles inland. First brewed for a Prague exhibition in 1891, **Pardubický Porter** ★★☆ is full of butterscotch and treacly malt, like a Christmas pudding with a shot of brandy on top.

PILSNER URQUELL (SABMILLER)
Plzeň

Modern descendant of the first pale lager and original role model for the style, from Plzeň (Pilsen) in western Bohemia. Still malt-driven and fairly well-hopped, bittersweet, with floral, citrus-scented Saaz notes, flagship **Pilsner Urquell** ★★★ is superior when served fresh and unpasteurized, as it is in numerous, mostly Czech pubs.

DESTINATION
PLZEŇ

Klub Malých Pivovarů (16 Nádražní) is a grungy, grimy beer bar with a "Small Breweries Club" that delights in serving unknown Czech and Bavarian beers, just a few steps from behemoth Pilsner Urquell.

PIVOVARSKÝ DŮM
Prague

Small Prague pub brewery making Czech classics as well as German, American and UK styles, some of which arrive hand-pulled. House pale lager **Štěpán Světlý Ležák** ★★★ is a riot of Saaz fireworks over pure Pilsner malt; dark-lager variation **Štěpán Tmavý Ležák** ★★☆ tastes of café au lait and gingerbread; and **Pšeničné Pivo** ★★☆ is a banana-scented German *hefeweizen*.

POLIČKA (MĚŠŤANSKÝ PIVOVAR V POLIČCE)
Polička, Pardubice

The old (1517) town brewery of the ancient walled city of Polička, in the Moravian highlands, has quietly flourished under the direction of hippie-era rock guitarist Karel Witz. The malting of classic dark lager, **Hradební Tmavé**

Pivo 10° ★★☆, is spicy and ginger; while in highly traditional pale lager **Záviš 12° ★★☆** it is biscuit-inflected.

PRIMÁTOR
Náchod, Hradec Králové

Regional brewery at Náchod in eastern Bohemia, with a diverse line of specialities that included the first widely available **Czech Stout ★★☆**, with smoky malt roastiness and a lightly sweet body; sharply bitter but sugary golden bock **Exklusiv 16° ★★**; and the Saaz-scented **Premium ★★☆**, among the best of the country's more industrial pale lagers.

PURKMISTR
Plzeň

Pub brewery in Plzeň (Pilsen), with a brand that echoes a long-gone local brew. Exemplary pale lager **Purkmistr Světlý Ležák ★★★** caps honey-scented malt with a bitter bite; **Tmavý Ležák ★★☆** is a rich and sugary dark beer; while *hefeweizen* style **Písař Pšeničné Pivo ★★☆** marries yeasty spice with crisp wheat body. The associated upmarket hotel offers a beer spa, tub and all.

RAMBOUSEK
Hradec Králové

A well-regarded small brewery at Hradec Králové, in eastern Bohemia, which is best known for its **Eliščino Královské Kaštanomedový Speciál 13° ★★☆**, a sweetly aromatic amber lager with a dose of chestnut honey

in the mash, a mouthful in both name and deed, named after medieval queen Elizabeth Richeza.

ROHOZEC
Malý Rohozec, Liberec

A small regional brewer based at Malý Rohozec in the the rolling hills of Český Raj, or Bohemian Paradise, where it is popular. Rarely seen elsewhere. **Skalák Světlý Ležák 12° ★★** is the premium pale lager, with crackery malt with a moderate noble hop aroma; while **Skalák Tmavý 13° ★★☆** is a cola-sweet dark lager with loads of roasted malt flavours.

RYCHTÁŘ (LOBKOWICZ)
Hlinsko ve Čechách, Pardubice

A small brewery at Hlinsko ve Čechách in the central highlands, halfway between the hop-growing region of northern Bohemia and the barley fields of the Haná Valley in southern Moravia, now in the **LOBKOWICZ** group. Unfiltered flagship pale lager **Rychtář Natur ★★☆** splits the geographical difference too, balancing Saaz hop

perfumes with toasty malt flavours, elevating both with a rich dose of bready yeast.

STRAHOV, KLÁŠTERNÍ PIVOVAR
Prague

A renovated brewpub located at a hilltop monastery near Prague Castle, making both trad Czech and contemporary craft brews in the name of Svatý ("St") Norbert. **Antidepressant** ★★☆ is a dark bock brightened by Saaz hops fresh from the harvest; the **IPA** ★★☆ leans on imported US hops; while the Vienna lager-esque **Amber Lager** ★★★ and *tmavé* **Dark Lager** ★★★ stick with Moravian malt and Bohemian hop zing.

ŠTRAMBERK
Štramberk, Moravia-Silesia

Pub brewery in the hilltop citadel of Štramberk, south of Ostrava in eastern Moravia, taking the brand name Trubač from the medieval watchtower across the town square. Its well-made, sweetish **Světlý Ležák** ★★☆ seems to get to travel more than the **Tmavý Ležák** ★★★, which is one of the Czech Republic's best darks, with a Java nose with bitter and sugary coffee flavours in the mouth.

SVIJANY
Svijany, Liberec

Successful regional brewer at Svijany in north Bohemia, the first to connect craft beer appeal to traditional techniques. The bready malt of pale lager **Svijanský**

Rytíř ★★ is balanced by grassy hops, while slightly turbid **Kvasničák** ★★☆ brightens noble-hop bite with a dose of fresh yeast.

U BULOVKY
Prague

Brewing entrepreneur František Richter's beachhead brewpub sits 200m (656ft) from the end of the E55 motorway in the north of Prague. Richter beers include house pale lager, **Ležák** ★★☆, where sugary malt meets peppery Saaz; a brave, hoppy and estery Czech take on an **Alt** ★★; and **Weizenbock** ★★☆, which offers a winter cocktail of boozy stewed-fruit flavours.

U FLEKŮ
Prague

Only one beer is made in the more than 500-year-old brewery attached to a massive, much touristed pub near the centre of Prague. Only available on

draught, barring occasional souvenir bottles, unaltered for 40 years and likely much longer. This fruity, roasty, rich and chocolaty dark lager, known officially as **Flekovský Tmavý Ležák ★★★★**, gains its fourth star for being an icon rather than a stunner. An essential line in any beer-drinking CV.

UHERSKÝ BROD (LOBKOWICZ)
Uherský Brod, Zlín

Regional brewer at Uherský Brod, not far from the Slovak border, now part of the LOBKOWICZ group. Most of its brews are solid, but the stronger pale lager, **Comenius Speciál 14° ★★☆** stands out, with loads of toffee malt balanced by bright, fragrant hop aroma.

ÚNĚTICE
Únětice, Central Bohemia

Renewed brewery in the village of Únětice just outside Prague, mainly producing two highly traditional Czech pale lagers. The base model, **Únětice 10° ★★★**, is surprisingly bitter for a session beer; highly hopped flagship **Únětice 12° ★★★☆** resembles pale ale as much as pils; while seasonal specials, like malty, amber **Vánoční Speciál 13° ★★**, offer variety but feel less self-assured.

U TÍ RŮŽÍ
Prague

Among the best of Prague's rash of new brewpubs, in one of the most touristic parts of the Old Town, close to Karlový Bridge. Beyond unusual seasonal specials, its pale lager, **Světlý Ležák ★★☆**, puts aromatic, citrus-scented Saaz to the fore; while the house **Vienna Red ★★☆** highlights bready, sugary malt.

DESTINATION PRAGUE

Pivovarský Klub (17 Křižíkova) is a well-lit beer bar and hearty-fare restaurant, just off the centre, with six independent Czech breweries on tap and 200 local and foreign brews in the bottle.

VYŠKOV
Vyškov, South Moravia

Regional brewer at Vyškov in southern Moravia, often overlooked despite its unusual Vyškovské Pivo range of brews, from pale *bock*-like **Jubiler 16,80 ★★☆**, a strong lager with unusually pronounced Saaz aroma; super-hoppy pale lager **Generál ★★☆**, that has won prizes as an IPA (!); and dark lager **Tmavý Džbán ★★☆** that dabs hoppy spice on molasses-like malt.

SLOVAK REPUBLIC

Before their amicable divorce in 1993, the two halves of the former Czechoslovakia had only been together for 75 years and had different traditions of beer making, the fanatical pivophiles being found more to the western (Bohemian) side of the Czech Republic.

As of 2013 the country has only one established top-quality craft brewery, though a few smaller ones are emerging and there remains a slender collection of better regional producers.

KALTENECKER
Rožňava, Košice

Founded in 1997 at Rožňava, near the Hungarian border, the country's most interesting brewery has an exceptional range of products, from simpler traditional lagers like amber-blond **Märzen 13°** ★★ and dark, sweet, coffee-tinged **Brokat Dark Lager 13°** ★★☆, via American-inspired ones such as its Imperial stout **Archa** ★★☆, to the country's strongest beer, **B27** ★★★, an old ale matured in Tokaji wine casks. Sadly some suffer from packaging in PET bottles.

ŠARIŠ (SABMILLER)
Vel'ký Šariš, Prešov

Although its pale lagers sell well they are far from special, while the dark beers from the Šariš (or Topvar) brewery at Vel'ký Šariš in the east of the country reach a better standard. **Šariš Tmavé 11°** ★★ is an easy-drinking *dunkel*; **Topvar 11° Tmavý Výčapný Ležiak** ★★ a more aromatic variant; and **Topvar Marina** ★★☆ has sufficient complexity to be an altogether more serious proposition.

SESSLER
Trnava

This small pub brewery, located at Trnava in the west, near Bratislava, was re-founded in 2004. It produces decent enough regular lagers like its **Svetlý Ležiak 11.5°** ★★ and its bready, caramelled, dark equivalent **Tmavý Ležiak 11.5°** ★★; plus frequent limited-edition heavier brown **Tmavý Špeciál** brews between **13°** and **21°** ★★→★★★.

URPINER
Banská Bystrica

Officially called the Banskobystrický brewery but known by its brand name, this well-organized firm at Banská Bystrica produces a workmanlike range of pale and dark lagers including reliable but unexciting blond **Ležiak Svetlý 12°** ★★, also called Premium; and the instantly appealing "draught" dark lager **Ležiak Výčapný Tmavý 11°** ★★☆, more often found bottled, and full of dried fruit, rich malt, chocolate, and other flavours.

POLAND

Some 80–85% of Polish beer is produced by subsidiaries of three global giants. SABMiller runs brands like Tyskie, Żubr, Lech, Dębowe, Książęce, Redd's and Gingers; Heineken has Żywiec, Warka, Tatra, Specjal and Leżajsk; and Carlsberg makes Okocim, Harnaś, Kasztelan and Karmi.

The rest is shared between 80 or so regional and smaller brewers, including over 30 pub breweries. Many older breweries remain conservative but there is a growing trend for home brewers to turn pro, opening small craft breweries, many brewing for others under contract, such as Pinta and AleBrowar.

After a slow start, the last couple of years have seen rapidly expanding awareness of better-quality beers, especially among young Poles, with pride in local products also noticeably increasing.

ALEBROWAR
Lebork, Pomerania

Beer seller commissioning craft beers from Browar Gościszewo, near Gdańsk. Mostly American styles thus far, like bittersweet, citrus and piney **Rowing Jack ★★★**, the best US-style IPA in Poland; American-hopped pale ale **Amber Boy ★★**; and Poland's first black IPA, with an intense hop aroma and roasted flavour, **Black Hope ★★☆**. In contrast **Sweet Cow ★★** is a soft milk stout that would pass for British.

AMBER BROWAR
Bielkówko, Pomerania

Medium-sized, modern brewery in Bielkówko, near Gdańsk. Sweet flagship **Żywe ★☆** began the trend toward unpasteurized and unfiltered beers; **Grand ★★** is a lighter weight, chocolate-malty

Baltic porter; and **Koźlak ★★** is a *bock*, complete with a painted goat's head on the bottle. Bottles of *hefeweizen*-style **Pszenicniak ★★** are similarly adorned.

DESTINATION
GDAŃSK

In the history-steeped Baltic port city, Degustatornia (16 Grodzka) and its associated Dom Piwa bottle-shop serve 150 mainly Polish and Czech beers, as does its eponymous sister bar and shop up the coast at Gdynia (130 Świętojańska).

ARTEZAN
Natolin, Masovia

Poland's first brewery to specialize in making Belgian and British styles of beer, created by home brewers at Natolin near Warsaw. Quality and accuracy can vary. Its first beer, **Wit ★★☆**, was based on Pierre Celis's original recipe for his Hoegaarden beer; **Dubbel ★★☆** ends up more a regular brown ale than in the fuller abbey style; its **India Pale Ale ★★**, fruity, slightly caramelized and of modest bitterness is English-style; with the best effort so far being a balanced but potent first Polish example of **Imperial Stout ★★★**.

DESTINATION KRAKÓW

The unofficial capital of the south is home to four fine beer bars. In Kazimierz, the old Jewish quarter, cool Omerta (3 Kupa) divides itself into Polish and international halves, and plainer Strefa Piwa (6 Józefa) concentrates on regional revivalists; while in the centre, Dominikańska (3 Ul. Dominikańska) and House of Beer (35 Ul. Św. Tomaszka) also chalk up 100+ brews.

BRACKI BROWAR ZAMKOWY (HEINEKEN)
Cieszyn, Silesia

Small traditional brewery within the Heineken-controlled Żywiec group, at Cieszyn on the Czech border, southwest of Cracow. Distinctly bitter *helles* lager **Brackie ★★** is only available locally, while dry, bitter and potent Baltic-style **Żywiec Porter ★★☆** is found throughout the country in better beer shops. This might one day happen for malty and lightly smoked **Bracki**

Rauch Bock ★★☆, 2012 winner of the national Festiwal Birofilia home brewing competition, rewarded with a one-off commercialization as Bracki Grand Champion beer, launched on 6 December each year.

CIECHAN
Ciechanów, Masovia

Small traditional brewery near Warsaw with good distribution in and around the capital. Flagship honeyed lager **Miodowe ★★☆** is golden and honey-sweet; *weizen* **Pszeniczne ★★** has an intense aroma of clove and banana; blond **Marcowe ★★** is a *märzen*; and its traditional, rich, malt-led and roasted Baltic porter is called simply **Porter 22 ★★★**.

FORTUNA
Miłosław, Greater Poland

Small traditional brewery at Miłosław, near Poznań. Best known for **Fortuna Czarne ★★**, an extremely sweet *dunkel* brewed with kola nuts, though its soothing dark and rich Baltic-style **Komes Porter ★★★** is far more interesting. The Komes brand has recently been expanded to include a couple of evolving bottle-conditioned beers, a *dubbel* called **Podwójny ★★☆** and *tripel* called **Potrójny ★★**.

KONSTANCIN
Konstancin-Jeziorna, Masovia

Small brewery at Konstancin-Jeziorna, near Warsaw, responsible for the production of **Żytnie ★★☆**, Poland's first, rather promising, rye beer.

KORMORAN
Olsztyn, Warmia-Masuria

Medium-sized independent brewery in the picturesque northeast achieving a national reputation following recent awards for its rich, roasted Baltic porter **Warmiński** ★★★☆ and light lager **Orkiszowe z Miodem** ★★☆, made with spelt and honey. Its weirdest concoction thus far has been **Orkiszowe z Czosnkiem** ★☆, a spelt beer with garlic.

LWÓWEK ŚLĄSKI
Lwówek Śląski, Lower Silesia

Small traditional brewery named after its home town, west of Wrocław, owned by the same people as CIECHAN. Although it claims an ancient heritage, its range points to the future, with a pleasant *helles* lager **Lwówek Książęce** ★★; and a caramelled pale ale named **Belg** ★★ but tasting rather more Brit.

PINTA
Wrocław, Lower Silesia

A firm of beer commissioners formed in 2011, seeking to create a range in styles largely unknown to Polish beer drinkers. In 2012 it even had beer brewed as a Finnish *sahti*, called **Koniec Świata** ★☆, almost flat, muddy and yeasty. More famously it conjured up **Atak Chmielu** ★★, the first Polish-made US-style IPA, with more caramel than most; also **Dobry Wieczór** ★★☆, a smooth oatmeal stout with dollops of chocolate and coffee; and the amazing **Viva la Wita** ★★★, a American-hopped "Imperial *witbier*".

WIDAWA
Chrząstawa Mała, Lower Silesia

Pub brewery with a restaurant, at Chrząstawa Mała near Wrocław, collaborating with a home brewer to produce beers that get into the best multi-tap pubs in the country. **Czarny Kur** ★★ is a well-roasted *schwarzbier*, better are **Kruk** ★★★, an American dry stout heavily hopped with Simcoe; US-style pale ale **Shark** ★★★, extremely bitter with a citrus aroma and currently the most highly hopped beer in Poland, just shy of 100 IBU; and **Kawka** ★★☆, a stout flavoured with coffee grounds.

**DESTINATION
OTHER CITIES**

Beer cafés are starting to crop up all round Poland. In Wrocław try Zakład Usług Piwnych (34 Ruska); in Poznań the extraordinary Setka (0 Ul. Św. Marcin); and in Łódź the Piwoteka Narodowa (1–3 Ul. 6 Sierpnia).

SLOVENIA

The northernmost province of the former Yugoslavia, now an independent state within the EU, has roughly two dozen pub-based breweries, each supplying a single outlet. We had been aware of only one small craft brewery, albeit a beauty, though recently we heard of two more.

HUMANFISH BREWERY
Slovenj Gradec, Styria

Named after an odd-looking local amphibian by an expat Australian, and operating since 2008 in the north of the country, hiring a brewhouse currently but set to get its own. The country's premier craft brewer makes a surprisingly excellent, US-UK, crisp, aromatic **Pale Ale ★★★**; and an unusually fresh-hoppy but enticing **Stout ★★☆**, said to be oatmeal-based.

DESTINATION
LJUBLJANA

Two central bars in the capital, a couple of blocks apart, make an excellent fist of accruing better beers from round the country and abroad, each topping 100 choices – Patrick's Irish Pub (6 Prečna Ul.) and Sir William's Pub (8a Tavčarjeva Ul.).

HUNGARY

In modern times, Hungary has been more a wine country, brewing being limited in the 20th century to restrained, mostly industrial lagers. However, since 1993 or so a new wave of entrepreneurial smaller brewers have taken root, supplying increasingly interesting beers to an increasingly interested public also enamoured of Czech and Belgian brews.

In addition to those listed below, look out for Grabanc brands, commissioned from a commercial brewery by a local entrepreneur; Bors beers from a contract brewer at Győrzámoly in the northwest; and brews from Serreforás of Miskolc, near the Tokaj wine region in the northeast, who either brew or commission – we are unclear which.

BÉKÉSSZENTANDRÁSI
Békésszentandrás, Békés

The first new *kézműves sörfőzde*,
or "craft brewery", back in 1993, at
Békésszentandrás in the southeast of
the country. Variable initially but more
hits than misses now, including perhaps
the best Hungarian pilsner, **Ogre Soren**
★★☆; an outstanding strong, plummy
dark lager dubbed **Black Rose** ★★★,
showcasing chocolate malt; an absurdly
strong reddish-brown lager, **Pöröly** ★★;
and a growing number of fruit beers.

CSOBÁNKAI
Csobánka, Pest

Impressive new brewery at Csobánka,
northwest of Budapest, gradually
unfolding a range of UK-inspired beers,
including Fuggles- and Goldings-hopped
Pastorale ★★☆, a legitimate take on
a darker English bitter; equally authentic,
slightly tart but elegant vanilla-edged
stout **Fekete Báry** ★★☆; and harder-
to-find **A Jó Éjjeli Portás** ★★☆, a
lighter black brew tasting a little of
autumn fruits, its name meaning "Good
Night Porter".

FÓTI
Fót, Pest

Another pioneer at Fót, northeast of
Budapest, since 1994. **Fóti Pils** ★★ is
a safe but decent enough blond lager;
pale-ale-inspired but bottom-fermented
Keserű Méz ★★★ is unfiltered
and golden, with biscuity malt and a
pronounced grassy aroma of Spalt,
perhaps the first beer to suggest a unique

Hungarian style; while its two strong
brown lagers, **Barcagi Dupla Bak**
★★☆ and winter's **Hammurapi 21+**
★★☆, both technically *doppelbocks*,
are given edge by a Champagne yeast.

RIZMAJER
Budapest

Another 1994 start-up, in Budapest,
now veering away from mainstream
styles like its light blond lager **Világos
Sör** ★☆ toward not-quite-Baltic, sweet
and caramelled **Cingulus Porter** ★★☆;
and newer, experimental Hopfanatic
brands like much-praised US-style IPA
Kiss-Bitterfly ★★★ and Imperial stout
Angry Beast ★★☆ that we believe are
commissioned from them.

> #### DESTINATION
> #### BUDAPEST
>
> The best beer bars in the capital
> still specialize in Czech or Belgian
> beers, so for Hungarian brews and
> the best international range head
> for Only Good Beer, or Csak a Jó
> Sör (42 Kertész Utca), a beer shop
> with a convivial small tasting area.

UKRAINE

The beer culture of western Ukraine, especially the area around the regional capital Lviv, is in some ways a continuum of that in neighbouring Poland to the west. It does not yet have a burgeoning craft brewing scene but this does not stop local tourist authorities promoting a five-brewery tour of the city, with tastings.

LVIVSKE (CARLSBERG)
Lviv

The largest brewery in Ukraine's beeriest city. Its mainstream beers, like stronger pale lager **Mitsne** ★★ are better balanced than some but do not survive export well; *witbier* **Bilyi Lev** ★★ is malt-accented with a big vanilla finish; and 8% ABV **Porter** ★★☆, intended to be Baltic but with German *dunkel* leanings, is another of Carlsberg's strong black local beers.

MIKULINETSKY
Mykulyntsi, Ternopil

Forward-thinking independent brewery in western Ukraine tracing its origins to 1457. Has a link with König Ludwig in Germany. Produces 17 mostly well-balanced and unpasteurized lagers, at the last count, among which the pilsner **Koruna Česka** ★★☆ has a rich Saaz aroma and hearty bitterness; lighter, more basic **Mikulin Svitle** ★★ has a bitter, mineral character; **Ukrainske Dark** ★★☆ is complex with lots of toffee and bread crust; and pale **Troyan** ★★ has a herbal, bitter character, underpinned by sweet malt.

PERSHA
Lviv

Small 2004 independent brewery in Lviv, its range including caramel-toffee **Chorne** ★★; a clean, refreshing pale lager **Stare Misto** ★★; stronger dark lager **Avtorske** ★★; and a plainish honey beer, **Medove** ★★.

STARGOROD
Lviv

Large brewpub in Lviv, making beers with a strong Czech accent. **Destika** ★★ has a nice pale malt balance and some herbal hop; its **Lager** ★★ is a slightly amber beer with a big malty nose; and **Chorne** ★★ is a toasty dark lager with too much diacetyl for some tastes.

GREECE

Something about craft beer seems to make it resilient in the face of hard economic times. Witness Greece, where a new clutch of small brewers are making gradual progress in a country unused to the joys of tasty beer.

Corfu Beer, opened in 2006 to make UK-style pale ales like darker toasty, nutty **Real Ale Bitter** ★★; grainy lagers like **Royal Ionian Pilsner** ★★ with a sweet malt finish; and a winter-only barley wine, **Ionian Epos** ★★☆.

Newer breweries on the rise include the Santorini Brewing Co, set up in 2011 by expats, whose brews thus far have included a blond **Yellow Donkey** ★★☆, a brown **Red Donkey** ★★☆, and Greece's first IPA, **Crazy Donkey** ★★★, all featuring US and New Zealand hops. Also Septem, on the near-island of Euboea, north of Athens, which names its beers by day of the week and has earned praise for **Friday's Pale Ale** ★★, **Sunday's Honey Golden Ale** ★★☆ and **Seasonal Winter's Day Porter** ★★.

On the island of Chios, just off the Turkish coast, Chios Micro makes a single bottled hazy blond **Fresh Chios Beer** ★★☆, which is getting about, as is the unpasteurized bottled version of **Zeos Pilsner** ★★☆ from Zeos Brewing Co at Argos on the Peloponnese. Currently we know of a dozen others either dipping a toe in the water in German *hausbrauerei* style or contemplating creating their own US-style craft beers.

If you're visiting, The Local Pub (25 Chaimanta, Chalandri) in the north of Athens, off the beaten track but two minutes from Xaimanta tram/bus stop, has the best range of craft beers in the capital, with 120+ including a dozen from Greek brewers. In Thessaloniki, The Prigipos (22 Apostolou Pavlou) is a traditional-style northern Greek drinks café with a a dozen or so Greek craft beers in a range of 100+, while out near the airport in the village of Trilofos the evenings-only Ipanema Beer Bar (Perikleous) does even more despite its obscure location.

RUSSIAN FEDERATION

Gathering information about brewing in the old Soviet Union was nigh impossible, a situation that continued in the first two decades after its break-up. In *The World Atlas of Beer* (Mitchell Beazley) we acknowledged these difficulties at the same time as recognizing that the fate of beer in the Russian Federation is of considerable importance to its future worldwide.

Carlsberg, Heineken and AB InBev all have clutches of breweries here but with the exception of the first, make no beers of interest.

The current crucible of craft beer revival is Saint Petersburg, home to an increasingly interesting variety of pub breweries, some of which are starting to sell their beers elsewhere. But as more young Russians take an interest in quality beers, information is starting to flow about brewers in far-flung corners that are cranking up after decades without investment. Watch this (massive) space.

AFANASIUS
Tver, Tver Oblast

Long-standing food and drink manufacturer at Tver, northwest of Moscow on the road to Saint Petersburg, that has added a few Afanasius-brand beers to its range: a safe-ish, mid-strength **Porter** ★★☆; unusual dark **Temnoe** ★★; and a lighter unfiltered wheat beer that seems unspiced.

BALTIKA (CARLSBERG)
Saint Petersburg

The Russian Federation's largest brewery company, formed by the merger and takeover of three large brewery plants in 2006, now with production facilities all over the country and in Azerbaijan. Most beers are instantly forgettable, as with those made by the country's other subsidiaries of multinationals, though there are exceptions. **No 8 Pschenichnoye** ★★ is a dryish, balanced and refreshing *weizen*; **No 6 Porter** ★★ is treacly, vinous and dark brown; and **Žatecký Gus Černý** ★★☆ is an oddly charming, low-strength dark lager that more resembles an English dark mild.

BALTIKA BREW (CARLSBERG)
Saint Petersburg

The Baltika group also operates a boisterous brewpub just off Nevsky Prospekt in Saint Petersburg. Beers include the toasty, honeyed, caramelled

Dark Ale ★★; a somewhat syrupy
Chocolate Stout ★★; and **Dark Velvet**
★★☆, which tastes strongly of rye.
Specials rotate frequently and have
included a floral **Honey Ale** ★★ with
a hint of hop character.

BIER HAUS
Ulan Ude, Buryatia

To prove that the German pub brewery
phenomenon has reached the ends of the
earth, this hotel and beer garden complex
on the outskirts of Ulan Ude, southeast
of Irkutsk, not far from the Mongolian
border in southern Siberia, makes one
of the better stouts in Asia. **Bagheera**
★★☆ is chocolaty, with a roast fudge
character and full body. Its other beers
are less successful, though 6% ABV pale
Hans ★☆ is a quirky example of a style
that is becoming an Eastern staple.

JOKER BAR
Kazan, Tatarstan

Brewpub at the Mirage Hotel in Kazan,
a long way east of Moscow, with an
excellent view of the Kazan Kremlin
UNESCO World Heritage site. Its **Helles**
★★☆ is fresh-tasting, with fruity hop
notes and a bready peach finish; the
Dunkel ★★☆ has a hearty bread-crust
character with cocoa notes; and the
Märzen ★★ is caramelly, nutty and
slightly toasty in the finish.

KARL & FRIEDRICH
Saint Petersburg

Saint Petersburg brewpub in a park on
Krestovsky Ostrov, Bavarian-themed
and fairly credible. Its yeasty, phenolic,
rich **Weizen** ★★☆ is currently one of
Russia's better wheat beers; while its
Pilsener ★★ is dry and yeasty, with
light malt presence.

MAXIMILIAN BRAUHAUS
Saint Petersburg

Quiet brewpub in a shopping mall on
a tram line at the outskirts of Saint
Petersburg. Bread-crusty **Temnoye**
★★ finishes off-dry; a balanced, fruity
Weizen ★★ is slightly yeasty; the
Lager ★☆ is somewhat doughy; and
MaxKriek ★☆ is a straightforward
cherried ale.

METROPOLE, BRASSERIE DE
Saint Petersburg

Upscale pub brewery in the heart
of Saint Petersburg specializing in
making Belgian-style ales. Still a work
in progress, its **Petit Lambic** ★☆
is more sweet than sour; **Rouge de
Flandres** ★★☆ has barrel-edged notes;
Kriek de Metropole is sweet and spicy
★★; and **Humuline** ★★ balances white
pepper notes, spicy hops and a pale
malt signature.

NORTH AMERICA & THE CARIBBEAN

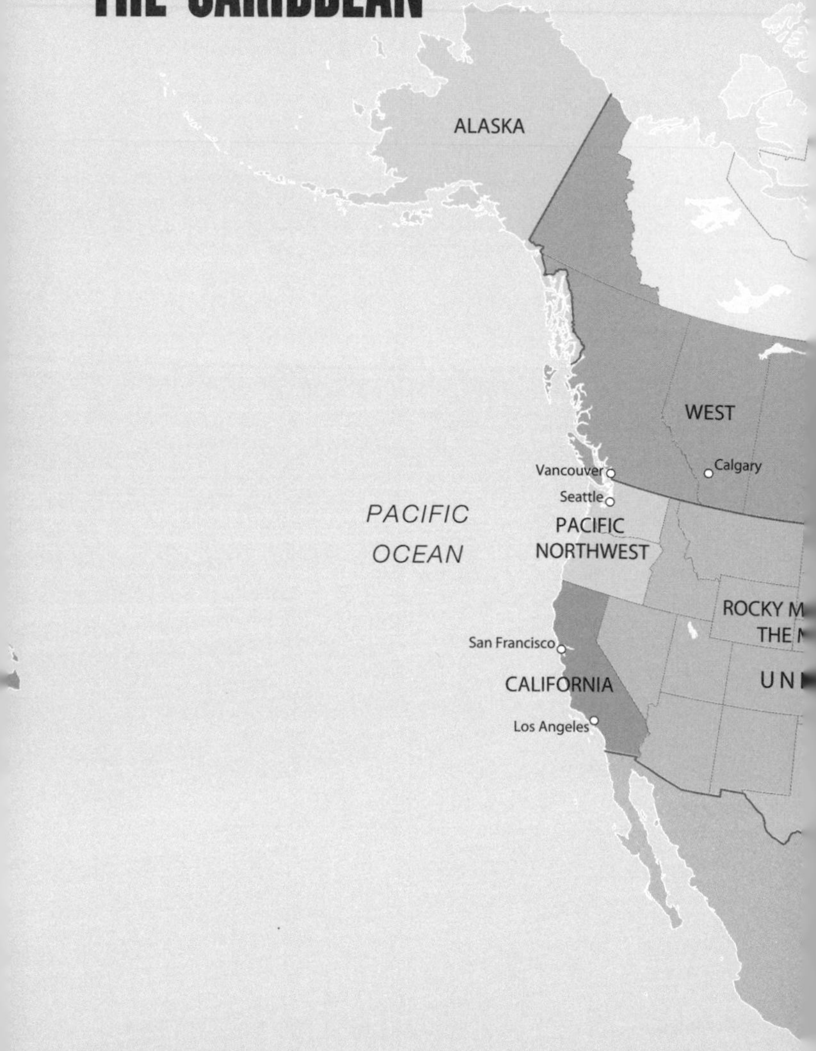

ALASKA

WEST

Calgary

Vancouver

Seattle

PACIFIC
OCEAN

PACIFIC
NORTHWEST

ROCKY M
THE N

San Francisco

U N

CALIFORNIA

Los Angeles

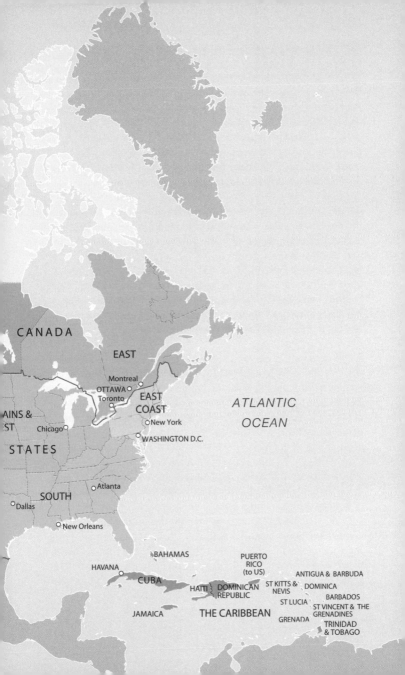

CANADA

EAST

Montreal

OTTAWA

Toronto

EAST
COAST

New York

WASHINGTON D.C.

*ATLANTIC
OCEAN*

AINS &
ST

Chicago

STATES

SOUTH

Atlanta

Dallas

New Orleans

BAHAMAS

PUERTO
RICO
(to US)

HAVANA

ANTIGUA & BARBUDA

CUBA

HAITI

DOMINICAN
REPUBLIC

ST KITTS &
NEVIS

DOMINICA

ST LUCIA

BARBADOS

ST VINCENT & THE
GRENADINES

JAMAICA

THE CARIBBEAN

GRENADA

TRINIDAD
& TOBAGO

UNITED STATES

Once upon a time, a mention of American beer would elicit nought but ridicule around the world. For although US breweries counted among the world's largest throughout most of the 20th century, or perhaps at least partially because of that fact, the nation's lagers had gone from light to lighter and even "lite", reaching their nadir when the Monty Python comedy troupe famously and with some justification compared them to "making love in a canoe".

But then, as the century drew to a close, entrepreneurial Americans did what they have always done best and began to transform the beer market not just in their own backyard, but also around the globe.

First, so-called "microbreweries" were unleashed, then they increased steadily in number, and once they grew too large for the "micro" label, they became craft breweries. Then they began to influence others to follow their lead, inspiring craft brewers near and far, in Canada and Japan, Brazil and Sweden.

By the dawn of the new millennium, the proverbial craft brewing "tail" had started to wag the brewing industry "dog". Making matters even worse for the big brewers, not only were they losing market share to the smaller guys, they were also losing national control of their own companies, with takeovers and mergers soon limiting domestic ownership of the now Big Two breweries to a mere 25% stake in one of the two.

Meanwhile, craft brewing continues to grow at a rapacious rate, escalating in number of breweries – some 2416 in operation at time of writing, with hundreds more in development – increasing in both volume and dollar market share and generally dominating the social beer consciousness. And with a brewery-to-population ratio well below that of countries like Belgium and the United Kingdom, there would seem to be still ample room for market growth in the immediate, perhaps even long-term future.

CALIFORNIA

By almost any measure, whether by Fritz Maytag's famous resuscitation of San Francisco's **ANCHOR BREWING** or Jack McAuliffe's ultimately unsuccessful founding of New Albion Brewing, modern American craft beer got its start in California. It is also in that state, particularly the north, that it first thrived.

Brewpubs were legalized in California in 1982 and shortly thereafter they proliferated across the state, notably so around the San Francisco Bay area, but also further north and, at the dawning of the 21st century, in the southern reaches around San Diego and Los Angeles, as well. Today, the state remains a craft beer leader, not only in terms of total number of breweries, with almost twice as many as the next most brewery-populated state, but also, and perhaps more importantly, as the enduring source of inspiration for others.

21ST AMENDMENT BREWERY
San Francisco, California

Brewpub in the shadow of a baseball stadium, now contract-brewing its major brands for canning. **Seasonal Hell** or **High Watermelon** ★★☆ is softly sweet with flavours of fresh watermelon; **Bitter American** ★★☆ is a quaffably light pale ale; piney and herbal **Brew Free! or Die IPA** ★★☆ is slightly sharp on the finish;

Back in Black ★★★ is a near-black IPA with a roasty body and hoppy finish.

DESTINATION
SAN FRANCISCO

The Toronado (547 Haight Street), a landmark in the area known as "Lower Haight", is a rough-around-the-edges bar with a passionate devotion to beer, evident in its extensive draught beer selection and frequent tasting events.

ALESMITH BREWING
San Diego, California

Fiercely local brewery only recently stretching sales beyond city borders. February seasonal **Bloody Valentine** ★★★ combines assertive hoppiness with red apple flavours, deliciously; pale

ale **X** ★★☆ is fragrant and very dry and quaffable; complex **Grand Cru** ★★★ uses Belgian yeast to coax flavours of dried fruit and spice; flagship **Horny Devil** ★★★☆ tweaks maltiness with peppery, citrus spice; **Old Numbskull** ★★★ barley wine is intense and warming.

ALPINE BEER
Alpine, California

This San Diego area brewery is justly well known for extremely hoppy beers like **Pure Hoppiness** ★★★☆, a classic double IPA with fruity mango/pineapple aromas and sticky pine character; and **Exponential Hoppiness** ★★★☆, another double that's dry-hopped twice, the second time with oak chips, for extreme hop character that's surprisingly well balanced. **Nelson** ★★☆ is a rye IPA that's spicy with Sauvignon Blanc flavours; and **Duet** ★★★ is a nicely balanced IPA with grassy, pineapple, mango notes.

ANCHOR BREWING
San Francisco, California

Prohibition-era San Francisco brewery revived by Fritz Maytag in the 1970s to become craft beer vanguard. Flagship **Steam Beer** ★★★★ mixes ale and lager characteristics in a most refreshing fashion; moderately strong and crisply hopped **Liberty Ale** ★★★ arguably set the stage for IPAs to come; mellow and warming **Old Foghorn Barley Wine** ★★★☆ pioneered the style in the US and remains maltier than most; newer **Humming Ale** ★★☆ screams hoppy freshness; and spiced **Christmas Ale** ★★★ changes annually, but remains reliably balanced.

ANDERSON VALLEY BREWING
Boonville, California

Stalwart northern California brewery, delighting in the use of local dialect "Boontling" on its labels. **Hop Ottin' IPA** ★★★ is an ale that mixes well bitter hop and sweet, fruity malt; **Barney Flats Oatmeal Stout** ★★★☆ is a smooth, silky, lightly sweet black ale with mild roastiness; **Brother David's Double** ★★★, brewed in cooperation with San Francisco's Toronado bar (*see* box, page 201), is rich with raisin and other dried-fruit flavours; **Poleeko Gold Pale Ale** ★★☆ is peachy and quaffable.

BALLAST POINT BREWING
San Diego, California

A San Diego brewery born out of a homebrew shop. Fish-named ales include the highly regarded, grapefruity **Fish Eye IPA** ★★★; and more roundly fruity, lighter-tasting **Sculpin IPA** ★★☆. Simply named **Pale Ale** ★★☆ pleases with easy quaffability; while food-friendly **Marlin Porter** ★★★ is mocha-ish and drying.

BEAR REPUBLIC BREWING
Healdsburg, California

Father-and-son brewery long a staple of California wine country. Flagship **Racer 5 IPA** ★★★☆ is a testament to US hops in its citrus appeal; **Hop Rod Rye** ★★★ was one of the first US beers successfully to combine the spiciness of rye with strength and hoppiness; seasonal **Racer X** ★★★ is a superbly balanced double IPA.

BISON BREWING
Berkeley, California

Born of a Berkeley brewpub, now contract-brewing a range of organic ales. Soft fruitiness of **Organic IPA ★★☆** underscores gently citrus hop; **Organic Chocolate Stout ★★★** combines plummy malt with chocolate and liquorice flavours; **Organic Honey Basil Ale ★★** speaks loudly of its herbal ingredient and pairs well with pizza.

DESTINATION
DAVIS

The Sudwerk Restaurant & Brewery (2001 Second Street) is a rare western US lager specialist, and one with ties to the brewing programme at the nearby University of California, making it a fine spot for sipping *märzen* and talking beer.

BRUERY, THE
Placentia, California

Brewer Patrick Rue punned on his name to create his brewery's moniker and

quickly earned a devoted following for his oft-quirky ales. Spicy-yeasty and faintly tart **Saison Rue ★★☆** and peppery, pear-ish **Mischief ★★☆** headline the core beers; while **Autumn Maple ★★★**, brewed with yams and complex with sweet maple, spice and yam flavours, and lightish, quenching, dryly tart Saison de Lente highlight seasonal offerings.

CRAFTSMAN BREWING
Pasadena, California

Under-the-radar brewery out of Pasadena, brewing a wide range of mostly draught-only ales. Unusual offerings include the herbaceous **Triple White Sage ★★★**, seasoned with wild white sage; and the suitably orangey **Orange Grove Ale ★★☆**.

DESTINATION
PASADENA

Lucky Baldwin's Pub (17 South Raymond Avenue), now with two sister bars, is a pioneering southern Californian beer bar opened by the late David Farnworth, offering a mix of British pub tradition and local and Belgian beers.

DEVIL'S CANYON BREWING
Belmont, California

Long-time brewery-for-hire in the San Francisco area, now making more of an effort with its own brands, including the variably peaty **Full Boar Scotch Ale ★★**, best when its smokiness is

UNITED STATES

restrained; **Deadicated Amber**
★★☆, a caramelly, nutty session
ale; the surprisingly soft and inviting
California Sunshine IPA ★★, with
only a moderate citrus hop character;
and work-in-progress **Belle** ★☆, a
Champagne-esque *bière brut* that
has real potential.

EL TORO BREWING
Morgan Hill, California

A family-owned and -operated brewery
and pub located south of San José.
Flagship **Poppy Jasper Amber Ale**
★★★ is a too-often-overlooked
caramelly ale with a fine drying and
bittering finish; **IPA** ★★☆ layers
orange and grapefruit hoppiness over
a firm malt backdrop; and **Negro
Oatmeal Stout** ★★☆ mixes smooth
oatiness with coffee flavours and light
vanilla-ish chocolate.

FIFTYFIFTY BREWING
Truckee, California

Nestled in the mountain town of
Truckee, near the Nevada border,
award-winning brewer Todd Ashman's
FiftyFifty Brewing creates snow-friendly
beers like the **Imperial Eclipse Stout**
★★★, with barrel-aged versions
matured in different used bourbon
barrels; the **Pappy Van Winkle**
★★★☆ and **Elijah Craig** ★★★☆
versions are particularly complex and
delicious. Other offerings include
RyePA ★★☆, with floral, citrus notes;
rich, bittersweet chocolate **Totality
Imperial Stout** ★★☆; and **Donner
Party Porter** ★★☆, a molasses,
espresso delight.

FIRESTONE WALKER BREWING
Paso Robles, California

Extraordinary Paso Robles brewery
specializing in all things barrel- and
blending-related. Flagship **DBA** ★★★☆
is remarkably rich for its modest strength
and arguably the most British beer
brewed in America; **Union Jack IPA**
★★★ blends juicy malt and orange
marmalade flavours with citrus hop;
and **Pale 31** ★★★ is light, mellow
and fruity. The Proprietor's Reserve line
includes **Double Jack** ★★★, with
resinous hops and overripe fruit; and the
always interesting, differently blended
Anniversary Series of ales, usually
stunning ★★★☆→★★★★.

GORDON BIERSCH BREWING
San José, California

Brewpub-chain-spawned brewery
based in northern California. German-
inspired beers include a lightly sweet,
crisply malty **Märzen** ★★★; stronger
Blonde Bock ★★, notable more for its
mouthfeel than its depth of character;
and a bready, slightly spicy **FestBier**
★★☆. Limited releases have included
a boozy, peppery, slightly candy-ish
Weizen Eisbock ★★.

GREEN FLASH BREWING
San Diego, California

San Diego brewery expanding at record
pace. Known for prodigiously hoppy ales
like the intensely piney **West Coast IPA**
★★★; the more intense but complex
Palate Wrecker ★★★; and the Belgian
tripel-American IPA mash-up known as

Le Freak ★★★☆. For all that bombast, it can still be nuanced in beers like **Fizzy Yellow Beer** ★★☆, a crisp and floral pilsner; and seasonal **Summer Saison** ★★, with honey-ish malt and spice.

DESTINATION
SAN DIEGO

Hamilton's (1521 30th Street) boasts a collection of 30 taps, including two casks, plus a litany of well-chosen bottles, making it one of southern California's ultimate beer destinations.

HERETIC BREWING
Pittsburg, California

Suitably unorthodox brewery located midway between San Francisco and Sacramento. Rye beer **Gramarye** ★★☆ combines bold hoppiness with rye spiciness and session beer strength; **Evil Twin Red Ale** ★★★ surprises with a richly hoppy aroma but maltier, fruity body; massive **Evil Cousin** ★★☆ is a hugely herbaceous, almost oily double IPA that's not dominatingly bitter; marvellously named **Shallow Grave** ★★★ is a porter with roasted fruit notes and well-disguised strength.

HIGH WATER BREWING
San Leandro, California

Veteran Californian brewer Steve Altimari's first self-run effort, contract-brewed at Drakes Brewing in San Leandro. Spiced winter ale **Blind Spot** ★★★ is gingerbready without

being confectionary; tropical-fruity **No Boundary IPA** ★★★ uses New Zealand hops to glorious effect; **Hop Riot IPA** ★★★ is strongly grapefruity but also oddly mellow; **Retribution** ★★★ is a fruity-hoppy double IPA swat at Altimari's former employers.

KARL STRAUSS BREWING
San Diego, California

Pioneering brewery producing southern California craft beer long before it was cool. Basic brands seem produced with mass market in mind, as with the sweetish, caramelly and slightly nutty **Karl Straus Amber** ★★. Speciality brands get more interesting: **Two Tortugas** ★★★, a spicy, toffee-ish fruitcake of an ale; spicy, tropical fruit and citrus **Blackball Belgian IPA** ★★☆; and various barrel-aged anniversary beers – including the bourbony **23rd Anniversary Old Ale** ★★★ – among them.

LAGUNITAS BREWING
Petaluma, California

Brewery north of San Francisco with a second facility in construction in Chicago.

Usually irreverent attitude held in check for **Pils ★★★**, a distinctly crisp yet floral lager, but in full evidence in potent **Hairy Eyeball ★★☆**, a malty, toffee-ish ale that stops just short of sweet. Chocolate and port-wine notes define dessert-like **Imperial Stout ★★★**; while basic **IPA ★★★** is dryly fruity and herbal; and **Brown Shugga ★★★** is a hoppy fruitcake of a beer.

LINDEN STREET BREWERY
Oakland, California

Draught-only brewery housed in an historic warehouse in Oakland. **Black Lager ★★★** is not a *schwarzbier*, but a crisp, tobacco-ish and lightly fruity cross of porter and *helles*; flagship **Urban People's Common Lager ★★☆** is a gently fruity brew in the steam beer style; **Deep Roots Red Lager ★★★** is a toasty, almost smoky lager with a refreshingly dry finish.

DESTINATION
OAKLAND

Beer Revolution (464 3rd Street), steps from Jack London Square, is technically a beer store, but when the crowds descend to sup from its 48 impressive draught taps, an observer could be forgiven for mistaking it for a great beer bar.

LOST ABBEY/PORT BREWING
San Marcos, California

Two storied breweries in one location, just north of San Diego. The Port line is more American in approach, evidenced by the strong and forcefully roasty and complex **Old Viscosity ★★★**; and perennially award-winning **Shark Attack★★★**, a "double red ale" of prodigious hoppiness. Belgian-inspired Lost Abbey brews include spiced and strong, but quenching, **Red Barn Ale ★★★**; barrel-aged, vanilla-streaked, complex and warming **Angel's Share ★★★★**; and the bold, lightly tart and deeply nuanced, although occasionally variable, **Cuvée de Tomme**, **★★★☆** when it is at its best.

MAD RIVER BREWING
Blue Lake, California

Hidden behind the Redwood Curtain in Humboldt County, about five hours north of San Francisco, in the tiny town of Blue Lake. Standouts include barley wine **John Barleycorn ★★★**, caramel-sweet with tons of US hops; **Serious Madness ★★☆**, a nutty, coffee-infused black ale; **Jamaica Red ★★** with toffee maltiness and spicy hopping; and **Steelhead Extra Stout ★★★**, a thick, creamy, chocolate delight.

MOONLIGHT BREWING
Santa Rosa, California

Santa Rosa draught-only, one-man operation is a true undiscovered gem of the San Francisco Bay area, with the toasty, complex **Death & Taxes ★★★☆** black lager a standout. **Reality Czeck ★★★** is a soft, floral/grassy pilsner; and **Bombay by Boat ★★☆** a worthy West Coast IPA with grapefruit notes. **Working For Tips** *gruut* **★★☆** features spicy redwood tips. New growler-filling station in downtown offers refills.

NAPA SMITH BREWERY
Napa, California

Legendary brewer Don Barkley was assistant brewer at New Albion, America's first microbrewery in 1977. Now brewing at Napa Smith, in the heart of wine country, with big beers like **Bonfire Imperial Porter ★★☆**, spicy, with nutty, figgy notes; **Grateful Dog Barleywine ★★**, a complex mélange of butterscotch, dark fruit and vanilla; **Lost Dog ★★**, a big tangy red ale; and **Hopageddon ★★☆**, a deliciously herbal Imperial oak-aged IPA, thick with pineapple, grapefruit and grassy hop character.

NORTH COAST BREWING
Fort Bragg, California

Long-standing brewery in far northern California. Best known for big beers, but excellent also when greater subtlety is called for, as in **Scrimshaw Pilsner ★★★**, a highly crisp and quaffable lager; and **Red Seal Ale ★★★☆**, a medium-bodied pale ale with a spicy

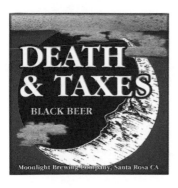

DEATH & TAXES
BLACK BEER
Moonlight Brewing Company, Santa Rosa CA

hop kick. Bolder offerings include the liquorice-accented, sweetly malty **Brother Thelonious ★★★**; Belgian-inspired **PranQster ★★★**, with dry fruitiness and a spicy finish; and **Old Rasputin Russian Imperial Stout ★★★☆**, with lusciously sweet and complex roastiness.

RUSSIAN RIVER BREWING
Santa Rosa, California

Much-lauded Santa Rosa brewery headed by Vinnie Cilurzo, presumed inventor of the double IPA, perhaps perfected in **Pliny the Elder ★★★★**, a startlingly hoppy beer with wondrous malty balance. Barrel-ageing produces many ales in the " tion" line, such as the earthy, sour cherry-ish, almost Burgundian **Supplication ★★★**; and subtly winey, tart and complex blond ale **Temptation ★★★**. **Redemption ★★★** eschews both barrel and strength for quaffability; while **Pliny the Younger ★★★** raises the bar in strength, hoppiness and cult appeal.

SIERRA NEVADA BREWING
Chico, California

Pioneering craft brewery located in the California interior. Flagship **Pale Ale ★★★★** arguably defined the American style, piney recent arrival **Torpedo ★★★** aims to do same to the IPA; **Stout ★★☆** balances sweet and bitter nicely; seasonal **Celebration ★★☆** remains a holiday landmark of hoppy aggression; **Bigfoot ★★★★** is a seminal hop-forward barley wine; new "Ovila" line of abbey ales shows promise.

SOCIETE BREWING
San Diego, California

Young San Diego brewery by veteran brewer Travis Smith, formerly with RUSSIAN RIVER and THE BRUERY, offering a trio of beer types: hoppy, Belgian-inspired and barrel-aged sour ales. Beers named for society's occupations, with the **Harlot** ★★★ a pale ale showing nice spicing and floral notes; **Pupil IPA** ★★☆ grassy and grapefruity dry; and **Everyman's IPA** ★★☆ a seriously complex, strong IPA with piney, tropical-fruit aromas.

STONE BREWING
Escondido, California

Mini-empire of craft brewing in southern California, built in part on the back of an unlikely flagship ale, **Arrogant Bastard** ★★★, combining hops, malt and alcohol in delicious near-balance, better still in its **Oaked Arrogant Bastard** ★★★☆ version. **IPA** ★★★ provides a lean, piney contrast, while **Ruination IPA** ★★☆ challenges with strongly assertive bitterness. Low-alcohol **Levitation Ale** ★★★ offers relative subtlety with characteristic Stone hoppiness, and numerous special releases and collaborations offer extreme variety.

TRUMER BRAUEREI (GAMBRINUS COMPANY)
Berkeley, California

This Berkeley brewery makes only one beer, based on German-style pilsner from sister brewery outside Salzburg, Austria. Since 2003, **Trumer Pils** ★★★☆, with beautiful golden colour, sweet, biscuity aromas and signature Saaz hop character, has won countless deserved awards, and is best on draught rather than in the green bottles.

UNCOMMON BREWERS
Santa Cruz, California

Santa Cruz brewer lives up to its name with unique interpretations of styles, all in 16-oz cans. Brands include a *dubbel*, **Siamese Twin** ★★★, with kaffir lime, lemongrass and coriander; **Golden State** ★★, a tasty, floral and tart Belgian-esque pale ale; **Bacon Brown** ★★, subtly smoky with fruit and nutty notes; and **Baltic Porter** ★★☆, with liquorice root and star anise, in equal parts traditional and inventive.

PACIFIC NORTHWEST

Despite California's claim to have the most breweries of any state, even it cannot boast the ubiquity of craft beer that is the reality in the Pacific Northwest, more specifically Washington and Oregon. Visit almost any town in either state, north or south, inland or coastal, and chances are high you will find a brewery. In all of the region, this commitment to craft beer is perhaps nowhere more in evidence than in Portland, OR, where it is estimated that nearly one out of every three beers consumed is craft.

Washington, home to the country's most prolific hop-growing region, the Yakima Valley, trails Oregon's mania for craft beer only slightly, and Alaska, for all its remoteness and transportation challenges, is not that far behind, with a brewery for roughly every 35,000 residents. Even Hawaii, included here but really standing alone geographically, has caught the craft brewery bug, with eight breweries of its own at the time of writing.

10 BARREL BREWING
Bend, Oregon

Home to several award-winning brewers in beer-centric Bend. Toasted malt restrains abundant tropical fruit grapefruit in **Apocalypse IPA ★★★**; India-style **Session Ale (ISA) ★★☆** deploys a blast of orange with grassy-lemon zest; rotating selection **Oregon Brown Ale ★★☆**, with a heavy dose of citrus, is not your grandfather's brown; winter's seasonal **Pray For Snow ★★★** is resplendent with dark fruits.

ALASKAN BREWING
Juneau, Alaska

Long-standing craft brewery in Juneau, perhaps most famous for its caramelly, smoky — although not intrusively so — and darkly fruity **Smoked Porter ★★★☆**. Year-round brews include **Amber ★★★**, meant to resemble an *altbier*, successfully so, with a faintly raisiny earthiness; a mildly fruity, slightly thin **Pale Ale ★★☆**; and a sweetish, mildly creamy **Stout ★★☆**. Occasional Pilot Series beers encourage creativity.

BARLEY BROWN'S BREWPUB
Baker City, Oregon

Multiple-award-winning brewery, with draught-only beers available mostly at the brewpub in Baker City and occasionally in Portland or Bend. Look for assertive yet deftly balanced **Turmoil Black IPA ★★★☆**, revealing hints of pine resin, grapefruit, roasted coffee and chocolate; effervescent, refreshing, citrus **Shredder's Wheat ★★★**, a multiple-award-winning American-style wheat beer; and citrus-dominant, slightly resinous **Pallet Jack IPA ★★☆**.

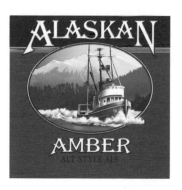

BEND BREWING
Bend, Oregon

A standout in this Oregon city of notable breweries, thanks to stellar seasonals. Locals' favourite **Hop Head Imperial IPA** ★★★ is a resin bomb with citrus rind. Fruity, caramel-rich **Outback X Old Ale** ★★★ and pink-lemonade-meets-grapefruit **Ching Ching Berliner Weiss** ★★☆ are two award-winning seasonals. Standards **Elk Lake IPA** ★★, grapefruity with hints of mango and orange marmalade, and caramel-nutty **Outback Old Ale** ★★ don't disappoint.

BLOCK 15 BREWERY & RESTAURANT
Corvallis, Oregon

Innovative brewery with strong barrel-ageing programme. Most beers are draught-only, some bottled. **Figgy Pudding** ★★★☆, a strong ale aged in brandy barrels, is a mouthful of figs, cinnamon, nutmeg; **Pappy's Dark** ★★★ is a strong ale replete with bourbon, baked bread, caramel; **Super Nebula Imperial Stout** ★★★ is aged on different origin-specific cocoa nibs each year, giving each version a slightly distinctive flavour.

BONEYARD BEER
Bend, Oregon

Draught-only brewery cranking out exceptional beers in Central Oregon. Many offerings are hop-heavy: **Hop Venom Double IPA** ★★★, a spicy-yet-resinous grapefruit bomb; and pineapple-citrus **RPM IPA** ★★★☆. Originally a THREE FLOYDS BREWING collaboration, **Armored Fist Imperial CDA** ★★★

keeps the citrus hops and deftly adds roasty depth. Tamer palates would enjoy **Diablo Rojo** ★★☆, an easy-going, slightly bready red ale.

BOUNDARY BAY BREWERY & BISTRO
Bellingham, Washington

Bellingham's oldest brewpub is still a locals' favourite known for assertive but balanced beers. Standouts include **Imperial IPA** ★★★, a hop bomb that sweetens up right before hitting the hop wall; **Oatmeal Stout** ★★☆ and the fruitier **Imperial Oatmeal Stout** ★★☆, both of which offer dark chocolate, espresso qualities with a silky backbone; and **ESB** ★★☆, a subtly hoppy brew with toasted nut notes.

BREAKSIDE BREWING
Portland, Oregon

Up-and-coming brewery celebrated for its one-offs and seasonals, also offering solid year-round beers. Multiple-award-winning **Dry Stout** ★★☆, with hints of Dutch-processed cocoa powder, could redefine the style; while Mexican-chocolaty **Aztec Ale** ★★★ could arguably define a new one. **English Session Brown** ★★★, with deep chocolate notes, proves brown doesn't mean boring; another seasonal, **Coconut Pumpkin Sweet Stout** ★★★, is very nearly a milkshake.

BRIDGEPORT BREWING (GAMBRINUS COMPANY)
Portland, Oregon

One of the Pacific Northwest's original breweries, now housed in a renovated

Portland complex that includes a bakery and restaurant. **India Pale Ale** ★★★ might seem tame by today's standards, but remains a classic; **Blue Heron Pale Ale** ★★ is lightish and a bit too fruity for some; annual **Ebenezer Ale** ★★☆ is a restrained model of maltiness; while **Old Knucklehead** ★★★ is a warming, raisiny barley wine.

DESTINATION PORTLAND

Bailey's Taproom (213 SW Broadway) might be small, but its attention to detail and hi-tech draught system – even viewable online – places it at the front of the highly saturated Rose City beer scene.

BURNSIDE BREWING
Portland, Oregon

Standard selections on draught and in bottles. More creative beers overshadow the expected IPA and other hoppy brews, like standards **Sweet Heat** ★★★☆, a Caribbean-chutney of a wheat beer with apricots and Scotch Bonnet peppers; and silky smooth, herbal **Oatmeal Pale Ale** ★★☆. Balanced, herbal, nutty **Stock Ale** ★★☆ and dry-finishing **Stout** ★★★ are solid selections for the less adventurous imbibers.

CASCADE BREWING BARREL HOUSE
Portland, Oregon

Spin-off from Portland beer veteran Art Larrance's Raccoon Lodge, specializing in barrel-conditioned ales. Beers are ever changing, but more regular offerings include the tart and funky, apricot-almond **Apricot** ★★★; a **Kriek** ★★★ that begins with cherry pie and grows progressively more tart to a spicy-dry finish; the grapey, vanilla-accented **The Vine** ★★★, aged on Muscat grapes; and the complex, peppery-fruity **Strawberry** ★★★.

CHUCKANUT BREWERY & KITCHEN
Bellingham, Washington

State-of-the-art craft brewery with roots in German lager styles located in northern Washington's college town of Bellingham. Only available on draught, award-winning beers include nearly flawless, clean-finishing **Vienna** ★★★ with toffee and caramel notes; crisp, slightly grassy German-style **Pilsner** ★★★; and softly subtle, fruity yet refreshing **Kölsch** ★★★. Intermittently brewed, smooth-as-silk and toffee-ish **Bock** ★★☆ is a delightful winter seasonal.

COMMONS BREWERY
Portland, Oregon

Small and ambitious new Portland brewery, focused mostly on draught sales. Early flagship is **Urban Farmhouse Ale** ★★, a spicy-sweet ale that may be a bit too much of the latter; irregularly released **Golden Harvest** ★★☆ is given an unusual floral jolt by the addition of lemon balm; *saison*-ish **Haver Bier** ★★★ is creamy with pronounced hop and a spicy finish; and **Flemish Kiss** ★★☆ is mildly tart and appley.

DESCHUTES BREWING
Bend, Oregon

Tremendously accomplished brewery. So many beers that a flagship is hard to identify, but perhaps it's floral, lemony-spicy **Mirror Pond Pale Ale** ★★☆ or mocha-ish **Black Butte Porter** ★★★☆, surely an American classic; or newer, Meyer lemony **Red Chair NWPA** ★★★. Fans anxiously await the annual return of fruity-tart **The Dissident**, ★★☆ at release and improving with age, and the stunning, multi-layered, high-strength anniversary edition of **Black Butte** ★★★.

DOUBLE MOUNTAIN BREWERY
Hood River, Oregon

Brewery better known for creative seasonal offerings than its solid standards. Piney-citrus **Hop Lava IPA** ★★☆, Northwest-hoppy **Kölsch** ★★☆ and lemon-zesty **The Vaporizor Pale Ale** ★★☆ are notable year-round beers. Winter favourite **Fa La La La La** ★★★ offers plenty of piney hop, but on a prodigiously malty base. A variety of seasonals like tart **Devil's Kriek** ★★★ reveals a flair with fruit.

ELYSIAN BREWING
Seattle, Washington

Long-time Seattle brewer Dick Cantwell and partners spun a single brewpub into a mini-empire that includes a production association with NEW BELGIUM BREWING. Beers at the pubs are many and diverse, but bottled line-up always includes the floral-spicy **Avatar Jasmine IPA** ★★★; the assertively hoppy but balanced **Immortal IPA** ★★★; and **Bête Blanche** ★★★, a *tripel* that progresses smoothly from sweet pear to dry, bittering hop.

DESTINATION
SEATTLE

Brouwer's Cafe (400 N 35th Street) is a beer-obsessed bar and restaurant in the city's Fremont district, with emphasis placed on Belgium in both food and drink, and one of the best draught systems in the whole of the United States.

FORT GEORGE BREWERY
Astoria, Oregon

Situated on the exact location in Astoria of the first American-owned settlement on the Pacific coast. Assertive, grapefruity **Vortex IPA** ★★★ is named for a tornado owners encountered when hauling their brewery cross-country. Crisp, grassy **1811 Pre-Prohibition Lager** ★★☆ honours the year Astoria was founded. Dark-chocolaty **Cavatica Imperial Stout** ★★☆ lends itself to many draught-only iterations; **Sunrise Oatmeal Pale Ale**

★★★ frames grapefruit-grassy hops with silky smoothness.

FULL SAIL BREWING
Hood River, Oregon

Employee-owned brewery on Hood River in Oregon, the fourth largest in the state. The Session line of beers is quaffable but mostly of limited interest, unlike main-line beers like the dry and mildly spicy **Amber** ★★☆; the rounded, spicy-citrus-peach **IPA** ★★☆; and **LTD Series Black Bock** ★★★, a strong and chocolaty, but curiously light on the palate, seasonal brew. Other occasional brews, like the Brewmaster Reserve series, are worth watching.

HAIR OF THE DOG BREWING
Portland, Oregon

Born in a Portland industrial park, this small brewery that bats way above its weight is now located closer to downtown. Flagship strong ale **Adam** ★★★☆ takes a gingerbready start through roasted apple and raisin to a long, warming finish; earthy-spicy **Greg** ★★☆ is fortified with squash; golden **Fred** ★★★ offers sweet yellow fruit tempered by growing hoppiness; and seasonal barley wine **Doggie Claws** ★★★ is a liquid fruitcake with bite.

HOPWORKS URBAN BREWERY
Portland, Oregon

Certified organic brewery with two locations. Intensely resinous-orange **Hopworks IPA** ★★★ is a local favourite; while citrus **Lager** ★★☆

suits gentler palates. Highly anticipated seasonals include piney, grapefruity **Abominable Winter Ale** ★★★; **Secession Cascadian Dark Ale** ★★★, which balances roastiness and grapefruit bitterness with supportive malts; and fiercely orange-hoppped, sticky-malt **Ace of Spades Imperial IPA** ★★★.

DESTINATION
PORTLAND

Horse Brass Pub (4534 SE Belmont Street), founded by the late Don Younger, was a craft beer destination even before the phrase "craft beer" was born, and remains a pre-eminent beer destination in a city full of brewpubs and beer bars.

KONA BREWING (CRAFT BREW ALLIANCE/AB INBEV)
Kailua-Kona, Hawaii

Father-and-son-founded brewery now producing beer on Hawaii's Big Island and by commission in two mainland locations. Lightly sweet **Longboard Lager** ★★ is the flagship; while more unconventional brews like **Pipeline Porter** ★★☆, flavoured to intensity with Kona coffee, and **Koko Brown** ★★☆, brewed with toasted coconut, provide greater complexity and interest.

LAURELWOOD PUBLIC HOUSE & BREWERY
Portland, Oregon

Mini-empire with several locations, including two at Portland's airport.

Flagship **Workhorse IPA** ★★★☆, classically Northwestern with grapefruit and pine notes, continues to draw fans; seasonals **Organic Deranger Imperial Red** ★★★, with toffee backbone and citrus-pine highlights, and floral-grapefruit **Green Elephant IPA** ★★★ showcase how well made organics can be. Softer **Hooligan Brown Ale** ★★☆ offers chocolate-nutty notes.

LOGSDON FARMHOUSE ALES
Hood River, Oregon

Overseen by the founder of Wyeast Laboratories, this young brewery is already shaping directions for farmhouse-style beers. Complex, fruity, spicy **Seizoen** ★★★ balances hop character with malt; **Seizoen Bretta** ★★★ offers a crisper, drier finish; seasonal **Peche 'n' Brett** ★★★ features lightly acidic peach flavours; lemongrass-herbal **Kili Wit** ★★☆ is an interesting example of a Belgian-style wheat beer.

MAUI BREWING
Lahaina, Hawaii

Award-winning brewery on Hawaii's second-largest island. Tropical-fruity, floral **Big Swell IPA** ★★☆ is what an exotic island brewery's IPA should be. Coriander-heavy **Le Perouse White** ★★☆ uses local mandarin oranges. Robust, dessert-in-a-glass **CoCoNut PorTer** ★★★ focuses on toasted coconut and chocolate; and draught-only, caramel-rich **Hawaii 90 Wee Heavy** ★★☆ proves the brewery makes some heavy-hitters despite the heat.

MIDNIGHT SUN BREWING
Anchorage, Alaska

Anchorage-based brewery steeped in the frontier spirit of Alaska. Winter is embraced through **Arctic Devil Barley Wine** ★★★, a malt-forward and age-worthy brew; while **Sockeye Red IPA** ★★☆ offers a year-round, hoppy yin to the barley wine's yang. The new addition of canned beer to the portfolio assures that beer quality remains in the lower 48.

NO-LI BREWHOUSE
Spokane, Washington

Northern Lights Brewing until a threatened lawsuit hastened a name change, this Spokane, Washington, operation is one to watch. Recently retooled ales include the faintly woodsy **Silent Treatment Pale Ale** ★★☆; the citrus, almost oily **Born & Raised IPA** ★★☆; a quaffable, fruity **Crystal Bitter Ale** ★★; and pine-forest and toasted lemon peel **Jet Star Imperial IPA** ★★★.

OAKSHIRE BREWING
Eugene, Oregon

Homebrewing brothers turned community-minded pro brewery in Eugene, Oregon. Year-round brands include a dry and toasty **Amber ★★☆**, with both nutty and citrus hop notes; and a predominantly citrus **Watershed IPA ★★★**. Seasonal **O'Dark:30 ★★★** is a sweet-to-bitter, chocolaty black IPA.

PELICAN PUB & BREWERY
Pacific City, Oregon

Thrice "brewery of the year" at the Great American Beer Festival, this coastal Oregon brewery offers an **Imperial Pelican Ale ★★★** that smacks the senses with citrus and pine while maintaining a surprising balance. Also available bottled: seasonal **Mother of All Storms ★★★☆**, a barley wine bundle of bourbon-barrel influence; year-round **Tsunami Stout ★★★**, offering dark chocolate-cream notes; and bready, fruity **Kiwanda Cream Ale ★★☆**.

PIKE BREWING
Seattle, Washington

Teaching lab for many accomplished Pacific Northwest brewers, this brewpub has gone through many guises en route to its present and somewhat iconic status. Classic Pike brews include nutty-fruity-floral **Pale ★★**; rich and robust **Extra Stout** (formerly XXXXX Stout) **★★★**; and malt-intense **Old Bawdy Barley Wine ★★★**. Newer are the sessionable **Naughty Nellie ★★☆**; and fruity, perhaps overly roasty **Tandem Double Ale ★★☆**.

DESTINATION SEATTLE

The Tap House Grill (1506 6th Avenue), perched on a hilltop, is the highest beer destination in Seattle, but its 160 taps make it well worth the climb.

ROGUE ALES
Newport, Oregon

Remarkably prolific brewery on the Oregon coast, known for big beers and silk-screened labels. **Juniper Pale Ale ★★★** fuses gin-like spice with spicy hop; **Mocha Porter ★★☆** is creamy and well named; **Morimoto Soba Ale ★★☆** is toasty with buckwheat and curiously savoury. Own farm provides ingredients for **Rogue Farms OREgasmic Ale ★★☆**, grapefruity and biscuity; and the roasty but medium-bodied **Rogue Farms Dirtoir Black Lager ★★★**.

SILVER CITY BREWING
Bremerton, Washington

This relatively unknown gem, located opposite Puget Sound from Seattle, continues to gain accolades without fanfare. Flagship **Fat Scotch Ale ★★☆** offers molasses notes with a touch of peat; newcomer **St Florian IPA ★★☆** balances malt with pine and citrus; the resinous, intensely hoppy **Whoop Pass DIPA ★★★** is locals' favourite; polar opposites **Ziggy Zoggy Summer Lager ★★☆**, a honey-like *kellerbier*, and limited-release **Imperial Stout ★★★** showcase brewery's breadth.

UPRIGHT BREWING
Portland, Oregon

A Portland brewery that combines
an admiration of French and Belgian
farmhouse brewing with an appreciation
of jazz great Charles Mingus (really).
Its beers are named in reference to
their starting gravities. The light-bodied
Four ★★ is citrus and peppery, with a
tangy finish; the herbal, hoppy
Five ★★★ is dryly appetizing; the
rye-based **Six** ★★☆ is toasty and
suitably spicy from the rye; and the
highly fruity **Seven** ★★★ is both
eye-opening and warming.

**WIDMER BROTHERS BREWING
(CRAFT BREW ALLIANCE/AB INBEV)**
Portland, Oregon

Best known for its near-opaque and
unBavarian, lemony **Hefeweizen** ★★,
Widmer Brothers lately stepped up the
interest quotient in its beers. While
peachy-pineappley **Nelson Imperial
IPA** ★★★ is worth seeking, Widmer
shines with seasonals: **Citra Blonde
Summer Brew** ★★☆, a lemony
session ale; and caramel-citrus **Brrr
Seasonal Ale** ★★☆. Occasional
Brothers Reserve and Rotating IPA
series are both worth seeking.

ROCKY MOUNTAINS & THE MIDWEST

Without doubt, the heart and soul of Rocky Mountain craft brewing is
Colorado. One of the country's earliest breweries (**BOULDER BEER**) was founded
there; the craft beer trade group, the Brewers Association, is based there;
the state ranks third and fourth respectively in total number of breweries
and breweries per population; and the country's most important beer
event, the Great American Beer Festival, is held in Denver every autumn.
Outside Colorado, the more sparsely populated mountain states might boast
correspondingly fewer breweries – a mere dozen in Wyoming, for instance –
but when weighted on a population basis prove that interest in craft brewing
is practically a mountain region trait.

The Midwestern equivalent of Colorado is perhaps Michigan, home to more
than 100 breweries, although residents of Illinois, Wisconsin and Missouri

might wish to take issue with that characterization. While the region was slow to take to craft beer – the city of Chicago, for example, was famously resistant to anything other than the familiar big brewery labels throughout most of the 1980s and 1990s – the Midwest has since the start of the new century made up for lost time to become, as it was once in the early and mid-20th century, an important centre of brewing in the United States.

3 SHEEPS BREWING
Sheboygan, Wisconsin

Young and promising brewery mixing fringe beer styles with great names. **Rebel Kent the First Amber Ale** ★★★ is a spicy and very dry mix of sessionable Belgian (*enkel*) and British (bitter) styles; **Really Cool Waterslides IPA** ★★☆ is a piney but mellow take on the style; and the inevitable **Baaad Boy Black Wheat Ale** ★★ is mocha-ish and lightly fruity. Brewery is draught-only.

4 HANDS BREWING
St. Louis, Missouri

Brewery, and tasting room, located short walk from Busch Stadium in St. Louis. Hop-centric beers like the fruity and floral

Reprise Centennial Red Ale ★★☆ are most popular, but diverse offerings include **Smoked Pigasus** ★★☆, a seamless smoked rye maple porter; **Cuvee Ange** ★★★, fermented with wild yeast, raspberries and blackberries in wine barrels; refreshing **Prussia Berliner Weiss** ★★★; and chocolate-rich **Cast Iron Oatmeal Brown** ★★.

5 RABBIT BREWING
Bedford Park, Illinois

Brewed in suburban Chicago, beers from first Latin American-inspired brewery in the country reflect the flavours of that culture. **5 Lizard Latin-Style Witbier** ★★★☆ is made with lime peel, passion fruit and spices, with New Zealand hops accentuating tropical flavours. Ancho chillies add a smoky twist to **5 Vulture Oaxacan-Style Dark Ale** ★★★; and hibiscus and ginger keep the warming **Huitzi Midwinter Ale** ★★★ floral and refreshing. Dulce de leche and various spices make **Vide y Muerte** ★★ a most unusual Oktoberfest.

ARCADIA BREWING
Battle Creek, Michigan

British-inspired brewery in Battle Creek, Michigan, a town better known as the home of Kellogg's cereals. Year-round picks include **Loch Down Scotch Ale** ★★★, raisiny, rich and roasty; the dry, peppery-earthy **Sky High Rye** ★★☆; and the pine-needles and caramel-apples **Hopmouth Double IPA** ★★☆. Irregular standouts are the liquorice and dark chocolaty **Imperial Stout** ★★☆; and outstanding, vanilla-chocolate-spicy-raisin **Barrel Aged Shipwreck Porter** ★★★☆.

AUGUST SCHELL BREWING
New Ulm, Minnesota

Venerable brewery dating from 1860 in New Ulm, Minnesota. Produces large quantities of forgettable, adjunct-y "Grain Belt" beers, but also legitimate craft offerings like the crisply malty **Pils** ★★★; the bready and surprisingly well-bodied, 150th anniversary brew, **Hopfenmalz** ★★☆; and the seasonal, perhaps overly full and malty **Schmaltz's Alt** ★★.

AVERY BREWING
Boulder, Colorado

Boulder, Colorado, brewery founded in 1993. First known for hoppy ales like still-popular, grapefruity **India Pale Ale** ★★★, but the years have seen a branching out to beers like the bold, hop-forward **Hog Heaven** ★★★ barley wine; the molasses and plum **The Reverend** ★★★; the variable-by-vintage Imperial stout **The Czar** ★★☆; and the intensely hoppy **duganA IPA** ★★★. Barrel-Aged series beers like the peppery, grapey, cinnamon **Dépuceleuse** ★★★★ are cause for excitement.

BELL'S BREWERY
Kalamazoo, Michigan

Instigator of the Michigan craft beer explosion, based in Kalamazoo. Wide range of beers from the apricoty, herbal **Amber Ale** ★★★ to the hops-and-honey **Hopslam** ★★★. Perhaps best known, however, for an almost endless parade of black ales, from the **Porter** ★★★, chocolaty and sessionable, to the bigger, roast-and-coffee **Kalamazoo Stout** ★★★, to the potent, intense and darkly fruity **Expedition Stout** ★★★☆.

BIG SKY BREWING
Missoula, Montana

Moose Drool Brown Ale ★★★, malt-rich and balanced, offers more than just a memorable name used to sell tee-shirts in nearby Montana national parks. Other equally solid brews include: **Big Sky IPA** ★★☆, caramelly-sweet upfront, then piney and floral; the chewy **Ivan the**

Terrible Imperial Stout ★★★; Bobo's Robust Porter ★★☆, dark, roasty and dessert-like; and Cowboy Coffee Porter ★★☆, espresso-like but restrained.

BOULDER BEER
Boulder, Colorado

Colorado's original craft brewery, founded in a goat shed in Boulder. Psychedelic designs adorn the labels of beers like the grapefruity, piney Mojo IPA ★★☆; the dry-hopped and fragrant Hazed & Infused ★★☆; and the seasonal, thinly malty double IPA Mojo Risin' ★★.

BOULEVARD BREWING
Kansas City, Missouri

The little Kansas City brewery that could is now one of the largest craft operations in the States. Regular brands include the accurately named 80-Acre Hoppy Wheat Beer ★★☆ and citrus, six-hop Single-Wide IPA ★★☆, but it's the Smokestack series beers that attract most attention, like the lemony spice of Tank 7 Farmhouse Ale ★★★; the peppery, tangy Saison Brett ★★★; and the warming but not weighty Harvest Dance Wheat Wine ★★★☆.

BRECKENRIDGE BREWING
Denver, Colorado

First a ski-town brewpub, one of Colorado's first, now a Denver brewery known for its YouTube spoofs of industrial brewers' advertising. Line includes Avalanche Ale ★★, an archetypal Colorado amber; the more

assertive and grapefruity 471 IPA ★★☆ and 471 ESB ★★★, both part of a Small Batch series of oversized beers; and Oatmeal Stout ★★, with roasted notes balancing abundant chocolate flavours.

BREWERY VIVANT
Grand Rapids, Michigan

Young brewery and pub in Grand Rapids, Michigan, fearlessly canning Belgian and northern French farmhouse-style ales. Brands include the hoppy, spicy orange-apple Triomphe ★★★, billed a "Belgian IPA"; the honey-ish Contemplation ★★, brewed with Michigan honey; the mildly barnyardy, citrus-fruit-salad Zaison ★★☆; and the dry, supremely quenching Farm Hand ★★★.

CAPITAL BREWERY
Middleton, Wisconsin

Early Wisconsin craft brewery, located just outside the state capital, Madison. Best when brewing German-influenced beers like slightly grainy, dryish Pilsner ★★ or faintly roasty, toasted malt Dark ★★★. Special edition beers like Autumnal Fire ★★★, a *doppelbock* with toffee-like maltiness and vague spicy-mocha notes, provide variety and excitement.

CROOKED STAVE BREWING
Denver, Colorado

Founder Chad Yakobson wrote his master's dissertation on brettanomyces, and different species of that "wild" yeast are a part of every beer at this Denver brewery, most the result of blending beers aged in wood barrels. They are generally tart, untamed and refreshingly dry, such as the tropical-fruity (tangerine, pineapple) **St Bretta** ★★★ and hazy golden **L'Brett d'Or** ★★★; or two *saisons*, **Saison Vielle Artisanal** ★★☆, low in alcohol and rustic, and **Surette** ★★★, fruity, earthy and acidic.

DRY DOCK BREWING
Aurora, Colorado

Fast-growing brewery founded in 2005 in Aurora, Colorado, next door to a suburban Denver homebrew shop. Excels at traditional European styles such as the light yet spicy **Hefeweizen** ★★★; and toasty **HMS Victory Amber** ★★☆, rather like a strong American take on a best bitter. **Vanilla Porter** ★★, mixing chocolate with prominent vanilla flavours, and **Paragon Apricot Blonde** ★★☆, crisp and fruity, find their own way.

EPIC BREWING
Salt Lake City, Utah

Unlike Utah's other breweries that make low-alcohol beer to serve in their brewpubs, EPIC brews only strong and stronger beers. **Hopulent IPA** ★★★ has an immense citrus character with bracing bitterness; **Brainless on Peaches** ★★★ is peachy, with Champagne-like notes; **Big Bad Baptist Imperial Stout** ★★☆, infused with coffee, gets aged in bourbon barrels; while **825 State Stout** ★★★ is a mocha delight; and **Utah Sage Saison** ★★★ offers tropical-fruit and peppery notes.

FOUNDERS BREWING
Grand Rapids, Michigan

Stubbornly enduring Michigan brewery with a growing international reputation. Seamless **Centennial IPA** ★★★☆ is both complex and quaffable; speciality **Curmudgeon Old Ale** ★★★☆ is decadent in its youthful maltiness and built for ageing; **Red's Rye PA** ★★★ balances citrus, spice and peppery accents; **Breakfast Stout** ★★☆ is soothing and warming, and outstanding in its stronger, barrel-aged **KBS** ★★★☆ and **CBS** ★★★★ versions.

FOUR PEAKS BREWING
Tempe, Arizona

Across a broad range, the core beers exhibit the balance you'd expect from recipes co-concocted by a British expat brewer. Flagship **Kilt Lifter Scottish-Style Ale** ★★★ is rich and a touch smoky; **8 Street Ale** ★★ is a mellow best bitter; **Oatmeal Stout** ★★☆ offers roasty malt and layered complexity; and **Hop Knot IPA** ★★☆ is floral with lingering fruity flavours.

FUNKWERKS BREWING
Fort Collins, Colorado

One of the smallest Fort Collins breweries, best known for *saisons*, but offering other Belgian-influenced beers like the golden **Deceit** ★★☆, a powerful combination of fruits and spices. Straightahead **Saison** ★★★ is earthy, complex, but delicate; the more robust **Tropic King** ★★☆, described as Imperial, is intense, filled with tropical-fruit aromas and flavours.

GOOSE ISLAND BEER (AB INBEV)
Chicago, Illinois

Brewpub expanded to two pubs plus a production brewery, then sold in 2011. Certain brands such as the mildly fruity **Honkers** ★★☆ now being brewed at other ABI facilities, but not (so far) Vintage Ales series beers like the Orval-inspired **Matilda** ★★☆ or the sparkling, somewhat winey **Sophie** ★★☆. Pioneering bourbon-barrel-aged brew, **Bourbon County Stout** ★★★☆, now part of a line of Bourbon County beers.

DESTINATION CHICAGO

The Hopleaf (5148 N Clark Street) is a wonderfully stocked beer bar in front and a commendable brasserie-style restaurant in the back, with slight Belgian leanings throughout.

GRAND TETON BREWING
Victor, Idaho

Idaho brewer based at the foot of the Teton Mountains, near Yellowstone National Park. Signature beers include **Bitch Creek ESB** ★★☆, which stands for Extra Special Brown, rather than Bitter, and is not American-hop-shy; and **Teton Ale** ★★☆, with toffee malt and spicy hoppiness. Brewers' series ales include the nutty, softly spicy **Pursuit of Hoppiness** ★★☆, an Imperial red ale; and the coffee-ish, herbal **Black Cauldron Imperial Stout** ★★☆.

GREAT DIVIDE BREWING
Denver, Colorado

Downtown 1994 brewery, now with a tasting room attached. Perhaps best known for the powerful yet approachable **Yeti Imperial Stout** ★★★ and all its many variations, including the whisky-accented **Oak Aged Yeti** ★★★☆. **Denver Pale Ale** ★★☆ provides a sessionable, perfumey contrast to the monster stout; as does the even lighter, delicate **Samurai** ★★★. **Titan IPA** ★★★ provides the obligatory wallop of hops.

GREAT LAKES BREWING
Cleveland, Ohio

Brewpub and production brewery that played a large part in the revival of Cleveland's Ohio City neighbourhood. **Dortmunder Gold Lager** ★★★☆ is an exceptional example of a style rarely brewed even in Germany; **Elliot Ness Amber Lager** ★★★ balances sweet and bitter and strength wonderfully; **Burning River Pale Ale** ★★☆ is a citrus quaffer; and perennial award-winner **Edmund Fitzgerald Porter** ★★★ is mocha-ish and satisfying.

GREAT NORTHERN BREWING
Whitefish, Montana

Montana brewery founded by the great-great grandson of Pacific Northwest brewing legend, Henry Weinhard. Flagship brand is **Black Star Double Hopped Lager** ★★☆, curiously reserved for a beer so described; while winter seasonal **Snow Ghost Winter Lager** ★★★ draws attention with its drying, roasty-nutty character and big malt-derived flavours.

HALF ACRE BEER
Chicago, Illinois

Largest of a new wave of Chicago breweries, sales fuelled by success of 16-oz "tallboy" cans, starting with **Daisy Cutter** ★★★☆, a pale ale brimming with grapefruit and pine; **Over Ale** ★★☆, a nutty chocolate brown ale; and crisp **Gossamer** ★★☆, a golden ale. Many specialities, like spicy rye stout, **Baumé** ★★★; and **Ambrosia** ★★, a wheat ale laced with oranges and hibiscus.

JOLLY PUMPKIN ARTISAN ALES
Dexter, Michigan

Idiosyncratic brewery near Detroit dedicated to oak-ageing and bottle-conditioning its beers. Stylistically unclassifiable beers include **La Roja** ★★★, a spicy mix of berry and vanilla notes with warming strength; fragrant and pineappley **Oro de Calabaza** ★★☆; cocoa, cinnamon and dried fruit **Maracaibo Especial** ★★★; and **Bam Bière** ★★★, a dry, tart and refreshing session beer that has spawned a line of similar Bam beers.

KUHNHENN BREWING
Warren, Michigan

Family-owned, Detroit-area hardware store that adjusted to the arrival of a "big box" store by transforming into a highly regarded brewery. Most famous for the potent and densely fruity **Raspberry Eisbock** ★★★☆, but worth noting, too, for the similarly powerful **Fourth Dementia Olde Ale** ★★★, caramelly and cherry-ish; and the highly hoppy, not-quite-balanced **American IPA** ★★☆.

LA CUMBRE BREWING
Albuquerque, New Mexico

Husband-and-wife brewery founded in 2009 in Albuquerque, New Mexico. Core brands include the piney and faintly nutty **Elevated IPA** ★★☆; the dry, Germanic **South Peak Pilsner** ★★☆; and the roasty, raisin-and-spice **Malpais Stout** ★★★. Limited release **Fievre d'Abricot** ("Apricot Fever") ★★☆ shows skill in complex, non-sweet fruit beer.

LAKEFRONT BREWING
Milwaukee, Wisconsin

Early Milwaukee brewery offering
excellent core beers and what may be
the best brewery tour in the business.
Their lagers remain a strength, with
Riverwest Stein Beer ★★★ teasing
with malty sweetness before finishing
dry; seasonal **Pumpkin Lager** ★★★
spicy but never overly so; and perfumey
Oktoberfest ★★★, an off-dry mix of
toffee and spice. Nutmeg and muddled
fruit notes of **Bridge Burner Special
Reserve Ale** ★★★ show skill at the
top of the fermenter.

LEFT HAND BREWING
Longmont, Colorado

The red left hand on its labels is one
of the most distinctive symbols in craft
beer, the brewery's name taken from
Arapahoe Chief Niwot or "Left Hand".
Their deep line-up includes **Sawtooth
Ale** ★★★, a soft but assertive special
bitter; **SmokeJumper** ★★☆, a
powerful smoked porter; **Milk Stout**
★★★, creamy in both its regular and
nitro versions; and the chocolaty **Black**

Jack Porter ★★☆. The intriguing
Fade to Black series highlights limited
edition black beers.

MARBLE BREWERY
Albuquerque, New Mexico

Young brewery founded by a trio of
brewpub veterans in Albuquerque, New
Mexico. **Red Ale** ★★ is replete with
rooty and resinous herbs and citrus oils,
almost an IPA in red ale form; while the
India Pale Ale ★★★ is spicy, juicy in
its fruitiness and admirably restrained in
bitterness. Much promise for the future.

MILWAUKEE BREWING
Milwaukee, Wisconsin

Durable late-1990s brewpub now a
production brewery not far from the city's
Historic Third Ward. Flagship **Louie's
Demise** ★★☆ is a toasty, toffee apple-
ish amber ale; fruity **Hop Happy IPA**
★★☆ is curiously subdued for a beer
with such a name; **Pull Chain Pale Ale**
★★ is similarly understated; and milk
stout **Polish Moon** ★★★ builds and
builds in dark chocolaty maltiness to a
long and lingering finish.

NEBRASKA BREWING
Papillion, Nebraska

Brewery making a solid range of beers, such as the peppery **Infinite Wit** ★★, but grabs attention with **Hop God** ★★☆, a double IPA fermented with Belgian yeast, peachy, citrus and bitter; **Melange A Trois** ★★★, a strong Belgian-inspired blond that spends six months in Chardonnay barrels; and barrel-aged **Apricot Au Poivre Saison** ★★, earthy and peppery.

NEW BELGIUM BREWING
Fort Collins, Colorado

Sustainability-obsessed (in a good way) brewery based in Fort Collins, Colorado, and building in North Carolina. Basic amber ale **Fat Tire** ★★ pays many of the bills, but newer **Ranger IPA** ★★★ is building fans with its fruity, piney hop character. **Trippel** ★★★, with its tangerine, spice and warming alcohol, and chocolaty, apricot **Abbey** ★★☆ fly the Belgian flag, while Lips of Faith beers like the tart, dryly fruity **La Folie** ★★★☆ excite experiential drinkers.

NEW GLARUS BREWING
New Glarus, Wisconsin

Famed brewery near Madison, Wisconsin, frustrating aficionados everywhere by distributing only within the state. Light ale **Spotted Cow** ★☆ pays the bills, but allows for delights like the intensely fruity **Wisconsin Belgian Red** ★★★★ (replaced in 2012 by the also stunning **Serendipity** ★★★☆, but hoped to return); the pleasantly restrained black

IPA **Black Top** ★★☆; and seasonals such as the almost Scotch-whisky-esque **Winter Warmer** ★★★.

NEW HOLLAND BREWING
Holland, Michigan

Brewery and distillery on the shores of Lake Michigan, in the small town of Holland. Flagship is the dried-peach and citrus **Mad Hatter IPA** ★★★, now the heart of a whole Hatter line of brands, including the spicy-fruity, almost brandy-ish **Imperial Hatter** ★★★. Other ales include the plummy, bracing **Dragon's Milk Ale** ★★☆; **Black Tulip Tripel** ★★★, which begins fruity and sweet but ends with a hoppy statement; and the light and *kölsch*-like **Full Circle** ★★☆.

O'SO BREWING
Plover, Wisconsin

Tiny brewery grown slightly larger in Plover, Wisconsin, 160km (100 miles) north of Madison, dedicated to brewing beer "differently". **3rd Wheel Summer Ale** ★★★ does just that, with floral rosehips accenting a light and quenching body; while **Hop Whoopin' IPA** ★★☆ steers a slightly more conventional course with grapefruity hoppiness. Special brews show promise for the future.

ODELL BREWING
Fort Collins, Colorado

Family-founded brewery in Fort Collins, Colorado, the second to open in the state. Original draught-only focus was dropped to bottle brews like earthy, citrus and apple **5 Barrel Ale ★★★**; the rich, sweet but never overbearing **90 Shilling ★★★**; the lightly creamy, mocha-ish **Cutthroat Porter ★★☆**; and the lime- and grapefruit-accented **IPA ★★☆**. The 4 Pack series beers up the ante in strength and body.

OSKAR BLUES BREWERY
Longmont, Colorado

Orchestrator of the "canned beer apocalypse", pioneering the canning of craft beer in Longmont, Colorado. First in the can was **Dale's Pale Ale ★★★**, a balanced, toasty-citrus ale, followed by the toffee maltiness of **Old Chub Scotch Ale ★★★**; **Ten Fidy ★★☆**, a bold and brash Imperial stout; the rather straightforward, sweetish **Mama's Little Yella Pils ★★**; and the herbaceous, almost chewy **Gubna Imperial IPA ★★☆**.

PERENNIAL ARTISAN ALES
St. Louis, Missouri

Southside St. Louis brewery that often uses yeasts from Belgium and locally sourced ingredients such as rhubarb and squash, resulting in beers like the summer seasonal **Peach Berliner Weisse ★★☆**, fermented on local peaches. Dizzying range: the delightfully dry and Belgian-esque **Hommel Bier ★★★**; **Abraxas ★★★**, an Imperial stout packed with spices and Ancho chillies; **Fantastic Voyage ★★★**, an Imperial milk stout aged on coconut flakes; and **Black Walnut Dunkel ★★☆**, a *dunkelweisse* made with Missouri walnuts.

REVOLUTION BREWING
Chicago, Illinois

Brewpub in Chicago's Logan Square neighbourhood opened a production facility a short distance away in 2012. As adept at bold beers like **Anti-Hero IPA ★★☆**, a resiny, fruity/pine punch, and the husky **Eugene ★★★**, a robust porter, as it is with lower-alcohol offerings such as **Cross of Gold ★★☆**, a floral and crisp golden ale, and the toffee-like, nutty **Workingman Mild ★★★**.

SAINT LOUIS BREWERY
St. Louis, Missouri

The downtown taproom, a brewpub, and a production brewery at close-in suburb Maplewood make about 50 varieties of Schlafly beer a year, including three rotating and distinct IPAs, the **Tasmanian India Pale Ale ★★★**, showcasing Australian hops rich with melon and passion-fruit, being one. Wide range, from coffee-and-cream **Oatmeal Stout ★★★** and delicate **Kölsch ★★☆** to popular spiced seasonals **Pumpkin Ale ★★☆** and **Christmas Ale ★★☆**.

DESTINATION
ST. LOUIS

The Bridge (1004 Locust Street) blends sophisticated surroundings with 55 taps, a couple of hundred bottled beers and a fine selection of charcuterie and cheese, plus 20 wines by the glass for the beer-phobic.

SANTA FE BREWING
Santa Fe, New Mexico

Began operations in a horse barn south of Santa Fe, New Mexico, with a square brewing kettle originally used by Boulder Brewing during its early days. **State Pen Porter** ★★ offers toffee notes balanced by a properly roasty character; colourfully named **Chicken Killer Barley Wine** ★★ can be reminiscent of fruitcake when aged; while **Imperial Java Stout** ★★☆ is suitably coffee-dominated and rich.

SHORT'S BREWING
Elk Rapids, Michigan

The original northern Michigan brewpub still operates, but a separate brewery has grown into a buzz-worthy regional producer. Numerous strong, uniquely flavoured beers like **Peaches & Crème** ★★★, peachy and tart; a true to its name **Key Lime Pie** ★★★; and molasses-rich Imperial-sized **Publican Porter** ★★☆. More traditional offerings include **Huma Lupa Licious IPA** ★★☆, packed with pine and grapefruit hoppiness; and **Local's Light Beer** ★★☆, a crisp light lager.

SKA BREWING
Durango, Colorado

The founders labelled their home brewed beer from Ska Brewing because they played ska music while brewing in Colorado's San Juan Mountains. Chequerboard labels still adorn beers: **Modus Hoperandi IPA** ★★★, full of pine and grapefruit; **Autumnal Mole Stout** ★★★, a balanced blend of cocoa and peppers; the spicy **Euphoria Pale Ale** ★★; and appropriately milky **Steel Toe Stout** ★★☆.

SNAKE RIVER BREWING
Jackson, Wyoming

Brewpub that also packages several beers, in the tourist destination of Jackson, Wyoming. **Zonker Stout** ★★★ offers intense roasty notes balanced by chocolate sweetness; **Vienna Lager** ★★★ is soft and faintly nutty; **Dortmunder** ★★☆ is a bready and spicy lager; barrel-aged **Le Serpent Cerise** ★★★☆ is cherry-laced and tart; and **Pako's Eye P-A** ★★ is floral and juicy.

SPRECHER BREWING
Milwaukee, Wisconsin

Eponymous brewery founded in Milwaukee by former Pabst brewer Randy Sprecher in 1985. Classic **Black Bavarian** ★★★ is the picture of balance in a black lager; special edition **Doppel Bock** ★★★ is a full-bodied, malty delight; **Hefe Weiss** ★★☆ tends toward the lighter side of the style; and decidedly unGermanic **IPA2** ★★☆ segues nicely from a sweet entry to a bitter but not aggressive finish.

SQUATTERS PUBS & BEERS
Salt Lake City, Utah

Long-established brewpub, now with three locations and bottling through the Utah Brewers Cooperative. Crisp and moderately bitter **Provo Girl Pilsner** ★★★ refreshes with low strength, as does the peppery, nutty **Full Suspension Pale Ale** ★★☆. Stronger brews include the indulgent **Hop Rising** double IPA ★★★; the dense, anise-accented **Outer Darkness** ★★★ Imperial stout; and the sweet, tart and funky spice of oak-conditioned **529** ★★★☆.

SUMMIT BREWING
Saint Paul, Minnesota

Focused on the Minnesota Twin Cities market from the outset in 1986, with a core of well-made beers, recently augmented by an Unchained series and excellent seasonals such as the restrained **Maibock** ★★☆. Core brands include **Great Northern Porter** ★★★, roasty but soft; creamy **Oatmeal Stout** ★★☆; and **Extra Pale Ale** ★★☆, with citrus/lemon notes leading to a dry finish.

SUN KING BREWING
Indianapolis, Indiana

Brewery with acclaim disproportional to the short time it has been open (since 2009). A long list of specialities and one-offs keep the beer raters active, but regular brands are fine on their own, such

as the floral, citrus **Sunlight Cream Ale** ★★☆; the admirably restrained **Osiris Pale Ale** ★★★; and the toffee and raisin, brown-spice-accented **Wee Mac Scottish-Style Ale** ★★★.

SURLY BREWING
Minneapolis, Minnesota

After opening in 2006, this Minnesota brewery quickly grabbed attention for its often "extreme" beers. Fans of **Darkness** ★★★☆, a chocolate-layered, dark-fruit Imperial stout, travel hundreds of miles to buy it on "Darkness Day". Piney IPA **Furious** ★★☆ is equally intense. More nuanced offerings include the creamy oatmeal brown ale **Bender** ★★☆; an unfiltered *helles* called **Hell** ★★★; and a malty **Mild** ★★☆.

TALLGRASS BREWING
Manhattan, Kansas

Young brewery near Topeka focused on draught, cans and community. Main brands include the citrus and refreshing **Halcyon Wheat** ★★; the improbably named **Buffalo Sweat** ★★, a sweet and chocolaty brown ale; and **Oasis** ★★☆, a fruity, vaguely grassy strong ale best described as an amped-up ESB.

THREE FLOYDS BREWING
Munster, Indiana

Founded by, you guessed it, three guys named Floyd – a father and two sons. Best known for their once pre-eminent hop bomb, **Alpha King** ★★★, still a solid illustration of the beauty of American hops. **Robert the**

Bruce ★★☆ is a strong and sweetly caramelly Scotch ale; **Dreadnaught** ★★★ is a chewy-hoppy, tropical-fruity double IPA; and **Gumballhead** ★★☆ is a love-or-hate wheat beer with a sharp shot of hoppiness.

DESTINATION
SCOTTSDALE

Papago Brewing Company (7107 East McDowell Road) is more beer bar than brewpub, with beers made off-site complemented by well over two dozen studiously selected taps.

TOMMYKNOCKER BREWERY
Idaho Springs, Colorado

Located in a former mining town west of Denver, taking its name from the term for the ghosts of buried miners. **Butt Head Bock** ★★☆ is a sweetish *doppelbock*; **Maple Nut Brown** ★★ offers restrained maple and roasted nut flavours; rye adds interesting spiciness to abundant citrus character in **Hop Strike Rye IPA** ★★☆.

TWISTED PINE BREWING
Boulder, Colorado

Started by local brewing legend, the late Gordon Knight, using equipment acquired from NEW BELGIUM BREWING. Broad range on offer: much-loved and perfectly named **Big Shot Espresso Stout** ★★★; love-it-or-hate-it **Ghost Face Killah** ★★, a tongue-scorching golden ale infused with six chilli peppers; **North Star Imperial Porter** ★★☆, with roasted notes balancing sweet chocolate.

TWO BROTHERS BREWING
Warrenville, Illinois

Like many in the 1990s, Jason and Jim Ebel started their brewery in suburban Chicago with a combination of new equipment and repurposed dairy tanks, designing it with **Ebel's Weiss** ★★☆, a soft, almost fluffy, *hefeweizen*, in mind. Diverse portfolio includes **Domaine DuPage**, a sweetish *bière de garde* ★★; roasty **Reprieve Schwarzbier Lager** ★★☆; and **Cane and Ebel** ★★★, a strong, spicy rye beer.

UINTA BREWING
Salt Lake City, Utah

Adept at low-alcohol beers, this wind-powered brewery produces three lines: Organic, Classic and Crooked, the last being the strongest. **Organic Baba Black Lager** ★★☆, a chocolaty *schwarzbier*, typifies the first, while the well-balanced **Cutthroat Pale Ale** ★★ highlights the Classic category. Crooked class brews include the **Anniversary Barley Wine** ★★☆, redolent of chewy caramel and citrus hops; and **Hop Notch IPA** ★★, leaner of body, floral and bitter.

URBAN CHESTNUT BREWING
St. Louis, Missouri

Founded by two former Anheuser-Busch employees, who preach "beer divergency" through Reverence and Revolution series. Former features **Zwickel** ★★★, a bready *helles*; and **Schnickelfritz** ★★★, a *weissbier* brimming with vanilla, banana and clove. Revolution includes **Hopfen** ★★★☆, a floral, grassy "Bavarian IPA"; **Winged Nut** ★★☆, a roasty *weissbier* infused with chestnuts; and **STLIPA** ★★, a double IPA laced with citrus notes.

WASATCH BREW PUB & BREWERY (SCHIRF BREWING)
Park City, Utah

Irreverent brewery known for poking fun at the local Mormon community. Soft, chocolaty **Polygamy Porter** ★★☆ is marketed with the slogan "why have just one"; while the label of thinnish, caramelly **Evolution Amber Ale** ★★ teases with a picture of Darwin. Bottled beers produced by the Utah Brewers Coop.

WYNKOOP BREWING
Denver, Colorado

Brewpub in Lower Downtown (LoDo) district once owned by now-Colorado governor John Hickenlooper, now canning its beers for distribution. Flagship **Railyard Ale** ★★☆ is dryly malty, appley and sessionable; newer **Belgorado** ★★★ is brewed with Colorado-grown malt and hops to a peachy, spicy, resinous body and bittersweet finish; while stronger **Colorojo** ★★☆ segues neatly from raisiny toffee to grapefruity hoppiness.

> ### DESTINATION DENVER
>
> Falling Rock Taphouse (1919 Blake Street), in the district known as LoDo, became a beer landmark by supporting local brewers, bringing in hard-to-find beers and generally serving as the hub of Colorado's booming craft beer scene.

EAST COAST

Craft brewing was born in California and brewpubs got their start in the Pacific Northwest, but the successful commercialization of craft beer began in the East, more specifically in Boston, home to the Boston Beer Company. Originally a beer commissioned at other breweries, Samuel Adams Boston Lager was the first craft beer to break down barriers and begin appearing on draught taps and in beer fridges across the nation, from sports bars to white-tablecloth restaurants.

It didn't take long for the idea to catch on. From Maine to Maryland, the northeast soon became a hotbed of craft brewing, oddly taking root last – but now quite solidly – in its most populated jurisdiction, New York City. And likely the hottest place in the region is Philadelphia, the self-proclaimed "America's Best Beer-Drinking City" and without question a hub of both modern American craft brewing and the beer bar movement.

508 GASTROBREWERY
New York City

In Manhattan's SoHo neighborhood, this relative newcomer is turning out flavourful brews in a tiny system in a restaurant's basement, and even more amazingly, bottling for retail sale. Thick and boozy **Montezuma Imperial Stout** ★★☆; funky yet bracing, lambic-inspired **Greenwich Gueuze** ★★★; fruity-spicy **Belgian-Style Golden Strong Ale** ★★☆; balanced and dry **Smoked Rye IPA** ★★☆; and chewy, nutty **American Strong Ale** ★★ are just a few of dozens released.

ALCHEMIST, THE
Waterbury, Vermont

Northeastern Vermont brewery currently producing just one beer year-round. The double IPA **Heady Topper** ★★★☆ is not so much a hoppy punch, like some others, but more of an unfolding dance with hops, holding notes of pineapple,

tropical fruit, lemon and citrus, and even a little alcoholic warmth.

ALLAGASH BREWING
Portland, Maine

Brewery in Portland, Maine, so preoccupied with all things Belgian it built a lambic-style coolship for spontaneous fermentation. Belgian-style wheat beer **White** ★★★ has great balance of citrus and peppery herbals; **Tripel** ★★★ segues nicely from perfumey fruit to drying hops, and is aged in oak to become the bizarrely attractive **Curieux** ★★★☆; limited-edition **Gargamel** ★★★☆ is tart, floral raspberry with vanilla and huge complexity; coolship beers are works in progress with great potential.

BERKSHIRE BREWING
South Deerfield, Massachusetts

Nestled in the western mountains of Massachusetts, this brewery

has garnered a reputation for uncompromised recipes and quality control. Brands include the bready and slightly hoppy **Steel Rail Extra Pale Ale ★★★**; the roasty, caffeinated **Dean's Beans Coffeehouse Porter ★★☆**; and the hoppy/malty **Shabadoo Black & Tan Ale ★★☆**, along with the summer perennial, crisp and biscuity-spicy **Czech Style Pilsner ★★★**.

BROOKLYN BREWING
New York City

New York brewery fronted by well-known brewer and sometimes author Garrett Oliver. Stalwarts include the **Lager ★★☆**, toasty and somewhat Vienna-like; **Brown Ale ★★★**, bold with nutty hoppiness; and **East India Pale Ale ★★★**, which skilfully mixes British influence with American hopheadedness. Seasonal **Black Chocolate Stout ★★★☆** is wonderfully chocolaty without the addition of chocolate; while **Local 1 ★★★** is a spicy, all-bottle-fermented restorative

DESTINATION
BROOKLYN

Spuyten Duyvil (359 Metropolitan Avenue) is a bare-bones bar in the Williamsburg area of Brooklyn serving cheese and charcuterie plates to complement an impressive selection of sometimes pricey but often extremely hard-to-find tap and cask beers from around the world.

CAMBRIDGE BREWING
Cambridge, Massachusetts

A small production brewery and pub located in the middle of Boston's college districts. The house beers, which are brewed by Will Meyers, include the mocha-ish, dryly bitter **Charles River Porter ★★☆**; and dry-hopped, sessionable **Tall Tale Pale Ale ★★☆**. But the brewery's strength is in occasional releases like **Cerise Cassée ★★★☆**, barrel-aged and loaded with tart cherry fruitiness, among others. Local draught and limited bottle distribution.

DESTINATION
CAMBRIDGE

Lord Hobo (92 Hampshire Street) caters to students and hipsters, beer aficionados and cocktail geeks, with 43 taps, a select bottled beer list and more-than-respectable cocktails and wines, all at prices that won't tax the budget.

CAPTAIN LAWRENCE BREWING
Elmsford, New York

Westchester brewery known for flavourful beers that often mask high strength. Regular offerings include the clovey, banana-ish and mildly funky **Liquid Gold ★★☆**; the massively piney and slightly citrus **Captain's Reserve Imperial IPA ★★★**; and the bonfire-like **Smoked Porter ★★☆**. Popular speciality releases include the funky **Cuvee de Castleton ★★★☆**, with pleasant notes of sour grapes; and **Nor'Easter: Winter Warmer ★★★**, brewed with elderberries and aged in bourbon barrels.

DOGFISH HEAD BREWING
Milton, Delaware

This Delaware brewery is known for experimentation and "extreme" brewing. Year-round brews include continuously hopped, aggressive yet balanced **90 Minute IPA ★★★**; raisiny and soothing **Raison d'Etre ★★★☆**; and complex, luxurious, Paraguayan-wood-aged **Palo Santo Maron ★★★★**. Irregular releases are highly sought, but less reliable, save for **Immort Ale ★★★**, a strong, faintly smoky beast; and the outrageous and potent fruit beer, **Black & Blue ★★★**.

FLYING FISH BREWING
Somerdale, New Jersey

Brewery near the Philadelphia–New Jersey border that evolved out of a web-based crowd-sourcing project in the mid-1990s. Spicy American hops add a local touch to **Exit 4 American Trippel ★★★**; while fragrant **Hopfish IPA ★★** portrays the gentle side of India pale ale. A hoppier, piney, caramelly bite is provided by newer **Redfish ★★☆**.

GEARY BREWING
(DL GEARY BREWING)
Portland, Maine

Early northeast brewery, established 1983 in Portland, Maine. **Pale Ale ★★☆** was an early standard by which others were judged, although UK rather than US in style; **Hampshire Ale ★★★** was born a winter warmer and is still best "when the weather sucks"; while the **IPA ★★☆** is arguably the British-leaning brewery's most American-style ale.

DESTINATION
LOVELL

Ebenezer's Pub (44 Allen Road) might be a little out of the way, situated as it is in rural Maine near the New Hampshire border, but its well-earned tradition of featuring obscure and arcane – and usually excellent! – ales and lagers makes it worth the detour.

HE'BREW (SHMALTZ BREWING)
Clifton Park, New York

Beer commissioner turned upstate New York brewer, mixing good-natured fun with respect for the Jewish religion. "Chosen beers" include the pomegranate-juice-fuelled **Origin** ★★★, a strong ale of powerful complexity; **Bittersweet Lenny's R.I.P.A.** ★★☆, an appealing car crash of caramel malt, spicy rye and hops; and the tamer, lower strength **Genesis** ★★. Newer arrival is **Hop Manna IPA** ★★★, an orangey ale with some finesse.

HIGH POINT BREWING (RAMSTEIN BEER)
Butler, New Jersey

Brewery making Ramstein beers from all-German ingredients at a New Jersey location chosen for its pristine water source. The **Blonde Wheat Beer** ★★☆ is a floral, hazy year-round bestseller; while the **Classic Wheat Beer** ★★★ is a dark marvel of sweet and creamy roasted malt flavour. Traditional German seasonals include the hazy, toasted caramel-like *märzen* **Oktoberfest** ★★☆; lightly hoppy and sweetly mellow **Mai Bock** ★★☆; and the lusciously boozy **Winter Wheat** ★★★.

HILL FARMSTEAD BREWERY
Greensboro, Vermont

Known for a skilful use of hops, this brewery has a near-cult-like following. Diverse offerings include the balanced, citrus-spicy pale ale **Edward** ★★★; chewy and tropical-fruity **Abner Double IPA** ★★★☆; the strongly roasty and dark chocolaty **Everett Porter** ★★★; the grapefruity and strong **Susan IPA** ★★★; and the gorgeous **Ann** ★★★★, a *saison* that blends flavours of honey, oak, acidic citrus, vanilla and white wine.

MAINE BEER
Freeport, Maine

Sparse bottle labels understate the elegant flavours within. **Peeper** ★★★, a balanced, citrus IPA; and thin but smooth **Mean Old Tom** ★★☆, a stout aged on vanilla beans, put spins on established styles. **Zoe** ★★☆, a hoppy, zesty and aromatic amber ale; **Lunch** ★★★, a tropically fruity and piney IPA; and the chocolaty, hoppy porter **King Titus** ★★☆ round out offerings from this small brewery with big buzz.

NARRAGANSETT BREWING
Providence, Rhode Island

Circa 1890 brewery, closed and demolished in the 1990s but reopened in 2005 as a beer commissioner. Only year-round brand of note is the fruity **Cream Ale** ★★, quenching and off-dry; but seasonals like the dark-chocolaty, pumpernickel-ish **Porter** ★★☆; caramelly **Fest Lager**; ★★ and the slightly honey-ish, mildly bitter **Summer Ale** ★★ keep the portfolio interesting.

NEW ENGLAND BREWING
Woodbridge, Connecticut

Canning craft brewery with three year-round offerings: English-style **Sea Hag IPA** ★★, caramelly with citrus hoppiness; **Elm City Lager** ★★, crisp and bready with hints of lemongrass; and caramelly, nutty flagship brew, **Atlantic Amber** ★★, fermented with lager yeast at ale temperatures. Special offerings include citrus and spiced **668**; **Neighbour of the Beast** ★★☆ and mocha-hued, darkly fruity **Imperial Stout Trooper** ★★★.

OMMEGANG (DUVEL MOORTGAT)
Cooperstown, New York

Near the Baseball Hall of Fame, this brewery was founded by a beer importer in collaboration with three Belgian breweries, including now-sole owner Duvel. Flagship **Abbey Ale** ★★☆ is perhaps not as malty-spicy as it once was; while **Rare Vos** ★★★ remains a mellow, fruity sipper; and the dryly spicy, crisp-finishing **Hennepin** ★★★ continues to please. Newer **BPA** ★★☆, billed a Belgian-style pale ale, seems to fall just short of the mark.

SAMUEL ADAMS (BOSTON BEER COMPANY)
Boston, Massachussetts

Pioneering beer commissioning company, now largest craft brewery in US. Flagship **Boston Lager** ★★★ is the dry, toasty meeting place of *dunkel* and pilsner; **Noble Pils** ★★★ is a masterfully aromatic use of five hop varieties; special or limited editions include the velvety and smooth **Double Bock** ★★★; the winey, barrel-aged *tripel* **New World** ★★★; and the world's strongest fully fermented beer, the hugely complex **Utopias** ★★★★, still and darkly fruity, with notes of cocoa nibs and star anise in its 10th anniversary edition.

SARANAC BEER (MATT BREWING)
Utica, New York

Upstate New York family brewery in business since before Prohibition. Rebranded with the craft-like Saranac line, including newer **White IPA** ★★☆, a curious mix of IPA and Belgian-style wheat beer; dry and biscuity, only gently hoppy **Pale Ale** ★★; and slightly unbalanced (on the hoppy side) **India Pale Ale** ★★. High Peak series beers bring something extra to the table.

SLY FOX BREWING
Pottstown, Pennsylvania

Philadelphia-area brewery and pub experiencing great local success with canned beers. Crisply flavourful, German-inspired **Pikeland Pils** ★★★ is a warmer-weather treat; while citrus **Phoenix Pale Ale** ★★☆ quenches a cool-weather thirst. Large-format bottled brews include the peppery-fruity **Saison Vos** ★★★; and quite sweet, darkly fruity and strong **Ichor** ★★☆.

SMUTTYNOSE BREWING
Portsmouth, New Hampshire

Named for an island off the coast of New Hampshire, this brewery was founded in 1994. Regular brands include the hugely popular **Old Brown Dog** ★★★, a brown ale with a dry, mildly bitter caramel character; **Star Island Single** ★★★, with mild sweetness balanced by spicy, citrus hop; and aptly named, chocolate-toffee **Robust Porter** ★★☆. Occasional Big Beer series fuels creativity.

SOUTHAMPTON PUBLICK HOUSE
Southampton, New York

Acclaimed Long Island brewpub turned beer commissioner, fronted for 15 years by acclaimed brewer Phil Markowski, who left in 2012. Year-round brands include the **Double White Ale ★★☆**, orangey up front, big, spicy and sweet in the finish; and the sweetish, borderline fruity **Altbier ★★☆**. Excellence is reserved for Farmhouse beers like the enticingly floral **Cuvée des Fleurs ★★★☆** and spicy, cooked caramel **Grand Cru ★★★**.

SOUTHERN TIER BREWING
Lakewood, New York

Upper New York State brewery with a solid regular line-up and sometimes inspired seasonals, including dessert-like **Crème Brûlée Imperial Milk Stout ★★**, a vanilla and butterscotch love-it-or-hate-it ale; and pumpkin-pie-in-a-glass spiced **Pumking ★★**. Regulars include **Iniquity ★★★**, a biscuity, toasted-orange-ish strong black ale; **Hop Sun ★★☆**, a full-bodied yet quaffable wheat; and slightly sweet and peppery **UnEarthly IPA ★★☆**.

DESTINATION
NEW YORK

dba (41 1st Avenue) is an East Village beer landmark which, although it has since been eclipsed by other destinations in terms of craft beer credentials, was one of the pioneers in bringing good beer to the Big Apple. It is still devoted to its motto, "drink good stuff".

STOUDT'S BREWING
Adamstown, Pennsylvania

Carol Stoudt fronts this family-owned brewery in Adamstown, Pennsylvania Dutch Country, and the softly perfumey **Scarlet Lady Ale ★★** exists to remind anyone who forgets that fact. The brewery's other brands include the *helles*-like **Gold Lager ★★☆**, with a kiss of malty sweetness; the snappy, dry, quenching **Pils ★★★**; and the fruity, caramelly **Triple ★★☆**.

SUSQUEHANNA BREWING
Pittston, Pennsylvania

The long-time SHINER brewmaster Jaime Jurado left that Texas brewery at the end of 2011 to be a partner in this Pittston, Pennsylvania concern. Its initial offerings include the dry, blond **Goldencold Lager ★★☆**; the style-bending, moderately bitter **Pils Noir ★★☆**; and the biscuity, nutty-hoppy **Stock Ale ★★★**, the last harkening back to early-20th-century American ales.

TRINITY BREWHOUSE
Providence, Rhode Island

A mainstay in Rhode Island's capital city, the brewery offers a diverse, mostly draught-only selection from its pub. Kegs are available, but one beer, the citrus hoppy **Trinity IPA ★★** is sold in bottles. It's one of the largest breweries in the small state.

TRÖEGS BREWING
Hershey, Pennsylvania

Long a well-kept Pennsylvania secret, this central state brewery is now becoming better known up and down the east coast. Beers like the winter seasonal **Mad Elf ★★★☆**, with fruit-derived complexity and well-contained strength; the dryly malty, almost bready **Troegenator Double Bock ★★★**; and the intensely hoppy, resiny **Nugget Nectar ★★☆** are helping to spread the word.

VICTORY BREWING
Downingtown, Pennsylvania

Versatile Philadelphia-area producer of many styles, including ales and lagers of both session-strength and considerable potency. Brands include crisp and fragrant, Bohemian-style **Prima Pils ★★★**; **HopDevil ★★★**, an assertive US-style IPA; the rich and oily **Storm King ★★★☆**, a roasty, almost chewy Imperial stout of strong character; the luxuriant **St Victorious Doppelbock ★★★☆**; and **Golden Monkey ★★★**, a strong and spicy Belgian-inspired golden ale.

DESTINATION PHILADELPHIA

Monk's Cafe (264 S 16th Street) is not only the perennial "Best Beer Bar in Philly", it's also arguably the source of the Belgian craft beer invasion of the United States and a laudable destination for reasonably priced, quality brasserie fare.

WHITE BIRCH BREWING
Hooksett, New Hampshire

Located between Concord and Manchester, this small, Belgian-inspired brewery boasts a growing profile. Three flagships are the pear-ish and yeasty **Belgian Style Pale Ale ★★**; the citrus and toffee-ish **Hooksett Ale ★★☆**; and the resinous **Hop Session Ale ★★☆**. Also brews three seasonals, notably the tangy summer **Berliner Weiss ★★** and winter **Ol'Cattywhompus** barley wine **★★★**, with dominant brown sugar and toffee flavours and earthy hops in the background.

WOLAVER'S (LONG TRAIL BREWING)
Bridgewater Corners, Vermont

Pioneering organic brewery that began as a beer commissioner, then bought a flagging Vermont brewery, Otter Creek, only to be itself bought out by a neighbouring brewery in 2010. The plummy, roasty **Oatmeal Stout ★★☆** continues in organic form; as does the appetizing, appley **India Pale Ale ★★☆** and light-bodied, slightly sweet **Pale Ale ★★**.

YUENGLING (DG YUENGLING & SON)
Pottsville, Pennsylvania

The oldest brewery in America, dating from 1829 and still independently owned. Best beer is a thinnish but dependable **Porter** ★☆; also a vaguely citrus and modestly sweet **Lord Chesterfield Ale** ★. Some seasonal releases stand out, including a slightly bready **Bock** ★, but mostly this is a sentimental favourite.

DESTINATION
NEWARK AND ELSEWHERE

Iron Hill Brewery (147 E Main Street) is a group of 10 perennially award-winning brewpubs spanning three states: Delaware, New Jersey and Pennsylvania. Always creative, seasonally adjusted draught selections are supplemented by an impressive "Bottled Reserve" programme.

SOUTH

Time was that the American south would be referred to by beer aficionados as a craft brewing wasteland, and small wonder, when even today southern states like Mississippi, Alabama and Arkansas remain mired at the bottom of the chart in terms of both breweries-to-population ratio and total number of breweries.

Still, it's not all bad beer news in the south. Following successful challenges to trade-constraining alcohol laws, states like Georgia and North Carolina have blossomed as craft brewing hotbeds, while Texas and Florida have witnessed the rise of significant brewing centres within their borders. Aiding the development of craft beer across the south are the efforts of a breed of impressive southern beer bars, led by the 16-outlet Flying Saucer Chain and proud independents such as Georgia's Brick Store.

---

512 BREWING
Austin, Texas

Largest of the new wave of breweries in Austin, Texas, minimizing its environmental footprint by using mostly organic ingredients and selling only draught beer. Uses local pecans in its unique **Pecan Porter** ★★★, the nutty notes complementing a rich coffee flavour; offers Old World floral notes and New World citrus aromas in its **IPA** ★★☆; grapefruit peel provides a bright twist to **Wit** ★★☆; while **Bruin** ★★☆, a "double brown ale", is malty and dangerously smooth.

ABITA BREWING
Abita Springs, Louisiana

Early southern craft brewery based outside New Orleans. Flagship **Amber** ★☆ enjoyed up and down Bourbon Street, but more savvy locals reach for **Turbodog** ★★, a darker, slightly stronger and maltier brew; the beautifully aromatic **Restoration Pale Ale** ★★☆; or the firmly bitter **Jockomo IPA** ★★☆. Brewed for the 25th anniversary, it is to be hoped that the intense, chocolate-fruity **Double Dog** ★★★ continues.

BIG BOSS BREWING
Raleigh, North Carolina

Brewery and taproom located in Raleigh, North Carolina. Core range of five brands is best at the lighter-hued end, as with the *kölsch*-like **Angry Angel** ★★★, which hints at fruitiness without ever becoming fruity; and **Hell's Belle** ★★★, with initial candied pear notes drying to a spicy, slightly boozy finish. The brown ale **Bad Penny** ★★☆ misses the mark only slightly with a bit too much toffee-ish sweetness.

> ### DESTINATION
> ### HENRICO
>
> Mekong Restaurant (6004 W Broad Street) might superficially appear an ordinary Richmond-area Vietnamese restaurant, but owner An "Mekong" Bui's passion for beer has transformed it into a true destination for the craft beer aficionado.

CIGAR CITY BREWING
Tampa, Florida

Floridian cult favourite, located not far from the Tampa Bay airport. Regular brands include **Maduro Brown Ale** ★★★, rich and creamy thanks to the use of oats in the mash; and **Jai Alai IPA** ★★★, smooth with soft fruitiness and measured bitterness. Big-bottle seasonals include **Big Sound Scotch Ale** ★★☆, port-wine-ish with plum and brown-spice flavours; and **Marshal Zhukov's Imperial Stout** ★★★☆, with lashings of liquorice, roasted spice, coffee and warming alcohol.

COOP ALE WORKS
Oklahoma City

Craft breweries are a bit of a rarity in Oklahoma, which left ample room for this draught-focused operation to open in Oklahoma City in late 2008. **Horny Toad Cerveza** ★★☆ might sound like a simple light lager, but its gentle fruitiness and integrated hop says otherwise; while the chocolate-caramelly **Native Amber** ★★☆ boasts drying, moderately bitter hoppiness. Territorial Reserve series beers allow brewery to push the envelope.

DEVILS BACKBONE BREWING
Roseland, Virginia

A newcomer, opened as a brewpub in only 2008, establishing a reputation for German-inspired beers brewed with continental precision. Added separate production facility in 2012, also in central Virginia. The seamless and slightly nutty **Vienna Lager** ★★★ and citus-laden **Eight Point IPA ★★☆** are most widely available. **Danzig ★★★☆**, a silky Baltic porter; **Dark Abby ★★☆**, a delicate and complex dubbel; and grainy **Gold Leaf Lager ★★** illustrate the brewery's diversity.

DUCK-RABBIT CRAFT BREWERY
Farmville, North Carolina

Calling itself a "dark beer specialist", this east North Carolina brewery is likely best known for its rounded, mocha-ish **Milk Stout ★★☆**. Other brands include a sweet-starting, dryly bitter-finishing **Brown Ale ★★★**; and a slightly winey, milk-chocolaty **Porter ★★☆**.

FULLSTEAM BREWING
Durham, North Carolina

Durham, NC, brewery intent on creating "a distinctly Southern beer style". So far, core brands like the sweetish and earthy **Carver Sweet Potato ★★** and corn-and-barley **El Toro Cream Ale ★☆** fall shy of the mark, but greater success has been achieved with seasonal and special brews. The fruity, cinnamon **First

The Duck-Rabbit
MILK STOUT
THE DARK BEER SPECIALIST

Frost Winter Ale ★★★**, brewed with persimmons foraged by pub patrons, shows the brewery's potential.

GREEN MAN BREWING
Asheville, North Carolina

Born in the mid-1990s, this draught-only brewery is both one of North Carolina's oldest and a cornerstone of the burgeoning Asheville craft beer scene. The tangerine and grapefruit flavours of **IPA ★★☆** fuels hophead joy; while the more restrained **Pale Ale ★★☆** blends both malty and hoppy fruitiness. Midpoint is the **ESB★★★**, with biscuity British maltiness meeting spicy-fruity American hoppiness.

HIGHLAND BREWING
Asheville, North Carolina

Almost-two-decade-old stalwart of the Asheville, North Carolina beer scene. Flagship **Gaelic Ale ★★★** starts fruity, turns toasty, then mildly bitter and finally softly roasty and dry; light-hued **St Terese's Pale Ale ★★☆** layers spicy hop atop nutty maltiness; and the unusual **Oatmeal Porter ★★** combines prune and plum notes with roasted malt and not quite enough silky smoothness.

JESTER KING
Austin, Texas

Young brewery overcoming adversity – including drought – to forge some outstanding beers. Known for big beers, but best might be a little one, **Le Petit Prince ★★★☆**, dry, peppery and quenching at less than 3% ABV. Others include fruity-bitter **Noble King ★★☆**;

a delicious mild aged on oak to a very gently smokiness, **Commercial Suicide** ★★★; and the hoppy but otherwise *bière de garde*-like **Mad Meg** ★★☆.

DESTINATION
DALLAS

The Meddlesome Moth (1621 Oak Lawn Avenue) is the "gastropub" spin-off of the multi-location chain of Flying Saucer beer bars. Unlike the tavern-like Saucers – also recommended – the Moth is more casual chic bistro, featuring creative cuisine and a carefully curated list of draught and bottled beers.

KARBACH BREWING
Houston, Texas

Former CEO of Flying Dog Brewing, Eric Warner left that company to co-found this Houston brewery in 2011. Canned beers produced thus far validate the move, with the floral, hoppy **Sympathy for the Lager** ★★ leading the way for such bigger beers as **Hopadillo IPA** ★★☆, with peachy fruit matched by citrus hop; and **Rodeo Clown Double IPA** ★★★, an ale that highlights fruity malt over aggressive hop. Seasonal **Karbachtoberfest** ★★★ showcases Warner's German brewing roots.

KREBS BREWING
Krebs, Oklahoma

If America has a living indigenous beer it is Choc, brewed in eastern Oklahoma since before Prohibition from a recipe said to come from Choctaw Nation Indians. The range goes beyond the **1919 Choc Beer** ★☆, a somewhat fruity wheat beer, to a Brewmaster Signature series that includes the tart, salty **Gose** ★★ and **Grätzer** ★★☆, a relatively bitter beer in the style known as *grodziskie*, made with smoked wheat and fermented with Polish yeast.

DESTINATION
OKLAHOMA CITY

Tapwerks Ale House & Cafe (121 E Sheridan Avenue), is a three-floor beer emporium that is all about beer selection, with no fewer than 212 beers on tap and a hundred or so more in the bottle.

LIVE OAK BREWING
Austin, Texas

A rare survivor from an original round of breweries that opened in Austin, Texas, in the mid-1990s, and still draught-only. Czech immigrants who settled in the region in the late 19th century would easily recognize the bready but crisp and spicy **Pilz** ★★★☆. Their other brands include **Big Bark** ★★, a food-friendly amber

lager; **HefeWeizen** ★★★, complex beneath its typical banana and clove flavours; and **Primus** ★★, an intense, spicy *weizenbock*.

rich and deep banana flavours; the subtly smoky Scotch ale, **Iron Thistle** ★★★; and the suitably strong and warming **Winter Warmer** ★★.

NOLA BREWING (NEW ORLEANS LAGER & ALE BREWING)
New Orleans, Louisiana

Young brewery bringing the brewing tradition back to the Big Easy. Launched in 2008 with two ales: a lightly fruity, faintly toasty **Blonde** ★★☆; and a roasty, southern US take on a mild, the light-bodied **Brown** ★★. The duo were joined later by **Hopitoulas IPA** ★★☆, with assertive citrus-spicy-fruity hoppiness.

> ### DESTINATION
> ### NEW ORLEANS
>
> The Avenue Pub (1732 St Charles Avenue), which is family-owned and housed in a century-and-a-half-old Garden District building, is simply the finest stop for beer in the Big Easy, open 24 hours a day, 365 days a year.

RAHR & SON BREWING
Fort Worth, Texas

The roof literally fell in on this Fort Worth brewery in 2010 after a record snowfall, knocking it out of business for a time. But it came back fighting with a line-up of mostly lagers and adventurous seasonals, including **Ugly Pug** ★★☆, a chocolaty *schwarzbier* with coffee bitterness; *weizenbock* **Angry Goat** ★★☆, offering

REAL ALE BREWING
Blanco, Texas

Long ago outgrew the Texas Hill Country antique-store basement that first housed the brewery. The golden **Fireman's #4** ★★, light and floral, has driven growth, but the brewery's line-up is diverse: **Full Moon Pale Rye Ale** ★★★, spicy and well suited to local barbecues; **Sisyphus** ★★☆, a rich, but balanced barley wine; **Hans Pils** ★★★, floral and unapologetically bitter; and the lightly fruity *tripel* **Devil's Backbone** ★★.

SAINT ARNOLD BREWING
Houston, Texas

Named after a brewing saint and founded by two former investment bankers. Grew into the largest brewery in Texas opened since Prohibition, crafting a wide range that includes the perfectly rounded **Oktoberfest** ★★☆; the *kölsch*-inspired **Fancy Lawnmower Ale** ★★, an ideal refresher for hot and humid Houston; **Weedwacker** ★★, in which Bavarian yeast turns Lawnmower base recipe into a *weissbier*; and the hop-forward but sensibly balanced **Elissa IPA** ★★☆.

ST SOMEWHERE BREWING
Tarpon Springs, Florida

Clearwater-area brewery that was one of the first to bring creative craft brewing to the state. Large format, cork-finished bottles adorned with ornate, art nouveau labels hold Belgian-inspired ales like the perfumey, herbal-spicy **Saison Athene** ★★☆; and the tart, sweet peach- and apricot-accented **Lectio Divina** ★★☆.

SHINER (SPOETZL BREWERY, OWNED BY GAMBRINUS COMPANY)
Shiner, Texas

Century-old Texas regional brewer best known for rather forgettable **Shiner Bock** ★, amber in colour but light lager-ish in taste. Better are more niche brands like the **Bohemian Black Lager** ★★★, medium-weight and crisp in character; and **Dortmunder** ★★★, a firmly malty lager with hints of buckwheat honey and alfalfa.

SWEETWATER BREWING
Atlanta, Georgia

Inspired by the Atlanta Olympics, two former college roommates founded this early southern brewery on Atlanta's west side. A half-dozen regulars include the nutty, drying **Georgia Brown** ★★☆; an **IPA** ★★☆ that balances citrus hoppiness atop peachy malt; the bready, caraway-ish and peppery **LowRYEder IPA** ★★★; and the chocolate and prune **Exodus Porter** ★★. Catch & Release seasonals include the almost mincemeat-like seasonal **Festive Ale** ★★☆.

TERRAPIN BEER
Athens, Georgia

Iconoclastic brewery opened in Athens, Georgia, over a decade ago with a mission to do things differently. Which it did, launching with a spicy, hop-accented

Rye Pale Ale ★★☆, a beer few were brewing at the time. Other brands include the spicier, grapefruity **Hopsecutioner** ★★, an IPA not shy in its hoppiness; and seasonal **Hop Karma** ★★☆, a brown ale with IPA-like hoppiness.

DESTINATION
DECATUR

The Brick Store (125 E Court Square) is a neighbourhood pub located a short transit ride from downtown Atlanta, with a community feel and an impressive selection of draught and bottled beers.

CANADA

Although it seldom receives the recognition accorded its neighbour to the south, Canada's craft brewing industry has been around for almost as long and has marked almost as many significant continental craft beer milestones, including first brewpub (the now-defunct Horseshoe Bay Brewing in British Columbia); first brewery specializing in cask-conditioned ale (Ontario's WELLINGTON COUNTY BREWERY); and first *eisbock* brewed outside Europe (Eisbock from the former Niagara Falls Brewing Company).

Born in the west, nurtured in major cities from Vancouver to Calgary to Toronto to Halifax, and best known internationally for its creative brewing forces clustered around Montréal, Canadian craft beer is today vibrant and expanding. A change to the taxation structure in Québec around the turn of the century caused a rapid increase in the number of breweries in that province – estimated at time of writing to be somewhere approaching 100 – while recent growth in local craft beer markets has caused new breweries to pop up with astonishing regularity in southern Ontario and the lower mainland of British Columbia, and to a lesser degree in Nova Scotia and Alberta.

Long self-identifying as a nation of beer drinkers, Canadians now seem prepared to embrace craft beer with the same enthusiasm they usually reserve for hockey or complaining about the weather.

WESTERN CANADA

Canadian craft brewing got its start in and around Vancouver, but it took some time for it to thrive anywhere in British Columbia outside of south Vancouver Island, remaining through most of the 1990s broadly defined by timid blond ales and hemp beers. Thankfully, all that changed with the dawn of the new millennium, as an emerging wave of craft brewers arrived on the scene, producing all manner of new and assertive styles of ale and lager.

Elsewhere in western Canada, however, progress was not nearly so swift.

Although it remains the only province in Canada with fully privatized beer sales, Alberta has not yet witnessed a significant expansion in the number of craft breweries it boasts, while both Saskatchewan and Manitoba remain largely craft beer-challenged, save for the odd oasis of characterful beer in Regina, Saskatoon and Winnipeg.

ALLEY KAT BREWING
Edmonton, Alberta

For close to two decades the craft beer standard-bearer in northern Alberta, this Edmonton stalwart seems to have found new creativity in recent years. Long-time brands like the appetizingly dry **Full Moon Pale Ale** ★★☆ and rich and complex **Old Deuteronomy Barley Wine** ★★★ have been joined by seasonals like the plummy, boozy, cellarable **Belgian Style Quad** ★★☆ and an impressive Dragon series of single-hop double IPAs, some of which merit greater regularity.

```
DESTINATION
CALGARY
```

Bottlescrew Bill's (140 10th Avenue SW) was one of Calgary's original good beer pubs, if not actually the first, and remains one of the best, with over 300 beers served in a cordial atmosphere.

CENTRAL CITY BREWING
Surrey, British Columbia

Suburban Surrey is a beloved butt of Vancouver jokes, but this expanding brewery can add a note of envy. **Red Racer ESB** ★★☆ is a piney but subtly fruity quaff; dry, grassy and citrus **Red Racer Pale Ale** ★★★☆ might be the best of its type in Canada; bigger **Red Racer IPA** ★★★ is more aggressive in its herbal-citrus hop bitterness; complex **Thor's Hammer Barley Wine** ★★★ hits the palate with spice, grows fruity then finishes off-dry and warming.

CRANNÓG ALES
Sorrento, British Columbia

Based on an operational farm in the BC interior, this all-organic brewery produces Irish-inspired, draught-only ales that are distributed only so far as the brewery truck can be driven in a day. Best bets are the **Back Hand of God Stout** ★★☆, roasty with a hint of tobacco leaf; and the unusual, deeply malty **Gael's Blood Potato Ale** ★★☆. Cask-conditioned specialities are usually worth a detour.

DRIFTWOOD BREWING
Victoria, British Columbia

Fast-expanding (over five years) Victoria brewery serving Vancouver Island and the lower mainland of BC. Brands include the perfumey and peppery **Farmhand Saison** ★★☆; fruity and herbal, almost lavender-evoking **White Bark Wit** ★★☆, a highly aromatic Belgian-style wheat beer; and foresty, almost oily **Fat**

Tug IPA ★★☆. **Old Cellar Dweller** ★★☆ is a darkly fruity and vanilla-ish barley wine that improves with ageing.

HALF PINTS BREWING
Winnipeg, Manitoba

Manitoba was a craft beer wasteland until this brewery came along, headed by a former brewer at Regina's Bushwakker Brewpub (*see* box, below right). Highlights include chocolate-cinnamon-cherry **Pothole Porter** ★★☆; citrus-spicy **Little Scrapper IPA** ★★☆; cellar-worthy barley wine **Burly Wine** ★★☆; and an ale that promises "ludicrous" hoppiness, but delivers something far more balanced, **Humulus Ludicrous** ★★★.

HOWE SOUND BREWING
Squamish, British Columbia

This Squamish brewpub-turned-production brewery displays a deft hand with strong ales packaged in large bottles. One that perhaps shouldn't work, but does, is the strong, fruity-sweet and spicy **King Heffy Imperial Hefeweizen**

CRAFT BREWED IN VICTORIA, BC. 102-450 Hillside Ave, V8T 1Y7

DRIFTWOOD BREWERY

Beer/Bière 650 mL 5.5 % alc./vol.

★★★; the more conventional **Pothole Filler Imperial Stout** ★★☆ doesn't disappoint with dried-fruit and espresso flavours; real pumpkin flavours add to the pleasure of the almost bourbon-ish **Pumpkineater** ★★☆; while a flagship of sorts is the berry-ish, nutty **Three Beavers Imperial Red Ale** ★★☆.

PADDOCK WOOD
Saskatoon, Saskatchewan

One of Saskatchewan's few and true home-grown craft beer options. Regulars include the nutty, toasted malt and apple-ish **Red Hammer** ★★★; and **Loki IPA** ★★, once intense in its citrus hop but now more malt-driven. When barrel-aged, Loki becomes the more rounded, hazelnutty **Oaky Loki** ★★☆; while other seasonals include the warming, sweet, vanilla-ish **Barrel Full of Monkeys Imperial Stout** ★★.

> ### DESTINATION
> ### REGINA
>
> Bushwakker (2206 Dewdney Avenue) was a pioneering brewpub on the Prairies and remains a craft beer oasis in a region mostly devoid of attractive beer-drinking options.

PARALLEL 49 BREWING
Vancouver, British Columbia

Born of a craft beer-friendly restaurant partnership, this east Vancouver brewery earned local attention from almost day one. Cartoon labels adorn beers like **Hoparazzi** ★★☆, an off-dry, spicy-fruity

IPA; **Old Boy** ★★☆, a nutty, lightly tannic ale that seems to grow drier with every sip; and **Gypsy Tears Ruby Ale** ★★☆, a robust brew with plum fruitiness hidden behind walnutty, citrus, spicy hoppiness.

PHILLIPS BREWING
Victoria, British Columbia

From shoestring beginnings, Matt Phillips has built his namesake brewery into one of the more influential on Canada's west coast. Flagship is the floral, peachy **Blue Buck** ★☆, but enthusiasts opt instead for the **Amnesiac Double IPA** ★★☆, an ale of spicy, grapefruity hoppiness atop a soft, fruity malt backbone. Other beers of note include a more assertive, herbal-citrus **Hop Circle IPA** ★★; and gingery but mellow **Ginger Beer** ★★☆.

> ### DESTINATION
> **VICTORIA**
>
> The Swans Suite Hotel (506 Pandora Avenue) is home to not just an impressive brewpub and attached bistro, but also luxurious loft-style suites where pints of Riley's Scotch Ale or Buckerfield's Bitter may be ordered through room service.

SPINNAKERS GASTRO BREWPUB & GUEST HOUSES
Victoria, British Columbia

Victoria is a hotbed of craft brewing at least in part thanks to Canada's longest-surviving brewpub. Bottling and distribution now allows others to try pub favourites like full and floral-fruity

Mitchell's Extra Special Bitter ★★★; the mildly nutty and sessionable **Nut Brown Ale** ★★☆; and newer **Blue Bridge Double Pale Ale** ★★, a surprisingly gentle and approachable take on what's usually an aggressive style. Pub beers offer greater variety.

STORM BREWING
Vancouver, British Columbia

Unconventional, draught-only brewery located in an industrial part of Vancouver. Past experiments with loosely controlled "wild" fermentations have yielded impressive lambic-like fruit beers ★★→★★★, while regular brands include the spicy-hoppy **Hurricane IPA** ★★☆; and a roasty, slightly off-balance **Black Plague Stout** ★★, usually poured from a tap topped by a rubber rat.

> ### DESTINATION
> **VANCOUVER**
>
> Alibi Room (157 Alexander Street) is Vancouver's go-to place for craft beer, with two floors of seating, 50 taps and a pub/restaurant menu.

TOFINO BREWING
Tofino, British Columbia

Environmentally aware Vancouver Island brewery located almost as far west as is possible in Canada. Flagship **Tuff Session Ale** ★★★ leads with a orange-peach fruitiness but softens and dries in the toasted malt finish; stronger **Hop Cretin IPA** ★★☆ packs a piney, grapefruity hop punch, growing more floral in the finish.

TOWNSITE BREWING
Powell River, British Columbia

Young but immediately impressive brewery on BC's "Sunshine Coast". **Pow Town Porter** ★★ is mocha-ish, nutty and lightly sweet; strong **Charleston** ★★ is a malty powerhouse in the guise of a *tripel*; **Zunga** ★★☆ is a peaches-and-cream golden ale that proves blond need not be boring. Summer seasonal **Blackberry Festive Ale** ★★★ evokes thoughts of sparkling rosé in its floral, off-dry fruitiness.

TREE BREWING
Kelowna, British Columbia

Once BC's most shape-shifting brewery, Tree has settled down of late into a comfortable guise. Best when embracing hops, as with highly aromatic, tangerine-herbal **Hop Head IPA** ★★★; caramel-chocolaty, bitterly roasty **Hop Head Black IPA** ★★☆; the rather heavy-handed **Hop Head Double IPA** ★★ is less successful. Greater subtlety is shown by the summer seasonal **Hefeweizen** ★★☆, a lemony interpretation of the style.

VANCOUVER ISLAND BREWING
Victoria, British Columbia

Enduring island brewery with beers that run the gamut from soft and approachable to complex and creative. Somewhere in the middle is the admirable **Hermann's Dark Lager** ★★☆, a stalwart *dunkel* with soft, off-dry, malty earthiness, while its big brother, the seasonal **Hermannator Ice Bock** ★★★, can vary year-to-year but remains solidly malty and warming throughout.

YUKON BREWING
Whitehorse, Yukon

The sole brewery in Canada's far northern Territories, based in Whitehorse. Beers tend toward the conventional, as with the soft, dryish and mildly bitter **Yukon Gold** ★★; and fruity, modestly warming **Yukon Red** ★★. Of greater interest to aficionados is the winter seasonal **Lead Dog Ale** ★★☆, with raisin and plum notes backed by cinnamon spice and a suggestion of hop.

EASTERN CANADA

It may have lagged behind much of the rest of the country in jumping on the craft beer bandwagon – the city didn't get a brewery of its own until 1987 – but Montréal has since leapfrogged Toronto, Halifax and other eastern cities to become the heart of creative Canadian craft brewing. Best known both domestically and abroad for their Belgian-influenced brews, Québec brewers have more lately embraced a spirit of unbridled creativity, brewing beers made with all manner of ingredients, aged in all sorts of barrels and fermented in any number of ways.

And the creativity is catching. Having been mired for years in conservative brewing traditions, brewers in southern Ontario and the Maritimes are branching finally into big beers, bold hoppiness, Belgian influences and unusual expressions of the brewing arts. Coupled with the recent growth in both size and numbers of craft breweries, it portends a rosy future for craft brewing in eastern Canada.

À LA FÛT
Saint-Tite, Québec

Small-town Québec brewery and pub thrust into the limelight by winning Beer of the Year at the 2012 Canadian Brewing Awards with **Co-Hop V ★★★**, a wonderfully balanced sweet-tart cherry beer. Others in the stable include **La British ★★★☆**, a very nutty brown ale with supreme sessionability; the spicy-hop, dry finishing **À la Belge Saison ★★★**; the citrus hop, peachy malt of **Cuvée Houblonnée IPA ★★★**; and the grassy, quenching **Ma Première Blonde Pilsner ★★☆**.

BEAU'S ALL NATURAL BREWING
Vankleek Hill, Ontario

A family operation based in eastern Ontario close to the Québec border. Excels at the Germanic approach to brewing, as with its homage to *kölsch*, the lightly fruity, suitably crisp **Lug-Tread Lagered Ale ★★☆**; the outstanding, toasted caramelly **Night Märzen ★★★**; and the leafy-nutty, malt-driven and *altbier*-inspired **FestiveAle ★★☆**. Numerous seasonals and one-offs, including a **Screamin' Beaver Oak Aged Double IPA ★★☆**, rich with alcoholic warmth and flavours of stewed fruit and hoppy herbals.

BELLWOODS BREWERY
Toronto, Ontario

In the spring of 2012, this funky and highly experimental brewery opened to take Toronto by storm, producing a wide range of mostly very good to excellent beers in a multitude of styles. An on-site store offers limited amounts of a variety of bottled beers, including the liquoricy **Lost River Baltic Porter ★★★**; the gently fruity, off-dry **Fortune Cookie Tripel ★★☆**; and the unexpectedly impressive smoked *Berliner weisse* **Mash Pipe ★★★**.

DESTINATION
TORONTO

Bar Volo (587 Yonge Street) began life as an Italian restaurant, morphing in the late 1990s into a beer bar and later becoming Toronto's top destination for local, often hard-to-find beers and home to the tiny but impressive House Ales brewery.

BLACK OAK BREWING
Toronto, Ontario

Originally based in the Toronto suburb of Oakville, hence the name, this now west-Toronto-located brewery produces a handful of regular, occasional and seasonal brands. Flagship offerings are a light and fruity **Pale Ale** ★★; and an appropriately nutty, medium-weight **Nut Brown Ale** ★★☆. The brewery's 10th anniversary beer, **Ten Bitter Years** ★★★, continues to cause line-ups at the brewery on the odd occasion when the intensely fruity, prodigiously hoppy IPA is released.

DESTINATION TORONTO

beerbistro (18 King Street East) is a pioneering beer cuisine restaurant with a creative menu, impressive list of bottled and draught beers, including many privately sourced, and a large library of cellared beers. (Disclosure: restaurant was co-founded by co-author of this book, Stephen Beaumont, although no ownership stake remains.)

BORÉALE (LES BRASSEURS DU NORD)
Blainville, Québec

This pioneering Québec craft brewery – the third to open in the province – is located north of Montréal and produces mostly accessible beers aimed at capturing the market from the big breweries. A case in point is the flagship **Rousse** ★★, a smooth, reddish ale with plenty of maltiness and a drying finish. Other brands worth sampling include a perfumey **Blonde** ★★☆; and a zesty, ginger-accented **Blanche** ★★☆.

BRASSEURS DU TEMPS, LES
Gatineau, Québec

Atmospheric brewery-restaurant just across the border from Ottawa, distributing mostly stronger ales on a limited basis. Summery **La Saison Haute** ★★★ pleases with peppery citrus and a dry finish; while **La Messe de Minuit** ★★☆ is a gingerbready ode to Christmas. In between come the flamed orange zest and hop resin of **Diable au Corps** ★★★, a double IPA; and **Obscur Désir** ★★★, an inky and warming Imperial stout aged in bourbon barrels.

BRASSEURS SANS GLUTEN
Montréal, Québec

Though a young brewery, this exclusively gluten-free brewing operation has impressed greatly. Hopheads like the intensely bitter **Glutenberg Pale Ale Américaine** ★★; more balanced and measured is the dryly citrus **Glutenberg Blonde** ★★☆; eight ingredients make up the **Glutenberg 8** ★★☆, an "atypical ale" with flavours of date and nuttiness;

while a buckwheat character is apparent in **Glutenberg Red Ale ★★☆**.

CHARLEVOIX
Baie-Saint-Paul, Québec

Québec-City-region brewery offering two lines: Belgium-inspired Dominus Vobiscum and broadly British-influenced Vache Folle. Of the former, **Triple ★★★** impresses with tropical-fruit flavours and spicy alcohol notes; **Saison ★★★** offers citrus and grapey notes atop more spice; the hoppy **Lupulus ★★★** is yeasty, peppery and refreshing despite its strength; and the Champagne-esque **Brut ★★★☆** is subtle and dryly fruity. Best of the Mad Cow line is a complex, intensely flavourful and surprisingly strong **Imperial Milk Stout ★★★**.

CREEMORE SPRINGS BREWING (MOLSONCOORS)
Creemore, Ontario

Early Ontario craft brewery that actually improved after its acquisition in 2005. Flagship **Premium Lager ★★☆** is crisp enough but veers toward ale-like fruitiness; while more recent arrival **Kellerbier ★★★** is less yeasty than at its introduction, but still a satisfying quaff. Convincingly Düsseldorf-esque **Altbier Collaboration Ale ★★★** was brewed with schlüssel in Germany.

DENISON'S BREWING
Toronto, Ontario

Once upon a time a brewpub in downtown Toronto, this Germanic brewery is contract brewing until a new facility is built in nearby Collingwood. Canned or draught **Weissbier ★★☆** is reliably spicy, if sometimes a bit too fruity; while draught-only (at time of writing) **Dunkel ★★☆** can err a bit on the sweet side, but otherwise shows good earthy, cocoa-ish complexity.

DIEU DU CIEL!
Montréal, Québec

Stunningly innovative (and successfully so) Montréal brewpub-spawned brewery. Wide range of impressive brands, including black pepper and rye beer that balances the spiciness with precision, **Route des Épices ★★★**; hibiscus-flower-flavoured and summery **Rosée d'Hibiscus ★★★**; coffee-accented and deliciously intense **Péché Mortel ★★★**; Belgian-inspired, fruity **Dernière Volonté ★★☆**, which finishes with a decidedly bitter twist; and the cocoa-and-vanilla masterpiece, **Aphrodisiaque ★★★**.

DESTINATION
MONTRÉAL

Brasserie Benelux (245 rue Sherbrooke ouest) is a brewpub of note in a city filled with quality brewpubs, producing a diverse and creative array of mostly ales punctuated by the occasional excellent lager.

GARRISON BREWING
Halifax, Nova Scotia

Sometimes locally polarizing brewery established in 1997, but only really hitting its stride a few years into the new century. Brews the lemony and herbal **Hop Yard Pale Ale** ★★☆; roundly fruity, bitter-finishing **Imperial IPA** ★★★; molasses- and liquorice-accented **Grand Baltic Porter** ★★★; toffee-ish but bitter-finishing **Ol' Fog Burner Barley Wine** ★★★; plus occasional specialities, like the unlikely-sounding but excellent 15th Anniversary Hops**, Mango & Ginger** ★★★.

GRANITE BREWERY
Toronto, Ontario

Granite is a long-established and growing midtown-Toronto brewpub-turned-brewery. It has a growing interest in experimental and US influenced beers, but is still at its best with the dry and leafy **Best Bitter** ★★☆, which becomes still better as the dry-hopped and cask-conditioned **Best Bitter Special** ★★★☆. Also impressive are the nitro-poured and roasty-creamy **Keefe's Irish Stout** ★★★; and the boldly hoppy but British-inspired **IPA** ★★★.

GREAT LAKES BREWING
Toronto, Ontario

Born a malt extract brewery in suburban Toronto, this brewery has moved downtown to evolve into a more serious craft-driven operation. **Crazy Canuck Pale Ale** ★★★ is emblematic of this shift, with a balance of fruit, citrus, caramel and light florals, while seasonals like **Pumpkin Ale** ★★☆, unapologetic in its pumpkin-pie spiciness, and the over-spiced **Winter Ale** ★☆ can be variable.

HELL BAY BREWING COMPANY
Cherry Hill, Nova Scotia

Promising young brewery located on the south coast of Nova Scotia, brewing primarily English-inspired ales with a New World attitude. Cocoa-ish and roasty **Brown Ale** ★★☆ is a seasonal expected to go year-round; while the ballsy **English Ale** ★★☆ applies aggressive hopping techniques to the best bitter style. A quaffable but slightly thinnish, seasonal **Oatmeal Stout** ★★☆ and experimental, campfire-and-spice **Smoked Rye Beer** ★★☆ show potential.

HOPFENSTARK
L'Assomption, Québec

While best known for its multiple interpretations of the *saison* style of beer, this small brewery and pub east of Montréal displays admirable breadth with such ales as the caramel-citrus **Post-Colonial IPA** ★★★☆; the rich, creamy and almost port-like **Greg American Foreign Stout** ★★★; the stylistic mash-up of *rauchbier*, *saison* and *Berliner weisse* known as **Boson de Higgs** ★★☆; and of course, the dry, spicy and pear-ish **Saison Station 55** ★★★.

KICHESIPPI BEER
Ottawa, Ontario

This once-contract brewery got off to a rough start, but a purchase of the brewery it was contracting and the importation of a seasoned western Canadian brewer has done wonders. **Heller High Water** ★★☆ is a seasonal *helles* with a crisp palate and mildly bitter finish; **Blonde**

★★☆ is a mildly fruity, slightly herbal and quaffable ale; and another summer seasonal, **Uncle Mark's Hopfen Weisse** ★★☆, combines a banana-intense front with a more hoppy middle and a dry and fast finish.

KING BREWERY
Nobleton, Ontario

North-of-Toronto brewery specializing in spot-on interpretation of European lager styles. Flagship **Pilsner** ★★★ is strongly Czech in character, with a slight butteriness and firm hop finish; second brand **Dark Lager** ★★☆ speaks strongly to Bavarian *dunkel* traditions with an earthy, cocoa-ish taste; and **Vienna Lager** ★★★ begins with malty sweetness but ends refreshingly dry and softly bitter.

MCAUSLAN BREWING/ BRASSERIE MCAUSLAN
Montréal, Québec

Over-two-decades-old company produces two lines of beer – St Ambroise and Griffon – the more successful named after the working

class district in which the brewery was founded. Flagship **St Ambroise Pale Ale** ★★☆ inspires memories of the Québécois ales of the 1950s; **St Ambroise Oatmeal Stout** ★★★☆ is a silken, roasty, mocha-ish delight; **St Ambroise Vintage Ale** ★★★ benefits well from several years of age; and **St Ambroise Imperial Stout** ★★★ solidifies the brewery's stout credentials with a complex, winey character.

DESTINATION MONTRÉAL

Cheval Blanc (809 rue Ontario est) is an old, family-owned and classically Québécois tavern turned in 1988 into the city's first brewpub and, although expanded significantly in recent years, it remains one of the best.

MILL STREET BREWING
Toronto, Ontario

Brewery founded in historic Distillery District, turned brewpub with separate production facility in city's east end. Flagship **Tankhouse Ale** ★★☆ layers lightly citrus hop on a firm malt base; nitro-canned **Cobblestone Stout** ★★★ mixes dark chocolate with appetizing roastiness; and *helles*-esque **Organic Lager** ★★☆ serves as a dryish quaffer. More variety available at the brewpub.

MUSKOKA BREWERY
Bracebridge, Ontario

Based in Toronto's northern "Cottage Country", this operation went from humdrum to impressive in a short time, spearheaded by the wonderfully fragrant, refreshingly hoppy **Mad Tom IPA** ★★★ and a reworking of core brands such as the slightly winey, raisiny **Dark Ale** ★★☆. Later releases include the bigger, burnt-orangey **Twice as Mad Tom** ★★☆ and seasonals like the judiciously spiced, Belgian-esque **Spring Oddity** ★★★ and autumnal, earthy **Harvest Ale** ★★☆.

PEI BREWING/THE GAHAN HOUSE
Charlottetown, Prince Edward Island

Working in a tough market, PEI Brewing of Charlottetown has successfully transitioned from tiny brewpub via larger brewery-restaurant to packaging brewery. Their brands include the overtly gimmicky, but genuinely *helles*-esque **BeachChair Lager** ★★; the apple-nutty **Island Red** ★★☆, reminiscent of Irish red ales of old; and the yeasty, nutty-citrus **1772 India Pale Ale** ★★.

PICAROONS BREWING
Fredericton, New Brunswick

This stalwart Maritime brewery has certainly been through its ups and downs, although it has been quite stable and reliable for the last several years, even winning Brewery of the Year honours at the Canadian Brewing Awards in 2011. Picaroons brews ales mostly in the English tradition, such as the dry, biscuity **Best Bitter** ★★☆, which is imbued with leafy hop notes, but can deviate at times, as with the fragrant and citrus **Yippee IPA** ★★☆.

PROPELLER BREWING
Halifax, Nova Scotia

Once unapologetically British in inspiration, this long-standing craft brewery has more recently branched into diverse styles, largely in support of a successful growler-filling programme at the brewery. Still, English styles remain the forte, such as the raw cocoa- and chocolate-accented **London-Style Porter** ★★★; appley **ESB** ★★, especially good on tap; and the more New World-styled, floral-fruity **IPA** ★★. A notable diversion is the impressive, mango-ish, nutty **Double IPA** ★★☆.

DESTINATION
HALIFAX

Rogue's Roost (5435 Spring Garden Road), established in 1999, is the good beer anchor on Halifax's well-known shopping street, with traditional and creative beers crafted by the only brewer the brewpub has ever known, Lorno Romano.

STEAM WHISTLE BREWING
Toronto, Ontario

Housed in the shadow of Toronto's CN Tower, the motto of this fast-growing brewery is "Do one thing really, really well", and it does. The lone beer is labelled a **Pilsner** ★★★, but is more akin to a Bavarian *helles*, fragrant and floral in its aroma, with a softly sweet graininess tempered by a moderately bitter, drying hoppiness.

TROIS MOUSQUETAIRES, LES
Brossard, Québec

Highly regarded for its cork-finished, large-bottle speciality beers, this brewery founded by a trio of friends maintains a fascination with lagers in general and German brewing traditions in particular. Great success has been experienced with the floral, chocolaty **Rauchbier** ★★★; the spicy and dryly fruity **Hopfenweisse** ★★☆; and the outstanding, chocolate-raisin-cinnamon **Porter Baltique** ★★★☆.

TROU DU DIABLE
Shawinigan, Québec

Experimental and graphically inclined brewery midway between Montréal and Québec City, ageing ales in oak, naming beers after political in-jokes and generally having a good time. Successes include the appealingly sweet and sour **La Buteuse** ★★★, strong and matured in apple brandy barrels; the snappy, slightly grapey **Dulcis Succubus** ★★★; a hybrid pale ale/*hefeweizen* called **Shawinigan Handshake** ★★☆, dedicated to a former Canadian prime minister; and the deceptively light-tasting and fruity **Saison du Tracteur** ★★.

UNIBROUE (SAPPORO)
Chambly, Québec

Now owned by Japan's Sapporo, this Montréal-area brewery has been a leader in both Belgian-inspired brewing and export development. Flagships are a coriander-ish, quenching **Blanche de Chambly** ★★; and spicy, dark and food-friendly **Maudite** ★★☆, which might have lost a bit of character through the years. Also fruity *tripel*, **Fin du Monde** ★★★; dark, rich and slightly cloying **Trois Pistoles** ★★☆; and humorously named **Terrible** ★★★☆, a strong ale that drinks like a fine brandy.

WELLINGTON COUNTY BREWERY
Guelph, Ontario

Conceived as a producer of cask-conditioned ale, Ontario's third craft brewery (opened in 1985) adjusted quickly to the hard realities of the market. **Arkell Best Bitter** ★★, softly fruity and gently bitter, remains best on cask ★★☆; while co-flagship **County Dark Ale** ★★☆ is nutty and faintly minerally in the finish. Local aficionados highlight the winey, dark plum flavours of the **Imperial Stout** ★★☆.

THE CARIBBEAN

Throughout the Caribbean, you will find the market dominated by light lagers, most brewed by one of a handful of regional brewing powers. Craft breweries do exist, but finding their beers can be like searching for a needle in a haystack, and not necessarily a needle worth the hunt.

The three powers of Caribbean beer are Jamaica's Desnoes & Geddes, owned by Diageo; Trinidad and Tobago's Carib; and the Guyana-headquartered brewery of Barbados, Banks. Best known is Desnoes & Geddes' Red Stripe ★, a slightly grainy lager refreshing when served very cold. Better by a small measure is the slightly spicy Carib ★☆; while Banks Caribbean Lager ★ tends toward the sweeter side.

Dark beers do exist, a legacy of the strong stouts brought to the islands over a century ago, now brewed as strong and sweet black lagers. Here, too, Desnoes & Geddes leads with Dragon Stout ★★, lightly roasty and thinnish with a hint of anise; while Royal Extra Stout ★★ from Carib offers a slight silkiness; and Banks offers Banks Amber Ale, as yet untasted.

What can appear to be craft brewing in the Caribbean can be misleading. Once independent Big City Brewing of Kingston, Jamaica, is now allied with Anheuser-Busch InBev. The St Vincent Brewery and the Antigua Brewery are both owned by Denmark's Royal Unibrew. Trinidad's Samba Brewing and the Bahamian Brewery of the Bahamas are each independent, but with little apparent craft brewing ambition.

One of the few successful craft beer concerns in the Caribbean is St John Brewers in the US Virgin Islands. Although the bulk of its beer is contract-brewed in Maine, and even sold in the northeastern US, the partners maintain a small Tap House bar on the island where they test new recipes on willing customers. Among their brands is one of the few IPAs sold in the West Indies, Island Hoppin' IPA ★★, a British-influenced brew with fruity and nutty flavours.

LATIN AMERICA

UNITED STATES
OF AMERICA

Gulf of
Mexico

MEXICO

MEXICO CITY

GUATEMA

MEXICO

Mexico gets its modern brewing traditions from Germany, thanks to the Germans and Swiss who set up post-independence commercial breweries in the 19th century. By the mid-to-late 20th century, the country was known for golden, *helles*-esque lagers, amber beers that resembled Vienna lagers and the occasional *Münchener* style dark beer, known locally as *cerveza obscura*.

Then came Corona.

The light lager in the clear bottle, back then sometimes served with a squeeze of lime and a dash of salt or hot pepper sauce, had existed in Mexico for decades, but when it arrived as an import to the Texas and California markets in the 1980s, it became a cultural phenomenon. From thence forward, Mexican beer was known by the lightness of its taste, the clarity of its container and the ubiquity of the slice of lime wedged into the bottle.

Against this backdrop are several emerging craft breweries, each struggling to introduce more characterful ales and lagers to Mexico. Standing in their way is not only a public conditioned to light-tasting lagers served ice-cold, but also a retail and distribution system that favours the oligarchs to a tremendous degree.

Progress has been slow but steady, with greatest access to the new craft beers being in the capital of Mexico City, the Baja California peninsula and Guadalajara. Should gains in availability be made, and quality continue to improve, there may yet be a day when the country's brewers are known more for spicy Mexican Imperial stout than bland golden lager.

CAMARADA
Oaxaca

This young Oaxacan brewery got off to a shaky start with a trio of mostly pedestrian beers, including a decidedly unBavarian **Weissbier** ★. Experimental and one-off brews, however, hint at possible successes to come, such as an off-dry and compellingly spicy **Red Ale** ★★, infused with local *rosita de cacao*; and a captivating and sweet corn beer called **Santería** ★★.

CUCAPÁ
Mexicali, Baja California

Almost as well known in the US as in Mexico, this northern Baja California brewery produces flagship **Cucapá Clásica** ★★, off-dry and mildly bitter, with citrusy notes; and **Lowrider Ale** ★★☆, spicy from the use of rye and warming with orange toffee flavours on the finish. **Chupacabras** ★★★ is an herbaceous midpoint between pale ale and IPA.

GOURMET CALAVERA
Mexico City

A creative, experimental and gastronomically influenced brewery in Mexico City. Belgian styles an obvious interest, as shown by the slightly thin, chocolaty **Dubbel** ★★ and faintly candied **Tripel** ★★☆. An **American Pale Ale** ★★☆ is fruity and quaffable; **Mexican Imperial Stout** ★★★ has wonderful dark chocolaty dryness; and special **Lovecraft Beer** ★★★ is spicy and molé-esque.

DESTINATION
MEXICO CITY

Pujol (Francisco Petrarca 254) is not just one of Mexico's most highly acclaimed restaurants, it is also a place where the gastronomic possibilities presented by craft beer are recognized through a rather extensive list of local labels.

JACK
Mexico City

Mexico City brewery branching out from its British-brewing-inspired roots with **Alebrije** ★★☆, an unusual take on a *weissbier* with strong mango and peach flavours. More typical are **Jack Stout** ★★, black, sweet and rounded, **Jack Chocolate Sweet Stout** ★★☆, strong and massively chocolaty with notes of cinnamon and allspice; and **Jack Clown Smile** ★★☆, a slightly roasty Scotch ale with flavours of toffee and plum and a hint of nutmeg.

LA CHINGONERÍA
Mexico City

Homebrewer from Mexico City who developed his passion into a business. Golden pilsner **Chekate Esta** ★★ is spicy-herbal and curiously lemony, but also oddly compelling; **Házmela Rusa** ★★★ is a lovely, plummy Mexican Imperial stout that warms beyond its strength; and **Amargator IPA** ★★ is a double IPA with a pleasing fruitiness interrupted by a sharp, hoppy bitterness and hit of alcohol.

MINERVA
Guadalajara, Jalisco

Relatively high-profile brewery. **Pale Ale** ★★ is malty upfront, hoppier in back; **Viena** ★★★ is a toasty, drying lager true to its style; **Rila** ★★★ is off-dry and a bit cherry pie-ish, but certainly sessionable, brewed to celebrate a bicycle festival; **Imperial Stout** ★★☆ is light for its billing but roasty and coffee-ish; tequila barrel-aged **Imperial Tequila Ale** ★★☆ derives peppery spiciness from its maturing process.

> ### DESTINATION
> ### GUADALAJARA
>
> The Tap Room (López Cotilla 1533), a "Pastrami-Beer-Store," is among the better beer bars in one of the few Mexican cities where a relatively large number of such places exist.

PRIMUS
Mexico City

Brewery known better by the name it gives its beers. **Tempus Dorada** ★★☆ offers aromas and rounded, sweetish flavours of canned peach and apricot leading to an off-dry finish; **Tempus Doble Malta** ★★★ is raisiny, with clove-edged spice showing toward the peppery finish.

PÚBLICA CONDESA
Mexico City

Mexico City brewery producing a single beer, but a good one. **Poe Brown Ale**

★★☆ is sweetly roasty on the nose and offers a creamy body with notes of dark chocolate and dried fruit.

RÁMURI
Tijuana, Baja California

Tijuana brewery on its way to mastering classic beer styles. Best so far are **Lágrimas Negras** ★★★, an intensely chocolaty oatmeal stout at a strength 10% more akin to an Imperial, and **Bucéfalo** ★★, a mildly herbaceous and curiously low-key Imperial stout. Experimental brews show some promise.

TIJUANA BEER
Tijuana, Baja California

Known informally as TJ Beer, this Baja California brewery produces clean, conventional brews such as **Rosarito Beach** ★☆, a dryish alternative to Corona; and **Güera** ★★☆, a floral pilsner evocative of the Czech Republic. More boundary-stretching are **Güera** ★★, a dark and sweetish *dunkel* with tobacco leaf notes; and **Bufadora** ★★★, a full and toffee-ish lager identified as a *maibock*.

> ### DESTINATION
> ### RIVIERA MAYA
>
> The Fairmont Mayakoba (298 Playa del Carmen) distinguishes itself by being one of the very few Mexican resorts to feature local craft beer, even hosting regular beer tastings with complementary food pairings.

BRAZIL

Brazil is the fourth-largest beer-producing nation in the world. Yet all but a very small minority of that beer is light lager brewed from a minimum of barley malt by one of three companies: Anheuser-Busch InBev, with an estimated 70% market share; Kirin Brazil; and Heineken-owned Kaiser. This leaves some 200 Brazilian craft brewers grappling for roughly 1% of the beer market, while hamstrung by tax laws that treat them the same as the big brewers!

Still, there is hope for the Brazilian craft beer future. An emerging and growing middle class in the country is actively seeking to upgrade its eating and drinking experiences, and the upcoming World Cup (2014) and Olympics (2016) will surely shine a light on at least some of the country's small breweries. Additionally, over the last few years, many Brazilian brewers have shown vast improvement in the quality, originality and consistency of their beers.

If the government ever decides to follow the lead of developed nations across the west and introduces a graduated system of taxation based on brewery size and output, the future of craft brewing in Brazil might become very bright indeed.

ABADESSA
Porto Alegre, Rio Grande do Sul

Located in Rio Grande do Sul, this brewery doesn't pasteurize or filter any of its beers (unusual for Brazil, even in craft beer circles). **Slava Pilsen** ★★ is a refreshing, yeasty and flowery lager; **Export** ★★ has a biscuit-like aroma and nutty maltiness balanced with discreet bitterness; **Helles** ★☆ offers an evident breadiness in the body and a yeasty finish; and **Dunkles Nektar** ★★ starts with intensely caramelly aromatics and finishes with a slight spiciness.

AMAZON BEER
Belém, Pará

Based in a tourism and cultural centre in Belém, Pará, this innovative brewery tweaks beer styles through the addition of different Amazonian fruits. Examples include **Witbier Taperebá** ★★, which is flavoured with *taperebá* fruit, also known as *cajá*, for a highly perfumey aroma and citrus, zesty, plummy body; and **Forest Bacuri** ★★★, a pilsner whose sweet yet crisp, pineappley flavour is thanks to the use of *bacuri* fruit.

BACKER/3 LOBOS
Belo Horizonte, Minas Gerais

Belo Horizonte operation producing two line-ups of beer, plus a stand-alone ale called **Medieval ★★**, with a bottle more striking than its spiced mandarin orange flavours. Of the two lines, Backer and 3 Lobos, the latter is more interesting, with a crisp, light and mildly spicy wheat ale called **Exterminador ★★**; and the spicy-vanilla **Bravo American Imperial Porter ★★★**, aged in Amazonian wood. Best of the Backer line is the thinly chocolaty **Brown ★★**.

BADEN BADEN (KIRIN BRAZIL)
Campos do Jordão, São Paulo

One of the first breweries of Brazil's craft beer renaissance, sold to what was then Schincariol in 2007. Brews a light, smooth and refreshing **Weiss ★★**; **Golden Ale ★★**, with delicate sweetness and cinnamon notes; **1999 ★★★**, a hop-accented ale well balanced with caramelly malt presence and fruitiness; **Red Ale ★★☆**, strong and warming with a heavy dose of hops moderated by roasted malt; and a densely oily, coffee-ish and dry-finishing **Stout ★★☆**.

> DESTINATION
> **SÃO PAULO**
>
> Melograno (436 Aspicuelta) is not just a bar with an outstanding selection of Brazilian and foreign beers, it is also a restaurant that offers beer-pairing suggestions for each dish, a rarity in Brazil.

BAMBERG BIER
Sorocaba, São Paulo

Highly regarded, much lauded and perhaps predictably German-influenced brewery situated not far from São Paulo. Beers include a light-tasting but decidedly *dunkel*-ish **München ★★**; a most credible **Alt ★★**, with off-dry caramel notes and a dry finish; a toffee-ish **Bock ★★☆**; the gently smoky, appley **Rauchbier ★★★**; and a surprising paean to Belgium, **Due ★★★**, a toffee, pomegranate and chocolate delight brewed for the Melograno Restaurant in São Paulo (*see* box, below left).

> DESTINATION
> **SÃO PAULO**
>
> FrangÓ (168 Largo da Matriz Nossa Senhora do Ó), although unimpressive from the outside, is a sprawling, multi-level jewel that is almost certainly the finest beer bar in all Brazil, and has been so for more than two decades.

BIERLAND
Blumenau, Santa Catarina

Brewery producing some of the most awarded beers in the country. **Vienna ★★☆** has a gentle citrus hop aroma balanced with smooth caramel malt flavours; **Pale Ale ★★★** has an abundance of passion-fruity hoppiness and a lingering, dryly bitter finish; **Weizen ★★** is quite lively, smooth and predominantly clovey; **Bock ★★★** offers nutty, brandy-ish flavours and a warming finish; and a very rich, syrupy **Imperial Stout** ★★★☆ attempts to redefine the style with chocolate liqueur, coffee and liquorice notes.

BODEBROWN
Curitiba, Paraná

Refreshingly irreverent brewer/teacher leading the drive to make Curitiba Brazil's craft beer capital. Style-bending brews include **Cerveja do Amer** ★★☆, a berry *hefeweizen* that morphed into a stronger, mildly peppery, berry-flavoured *tripel*; while the more conventional **Wee Heavy** ★★★ is a very rich, warming and fudge-evoking Scotch ale. Improbable flagship is the strong, orangey and passion-fruity **Perigosa** ★★★, developed as Brazil's first double IPA.

DESTINATION
CURITIBA

Cervejaria da Vila (2631 Rua Mateus Leme), open since 2004 in the city and fast becoming the heart of Brazilian craft brewing, is one of the region's most impressive beer bars, often featuring hard-to-find American and Belgian beers.

BURGMAN
Sorocaba, São Paulo

New brewery in Sorocaba, near São Paulo, has a restaurant with excellent Bavarian and Brazilian national food. Best beer is a soothing, perfumey and floral **Weiss** ★★, with soft, clovey spiciness and a bitter accent on the finish.

COLORADO
Ribeirão Preto, São Paulo

A pioneer of the Brazilian craft beer movement, based in Ribeirão Preto. Local ingredients feature in beers like the honey-ish, lemony **Appia** ★★, brewed with honey; the gently bitter IPA, **Indica** ★★☆, which is fortified with a hard sugar called *rapadura* and better on tap than bottled; and the coffee porter **Demoiselle** ★★, an intense, espresso-ish jolt of flavour. Newer is the very successful **Vixnu** ★★★, a firmly bitter, apricot-and-allspice double IPA.

CORUJA
Porto Alegre, Rio Grande do Sul

Marketing-conscious brewery packaging some beers in eye-catching 1l (1¾ pint) bottles. Brews a sweet, biscuity and warming **Strix Extra** ★☆; the unusual, softly smoky and robustly clovey **Alba Weizen** ★★; and **Labareda** ★★, a chilli-spiced *kellerbier*-style lager with hints of smoke in the body and a gentle burn on the finish.

DADO BIER
Porto Alegre, Rio Grande do Sul

This pioneering craft brewery, from Porto Alegre, has been in production since 1995. Its beers include **Ilex** ★★, brewed with local yerba mate and boasting an herbal, minty aroma and light flavour; the caramelly and modestly bitter **Red Ale** ★; a sweet and spicy **Weiss** ★; and an intensely fruity and delicate **Belgian Ale** ★☆.

DAMA BIER
Piracicaba, São Paulo

Modern, well-organized, three-year-old brewery northwest of São Paulo. Brews a malty and slightly spicy *dunkel*, **Amber Lady** ★★; **Indian Lady IPA** ★★, with robust balance between intense, resiny hop bitterness and caramel malt flavours; **Summer Lady** ★☆, with a rich sweetness and evident banana-like fruitiness; and a sociable, smooth, cocoa-and-coffee-tasting **Dark Lady** ★★☆.

EISENBAHN (KIRIN BRAZIL)
Blumenau, Santa Catarina

Early brewer and exporter of Brazilian craft beer, sold in 2008. Flavours seem slightly lessened of late, as with the more malty than hoppy **Pale Ale** ★☆ and the modestly fruity **Golden Ale** ★★. (The latter is given traditional-method sparkling wine treatment to become the effervescent yet somewhat dull-tasting **Lust** ★★.) Better are more traditionally German brands such as the satisfyingly roasty, yet light **Dunkel** ★★☆.

FALKE BIER
Ribeirão das Neves, Minas Gerais

Belo Horizonte brewery founded by three brothers, producing a wide range of styles. **Ouro Preto** ★★☆ is a *schwarzbier* offering pumpernickel aromas and dry molasses and mocha notes in the body; **ER India Pale Ale** ★★☆ is more ESB than IPA, with notes of apple and fig; **Monasterium** ★★☆ is a spicy ale billed a *tripel* but really more a dryish *dubbel*; while **Vivre Pour Vivre**

★★★ is an outstanding, tartly spicy fruit beer using native *jabuticaba* fruit.

KLEIN BIER
Campo Largo, Paraná

This 2009 brewery close to Curitiba focuses on classic beer styles. **Brown Ale** ★☆ combines caramel, medium-low roastiness and some fruitiness to a refreshing end; **Stout** ★★ has bitter chocolate and coffee notes in the body and a roasty dryness on the finish; and the use of Saaz hops in **Tchec** ★★☆ imparts a flowery aroma and bitter finish.

OPA BIER (JOINVILLE)
Joinville, Santa Catarina

Historically minded coastal brewery. *Reinheitsgebot*-adhering beers include

a mocha-ish and plummy, but oddly thin **Porter** ★★; and a sweet-ish, lively **Weizen** ★☆. Better are the twin Göttlich Divina! beers brewed with *guaraná*, including an attractively floral and mildly fruity **Pilsner** ★★☆. The other Göttlich beer is a *weisse*, not yet tasted.

DESTINATION
RIO DE JANEIRO

BeerJack HideOut (Rua Martins Ferreira, 71) is an out-of-the-way bar with an impressive present and a promising future, enthusiastically devoted to exploring good beer.

SEASONS
Porto Alegre, Rio Grande do Sul

Creative, innovative brewery, focused on intensity and balance. **Wallace Amber** ★★★ balances herbal hop freshness with biscuit-like flavours; **Green Cow IPA** ★★☆, offers a citrus hop aroma and assertive bitterness; **Cirilo Coffee Stout** ★★★ is pungent with green coffee bean aromas and flavours; and **Bigfoot Russian Imperial Stout** ★★☆, is partially oak-aged to a rich, vanilla-accented, chocolaty and woody aroma and a flavour approaching that of a liqueur.

WÄLS
Belo Horizonte, Minas Gerais

Prolific brewery at its best with ales like mocha, raisin and liquorice **Wäls Dubbel** ★★☆; fruity-spicy, herbaceous **Wäls Trippel** ★★★; dried fruit and brandy-ish **Wäls Quadruppel** ★★★;

and outstanding **Petroleum** ★★★☆, a concentrated, gingerbready, chocolaty powerhouse brewed with DUM Cervejaria.

WAY BEER
Pinhais, Paraná

Flashy brewery located near the craft beer hub of Curitiba. Early proponent of using Amazonian woods for the ageing of beer, as with its faintly smoky, spicy chocolate **Amburana Lager** ★★★, aged in the wood for which it is named. Other beers include a nutty, lightly toffee-ish **Irish Red Ale** ★★☆; and a balanced, toasty, dry-finishing **American Pale Ale** ★★☆.

WENSKY BEER
Araucária, Paraná

A family of Polish descent opened this brewery in 2009. Brands include dry-hopped, earthy **Vienna Lager** ★★; **Chopin Tripel** ★★, with a remarkably lemony aroma and malty body; clean, nutty and toffee-ish **Munich Dunkel** ★★☆; fine **Baltic Porter** ★★★ with cocoa, raisin and coffee aroma and body; and superb **Dreu'na Piva Old Ale** ★★★☆, matured in French oak to an elegant vanilla and coconut character.

DESTINATION
BLUMENAU

The Basement English Pub (35 Rua Paul Hering) is a homey bar and restaurant with a good selection of beers from local brewery EISENBAHN and Kirin Brazil stablemates, BADEN BADEN and Devassa.

ARGENTINA

Argentinians are mostly descended from European settlers, so it makes sense that since the late 1980s roughly 500 new small breweries have been opened. Unfortunately, roughly half that number have also closed, though not for lack of enthusiasm.

On the plus side, it is not unusual even in provincial towns to find a couple of local beers on the menu of any respectable dining or drinking establishment. On the downside, the absence of an independently owned, quality network of wholesalers with refrigerated local depots means beer quality can suffer away from its locality.

A typical Argentine brewer makes three beers – one gold, one red and one black. The interesting part is that gold can mean anything from a light lager to a Belgian-style *tripel*, red could encompass anything from a pale ale or IPA to a Vienna lager, and black might vary from *schwarzbier* to Imperial stout.

While craft beer is still quite rare in hectic, sprawling Buenos Aires, the area around Río Negro, the Patagonian Lake District (including Bariloche), Llao-Llao and the hop-growing area of El Bolsón constitutes one of the most spectacular brewery crawls in the world.

ANTARES
Mar del Plata, Buenos Aires

The country's leading craft brewer since 1998, brewing at various locales for both on- and off-premises trade. Main brands include a true-to-style, thirst-quenching **Kölsch** ★★; a lightish **Porter** ★★☆, with sweet chestnut notes; a chocolaty, nutty and warming **Cream Stout** ★★☆; a boozy, tropical fruit and rounded malt **Barley Wine** ★★☆; and an oddly refreshing but strong **Wee Heavy** ★★.

BEAGLE
Ushuaia, Tierra del Fuego

Included for its location rather than for its excellence, as it is currently the world's southernmost brewery, in the port town of Ushuaia on Tierra del Fuego, the southern tip of Patagonia. **Rubia Ale** ★☆ is a safe blond ale; **Roja India Pale Ale** ★★ is more amber ale than IPA; and the **Negra Stout** ★★ is the biggest and boldest of the trio.

BERLINA
San Carlos de Bariloche, Río Negro

One of Bariloche's better established pub breweries, occasionally making cask ales. Best of the regular beers are **Patagonia Golden Ale ★★**, an intense golden ale with mild flowery bitterness balanced by a dab of caramel; and **Patagonia Foreign Stout ★★☆**, a moderately warming, mocha-ish ale with dark fruit notes and a long, ultra-dry finish.

DESTINATION EL BOLSÓN

The Fiesta Nacional del Lúpulo (www.patagonia.com.ar), or National Hops Festival, is one of numerous festivals held throughout the year in this beautiful town that is also the heart of Argentina's hop-growing region.

BLEST
San Carlos de Bariloche, Río Negro

Established in 1989 within walking distance of **BERLINA**, said to be the first of the area's 20+ brewpubs. Among its regulars, **Pilsen ★★☆** is considered among the best blond beers in the country; **Scotch Ale ★★** is a good example of a staple style in the Argentinian craft landscape; and prize-winning **Bock ★★☆** is a classically malt-forward beer. Seasonal **Frambuesa ★★☆**, with local raspberries, is easy-drinking despite 7.5% ARV

BULLER
Buenos Aires

Started as a brewpub in Buenos Aires' fanciest neighbourhood, Recoleta, and now branching out as a franchise, following Antares' example on consistent quality. Reliable performers include **Oktoberfest ★★**, similar in character to a *märzen* but low in bitterness; and a by-the-numbers **IPA ★★☆** that ticks all the right boxes.

GAMBRINUS
Zárate, Buenos Aires

Small, reclusive brewery upstream from Buenos Aires making some impressive beers that find their way into a number of the capital's specialist bars. **Celtic Stout ★★☆** is lighter than it seems, creamy and roasted with touches of vanilla and chocolate; **Gaelic Pale Ale ★★☆**, although stronger, is more quaffable with a good balance of malt, fruit and bitterness.

GÜLMEN
Viedma, Río Negro

Brewery with strong ties to its region.
Like ANTARES, its intention is to grow
smartly, expanding a network of reliable
distributors in a way that retains quality.
Lager Ahumada ★★ is a mildly smoked
amber beer with balancing bitterness; and
Trigo ★★ has clove and vanilla in the
nose, mild bitterness and a smooth finish,
with a deliberate but subtle sour touch.

JEROME
Mendoza

National music legend and Oscar-winner
Gustavo Santaolalla hooked up with this
craft brewery to make some seriously
interesting beers. **Negra ★★**, a dry mid-
weight stout, is the best of the standard
beers; **Diablo ★★☆** is a pale ale with a
whisky kick; and complex, daring **Grosa
★★★** is a grapey, spicy-finishing strong ale
that spends 18 months in Malbec barrels.

KRAKEN
Buenos Aires

Young brewery with much-praised
beers that are favourites in the local
beer community. **Red Ale ★★☆** has
handsome copper tones reflecting a solid
mix of caramel and dried-fruit maltiness
that barely holds its sharp bitterness; and
Stout ★★☆ is a highly approachable,
quaffable beer that hides its 6% ABV well.

OTRO MUNDO
San Carlos Sud, Santa Fe

Ambitious company that brought the old
San Carlos brewery in Santa Fe back to
life, with the help of its part-owner, the
Chilean brewing giant CCU. Most beer is
bottled and widely available, including the
aromatic, balanced and refreshing **Golden
Ale ★★**; and no-style **Strong Red Ale
★★**, which is both intense and confident.

PATAGONIA (AB INBEV)
Quilmes, Buenos Aires

Argentina's largest brewery is Quilmes,
part of AB InBev; Patagonia is its craft beer
wing. In contrast to beers like **Quilmes
Cristal ★**, **Patagonia's Bohemian
Pilsner ★☆** nudges above the industrial
standard; **Amber Lager ★☆** is more
malt-forward, though unpretentious; and
Weisse ★★ balances between German
and Belgian wheat beer styles.

CHILE

In the pecking order of Latin American craft beer, Chile sits somewhere after leader Brazil and number two Argentina, perhaps tied for third with Mexico. But as the country's growing number of craft brewers shake off their minor obsession with the *rubia, roja y negra* triptych of Central and South American beer styles/colours and start to follow in the more experimental footsteps of breweries like Szot and Rothhammer, progress could come very quickly.

CERVEZA DE AUTOR
Valparaíso

Brewery operated by chef and British-trained brewer, Ricardo Solis. Most interesting beers arrive at the darker end of the colour spectrum, with the **Brown Ale ★★** being slightly toffee-ish, raisiny and moderately bitter; and the **Stout ★★** being milk chocolaty, creamy from the use of oats in the mash and dry on the finish.

> DESTINATION
> **VALPARAÍSO**
>
> The El Irlandés bar (1279 Blanco) might sound like a faux Irish pub, but it is in fact Chile's finest beer bar.

GUAYACAN
Elqui Valley, Valparaíso

Brewery located in one of Chile's most popular tourist regions. Brands include the sweet and fruity **Pale Ale ★**, but also more robust offerings like the dryly malty **Golden Ale ★★☆**; the vanilla and mocha **Stout ★★**; and the light,

citrus-spicy **Uno ★★**, with tropical-fruit notes and delicate hoppiness.

KROSS CERVEZA INDEPENDIENTE
Santiago

Founded by a German in search of brewing freedom, this is likely to be Chile's most awarded brewery, now partly owned by Concha y Toro. Beers include a perfumey **Pilsner ★★**; a slightly sweet and chocolaty, dry-finishing **Stout ★★☆**; and a beer brewed first for the brewery's fifth anniversary, **Kross 5 ★★★**, with an oaky vanilla nose and a flavour of sweet malt, berry fruit and tobacco.

MESTIZA CERVEZA GOURMET
Valparaíso

Located close to where the first Chilean beer was brewed in 1825, this brewery focuses on beers that pair well with the local cuisine, including a hoppy, herbal **American Pale Ale ★★☆** to match spicy food; a copper-coloured, bittersweet **Deutsches Altbier ★★** for grilled meat; and a roasty, coffee-ish **Irish Dry Stout ★★** for lamb or pork.

RAPA NUI
Hanga Roa, Rapa Nui

The most remote craft brewery in the world, on Easter Island, 3200km (1988 miles) off the Chilean coast, from where it imports ingredients for its two Mahina beers, though barley cultivation is being tried on the island. Lightish, gently hopped US-style **Pale Ale ★★** and middleweight dryish, less extensively hopped **Stout ★★** warrant trying on merit alone.

ROTHHAMMER
Pudahel, Santiago

Young brewery started by two brothers with a deep affection for hops. **Meantime ★★** is a dry and citrus blond ale; **Bones of Oak Stout ★★** is a lightly cocoa-ish stout; strong IPA **Brutal Hops ★★★** is floral and well balanced; **Cosmos ★★☆** is a sweetly aromatic and full-bodied barley wine and the star of the brewery.

SOMA
San Bernado, Maipo

Brewery near Santiago producing only bottle-conditioned beers. **Gama Pale Ale ★★** is floral and off-dry, meant to resemble a sparkling wine; **Alfa Brown Ale ★★ +** is sweet and fruity with bitterness on the finish; and **Beta Sweet Stout ★★** is chocolaty and full-bodied.

SZOT
Santiago

Boundary-stretching brewery founded and run by an expat Californian and his Chilean wife. Caramelly **Amber Ale ★★** and lightly spicy **Rubia al Vapor ★★** are among the more accessible brews; while darkly fruity, port-wine-ish **Barley Wine ★★☆** and densely fruity, intensely malty **Strong Ale ★★★** are among the best.

TÜBINGER
Santiago

Brewery led by a Brazilian-born brewer of German descent, producing a variety of ales rather than lagers, including the off-dry and toasty **Red Ale ★★**; a **Pale Ale ★★** that is more a sweetish best bitter in character; the nutty, slightly chocolaty-sweet **Brown Ale ★★☆**; and the strong, wildly successful **Tubinator ★★☆**, a roasty, raisiny ale with an off-dry finish.

DESTINATION **SANTIAGO (AND ELSEWHERE)**

Oddly, supermarket chain Jumbo, with 13 outlets in Santiago and 15 elsewhere in the country, is likely the best bet for buying a variety of Chilean craft beers.

REST OF LATIN AMERICA

Blond, red and black, the *tricolores*, have been for years a running gag in Latin American *cerveza artesanal*. Roughly analogous to the pale ales, ambers and stouts that dominated North American craft in the early days, one measure of maturity is when breweries start to break the moulds and try new things. It's happening, even as the scattered brewpubs that came and went over the past two decades find more permanent footing and multiply. Genuine production breweries, small as they may be, are appearing with more frequency.

Colombia is beginning to show its neighbours what's possible. Local brewery-watchers report that more than 35 new breweries have appeared from 2009 to 2012 in various parts of the country, ranging from miniscule to small but ambitious. As the country's security has improved, so have its beer options.

Bogotá Beer Company was one of the first, overcoming a guerrilla's grenade attack in 2003 to become a thriving chain of 13 BBC pubs. Bogotá ★ is the safe lager, while the balanced Chapinero Porter ★★ is liked by craft-conscious visitors. Colón started in 1997, and while co-founder Berny Silberwasser left to start the BBC, the company followed the predictable path, making safe beers in atmospheric Palos de Moguer pubs: Roja, Rubia, Negra, and so on. Meanwhile, 3 Cordilleras in Medellín, launched in 2008, is a proper production brewery with a line-up more interesting than most in the region, including the citrus pale ale Mestizo and seasonals that include an IPA and a *saison*.

Uruguay has a few splashes of *cerveza artesanal*. Mastra is perhaps the most visible, with clever packaging of its gold, red and black ales, while Davok, born of the Shannon Irish Pub in Montevideo, offers a wider range of styles and has won awards in Argentina and Brazil. Cabesas Bier is a brewpub that bottles in Tacuarembó, with Trigo ★★☆, a seductively sweet Belgian-style wheat beer, and the chocolaty, brown ale-like Brown Porter ★★ among its better beers.

In Paraguay, Asunción has a German-style brewpub called Astoria that appears to promote its sangria as much as the house lager. Bolivia's Saya Beer has been around since 1997, with a brewery in Cochabamba and popular sales outlet at the Adventure Brew Hostel in La Paz. Peru's Arte Cerveza is a Lima brewery with a beer club, selling ingredients and renting out its equipment for personalized brews. Also in Lima, Cebi-Chela specializes in ceviche and house-made beer, including a disturbingly green Cerveza de Menta, or "mint beer".

There are stirrings in Ecuador. The tiny Umiña brewery is putting blackberries in a *tripel* and passion-fruit in an IPA. Cuenca has the Compañia brewpub, with three main beers named after the usual colours. In Baños, a mini-brewery called Cascada is making beer for the owners of the Posada del Arte hotel and their son's Stray Dog pub.

Venezuela is not the most hospitable place these days for entrepreneurs with capital, but Destilo brews an eponymous, slickly marketed amber ale, while Tovar makes a German-style pils in the "Germany of the Caribbean".

Central America presents some interesting cases, including a few brewpubs in Panama.

Istmo opened in 2005 in Panama City's Cangrejo neighbourhood. The best there is the dark Coclé ★☆, with dryish roasted malt helping to balance its residual sugar, while Veraguas ★ is an amber blend of Coclé and the sweet blond Colon, and better than the latter because of it.

Rana Dorada is newer to the capital, having opened in the historic Casco Viejo in February 2012. Ambition is present; the founders include Silberwasser of the Bogotá Beer Company (*see* page 271). There is a pils with some hoppy oomph and a Belgian-style wheat beer that gets the French name Blanche. Meanwhile, in western Panama near the Volcan Barú national park, Rock Boquete is an upmarket restaurant serving house-made beers.

Costa Rica's Craft Brewing Company (CRCB) is Central America's most successful microbrewery to date, with dozens of draught and bottle accounts dotted around the country. The one to convert lifelong lager drinkers is the crisp blond Libertas ★★; the challenging one is the bitter and fruity red-amber Segua ★★☆; the stable's newer member is sweet and malty Malacrianza ★☆. Seasonals have appeared on draught only, the most distinctive and impressive being the Trigo con Cas ★★★, a refreshingly acidic wheat beer made with sour guava.

Volcano Brewing Company is in Guanacaste, across the lake from Costa Rica's photogenic Arenal cone. Rooms are basic, but inclusive rates at this brewpub-hotel cover all the house beer and "farm-to-table" food one can consume. Regulars are the citrus-hopped Witch's Rock Pale Ale ★★; and the brown Gato Malo ★☆, malty but light and dry enough for the climate.

A couple of brewpubs in Honduras meet the needs of adventure travellers, both removed from the bustle of Tegucigalpa. D&D is a secluded and rustic hotel-brewpub on Lake Yojoa, in central Honduras. Sol de Copán, near the Copán ruins, is where German expat Thomas Wagner sticks to traditional German styles, served with equally loyal dishes like sausage and *spätzle*.

El Salvador's growing economy has allowed some beery happenings. Brew Revolution, in the surf town of El Tunco, is a Pacific beach brewpub that distributes bottles to a few shops and bars in San Salvador. The enthusiastic American owner is openly learning on the job, sometimes putting out well-received IPAs like Mercurio, other times brewing with seawater. In the capital, the Cadejo microbrewery was set to open in early 2013, fronted by a Salvadoran brewer/co-owner who studied engineering at Cornell. Its two main beers are expected to be a citrus-hopped wheat beer, Wapa, and a spicy-hopped Roja.

ASIA & THE MIDDLE EAST

Istanbul

TURKEY
• ANKARA

LEBANON • BEIRUT
ISRAEL • JERUSALEM

NEW DELHI •

HIMALA

*Arabian
Sea*

Mumbai •

INDIA

Bangalore • • Chennai

Colombo •

SRI
LANKA

*INDIAN
OCEAN*

JAPAN

Beer brewing did not arrive in Japan until 1869 and through much of the 20th century was subject to peculiar legislative measures that meant in effect it was inevitable the market would be dominated by a small number of indigenous companies, which came to be Asahi, Kirin, Sapporo and Suntory.

It was not until the mid-1990s that smaller breweries were enabled to set up, though since then entrepreneurs and industrialists, home brewers and idealists, long-established brewers of traditional sake and existing national brewers keen to experiment have established over 200 functioning small breweries, in every prefecture from Hokkaido to Nagasaki.

That Japan should become an important world centre of craft brewing is even more remarkable because *jibiiru*, the collective name for locally made beers of interest, usually costs at least three times as much as regular beers.

In the early days these new brewhouses were influenced strongly by German practices in particular, though with British, Czech or American influences too, often employing expat brewing staff to aid authenticity.

The spread of specialist beer bars and the direct sale of beer to consumers via the internet has led to steady year-on-year growth despite an economy in constant struggle, showing that *jibiiru* is no fad. This in turn has led the second generation of Japanese craft brewers to find its own way, including creating some indigenous Japanese beer styles.

Rice, particularly the highly polished preparations used in sake production, or else in its red and wild varieties, is finding its way into Japanese interpretations of foreign styles. Japanese hop strains are being developed, exotic local ingredients appear as flavourings and, most interesting of all, wild yeast harvested from cherry blossom is being trialled in slow-fermentation beers, sometimes matured in sake-style cedar casks.

AKASHI
Akashi, Hyōgo

A small brewery that can be found in a museum of sake cups, at Akashi, west of Kobe in Hyōgo prefecture. It is better at lagers than ales thus far. **Kaigan Beer** ★★ is a clean German-style pilsner with bitter hopping, appearing richer and unfiltered as **Meriken Beer** ★★☆; while **Yukyu no Toki** ★★★ is a creamy, chocolaty *schwarzbier*.

AQULA
Akita

A small brewery located at Akita on the northwest coast of Honshu. The regular line-up of beers on offer includes the rich, moderately strengthened dark *bock*, **Namahage** ★★☆; the mildly tart, cherry-blossom-yeast beer **Sakura Kobo** ★★, the entertaining and hoppier wheat beer **Citra Weisse** ★★☆; and the more experimental **Kiwi IPA** ★★☆, which highlights Nelson Sauvin.

BAEREN
Morioka, Iwate

Located in Iwate on the north of Honshu, Baeren avoided any major earthquake damage in 2011 to continue producing its solid German-influenced range of beers, like summer seasonal **Weizen** ★★; year-round flagship **Schwarz** ★★; and hoppy, stronger blond lager **Classic** ★★☆, the cult version of which, the unfiltered **Kellerbier** ★★★, might be Japan's best simple beer.

BAIRD BREWING
Numazu, Shizuoka

American expat Chris Baird is a leader in the business for both consistent quality and perpetual experimentation. Nearly 300 beers have come out of his brewery at Numazu in Shizuoka, southwest of Yokohama. Favourites include double-strength **Angry Boy Brown Ale** ★★☆; up-hopped and strong **Suruga Bay Imperial IPA** ★★☆; springtime's tart, other-worldly, religious-bathsalts-infused **Yuzu Garden Temple Ale** ★★★; and occasional, elusive, just plain clever **Brewer's Secret Handshake** ★★★ is an impressively Düsseldorfer *alt*.

BRIMMER
Kawasaki, Kanagawa

Start-up (2012) by a former brewer at SIERRA NEVADA BREWING in the US who had spent time brewing at a golf resort near Mount Fuji. His clean **Pale Ale** ★★☆ shows balance and moderate bitterness; while the off-dry, nutty **Porter** ★★☆ has excellent depth. Thus far, seasonals have included a leafy **Strong**

Pale Ale ★★; and softer, gentler **English IPA** ★★☆ that stays true to its British influences.

CHATEAU KAMIYA
Ushiku, Ibaraki

Japan's oldest winery, northeast of Tokyo at Ushiku in Ibaraki, has produced beer since the 1990s. Its **Helles** ★★★ is a delightfully balanced exemplar of the Munich original; spring brings **Sakura Kobo** ★★☆, a cherry-blossom-yeast beer that could only be Japanese; autumn prefers a UK-inspired **Brown Ale** ★★☆, which could pass as native; while winter's heavy, succulent, dark **Christmas Bock** ★★★ is a kind of pan-European winter warmer.

DESTINATION
TOKYO

In the enormous, sprawling capital international beers of quality are now commonplace but the go-to bar for draught Japanese craft beers, some cask-conditioned, is Popeye (2–18–7 Ryogoku) near Ryogoku railway station, with Ushi-Tora (2–9–3 Kitazawa) near Shimo-Kitazawa station not far behind.

DAISEN G BEER
Tottori

Small brewery on the slopes of Daisen, a deceased volcano in western Japan, making extraordinary beers that sometimes travel poorly. Its regular **Weizen** ★★☆ was voted the world's best in a US competition; though fruity and rich **Wheat Wine** ★★★☆, as complex as they come, has a more legitimate shout; with the malt-led, UK-style **Barley Wine** ★★★ impressing too. Spicy, innovative **Yago** ★★☆ is what happens when the grain bill has a lot of home-grown sake rice and fermentation is seeded with a spicy Belgian yeast.

FUJIZAKURA HEIGHTS BEER
Kawaguchiko, Yamanashi

Masterful and expanding brewery near the foot of Mount Fuji, in Yamanashi, setting the standard for German beer styles in Japan. Its **Weizen** ★★★ is sweet, malty and as good as they come; **Rauch** ★★★ is milder than Bamberg's smokiest but Japan's best; **Rauchbock** ★★★☆ has full-on smoked and chocolate malts; **Mori no Weizen Oktoberfest** ★★★☆ is a perfectly balanced smoked *weizen*; and winter's sweet, spicy **Weizenbock** ★★☆ is made for dessert.

HARVESTMOON
Maihama, Chiba

In a suburban shopping centre, a stone's throw from Tokyo Disneyland, the regular line-up includes a dry, roasty **Schwarz** ★★☆ and easy-drinking **Wit** ★★; while winter sees a rich, sweet **Barley Wine** ★★☆; and big roasted **Imperial Stout** ★★★ that are more captivating.

HIDA TAKAYAMA BEER
Takayama, Gifu

Impressive small brewery in the mountains of Gifu, deserving of greater renown.

Its **Weizen** ★★☆ is sweet and estery; the complex **Stout** ★★★ is rich, chewy and slightly vinous; lighter, UK-leaning **Dark Ale** ★★☆ has rich, nutty cereals and chocolate; while strong, dark and handsome **Karumina** ★★★☆ is a barley wine spiced by Belgian yeast.

HIDEJI BEER
Nobeoka, Miyazaki

Creative brewery at Nobeoka, east of Nagasaki in Miyazaki, often employing local fruits and their distillates. Nicely hopped **Taiyo no Lager** ★★☆ tops a seasonal list of characterful pale lagers; **Natsumikan Lager** ★★ involves local tangerines; export-strength **Kemurihige Stout** ★★★ is creamy and nutty; and **White Weizen** ★★ falls somewhere between Belgium and Germany.

ISE KADOYA
Ise, Mie

Newish small brewery within a 450-year-old family business at the pilgrimage centre of Ise, in Mie prefecture. Makes 40+ beers every year, including US-style, light and fruity **Pale Ale** ★★, sometimes found dry-hopped in the cask; strong, aggressively hopped, amber **Imperial Red Ale** ★★☆ tasting of cherries and caramel; and gently **Smoked Porter** ★★☆, which has coffee and chocolate flavours.

IWATE KURA
Ichinoseki, Iwate

Located in Ichinoseki, Iwate, one of the first Japanese craft breweries, from 1995, an early leader with a background in sake brewing. Its **IPA** ★★☆ shows restraint, though soft hops are elegantly balanced; the off-dry **Stout** ★★ has a lot of chocolaty character, but subdued roastiness; while autumn's heavier, roasty **Oyster Stout** ★★★ is briny to the palate or perhaps the imagination, accompanying the season's fresh oysters swimmingly.

KIUCHI
Naka, Ibaraki

Some brewers live twice. What to the Japanese is the Kiuchi sake brewery's 1996 beer-brewing arm is, to the rest of the world, rock-star Nippon craft brewer Hitachino Nest, its beers easier to find abroad than at home. The blond, bottom-fermented **Ancient Nipponia** ★★★ is made from Kanego Golden barley malt with Japanese Sorachi Ace hops; its **Espresso Coffee Stout** ★★★ is famously full-on; the ginger and coriander-tipped **Wit** ★★★ goes well with sushi; while the **Japanese Classic Ale** ★★☆ is a UK-edged American IPA aged in cedar casks and scoring high on imagination.

DESTINATION NATIONAL

Many Japanese craft beers can be purchased on-line, with many if not most *jibiiru* brewers offering direct sale, sometimes for export too, though carriage is expensive. In Japan, to source the best range of imports easily, go to www.ezo-beer.com.

MINOH BEER
Osaka

An innovative small brewery in Osaka that is run by two sisters, and is willing to experiment in many international styles, at its best locally. Excellent pale ales and stouts peak with **W-IPA** ★★★☆, a US-style double IPA with an immaculate malt body behind the hop hit; and brawny yet still smooth **Imperial Stout** ★★★, with chocolate and café-au-lait aromas. Downscale, hoppy **BB Gold** ★★★ is a Belgian blond you can drink all night; and **Yuzu White** ★★★ is a dry, tangy *witbier* using citrus peel.

DESTINATION
OSAKA

Q-Brick (4–6–12 Hiranomachi) is a small, friendly café near the Goryō Shrine in the north of the centre, with a fine range of Japanese beers on draught and 200+ mainly imported bottles, while near Nakamozu station to the south Eni-Bru (Kita-ku, 2–71 Nakamozu) is building a range of hard-to-find *jibiiru* at its 30-tap bar and upstairs shop.

MOJIKO RETRO BEER
Kitakyushu, Fukuoka

Pub brewery at Kitakyushu in Fukuoka, specializing in making top-quality beers in German-derived styles. A biscuity, fruity **Pilsner** comes filtered or not ★★→★★☆; the classy **Weizen** ★★☆ balances banana, clove and citrus flavours perfectly; its **Rauch** ★★★ is almost black with big smoke and rich chocolate; and **Weizen Strong** ★★★★ is a unique take on a wheat *bock* with mango and cherry alongside banana and clove flavours.

MOKU MOKU
Iga Iga, Mie

The brewing wing of an agricultural park at Iga Iga, in Mie. High quality but hard to find, even locally. The crisp, hoppy **Golden Pilsner** ★★☆ is very German; US-nudged *weizen* **Haru Urara** ★★★ gives spicy wheat and citrus hops; **Smoke Ale** ★★★☆ has sweet chocolate, caramel and big smoke flavours; and the **Barley Wine ★★★** is a malt-driven, UK-style winter warmer.

NORTH ISLAND BEER
Sapporo, Hokkaido

Adventurous small brewery at Sapporo on Hokkaido, with a tendency to add stuff. Hence its stronger-end **India Pale Ale ★★☆** sometimes comes out as bracingly bitter **Grapefruit IPA ★★☆**; herbaceous **Coriander Black ★★☆** is always that way; while the slightly tart **Stout ★★** achieves it notes of cacao and espresso unaided, we think.

OH! LA! HO BEER
Tōmi, Nagano

Constantly improving small brewery on an agricultural park in Tōmi, in central Nagano. **Bossa Nova ★★☆** is the latest name for its single but evolving lower-strength IPA; winter-released **Porter ★★★** is fruity and hoppy; **White Ale ★★☆** has citrus hops and light banana flavours; while **Amber Ale ★★☆** balances earthy hopping with rich caramel malt.

OKU NOTO BEER
Noto, Ishikawa

Small brewery employing Czech brewers, on the Noto peninsula in Ishikawa. Takes its brand, Nihonkai Club, from its base. The simple **Pilsner ★★** is sweet and malty, with Saaz hops; **Dark Lager ★★** is also Bohemian in style but dry and bready; while the new **IPA** may be unique in sporting bespoke sub-brands

with dry-hopping on a scale of 1–10 **★★→★★★**.

OTARU BREWING
Otaru, Hokkaido

Brewery (1995) on Hokkaido, staring across the ocean at Russia but thinking of Germany. Its conventional line-up includes an off-dry organic **Dunkel ★★**; and pleasantly smooth and cloved **Weisse ★★**; though the fireworks are reserved for its *doppelbock*-strength, four-month seasoned **Dunkel Bock ★★★**, baby brother of wooden-casked New Year treat, the seven-month, matured at low temperature, 13.5% ABV, heavy, malty **Eisbock ★★★☆**.

OUTSIDER BREWING
Kofu, Yamanashi

New brewery at Kofu in Yamanashi, already established as a creative. Use of wild yeast fermentation gives its **Belgian White ★★** dry citrus flavours; and **Plum Ale ★★☆**, made with Japanese apricot (*Prunus mume*) fruits, dry and tangy; the **Pale Ale ★★★** matches rich caramel malts with Styrian Goldings; and **Innkeeper Bitter Lager ★★☆** is full of prickly hops. More is inevitable.

SANKT GALLEN
Atsugi, Kanagawa

Pioneer craft brewer at Atsugi in Kanagawa, focusing heavily on the sweeter, darker side, a tendency seen at its best in the rich and hefty **Imperial Chocolate Stout ★★★**; more modestly in **Sweet Vanilla Stout ★★☆** and

Kokutou Sweet Stout, ★★, which contains locally created brown sugar.

SHIGA KOGEN BEER
Yamanouchi, Nagano

The ale-brewing wing of the Tamamura-Honten sake brewery, in the mountains of northern Nagano. Its ever-evolving, coyly named **House IPA ★★★☆** is always at least double strength and with lovely hop aromas; **African Pale Ale ★★★** is dry, hoppy and US-style; while its range of Japanese-tweaked *saison* beers include home-grown sake rice and heavy hop-loading, seen simply in **Saison One ★★☆**; and most assertively in **Isseki Nicho ★★★**, a strong black variant that could pass as a heavy stout with Belgian spiciness.

SHIMANE
Matsue, Shimane

Small brewery at Matsue in Shimane, sometimes called Hearn Beer. Its **Pilsner**

★★ is nicely hopped and balanced; cocoa-infused **Chocolat No 7 ★★** goes well with dessert but is otherwise unfashionably sweet; a quality that winter-seasonal pick of the bunch **Honey Weizen Bock ★★☆** carries off with great refinement.

SHONAN
Chigasaki, Kanagawa

Original 1990s *jibiiru* brewery in a popular beach area south of metropolitan Tokyo, now expanded to include two taprooms that allow it to play, making experimental beers that push it up to Japan's top flight. A large number of excellent IPAs have been joined by a clean, metallic **Alt ★★**; an **Imperial Stout ★★★** that had the smell of the sea over roasted malt flavours on a background of liquorice; a Valentine's Day chocolate beer called **Shonan's Chocolate Porter ★★★**; and a rich and hefty, malt-led **Belgian Stout ★★★** with amazing depth and character.

SWAN LAKE BEER
Agano, Niigata

Brewery (1997) attached to a lovely old hotel-restaurant at Agano in Niigata, producing some of the country's most consistently fine brews. **Amber Ale ★★★☆** and **Porter ★★★** are exemplars of its styles, and international medal-winners; the autumnal **IPA ★★★** is floral, fruity and balanced; while winter's **B-IPA ★★★☆** uses Belgian yeast and is even better. Relative newcomer **Imperial Stout ★★★** is tangy, spicy and highly complex.

TAZAWAKO
Senboku, Akita

Based at a hotel and natural hot springs next to Japan's deepest lake, Tawaka, in Akita. Highlight of the regular line-up is **Dark Lager ★★☆**, showing deep roasted malts and caramel with moderate bitterness; the dry, slightly fruity **Alt ★★** is more restrained; while the highlight is a silky smooth **Rauch ★★★** – imagine meat dipped in molasses cooking on a campfire – aged versions of which show even more depth.

THRASH ZONE LABO
Yokohama, Kanagawa

A cultural phenomenon of sorts, in Yokohama. This keg-only pub brewery started in 2012 to produce solely IPAs, a task which it has not shirked. Production is increasing rapidly thanks to some surprisingly approachable heavyweights of the style such as double IPA, **Hopslave ★★☆**, and an equally enjoyable regular IPA, **Hama-Cisco ★★☆**.

YO-HO BREWING
Karuizawa, Nagano

Pioneer of the Japanese craft brewing scene, at Karuizawa in Nagano, losing its way for a time but now back on track. Canned US-style pale **Yona Yona Ale ★★** is the best-known craft beer in the land, though hoppy, American-style porter **Tokyo Black ★★★** is far better; the IPA, **Aooni ★★**, is reliable rather than memorable; while its ever-changing, year-dated **Barley Wine ★★☆→★★★** is invariably as English as it is good.

YOKOHAMA
Yokohama, Kanagawa

Pub brewery at a central Yokohama restaurant, initially Czech-influenced but become more eclectic. Deep golden **Yokohama Lager ★★☆** shines with New Zealand hops; solidly Bohemian mainstay **Pilsner ★★☆** has biscuit malt and Saaz; while stronger *witbier* **White Joker ★★☆** is its best Belgian effort so far, using citrus hops as spicing.

ZAKKOKU KOBO
Ogawa, Saitama

Small brewery in Saitama outside Tokyo, experimenting with alternative brewing grains, many of which it grows. **Zakkoku Weizen ★★☆** includes rye and two kinds of millet; spicy **Sansho Porter ★★** uses Szechuan pepper for a citrus nuance; tart, lambic-like **Yamamomo Ale ★★☆** uses Japanese bayberry fruits; while more standard **Akane Red Ale ★★** blends earthy hops with bready malt.

CHINA

China is extremely important to the future of beer. In recent years it has become the largest producer and consumer of beer in the world. In 2013, it may well also become the world's largest grower of hops. If each Chinese adult drinks a mouthful of beer each week, this is equal to the combined output of all the craft brewers in the US.

However, until recently the growth in volume was not accompanied by any better understanding or appreciation of the quality and diversity of beer. Unsurprisingly, much of the market is being taken by major commercial brands, mostly owned by large foreign companies.

At one end of the Chinese beer scene are the beer stalls dotted along rural roadsides, selling cheap beers, the poor quality of which is legendary. A single mash may be used to make six or seven run-offs, the later ones creating a drink so watery that it is humiliating to call it beer at all. Many Chinese say that they "drink beer instead of water because at least it is sanitized".

Fortunately for those who prefer good beer, brewmasters from the New World, and increasingly from China itself, are starting to transform the Chinese beer landscape, most noticeably in major cities.

As the economy and spending power grows in China, German-style brewpubs have become popular to serve the growing appreciation of beer among white-collar consumers. The Paulaner chain of pub breweries in Shanghai enjoys great success, local people enjoying the fresh, malty flavours of authentically styled Bavarian beers that also serve as implicit symbols of higher status and class.

In an impressive show of foresight, several of China's best schools of brewing were founded and are run by German brewers.

American-style craft brewing did not arrive in China until 2008, when a few pioneering American-born Chinese from California crossed the Pacific to set up shop in the country's business capital, Shanghai, as BOXING CAT BREWERY.

In the beginning, these emerging breweries and their taphouses attracted mainly a foreign, expat crowd but slowly more and more locals have learned to appreciate the diversity, depth and creativity of the beers they brought. As this niche market was discovered and grew, further investment poured in, leading to the birth of more top-quality beer makers.

When GREAT LEAP BREWERY established itself as the first craft brewery in the national capital, Beijing, aiming at the same niche, instant success ensued, the more so when it started to add local flair to its beers by incorporating Chinese ingredients to create interesting local variations that enchant the palate.

The newcomers are still a relatively small part of the overall Chinese beer scene but their growth is impressive. Since 2010, appreciation of more interesting beers has blossomed and a wave of brewpubs and small commercial breweries has been hitting several more major cities across China. Even Taiwan's LE BLÉ D'OR operation has set up a branch at Suzhou in Jiangsu province, southwest of Shanghai.

Local home brewers are taking advantage of the tide to take the movement to new heights. This began with a brewer in Nanjing, who started a German-style bottle beer operation and has inspired others to try. Further developments have included the first genuinely independent Chinese-owned pub brewery, in Beijing, serving diverse ales. Amazingly, the first Chinese magazine on beer appeared in spring 2013.

The quality beer scene in China may be small but it is energetic, rapidly expanding, has huge potential and is anticipated to have a major impact in time.

BOXING CAT BREWERY
Shanghai

Long-standing leader of the Shanghai craft beer scene with two locations offering a variety of beers and American food. **Standing 8 Pilsner** ★★☆ is a well-conditioned blond lager beer; and **TKO India Pale Ale** ★★☆ is a US-style IPA with citrus and piney flavours. Seasonals include **Southpaw Winter Warme**r ★★★, an English brown ale spiced with star anise and others. Impressive **Yunnan Amber Ale** ★★☆ marked a first collaboration, with GREAT LEAP BREWERY.

BREW, THE
Shanghai

Australian-designed pub brewery at an upscale hotel in Shanghai's Pudong New District. An award-winning range includes crisp and fragrant **Skinny Green Lager** ★★☆, with assertive bitterness; Australasian-style **India Pale Ale** ★★☆ has bold fresh tropical-fruit flavours; gently spiced *witbier* **White Ant** ★★☆, with home-made dried orange peel; and cleverly spiced, light-bodied but weighty seasonal **Pumpkin Ale** ★★★.

DR. BEER
Shanghai

Trendy Shanghai brewpub known for serving fresh beer, direct from tank to tap. Its six permanent beers include German-style **Wheat** ★★, with a bubblegum flavour; sweet and fuller-bodied **Pilsner** ★★; and the easy-drinking **Pale Ale** ★★.

GREAT LEAP BREWERY
Beijing

Beijing's first pub brewery, a defining pioneer among new-generation Chinese brewers. Uses mainly locally sourced ingredients for a wide range that includes the distinctive **Iron Buddha Blonde** ★★★☆, infused with the famous Chinese tea; **Little General IPA** ★★★, which uses only Chinese hops and no dry-hopping to create a clean, crisp and distinctive bitterness; **Honey Ma Gold** ★★, with dried Szechuan peppercorns and Shandon honey, gentle but surprising; and a big but workaday **Imperial Stout** ★★.

MALTY DOG
Beijing

Beijing's newest taproom is the first to have a young Chinese owner. Inspired by the local home brewers' association, its **Hops American Ale** ★★☆ is a nicely balanced, hoppy US-style pale ale; **Blueberry Lady** ★★ incorporates local

blueberry juice to be fresh and appetizing; while the **Chocolate Stout ★★** and **IPA In Black ★★☆** are each deliberately aggressive and tangy, with roasted notes.

SLOW BOAT BREWERY
Beijing

Versatile small Beijing brewery making an international range of craft beers, among which are Australasian style **Monkey's Mango First IPA ★★☆**, with pungent mango but tender bitterness; a **Porter ★★** with a fine coffee edge; and **Safe Harbour Christmas Ale ★★☆**, a light-bodied amber ale flattered by spices. At its taproom the draught beers are unfiltered.

STRONG ALE WORKS
Qingdao, Shandong

Fervent home brewer based at Qingdao, where the world-famous Tsingtao brands are produced. His surprisingly good bottled beers are made in 100-litre runs, currently in five varieties, among which are **Bitter Ale ★★☆**, with a creamy mouthfeel

and nice bitterness; and **Smoky Dark Beer★★**, which has a smoky bacon flavour and fruit candy finish.

TYPHOON BREWERY
Lantau, Hong Kong

Small brewery located at Lantau in Hong Kong, the first to attempt to brew English-style cask ales in China. The brewery has no taproom, but its beers are distributed to a few pubs in the former British colony. **T8 English Bitter ★★** is the flagship product, with a mellow but traditional character; while **Eastern Lightning ★★☆** is a US-influenced IPA with a pleasant bittersweet balance.

SOUTHEAST ASIA

Let's get this much straight right away: craft beer has indeed arrived in southeast Asia. In some areas, like Singapore, it is even showing signs of beginning to thrive.

However, as there is no real tradition of brewing in this part of the world, save for what largely German breweries brought to the region, development of a craft brewing culture has been slow, sometimes glacially so. Part of this is due to bureaucratic constraints – see South Korea for a fine example of this – but the majority, to our minds, is cultural. Simply, in nations with relatively low per capita beer consumption, the impetus to shake up the large-brewery-dominated state of affairs is minimal.

Still, there are bright spots here and there, with potential as yet unrealized in Singapore, South Korea and Thailand, in particular. Within a matter of a few years, we suspect the beer picture in southeast Asia could be very different indeed.

SOUTH KOREA

It's not easy being a Korean craft brewer. By most estimates, within the last decade as many as 100 or more craft breweries have ceased operation, most of them brewpubs. This leaves fewer than 40 remaining craft breweries today, battling for a small fraction of a market controlled by two major brewing concerns, Hite and Oriental Brewery, the latter known as OB. Complicating matters further, a third large and well-financed corporation, the consumer goods company Lotte, is expected to break ground on a large-scale brewery in 2015.

Part of the challenge facing craft brewers is South Korea's curious set of requirements necessary for a licence to sell beer off-premises. In order to become a production brewery, a facility must have fermentation and storage capacity equalling or exceeding 150,000 litres, no small amount for a country in which craft beer accounts for under 1% of the total market.

Still, there is some reason for optimism. Sales of imported beer have in recent years been on the rise – "changing monthly", according to one correspondent – with growth in US craft, Belgian and German brands suggesting an awareness among Koreans in styles beyond the pale and pallid lagers that dominate beers sales, particularly Cass (OB) and Hite.

Outside of the big breweries, only two companies have the facilities necessary to brew and distribute beer, 7 Brau and Ka-Brew. The former produces a small handful of beers, including a canned IPA, of which local beer aficionados speak without enthusiasm. Ka Brew, sometimes known as the Kapa Brewery, serves primarily as a contract brewery for three beer commissioning agents, all based in Seoul and all favoured by the expat community, with growing interest among native Koreans: Reilly's Brewing, an offshoot of Reilly's Taphouse & Gastropub; Magpie Brewing; and Korea's best-known beer outlet, Craftworks Taphouse and Bistro.

Taiwan, CHINA

In brewing terms the island of Taiwan is a place to watch. The interest in beers that are off the industrial norm is reflected in the growth of organized and collaborative home brewing, and expansion of the commercial craft brewing scene is expected with at least one US-inspired supply brewery in the works.

BLÉ D'OR, LE
Taipei City

Despite the French name, this is a chain of German-style pub breweries appearing across Taiwan – seven at the last count – with one also at Suchou on mainland China. All make and serve an easy-drinking **Dunkel ★★** that contains smoked logan wood; **Hell ★☆**, a *helles*-style beer that impresses expats; a banana-imbued *weizen* called **Weiss ★★** that impresses ex-pats; and a more distinctive **Honey Beer ★★☆**, which is nicely infused with local logan honey.

JOLLY
Taipei City

Pioneering pub brewery in the capital, Taipei, with a long history of producing safer beers in a variety of styles to accompany its Thai cuisine. The **Pilsner ★☆** is rounded; the **Pale Ale ★☆** is a smooth but unsurprising amber ale; and the stronger **Scotch Ale ★★** uses understated peat-baked malt; though best by far is the unsweetened **Witbier ★★☆**, with a whiff of freshness and an appetizing underlay from the infusion of passion-fruit.

NORTH TAIWAN
Taoyuan, Taoyuan County

New small brewery at Taoyuan, with close links to the Taiwanese craft beer movement. Creates bottled beers based on Belgian styles, which appear in local supermarkets. Its **Weizen ★★** is a mutation of Belgian and German wheat beer styles, with clove, spice and yeasty flavours; popular **Lychee Beer ★★** is fruity and sweetened; **Melon Beer ★☆** similarly; while **6 ★★** is an attempt at a *dubbel* but with pronounced fruit flavours.

VIETNAM

Despite two millennia of Chinese rule, two centuries of French and two decades of American, the dominant influence in modern Vietnamese brewing is Czech, many Vietnamese having emigrated to Czechoslovakia after both countries achieved independence. The swathe of brewpubs opening in cities the length of the country is replacing an older tradition of 300 or so small brewhouses producing mostly beers high in rice but low in alcohol and colour, collectively known as *bia hơi*. Easier to find in the north, the routine is that draught beer is packaged immediately fermentation is complete and delivered daily to shack-like bars, where it is served uncarbonated directly from metal kegs that are emptied in a single session.

COI XAY GIO
Hanoi

This brewpub, attached to the Windmill restaurant, is the best example from dozens, particularly here and in Ho Chi Minh City, typically making only two types of beer – "Yellow" and "Black". The paler, rustic, fruity, herbal **Sèc ★★☆** has a mineral palate; while darker **Đen ★★☆** has rich sugars and a lot of fruitiness.

GOLDMALT
Hanoi

Small chain of pub breweries in Hanoi and the north, using Czech brewing kit to make Bohemian lagers that include herbal and modestly bitter **Pilsner 12º ★★☆**; lightly chocolated **Black ★★**, with a hint of smoke; and stronger, golden **Special ★★☆**, with a yeasty, herbal, spicy taste and doughy malt.

HOA VIÊN
Ho Chi Minh City

Pub brewery established in 1995 in Ho Chi Minh City, with offshoots in Hanoi and beach town Mui Ne. Shares space with the Czech embassy and produces two distinctly Bohemian beers, a pilsner called **Lager** ★★★, with a big Saaz nose, bready malts and a long, hoppy finish; and a classic Czech *tmavý* dark lager called **Bia Đen** ★★☆, soft, nutty and a little buttery.

LOUISIANE BREWHOUSE
Nha Trang, Binh Thuan

Australian-run pub brewery in Nha Trang that spills out onto the beach. Its **Witbier** ★★ has balanced fruit and coriander with a light spicy finish; the rich, woody **Pilsener** ★★☆, with New Zealand hops, has enough bitterness to taste; pale **Crystal Ale** ★★ has light bitterness and tropical-fruit character on the palate; and full-bodied **Dark Lager** ★★☆ is chocolaty.

SINGAPORE

Singapore's tiny land mass belies its prodigious thirst for beer, despite its notoriously high duties on alcohol. While the beer scene is still largely dominated by home grown Asia Pacific Breweries – brewer of Tiger Beer and owner of the country's largest craft brewery – as well as global players Carlsberg and Heineken, the past decade has seen the rise of a number of microbreweries and brewery pubs, as well as a burgeoning import market.

The annual Beerfest Asia, first introduced in 2009, saw over 30,000 visitors sample some 350 local and international beers over four days in 2012, while a newly introduced Singapore Craft Beer Week last year sought to inculcate the virtues of craft beer to both bar owners and the general populace.

ARCHIPELAGO BREWERY (ASIA PACIFIC BREWERIES)
Singapore

Craft beer division of Singapore's largest brewer, producing approachable beers. **Belgian Wit** ★★ is light and citrus; **Summer Ale** ★★ features US and NZ hops for light bitterness; Kiwi hops add a fruity twist to the otherwise Czech-style **Bohemian Lager** ★★; while toasty toffee, chocolate and caramel notes infuse a highly quaffable **Irish Ale** ★★.

BREWERKZ
Singapore

Pioneering 1997 brewpub now bottling and kegging for distribution as far as

Bangkok. Signature beers include a lightly bitter **Golden Ale** ★★; Germanic, bone-dry **Pilsner** ★★☆; and balanced, fruity and citrus-hoppy **India Pale Ale** ★★☆. Seasonal **Steam Beer** ★★☆ follows canned-peach fruitiness with slight bitterness and a dry, lightly woody finish.

DESTINATION
SINGAPORE

SQUE Rotisserie & Alehouse (6 Eu Tong Sen Street, #01–70 The Central) is Singapore's leader in beer variety, with 10 taps and in excess of 200 bottles in stock, and ambitions to carry many more.

JUNGLE BEER
Sembawang

New brewery experimenting in a range of styles. The malty, full-bodied **Kiasu Stout** ★★☆ exudes rich coffee and chocolate characters; a similarly malt-forward **English Pale Ale** ★★☆ combines

complexity and quaffability; and a variety of **Tropical Wheat** ★★ fruit-infused beers such as Mango & Orange, Mango & Rose and Guava & Soursop pander to local preferences for lighter, sweeter brews.

RED DOT BREWHOUSE
Singapore

Brewpub with two outlets. Spirulina adds colour and health benefits to low-hopped lager **Green Monster** ★★; crisp **Czech Pilsner** ★★ has minimal bitterness and a dry finish; and estery **Lime Wheat** ★★ is refreshingly citrus if understated.

DESTINATION
SINGAPORE

The Good Beer Company (Blk 335 Smith Street, #02–58 Chinatown Complex) is a bar operated out of a "hawker stand" in Chinatown, allowing patrons to mix craft beer with traditional foods served from the surrounding stands.

REST OF SOUTHEAST ASIA

For years now, backpackers have been returning from northern Thailand with Chang Beer T-shirts in tow, leading much of the western public to believe that Thai beer – indeed, Southeast Asian beer in general – begins and ends with that largely unexceptional lager. But there is more to Thailand than Chang, and potentially more to Cambodia and Laos, as well. We're not saying that a craft beer paradise is likely to arise in any of these nations in the near future, but with a handful of breweries and beers now established, and sporadic brewpub sightings becoming of late slightly less so, better beer times do seem to be on the horizon.

BEERLAO (CARLSBERG)
Vientiane, Laos

Co-owned by the Laotian government and Carlsberg, this chain of smallish breweries runs the length of Laos and produces blond **Beerlao Lager Beer** ★★☆ that in large bottles in its home country holds its delicate, slightly citrus flavour to the last gulp, while elsewhere or in other formats it does not. **Dark** ★★, though it is short on caramel, makes a change from everything else that is around.

BOON RAWD BREWERY
Bangkok, Thailand

Long-standing regional brewer with solid export sales in its flagship brew, the roundly malty, faintly peppery **Singha** ★★. Seldom-brewed **Singha 70** ★★, created for the brewery's 70th anniversary, mixes florals with rich caramel; while

perfumey **Kloster** ★★☆ is slightly easier to find and worth seeking out.

CAMBODIA BREWERY (HEINEKEN)
Phnom Penh, Cambodia

Although Cambodia has its first craft brewery, Kingdom Breweries of Phnom Penh, its products are so far too timid to be included here. However, the country enjoys a legacy from the 19th-century trade in strong porters and stouts, of which the remorseless best is **ABC Stout** ★★★, thick, black, sweet and burnt with a dollop of liquorice, brewed to a stronger recipe than the Singapore original.

STORM BALI
Denpasar, Indonesia

A rare example of a small Southeast Asian brewery of reasonable quality, on Bali in Indonesia. The **Pale Ale** ★★☆ is easy-drinking, vaguely American in style with a light yeastiness; **Red Dawn Bronze Ale** ★★ is light and fruity with good balance; **Black Moon Iron Stout** ★★☆ has a chocolate-fudge palate; and **Sand Storm Golden Ale** ★★ has orange and tropical-fruit notes undermined by a yeasty finish.

TAWANDANG MICROBREWERY
Bangkok, Thailand

Massive brewpub and concert hall with two Bangkok locations and now also open in Singapore, producing acceptable versions of Bavarian standards. **Weisse** ★☆ is bubblegummy, but with a bit of sourness; while the **Lager** ★★ is sweetish and floral. Best is the chocolaty, off-dry **Dunkel** ★★☆.

INDIA

India is not a beer-drinking country. In 2011, the average annual consumption was less than 2l (3½ pints) per capita, just a tiny fraction of that of every other significant beer-producing nation in the world. (And India's volume production is significant, totalling 18.5m hectolitres of beer in 2011, more than that of Belgium or the Czech Republic.)

Where alcohol is consumed in Indian society, mostly among the middle and upper classes, the drink of choice tends to be spirits, a fact which has contributed to India's UB Group becoming one of the largest spirits producers worldwide. The company's brewing division, United Breweries, produces over half of all the beer consumed in India. Still, there are signs that this situation is changing, with the rising popularity of imported beers in urban areas and an emerging craft beer sector. Institutional barriers and a government structure derided as hopelessly bureaucratic, however, are slowing the pace of change to a crawl.

As each state controls its own licensing and excise rules, and municipalities can further complicate matters with permits from all manner of development boards or committees, growth of the craft brewery segment has been uneven, to say the least. Indian beer insiders talk of brewpub cultures emerging in places like Gurgoan, an affluent suburb of New Dehli, where Rockman's Beer Island and Lemp Brewpub & Kitchen lead the charge, and Bangalore, with brewpubs like the Biere Club and Toit Brewpub.

As of the start of 2013, however, Mumbai was awaiting the imminent opening of what is thought to be India's first production craft brewery, Gateway Brewing, expected to launch in the spring with kegs of a *hefeweizen* called White Zen, the US-styled IPA and a pale ale named for a common Indian phrase, Like That Only.

Also in the planning stages at the time of writing are The Barking Deer, a Mumbai brewpub helmed by a US expat brewer, and Independence Brewing in Pune, developed in partnership with Stone Brewing's Greg Koch. Also in Pune is the pioneering Doolally brewpub, established when two Indian graduates met a German brewer in Singapore.

THE MIDDLE EAST

For political and religious reasons, the majority of the Middle East is understandably a less than hospitable place where alcohol is concerned. We know of a handful of respectable bars and restaurants catering principally to visitors and expats, with reasonable selections of imported beers, but aside from Israel and Turkey (*see* below), are only aware of a pair of small, independent breweries.

There is an increase in interest in non-alcoholic malt-based drinks, some produced by small breweries based in western Europe.

Historically there was certainly a tradition of beer brewing in the region going back millennia, and craft brewers as far apart as Belgium, the US and Japan have attempted to recreate lightly spiced, low alcohol wheat beers from apparently authentic ancient recipes.

TURKEY

Beer is both produced and enjoyed in officially secular Turkey, but that market with a per capita consumption of roughly 12 litres per annum – high for the Middle East, but very low relative to the rest of the world – is dominated utterly by Efes, partly owned by SABMiller, and the Turkish division of Tuborg, part of the Carlsberg Group.

Recent Istanbul brewpub arrival, Bosphorus Brewing Company, British-inspired and with five house taps, was greeted with much enthusiasm, particularly by the expat community, while the five-year-old, five-outlet chain of Taps Restaurants in Istanbul, Ankara and Bursa feeds four core and three seasonal brews to its establishments from a central brewery. Germanic Khoffner Brewery sates thirsts in Antalya, as does the similarly Teutonically inspired Red Tower Brewery in Alanya.

ISRAEL

Although the "fertile crescent" at the eastern end of the Mediterranean was the cradle of modern brewing thousands of years ago, it is 21st-century US craft brewers who are credited with kick-starting a trend that thus far has seen around two dozen smaller breweries set up in Israel since 2005.

DANCING CAMEL
Tel Aviv

The best known of the Israeli craft breweries, run by a US expat, with its own pubs in Tel Aviv. The regular beers are **American Pale Ale** ★★☆ with abundant tropical-fruit character; an oddly minty **India Pale Ale** ★★ with decent bitterness; **Midnight Stout** ★★☆ with fudge, chocolate and a touch of leafy hop; while in a clutch of more occasional, unusual beers monthly 11% ABV IPA **The Golem** is a burly brew that varies with each batch ★★→★★★.

HADUBIM
Even Yehuda, Central District

Beer commissioner that is ordering up some of the most interesting, hop-forward beers in Israel, brewed at Mivshelet Ha'Am, north of Tel Aviv. Flagship **Indira IPA** ★★☆, has a woody, slightly fruity hop aroma and a well-balanced palate; while **Oketz Bitter** ★★ is a surprisingly English lighter pale ale.

JEM'S BEER FACTORY
Petah Tikva, Central District

A small, orderly brewery located in Petah Tikva, east of Tel Aviv,

and making six regular Jem's beers, including an above average **Pils** ★★☆ with herbal hop character and gentle bitterness; a less impressive, thinnish **Dark Lager** ★☆; a complex **Stout** ★★☆ with gentle dark malt; and a possibly deceased, double-breasted **Blazer Brown Ale** ★★☆ with a nutty aroma punctuated with caramel.

MALKA
Kibbutz Yehiam, Northern District

A kibbutz brewery located at Yehiam, northeast of Haifa, which is producing beers that make it to the world beyond, such as its English-leaning **Admonit Pale Ale** ★★, which has a biscuity nose and some coriander in the finish; the hoppy, roasty and quaffable **Keha Stout** ★★☆; and the stronger seasonal **Behira** ★★☆, made like a fresh-tasting *saison* but with added coriander.

NEGEV
Kiryat Gat, Southern District

Small brewery making three regular beers, a sweet and soft, fruity **Amber Ale** ★★; weird but rather lovely passion-fruit-infused light amber **Passiflora** ★★☆; and lighter-bodied but full-flavoured black, oaky **Porter Alon** ★★★.

REST OF ASIA & THE MIDDLE EAST

Beer brewing likely originated in the modern Middle East. Religion and politics dictate it may not return, other than in Israel, for some time yet, though developments in Turkey are interesting. Elsewhere in non-Islamic Asia, wherever industrial beers have settled, so craft brewing may follow.

CHINGGIS CLUB
Ulaanbaatar, Mongolia

In 1998 the Chinggis Club brewery set up in the capital to brew beers that obeyed the rules of the *Reinheitsgebot*. Its **Dunkel** ★★☆ has a fairly toasty, light chocolate character; the basic, filtered **Pale Lager** ★★ is a bready *helles* with a slight fruity hop, better when allowed out on Friday nights in *zwickelbier* format as **Unfiltered Pale** ★★★, bready and yeasty but fresh and clean.

961 BEER (GRAVITY BREWING)
Mazraat Yachoua, Lebanon

Craft brewery started as a home brewing set-up during the 2006 Lebanon war. Basic **Lager** ★☆ is dryish and faintly bitter, while the mocha-ish **Porter** ★★ is light of body and seems styled to be more refreshing than satisfying. Brewmaster's Select **Lebanese Pale Ale** ★★☆ is hop-shy but flavoured with six herbs that come through in both aroma and flavour, particularly the thyme and sage.

TAYBEH BREWING
West Bank, Palestine

Brewery operating for almost two decades in Palestine, which alone makes it worthy of consideration. Beers include a Dark, Amber, Light and Non-Alcoholic, not tasted. **Golden** ★☆ is billed as in the *kölsch* style, but tastes more like a light pilsner with a crisp, drying palate and no discernible fruitiness. Some beers, particularly the Golden, have been brewed under licence internationally.

AUSTRALASIA

MICRONESIA

PAPUA NEW GUINEA

PORT MORESBY

INDIAN OCEAN

AUSTRALIA

Brisbane

Perth

Sydney

Adelaide

CANBERRA

Melbourne

NAURU

K I R I B A T I

SOLOMON
ISLANDS
HONIARA

oFONGAFALE
TUVALU

APIA
SAMOA

FIJI
SUVA

VANUATU

NUKU' ALOFA
TONGA

NEW
CALEDONIA

PACIFIC
OCEAN

Auckland

NEW
ZEALAND   WELLINGTON

AUSTRALIA

By the 1980s few Australians could give a XXXX about beer, the land of opportunity having succumbed to standardization on a massive scale. Only Coopers of Adelaide offered a range of beers outside a narrow spectrum of thin, ice-cold, light, pale lagers involved in testosterone-fuelled brand battles.

In contrast, the last 15 years has seen the emergence of a nascent Australian craft brewing scene that now boasts well north of a hundred breweries, some attracting investment from the country's successful wineries, making beers in styles from all over the world, with twists that it can increasingly call its own. In a nation of straight-talkers, most beers are named for the company and beer style, though the description "American" often encompasses both beers made with citrus, aromatic US hops and those that lead with fruity, tropical antipodean varieties.

2 BROTHERS
Moorabbin, Victoria

Small US-influenced pub brewery whose regulars include **Taxi ★★**, a crisp, hot-weather pilsner; and **Growler ★★**, a medium-bodied American brown ale with satisfying malt depth. Occasionals feature **James Brown ★★★**, a complex Belgian-leaning strong brown ale; and **Guvnor ★★★☆**, a huge barley wine suited to quiet contemplation.

4 PINES BREWING
Sydney, New South Wales

Pub brewery recently expanded into a 50-hl facility – large by Australian standards. Its **Kolsch ★★** is an affable, if unchallenging starter beer; its US-style **Pale Ale ★★** is gently bitter; its dry

Irish Stout ★★★ was famously researched for suitability for space travel.

> ### DESTINATION
> ### SYDNEY
>
> The Australian Hotel is a century-old, colonial-style beer hotel in The Rocks district (100 Cumberland St), gradually building an interest in craftier, broader-based, reliable Australian craft beers.

BOOTLEG BREWERY
Wilyabrup, Western Australia

Well-established small brewery standing out among the wineries. **Sou West Wheat ★★**, a refreshing, slightly fruity,

US-influenced wheat beer less interesting than **Raging Bull** ★★☆, a robust, intensely malty, not-quite roasty porter.

BREW BOYS
Adelaide, South Australia

Adelaide-based beer commissioners creating well-thought-through beers. **Maiden Ale** ★★ is a mid-Atlantic amber ale with New World hopping; **Ace of Spades** ★★☆ a dark, earthy, rich stout; and **Seeing Double** ★★★, a fumy, wee heavy type of Scotch ale, made with a dash of peated malt.

DESTINATION
ADELAIDE

If Australians did shabby chic the Wheatsheaf (39 George St) in Thebarton would be it. Not slick or fancy, and aspiring only to be a relaxed place to drink an ever-changing line-up of Australia's best beers. Live music too.

BRIDGE ROAD BREWERS
Beechworth, Victoria

Small brewery at Beechworth in Victoria, scene of outlaw Ned Kelly's adventures. Its original **Australian Ale** ★★ is a light-bodied pale ale with an aroma of apricots; **Chestnut Pilsener** ★★ is a characterful interpretation involving chestnuts and locally grown Galaxy hops; **Bling IPA** ★★☆ screams hops as the malt tries to keep up; while the upmarket Chevalier range is led by a brave, authentically tart and phenolic **Saison** ★★★.

BURLEIGH BREWING
West Burleigh, Queensland

Larger format craft brewer on Queensland's Gold Coast, south of Brisbane, making classic styles consistently well. German-style *hefeweizen*, **HEF** ★★★, is the best of its regulars, gaining international recognition; with US-style **28 Pale Ale** ★★ biscuity and balanced. More variable annual releases include unusual but reliably excellent coffee-infused *schwarzbier*, **Black Giraffe** ★★★.

CASCADE BREWERY (SABMILLER)
South Hobart, Tasmania

Scenic, historic brewery nestling in the foothills of Hobart's Mount Wellington.

Beers are mainstream, except for middle-strength **Cascade Stout** ★★☆, with chocolate-toffee highlights and lingering dry bitterness. Annual release **First Harvest** ★★ pioneered fresh-hopped ales a decade ago but has not kept up.

COOPERS BREWERY
Regency Park, South Australia

This 1862 family-owned brewery near Adelaide inspired a generation. Traditional brews include red-labelled **Sparkling Ale** ★★★, arguably Australia's first gift to world brewing styles; though green-labelled **Pale Ale** ★★ is the bigger seller. **Best Extra Stout** ★★☆ is a rich export stout; and the annual red-brown, old English-style **Vintage Ale**, a bit clunky when fresh, ages superbly ★★→★★★.

FERAL BREWING
Baskerville, Western Australia

One of Australia's best craft breweries, in the Swan Valley near Perth. Its first beer, **Feral White** ★★☆, is one of Australia's best interpretations of *witbier*; American

IPA **Hop Hog** ★★★☆ is consistently a critical and popular favourite; with **The Runt** ★★★ playing the smaller version. Playing with sour and barrel-aged beers helped create a plausible *Berliner weisse*, **Watermelon Warhead** ★★☆, with help from said fruit.

GRAND RIDGE BREWERY
Mirboo North, Victoria

Early craft pioneer at Mirboo North, some way southeast of Melbourne. **Gippsland** *Gold* ★★ is a UK-style pale ale finished with Australian and NZ hops; **Hatlifter Stout** ★★☆ is rich and full despite lowish strength, while **Moonshine** ★★★ is a strong Scotch ale smelling vaguely of Vegemite and tasting of dark fruit and brown sugar. All are best locally.

HARGREAVES HILL
Steels Creek, Victoria

Now back at Steels Creek, northeast of Melbourne, after being destroyed in the 2009 bushfires. Its idiosyncratic beers include a New World take on English **ESB** ★★☆; a Bavarian-style **Hefeweizen** ★★ with banana aroma; a light-bodied but flavoursome **Stout** ★★; and annually brewed, bold **Imperial Stout** ★★★ filled with roast malt, with coffee overtones.

HOLGATE BREWHOUSE
Woodend, Victoria

Small brewery at Woodend in Victoria. Its staple, **Mt Macedon Ale** ★★★, is a beautiful hybrid pale ale, with a citrus aroma despite German hopping, and an unusual malt character; **ESB** ★★☆ is a fine English ale made with East Kent Goldings; **Temptress** porter ★★★ is infused with chocolate and vanilla; and much sought-after annual blockbuster **Beelzebub's Jewels** ★★★ is a Belgian-angled barley wine.

KNAPPSTEIN ENTERPRISE BREWERY (KIRIN)
Clare, South Australia

Production of a single beer is shared between Malt Shovel and a boutique brewery at Knappstein's Clare Valley winery north of Adelaide. **Knappstein Reserve Lager** ★★★☆ is a Bavarian-styled blond lager, its complex palate lifted by slightly higher alcohol, New Zealand's Nelson Sauvin hops being wonderfully expressed to give it a distinctly New World aroma. Australia's best lager and among the finest anywhere.

KOOINDA BOUTIQUE BREWERY
Heidelberg West, Victoria

Started as a backyard brewery by two home brewers, at Rosanna in Victoria, and come good. Its **American Pale Ale** ★★☆ is a ballsy beer with great malt character; the **Belgian Witbier** ★★ is milky smooth, with coriander and dried, sweet orange peel; while black IPA **Full Nelson** ★★★ is a powerful, resinous, hop-driven beer that balances well.

DESTINATION BRISBANE

The Scratch (8/1 Park Road) is a great little beer bar in Milton, spearheading craft brewing and beer's inherent egalitarian sociability in the Queensland state capital, majoring smaller Australian brews with an occasional exotic import.

LITTLE BREWING CO, THE
Port Macquarie, New South Wales

Scrappy little brewery at Port Macquarie on the northern New South Wales coast, making solid beers that deserve to be better known. The Wicked Elf range includes a citrus, piney US-style **Pale Ale** ★★; a nicely to-style **Pilsener** ★★ with floral but firm bitterness; and a good Belgian interpretation of **Witbier** ★★. The same can be said of its Mad Abbot brand's high-quality interpretations of **Dubbel** ★★★ and excellent, fruity **Tripel** ★★★☆, which manages the Belgian trick of carrying its alcohol well.

LITTLE CREATURES BREWING (KIRIN)
Fremantle, Western Australia

Sizeable operation at Fremantle in Western Australia. Holds a similar place in the Australian brewing scene to that occupied by Sierra Nevada in the US, its 1999 launch beer, **Little Creatures Pale Ale** ★★★, being a tropically toned homage to its Californian predecessor. Golden-coloured **Bright Ale** ★☆ on the other hand is muted; the **Pilsener** ★★ is a well-measured light lager; but light,

AUSTRALIA

amber-coloured **Rogers' Beer** ★★☆ packs satisfying flavour without high strength. Let us hope its new owners do not cut corners.

LORD NELSON BREWERY
Sydney, New South Wales

One of the first Australian pub breweries, based at a beautiful old hotel in Sydney. **Quayle Ale** ★★ is an easy-drinking summer ale with restrained bitterness; **Three Sheets** ★★ is an Australian pale ale delivering gentle citrus fruits on its nose; and **Nelson's Blood** ★★☆ is a creamy smooth, roasty porter.

MCLAREN VALE BEER
McLaren Vale, South Australia

Beer commissioner recently turned brewer, in South Australia's McLaren Vale wine region. Launched its Vale range with an easy-going Australian pale called simply **Ale** ★★; hit its stride with an **IPA** ★★★ that bordered on US-style but showcased hops with summer fruit aromas; then added **DRK** ★★☆, a surprisingly rich *dunkel* for its strength.

MALT SHOVEL BREWERY (KIRIN)
Camperdown, New South Wales

The James Squire range is named after but unrelated to Australia's first brewer. His most prodigious offspring are light and under-hopped **Chancer Golden Ale** ★☆ and malty **Amber Ale** ★★; more interest coming from a good Czech-style pilsner, **Four Wives** ★★★; and inky porter, **Jack of Spades** ★★☆.

MATILDA BAY BREWING (SABMILLER)
Melbourne, Victoria

Early craft label, long since owned by multinationals. Bestselling **Fat Yak** ★☆ is made at an industrial brewery in Yatala but a new small brewery in Melbourne now produces **Alpha** ★★★, one of Australia's best US-style pale ales; a rich and chocolaty *dunkel* called **Dogbolter** ★★★; and a filtered *weizen* **Redback** that appear unfiltered at the brewery tap as **Redback Pale** ★★→★★★.

> ### DESTINATION
> ### MELBOURNE
>
> The Local (184 Carlisle St) is a popular neighbourhood taphouse with a large range of bottled and draught beers from across Australia, plus imports, while Slow Beer (468 Bridge Road) is currently the best beer shop to be found in the east.

MOO BREW
Berriedale, Tasmania

Tasmania's largest craft brewery is well resourced with winery connections but still small. Its **Hefeweizen** ★★ is a true-to-style Bavarian wheat beer; **Pilsener** ★★ is well rounded, floral and moderately bitter; **Dark Ale** ★★☆ is a satisfying American brown ale with rich malt character; its heavy **Stout** ★★☆ reaches higher when barrel-aged and released in numbered bottles as annual, limited edition **Imperial Stout** ★★★.

MORNINGTON PENINSULA BREWERY
Mornington, Victoria

New small brewery of potential, near Red Hill. Its US-style **IPA ★★☆** sees Citra, Amarillo and Centennial hops adding stonefruit character; while the **Pale Ale ★★** is toned down enough to make a session beer; **Witbier ★★** is big on citrus and spice; and the beautiful English-style **Brown Ale ★★★**, full of toffee and raisins, may appear on hand-pull in specialist beer pubs.

MOUNTAIN GOAT BEER
Melbourne, Victoria

Pioneering 1997 Melbourne craft brewery, with enough success to cause capacity issues. Its fruity, crisp **Steam Ale ★★** is brewed off-site for now; old-fashioned, grassy, malty English pale, **Hightail Ale ★★☆**, has gone national; and the up-hopped, previously occasional **IPA ★★☆** has gone full-time. Its seasonal beers are labelled Rare Breed and include strong golden, yeast-spiced **Rapunzel ★★★**, a *tripel* in all but name.

MURRAY'S CRAFT BREWING
Port Stephens, New South Wales

Innovative craft brewery on the New South Wales coast, north of Newcastle, creating numerous beers in hybrid styles. Highlights include golden Anglo-American pale ale **Angry Man ★★☆**; the similarly mid-Atlantic **Icon 2 IPA ★★★**, a boldly hopped double IPA; a Belgian *tripel*, **Grand Cru ★★★**, sent whizzy with lashings of New Zealand hops; and **Heart of Darkness ★★★**,

an Australian take on how a Belgian might ape Imperial stout. Put your name down early for a bottle of its ever-changing, annual, limited edition **Anniversary Ale ★★★**, always an intriguing, heavyweight, oak-aged barley wine.

NAIL BREWING
Perth, Western Australia

Founded in 2000 at Perth. One of the first exponents of a distinctively Australian type of pale ale, its starter brew **Nail Ale ★★** being easy-drinking, with malt and fruit esters; multiple prize-winning, mid-strength oatmeal **Stout ★★★** has satisfying complexity; while annual, limited edition, Imperial-strength **Clout Stout ★★★☆** is an evolving classic.

DESTINATION PERTH

No world-class beer bars yet but a fine array of stores, the two standouts, each with 1000+ brands in stock, being Mane Liquor (237 Great Eastern Highway) in Belmont and the International Beer Shop (69 McCourt St) in West Leederville.

RED HILL BREWERY
Red Hill South, Victoria

Obscure local planning laws mean that this small brewery on the Mornington Peninsula, south of Melbourne, sits in its own hop garden. A strong range of beers includes light-bodied bestseller **Golden Ale ★★**; a six-week-lagered, clear but unfiltered **Bohemian Pilsner**

★★ with real hop bite and nice malt body; **Scotch Ale** ★★☆ with a complex mix of caramel and dried fruit; and prize-winning seasonal **Christmas Ale** ★★★, brewed like a strong Belgian *dubbel*.

SEVEN SHEDS
Railton, Tasmania

Hidden in tiny Railton, near the north Tasmanian coast, Seven Sheds is run by the elder statesman of Australian beer writing, Willie Simpson. **Kentish Ale** ★★☆ is a rewarding traditional English-style pale ale; **Elephant's Trunk** ★★☆ is a middle-strength, rich and long-finishing, full-flavoured blond that would pass as Belgian; and **Willie Warmer** ★★★ is a medium-strength dark ale spiced with cassia bark and star anise.

SOUTH AUSTRALIA BREWING (KIRIN)
Adelaide, South Australia

Industrial brewery in Adelaide, making little of note beyond a single beer that refuses to go away. Perfected in the 1950s, coffee-tinged, rich, beefy **Southwark Old Stout** ★★★ is a lighter Imperial sometimes compared to port. Killed more often than Kenny and still on life support, badly in need of an owner that can spot a national treasure.

STONE & WOOD
Byron Bay, New South Wales

Successful brewery at Byron Bay in the coast a few miles south of Burleigh. Making a name for engaging beers like cloudy Australian pale **Pacific Ale** ★★★☆, which generously expresses Australian Galaxy hop aroma; **Jasper Ale** ★★☆, an English brown ale with spicy German hop character; and classic *helles*, **Pale Lager** ★★. Impressive flair is added annually with the volcanic-rock-seared, caramelized, faintly burnt, Austrian-style **Stone Beer** ★★★.

TEMPLE BREWING
Melbourne, Victoria

Pub brewery recently opened by a former gypsy brewer. Bold but balanced US-style **Pale Ale** ★★ features Amarillo and Cascade; **ESB** ★★☆ is earthy with a dry bitterness; **Saison** ★★☆ is spiked with Brazilian pepper; *weizenbock* **Unifikator** ★★★, originally from a collaboration with Bavarian Weihenstephaner, is now an in-house regular.

NEW ZEALAND

Craft brewing in New Zealand since the 1990s has been a series of ups and downs. By the end of the millennium there were some 60 or more breweries in the country, of which about half had closed a mere decade later. Fortunately, waiting in the wings were sufficient young, creative and enthusiastic brewers that by the time the second decade of the 21st century was well underway, Kiwi craft brewing was once again looking forward with hope and promise.

The key to the present and most probably the future of New Zealand craft beer may be found in two elements: contract brewing and native hops. The former, sometimes still derided by certain craft beer aficionados, is practically a New Zealand necessity, considering the variety of costs associated with serving a nation of 4.3m people living on two islands that stretch about 2000km (1240 miles) north to south. The contract arrangement, of which there are many in New Zealand, thus works to the benefit both the contracting brewery – in additional revenue – and the commissioning brewer – in terms of lower costs.

New Zealand's hop industry, on the other hand, has thrived precisely because of the country's isolation, with island-specific varieties such as **Nelson Sauvin** and **Riwaka** boasting distinctive tropical-fruit characteristics all their own. Local brewers, skilled as they are in coaxing flavours out of their native hops, have turned these traits into uniquely Kiwi styles, beginning with the perfumey New Zealand pilsner and tropical-fruity New Zealand pale ale, and finishing only at the limit of Kiwi brewers' imaginations.

---

8 WIRED BREWING
Blenheim, Marlborough

South Island beer commissioners with a deserved reputation for quality and innovation, illustrated by **Hopwired IPA ★★★☆**, a restrained fruit bowl of a beer credited as the first IPA to be brewed from all-Kiwi ingredients. Others include **Rewired Brown Ale ★★☆**, a keen balance of nutty malt and fruity-floral hop; **Super Conductor Double IPA ★★★**, an amped-up mingling of US and NZ hoppiness; and **The Big Smoke ★★☆**, an unambiguous smoked porter.

BREW MOON BREWERY
Amberley, Canterbury

Tucked in behind a nondescript café in the north Canterbury township of Amberley, Brew Moon has been producing English-inspired beers for over a decade. The smooth caramel flavours of **Broomfield Brown Ale ★★☆** are popular with locals, but most accolades are reserved for the orange-marmalade notes of **Hophead IPA ★★★** and the silky, milk-chocolate decadence of **Dark Side Stout ★★★**.

EMERSON'S BREWING (KIRIN)
Dunedin, Otago

Dunedin-based Richard Emerson was the originator of the New Zealand pilsner style, hopping his **Pilsner ★★★★** with Nelson-grown Riwaka hops for a flowery and passion-fruity character. Almost as influential is his **Bookbinder ★★★**,

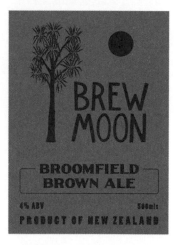

a session-strength ale with a firm maltiness and a dry finish; while the roasty, faintly briny **London Porter ★★** tends toward the thinner edge of the style. The brewery was sold in late 2012.

EPIC BREWING
Otahuhu, Auckland

Auckland-based beer commissioners led by Kiwi beer stalwart Luke Nicholas. Best known for big beers like **Hop Zombie ★★☆**, piney, lemony and pearish; **Larger ★★**, a strong pilsner that begins almost honeyed, but finishes with a serious bitterness; the massively citrus, all-US-hopped **Armageddon IPA ★★☆**; and the relatively nuanced **Coffee & Fig Imperial Oatmeal Stout ★★★**, part of the well-named Epicurean series.

> ### DESTINATION AUCKLAND
>
> Brew on Quay (102 Quay Street) is a wood-panelled oasis of beer in the heart of the city, with nine draught taps supplementing an extensive selection of bottled beers and a select "Cellar List".

FORK & BREWER
Wellington

Brewery and restaurant operating in the heart of Wellington, with a limited number of kegs supplied to other venues. Range is constantly changing and developing, but favourites include the dry grassiness and balance of the **Bohemian Hipster Pilsner ★★★**;

and the grapefruit punchiness of **Base Isolator IPA ★★★**. Seasonal, speciality and collaboration brews are common.

DESTINATION
WELLINGTON

The Malthouse (48 Courtenay Place) is Wellington's original beer bar on Courtenay Place, hub of the city's rollicking nightlife, with 27 taps, two hand pumps, a lengthy list of bottled beers and one of Australasia's only vintage beer lists.

GALBRAITH'S BREWING
Auckland

New Zealand's first modern brewpub, housed in an Auckland building that was once a public library, is renowned for its traditional ales, including the nutty **Bob Hudson's Bitter ★★☆**; the bittersweet yet earthy **Bitter and Twisted ESB ★★☆**; and the spicy, yeasty Belgian monster **Resurrection Tripel ★★★**. Kegs are distributed, as are bottled lagers such as **Galbraith's Munich Lager ★★**, with a herbaceous nose, lemony and floral hoppiness and a gentle bitterness.

GARAGE PROJECT
Wellington

Self-styled "ongoing project" brewery brewing a seemingly endless variety of ales. No telling what might stick long term, but impressive appearances have been made by honey-ish, perfumey

and almost buckwheat-like **Double Summer Ale ★★☆**; the inspired, boozy toffee **Rum & Raisin ★★★**, aged on rum-soaked raisins; and the hop-soaked **Pernicious Weed ★★**, a brew strictly for hop fanatics.

GOOD GEORGE BREWING
Hamilton, Waikato

Located in a former church, this young Hamilton brewpub with grand ambitions keeps a steady focus on flavour. Best offerings from highly regarded young brewer Kelly Ryan include a spicy, navel-orange **New Zealand White Ale ★★**; a citrus zest and biscuity **Sparkling Ale ★★★**; and the punchy **Good George IPA ★★☆**, bursting with lemony German hops. It also brews for the Green Dragon pub at the nearby Hobbiton attraction.

HARRINGTON'S BREWERY
Christchurch, Canterbury

Crowned New Zealand Champion Brewery of 2012, this sizeable Christchurch operation consistently produces the largest range of beers in the country. The best include the bourbon-infused Scotch ale **Big John Special Reserve ★★★** with notes of vanilla and oak; multi-award-winning dark ale **Pig and Whistle ★★☆**; and a zesty, orangey hop bomb called **Hop Tremor IPA ★★★**.

INVERCARGILL BREWERY
Invercargill, Southland

Located in provincial Invercargill, the southernmost brewery in New Zealand

NEW ZEALAND

was founded in 1999. Popular brands include a tasty UK-style pale ale with hints of fruitcake, called **Stanley Green** ★★☆, but aficionados search for brewer Steve Nally's darker brews, including the chocolate/caramel kiss of **Pitch Black Stout** ★★★; and **Smokin' Bishop** ★★★, a seasonal *rauchbier* made with malt that has been house-smoked over native manuka branches.

LIBERTY BREWING COMPANY
New Plymouth, Taranaki

One of the smallest commercial breweries in New Zealand enjoys one of the best reputations, especially when pushing the boundaries of flavours and styles. This New Plymouth brewery is best known for the hugely hopped **C!tra Imperial IPA** ★★★☆, with lashings of orange and grapefruit; the proudly politically incorrect **High Carb Ale** ★★★; and the robust coffee smokiness of **Never Go Back Imperial Oak Stout** ★★★.

MIKE'S ORGANIC BREWERY
Urenui, Taranaki

Nestled in farmland near the Taranaki hamlet of Urenui, the over-two-decades-old mike's was the second fully accredited organic brewery in the country. Its core range includes a quenching, grassy **Pilsner** ★★☆; the famous **Organic Ale** ★★☆ with caramel notes and faultless balance; and the robust raisin and toffee flavours of the whisky-barrel-aged **Whisky Porter** ★★★. The brewery also produces a rotating range of excellent non-organic pale ales.

MOA BREWING
Blenheim, Marlborough

High-profile and sometime controversial brewery in Marlborough wine country. All Kiwi-hopped **5 Hop** ★★★ combines tropical fruitiness with biscuit malt; two rather than five NZ hops give the **Pale Ale** ★★☆ a citrus, gooseberry-ish character; light and spritzy **Breakfast Beer** ★★☆ is made with 65% wheat malt; vaguely *saison*-esque **Méthode** ★★☆ is bottle-fermented to a spicy crispness; and darkly fruity, coffee-ish **Imperial Stout** ★★☆ brings strength to the finish.

MUSSEL INN
Onekaka, Tasman

On the edge of two national parks on the South Island's Golden Bay, the Mussel Inn operates a brewery rightly revered for a single beer, although others are also brewed. Amber-hued **Captain Cooker Manuka Beer** ★★★☆ is flavoured to great complexity with tips from the native manuka tree, giving it cinnamon-ish aroma notes and

a leafy-herbal-spicy flavour built on a backdrop of caramel apple malt.

PARROTDOG BREWERY
Te Aro, Wellington

The brewery founders – three twentysomething guys, all named Matt – moved from being home brewers to Wellington brewery owners in less than four years. First beer, **BitterBitch IPA** ★★★☆, rightly remains the flagship product with punchy grapefruit notes and dry, cleansing bitterness. It is joined by **Bloodhound** ★★, a soft caramel red ale; and the outrageously named **DeadCanary** ★★☆, a contemporary NZ pale ale with plenty of tropical fruit and caramel.

RENAISSANCE BREWING
Blenheim, Marlborough

Marlborough-based operation producing elegant, sophisticated beers. Nelson-grown American hop strains flavour the citrus-fruity **American Pale Ale** ★★; multi-award-winner **Elemental Porter** ★★★ is plummy and mocha-ish; hugely aromatic **Craftsman Chocolate Oatmeal Stout** ★★ remains sessionable despite its big chocolate character; and **Stonecutter Scotch Ale** ★★★☆ offers soothing layers of caramelly, lightly roasty and date- and raisin-accented maltiness, with a drying finish.

THREE BOYS BREWERY
Christchurch, Canterbury

Christchurch operation named for the founder and his two sons, rather than three partners. **Oyster Stout** ★★★ is a rich, figgy, lightly smoky ale brewed only when local Southland Bluff oysters are in season; light **Wheat** ★★ is a thinnish Belgian-style wheat beer with strong, spicy lemon notes; and the fresh and floral **Pils** ★★☆ proves that Kiwi hops aren't only about tropical fruit.

DESTINATION CHRISTCHURCH

Pomeroy's Old Brewery Inn (292 Kilmore Street), located in a heritage building that formerly housed the original Harrington's Brewery, is a popular destination boasting over 20 craft taps, including its own Four Avenues brands, outstanding food and boutique accommodation next door.

TUATARA BREWING
Paraparaumu, Wellington

Wellington-area brewery recently relocated from the brewer's backyard to somewhat more sophisticated surroundings. A shortage of American hops led to the fortuitous creation of **Aotearoa Pale Ale ★★★**, bold and fruity with local hops; also Kiwi-hopped, **Bohemian Pilsner ★★☆** is a fine, tropical-fruity example of an emerging NZ style; soft bitterness but high quaffability define the **Munich Helles ★★**; and perhaps overly gentle **Bavarian Hefe ★★** nonetheless offers authentically spicy-banana flavours.

TWISTED HOP, THE
Wigram, Canterbury

This Christchurch brewery was destroyed by the 2011 earthquake, which left the owners loaning other breweries for production while rebuilding their own. Beers like the quaffable, tropical fruit **Hopback IPA ★★★** and toffee-ish dark ale **Twisted Ankle ★★☆** will no doubt benefit further from the stability a permanent home provides.

YEASTIE BOYS
Wellington

Audacious beer commissioners based in Wellington, showing a deft hand with utterly unconventional brews like **Rex Attitude ★★**, an intensely phenolic ale made entirely from peated malt, which becomes oddly more balanced and predictably whisky-ish in its stronger guise as **Rex ★★☆**. Flagship is the

hoppy porter **Pot Kettle Black ★★★**, evocative of baker's chocolate; while **Hud-a-wa' Strong ★★☆** mixes tropical-fruit notes with toffee and honey-ish malt.

DESTINATION WELLINGTON

Hashigo Zake (25 Taranaki Street) is a the Japanese-themed bar and restaurant that doubles as one of the city's finest beer destinations, with a beer list that boasts an impressive number of obscure and much-lauded ales and lagers from New Zealand and well beyond, many of which the bar imports direct.

THE SOUTH PACIFIC

That part of the southwestern Pacific known as Oceania is supplied mainly by locally based breweries that are part of global groups, making mostly lighter blond lagers. However, a few entrepreneurial smaller breweries are now cropping up across the region.

The Norfolk Island Brewery Company supplies its beers to local bars and restaurants from a brewpub base next to the island's airport, 1400km (870 miles) off the Australian coast, its honeyed blond ale Bee Sting, pale ale Mutineer and stronger dark ale Bligh's Revenge earning prizes for authenticity.

We think Fiji is now down to just one smaller brewery, a boutique lager maker called Island Brewing, at Nadi on the west coast of the main island in the group, which makes a tasty, crisp Vonu Lager and up-strength but unsubtle Eight.

Likewise, the Cook Islands are now down to a single small producer, the Matutu Brewing Company at Tikioki on Rarotonga, which makes UK-style Kiva Pale Ale, a German-hopped Mai Lager and draught Matutu, all best sampled locally and fresh.

For brewing in real isolation it is hard to beat Stone Money Brewing Company, on the island of Yap in Micronesia since 1999, making Manta Gold and Hammerhead Amber, while one to watch is Nambawan Brewing in Vanuatu, the former New Hebrides, a recent set-up that styles itself a craft brewery and intends to brew a bitter and a porter, among others.

Finally, further north, on the US dependency of Guam, Great Deep Brewing regularly rings the changes through 16 draught beers, at the Mermaid Tavern in Hagatna, that would pass muster in any North American brewpub. It has recently been joined on the island by Ishii Brewing Company at Tamuning, which supplies Minagof Pale Ale and IPA to a dozen local bars and last year audaciously licensed Marstons of Burton upon Trent to do the same for the Wetherspoon pub chain in the UK.

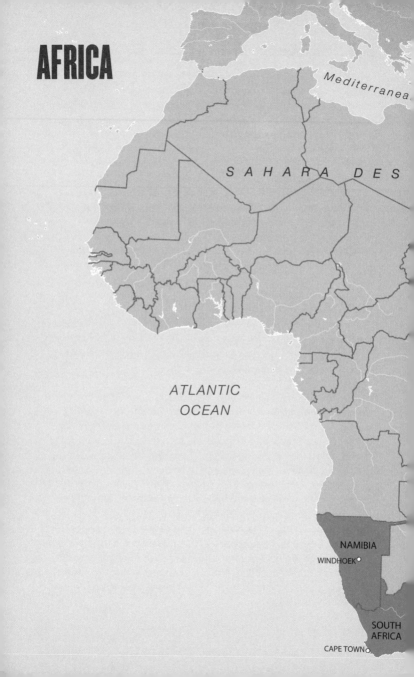

AFRICA

Mediterranea

S A H A R A   D E S

ATLANTIC
OCEAN

NAMIBIA
WINDHOEK○

SOUTH
AFRICA

CAPE TOWN○

Sea

R T

Red Sea

INDIAN
OCEAN

PRETORIA
Johannesburg

Durban

SOUTH AFRICA

The rainbow nation had more than its fair share of obstacles to building a modern beer culture, not least the extraordinary power over all aspects of the beer trade, from ingredients to point of sale, invested until recently in a single producer.

All that is changing slowly, with the emergence of 20 or so craft breweries, mainly around Cape Town, Durban and metropolitan Johannesburg, plus a dozen or more beer commissioners, most intent on brewing for themselves in future but currently just pushing the boundaries in a country where the abiding culture is to drink beer for effect rather than pleasure.

ANVIL ALE
Dullstroom, Mpumalanga

Tiny pub brewery breaking traditions in Mpumalanga province east of Pretoria. **White Ale** ★★★ is made with local tangerines, peeled and dried here, then added with ginger and coriander to this fresh, spicy, refreshing and absurdly multi-layered *witbier*, while the regular **Blonde Ale** ★★☆ is clean and sweet, with a healthy dose of spicy hop.

BIERWERK
Western Cape

Beer commissioner based south of Cape Town, getting its two regular ales brewed at **BOSTON BREWERIES SA**, we think. Bottle-conditioned ordinary bitter **Vlakvark** ★★☆ is made with Southern Promise hops; while heavyweight coffee porter **Aardwolf** ★★★ packs in five different grains, molasses and roasted coffee beans.

BOSTON BREWERIES SA
Cape Town, Western Cape

Smart Cape Town brewery making its own beers since 2000 and now contract brewing for numerous aspiring craft brewers. Clean but tasty **Boston Premium Lager** ★★ is the backbone; soft, balanced **Johnny Gold Weiss** ★★☆ is tied together by a little acidity in its finish; **Van Hunk's Pumpkin Ale** ★★☆ is a sweet and spicy pumpkin pie beer; and dark ruby barley wine **Hazzard Ten** ★★, while balanced enough could do a bit more.

DARLING BREW
Darling, Western Cape

Beer commissioner and wannabe brewer at Darling north of Cape Town, selling beers made by **BOSTON BREWERIES SA**. These include orange-tinged *witbier* **Bonecrusher ★★☆** with nice spiciness and a light body; while *dunkelweisse* **Silverback ★★** has a subtle fruitiness and a character somewhere between coriander and liquorice.

DEVIL'S PEAK
Somerset West, Western Cape

Beer commissioner at Somerset West in the Western Cape. **King's Blockhouse IPA ★★★** is South Africa's hoppiest beer, American in style with abundant C-hops; **Woodhead Amber ★★★** is fresh, with chewy crystal malt and a fair amount of leafy hop character; and **First Light Golden ★★** has light floral hop with kiwi fruit and slightly doughy pale malts.

DRAYMAN'S
Pretoria, Gauteng

Pioneering 1997 brewery in Pretoria, making mostly session beers in both German and British styles. Commonest is so-so light blond **Berghof ★☆**; the most accomplished is an authentic *hefeweizen* called **Altstadt Weissbier ★★☆**, with gentle clove and banana lacing a fresh character; with darker than average, English-style **Goblin's Bitter ★★☆** not far behind; and pretty passable **Düssel Altbier ★★** found only on draught.

GILROY
Muldersdrift, Gauteng

A pioneering pub brewery that is located at Muldersdrift, northwest of Johannesburg. The light **Lager ★★** is malt-accented; the **Favourite Pale Ale ★★** is malty with a touch of diacetyl; the **Traditional Ruby Ale ★★☆** has a lot of malt on the nose, with a soft, juicy palate; and the unplaceable but mostly English **Serious Dark Ale ★★★** has an appetizing dark-sugar character with light fruitiness.

JACK BLACK
Cape Town, Western Cape

A Cape Town contract brewer selling beers that are made at **BOSTON BREWERIES SA**. Its **Amber ★★** has a biscuity fresh-grain aroma; the **Pilsner ★★** has doughy malts and a light continental hop character; and the **Pale Ale ★★** has mild bitterness and a fair bit of fruitiness, more amber ale than pale.

MITCHELL'S
Knysna, Western Cape

Brewing at Knysna in Western Cape since 1983 and showcased at its pub on Cape Town's V&A Waterfront. **Bosun's Bitter** ★★ is a soft, subtle, balanced UK bitter with gentle spiciness; **Raven Stout** ★★★ has a chocolaty, fruity nose and sweet chocolate on the palate; strong Scotch ale **90/-** ★★☆ has a caramelled, slightly smoky palate with a touch of dryness in the finish; and barley wine **Old Wobbly** ★★☆ is 11% ABV with a strong pale malt character.

PORCUPINE QUILL
Botha's Hill, KwaZulu-Natal

Small brewery in Durban's northern suburbs brewing lighter Quills, mid-strength African Moon and heavier Dam Wolf brands, represented by sweet, caramel and toasty **Karoo Red** ★★; sweet toffee, slightly nutty **African Moon Amber** ★★; and strong, sweet and fruity old ale **Black Buck Bitter** ★★☆; and

Wolf in Sheep's Clothing ★★☆, a strong ale with chocolate notes, leafy hop and subtle apple and plum fruitiness.

SHONGWENI
Hillcrest, KwaZulu-Natal

Small brewery northwest of Durban that making Robson;s beers. **East Coast Ale** ★★☆ is a slightly fruity pale ale hopped lightly with Brewers Gold and Challenger; **West Coast Ale** ★★ is slightly stronger and intended to be American but leans more toward malt, with only light bitterness; while the boldest is **Durban Pale Ale** ★★★, dry, with a bright hop character and a fair bit of complexity.

STANDEAVEN
Alverstone, KwaZulu-Natal

Newish brewery near Durban with a range that includes a yeasty **No 3 Bohemian Pilsner** ★★ with a light hop character; **No 5 Press Club Stout** ★★☆ with a hearty body and fudge character; and **No 7 African Pale Ale** ★★ with modest bitterness.

TRIGGERFISH
Somerset West, Western Cape

Brewery company in the same town as DEVIL'S PEAK. Produces a wide range, some in bottle. **Hammerhead IPA** ★★ is malt-accented; **Titan Imperial IPA** ★★☆ is big and chewy with plenty of crystal malt; **Empowered Stout** ★★☆ is buttery and slightly nutty. Harder to find is **Black Marlin Imperial Stout** ★★☆, worth hunting for, rich chocolate in character with good balance and classical intensity.

REST OF AFRICA

While it would be a mistake to say that, outside of South Africa and Namibia, the African continent is a desert for characterful beer, it would not be too much of one. We know of brewpubs scattered here and there – in Kenya and Ethiopia, for instance – but nothing that appears particularly attention-worthy. And while some craft beer aficionados remain enamoured with the legend of Nigerian-brewed Guinness, our limited encounters with the beer have left us less than impressed.

So, for the time being, at least, the vast majority of Africa remains awash in a sea of light golden lagers designed more to slake thirst than deliver flavour, plus one expat Irish stout.

CAMELTHORN BREWING
Windhoek, Namibia

Namibia's only small brewery, in the capital Windhoek, impacting in South Africa too. Four regular beers include a yeasty **Weizen** ★★ with just a hint of banana; and American amber ale **Red** ★★ with hops imported from Oregon. Seasonal **Summer Ale** ★★☆ has a fruity, juicy, refreshing character; and a tougher dark **Bok** ★★ appears in the winter months.

ACKNOWLEDGEMENTS

We have each been fortunate over the years to have met and got to know many of the world's best beer writers and consumer champions, though neither of us understood how grateful we would one day become for their knowledge, wisdom and insights until the time came to compile this book.

We wish to thank the following for their invaluable help in compiling our regional and national information:

USA: Stan Hieronymus (*www.appellationbeer. com*), Lisa Morrison (*www. beergoddess.com*), John Holl (*www.johnholl.com*) & Jay Brooks (*www.brookstonbeerbulletin.com*)

UK & Northern Ireland: Des de Moor (*www.desdemoor.co.uk*)

Germany: Steve Thomas (*www.german-breweries.com*)

Czech Republic: Evan Rail (*www.evanrail.com*)

Italy: Lorenzo Dabove (*www.kuaska.it*)

Netherlands: Tim Skelton (*www.facebook.com/tim.skelton.399*)

France: Elisabeth Pierre (*www.lafilledelorge.com*)

Denmark: Henrik Papsø (*www.facebook.com/henrik.papso*)

Sweden: Andreas Fält (*twitter.com/BAambassador*)

Finland: Patrik Willfor

Austria: Conrad Seidl (*www.bierpapst.com*)

Switzerland: Laurent Mousson (*libieration.blogspot.co.uk*)

Lithuania: Martin Thibault (*www.lescoureursdesboires.blogspot.co.uk*)

Republic of Ireland & Latvia: Krystian Hughes (*www.booksaboutbeer.com*)

Poland: Tomasz Kopyra & Jan Lichota (*www.bractwopiwne.pl*)

Australia: Matt Kirkegaard (*www.brewsnews.com.au*)

New Zealand: Neil Miller (*www.beerandbrewer.com*)

Japan: Mark Meli & Tim Eustace

China & Taiwan: Elaine Hseih (*www.facebook.com/elainecraftbeer*)

Spain & Argentina: Max Bahnson (*www.pivni-filosof.com*)

Latin America: Joe Stange (*www.thirstypilgrim.com*)

Brazil: Kathia Zanatta (*www.institutodacerveja.com.br*)

Far-flung outposts: Josh Oakes (Editor-in-chief, *www.ratebeer.com*)

Chile: Felipe Pizarro (*www.sommelierdechile.cl*)

Singapore: Daniel Goh (*www.facebook.com/goodbeersg*)

We also wish to thank Erik Dahl, Joris Pattyn, David Cryer, Doug Donelan, Junghoon Yoon, Chul Park, Bill Miller, Troy Zitzelsberger, Ankur Jain, Navin Mittal, Benjamin Johnson, Manuele Colonna, Luca & Ivan at Domus Birrae in Rome, Luis Garcés and the Fairmont Mayakoba Resort.

PICTURE CREDITS

Octopus Publishing Group would like to acknowledge and thank all those breweries and their agents, credited on the page, who kindly supplied labels for use in this book.

Additional picture credits
8 Peter Adams/Getty Images; 11 Jerry McBride/AP/Press Association Images; 14 WoodyStock/Alamy; 18 courtesy www.carlsberggroup.com